Sanborn's Travelog Series:

D0885595

MEXICO'S
PACIFIC COAST
& COPPER CANYON
A Driver's Guide

Wanderlust
Publications
2009 S. 10th McAllen TX 78503
Ph: (956) 682-7433
Fax: (956) 686-0732

Wanderlust Publications, McAllen, Texas

Copyright © 1996,1997, 1998, 1999, 2000, 2001, 2002, 2003, 2004 by Wanderlust Publications

Maps Copyright © Travco Services, Inc.

All rights reserved. No part of this book may be reproduced or utilized in any form or by any means, electronic or mechanical, including photocopying, or recording by any information storage and retrieval system, without permission in writing from the publisher. However, members of the news media may freely use excerpts of a reasonable length as long as credit is given, including where to obtain this book.

Inquiries should be addressed to: Wanderlust Publications, 2009 South 10th Street, McAllen, TX 78503-5405 Ph: (956) 682-7433 Fax: (956) 686-0732.

Our web page address: http://www.sanbornsinsurance.com

E-mail: info@sanbornsinsurance.com

First Edition: May, 1996

Second Edition: May, 1997

Third Edition: February, 1998

Fourth Edition: December, 1998

Fifth Edition: April, 1999

Sixth Edition: January, 2002

Sixth Edition Reprint: June, 2002

Seventh Edition: May, 2003

Eighth Edition: July, 2003

Ninth Edition: January, 2004

Ninth Edition Reprint: June, 2005

Printed in the United States of America

Mexico's Pacific Coast & Copper Canyon
 A Driver's Guide
Sanborn's Travelog Series
ISBN: 1-878166-53-0

If you've got a minute ...

We truly hope you had a wonderful trip and that our *Travelog* helped. You can help other folks by passing on information you may have learned. It's from your feedback that we can improve, so send us your suggestions and observations. If possible, please refer to name of book, page #, and the mile #. The whole *Travelog* covers all of Mexico and is contained in nine books, so we need some way to track it. **YOUR PHONE #, POR FAVOR!** We may have a question, or want to thank you personally!

Praise or complaints for Mexican individuals or companies should be sent to : **Secretaria de Turismo, Dirección General de Servicios al Turismo, Presidente Masaryk – 3er Piso, C.P. 11587, Mexico D.F.** Each year, the government honors a citizen who helped tourists. Your complaint or praise will be recorded and sent to the right agency. You'd be surprised at what good it can do.

Hasta luego from all the staff at Sanborn's.

Today's date:_____ Date entered Mexico: _____ Exit date: _____

Which Sanborn's office served you? _____

Were they friendly?_____ Helpful?_____ Knowledgeable?_____ How could they improve service? _____

_____

_____

Did you have a good time – overall? YES! _____NO _____Was any facility or individual especially helpful? _____

Was your *Travelog* in order? YES_____NO_____ Did it make sense? YES_____NO_____

Excellent? _____ Good? _____ Fair?_____

Was the **HIGHWAY INFORMATION** essentially accurate? YES_____NO_____

Do you have new info for us?_____

_____

_____

_____

Was the **EAT & STRAY** section essentially accurate? YES_____ NO_____

Do you have new places for us or some that should be edited?_____

_____

_____

_____

_____

What would YOU like to see that WASN'T there?_____

Will you return to Mexico some day?_____

Name:_____

Address, City, State, Zip :_____

Country_____**TELEPHONE** # (_____)_____

How many travelling?_____ First trip? YES_____NO_____

Where did you hear about Sanborn's?_____

_____

FROM:

NO POSTAGE
NECESSARY
IF MAILED
IN THE
UNITED STATES

BUSINESS REPLY MAIL
FIRST CLASS PERMIT NO. 57 McALLEN, TEXAS

POSTAGE WILL BE PAID BY ADDRESSEE

SANBORN'S

MEXICO   INSURANCE   SERVICE

DEPT. COMMENTS
P.O. BOX 310
McALLEN, TX 78505-0310

Table of Contents

Maps

Logs

Specials

Eat & Strays

Return Logs

WELCOME TO MEXICO!

HOW TO READ THIS BOOK

First of all, take some time to get familiar with our format. The information is presented in varying detail, depending on where you are in your journey. In cities, we tend to give you several landmarks in case one has disappeared since our last visit.

Remember, always read ahead in the log! You should look at it the night before to plan your trip and mark appropriate highlights. On the road, the navigator should read ahead about four or five entries, but don't give them all to the driver. Work this out with your pilot.

With this *Travelog*, we have attempted to include every route that you could take while exploring this region of Mexico. Since there is sometimes more than one way you could go, we've included alternate routes. Every time you come to a major intersection or a major new highway, there should be a new log. Pay special attention to the **"IF TO:"** paragraphs which will indicate a page number if the next log you need is on a different page.

The mileage numbers represent miles and kilometers, respectively. We've listed both so our Canadian friends can use this book. The numbers start at 0.0 at a major intersection. The "KM XXX" stands for the kilometer markings you'll see on Mexico's highways. They aren't always visible, but when they are, they give you a great reference point.

The scenic ratings of roads are subjective. A "5" is very close to heaven. A "0" is either hell or a tollroad. These have nothing to do with driving ease. Some toll roads are actually pretty, but most are not. Take the scenic route if you want to take your time and enjoy. Take the direct route if you just want to get from point A to point B in a hurry.

EAT AND STRAY LEGEND

We gave up listing exact prices years ago. That's the one thing that people are most likely to complain about in any guidebook. Prices change but often stay within the same range. A moderately priced restaurant or hotel will stay in the same category relative to others in the same city.

AE = American Express, MC = MasterCard, VI = Visa, SATV = Satellite TV.

PRICES – Always look at the room first and ask for the best price. Prices are in U.S. Dollars.

ECON – under $25 MOD – $25-$60 UPPER $60 and above

Restaurants are rated for quality and service. Prices are approximate for two people to eat dinner there. Drinks, tips and appetizers are not included. If breakfast is the specialty, cut prices in half.

ECON – under $10 MOD – $10-$25 UPPER – $25 and above

For RV parks, we list approximate rates when known.

ECON – under $8 MOD – $8-10 UPPER – $10 and above

CAR PERMITS AND IMMIGRATION DOCUMENTS

If you are driving your car or a rented car from the border, you'll need a vehicle permit to drive to the interior of Mexico with the exception of Baja California (If you fly to the interior and rent a car, you won't need a permit).

To get your permit, you'll need the vehicle title or registration, which must be in the same name as your credit card (Visa©, MasterCard©, American Express© or Diner's Club©). If your chariot is financed, you'll need a notarized letter of permission from the lien holder to take it into Mexico. You can't loan your car to a friend. If you have a boat and a trailer, they must also be in the same name as the vehicle. You need the credit card to pay a $18 fee to Banjército for your permit. If you don't have a credit card, you can still get a permit by posting a bond, but it's a lot more trouble. Get a credit card if you possibly can. The permit is good for multiple entries during 180 days.

You must turn in your permit and tourist card before you leave the country for the last time. Forgetting to do so could result in your being refused entry again or subject you to a high fine. You must turn in your permit at the Banjército office, either at the 21 kilometer checkpoint or at the border station. The Banjército offices are generally close to the bridge. You do not need to return to the U.S. at the same border crossing where you started.

Everyone must have proof of citizenship: A picture ID with a birth certificate, voter's registration card or a notarized proof of citizenship. Even little children must have birth certificates. If a child is traveling with only one parent, it is necessary to have notarized permission of the absent parent (even if divorced). Pets need current vaccination records and health certificates.

Effective July 1, 1999, a fee of $150.00 pesos (about $18.00 dollars) will be charged for each tourist permit (FMT), Business-person permit (FMN) or transmigrante (those passing thru Mexico to Central America) permit. Any non-Mexican tourist traveling beyond the designated 20-mile free zone will be subject to the tourist tax. Tourists will be charged on a per person basis but the tourist card will still be multiple entry and the fee will be charged only at the tourist's initial internment. The validity period for a tourist card will continue to be 180 days, but may be limited to a shorter period at the discretion of immigration officials.

WHAT CAN I TAKE INTO MEXICO?

When crossing into Mexico, if you have no merchandise to declare, you must go through the stop and go light check point. A green light means proceed ahead without inspection. A red light means stop for inspection.

When you travel to Mexico by airplane or by ship, you are allowed to import duty free one or various items worth up to $300 dollars per person (including children). For example, a family of five members consisting of the parents and three minor children, can import up to $1,500 Dollars worth of merchandise, duty free. However, if you are traveling by land, you are allowed only $50.00 Dollars (per person) worth of merchandise duty free.

When you bring items whose value exceeds the above mentioned limits, but not more than $1,000.00 Dollars, you can pay your personal taxes. If your merchandise is worth more than $1,000.00 Dollars, you must use the services of a customs broker.

If the flight by which you arrive come from the border zone you are allowed only $50.00 Dollars of new items per person.

If you are a resident in Mexico you are allowed to bring in free of duty the following items for your personal use: One camera or video camera if it can be carried by the passenger; up to 12 rolls of virgin film, video cassettes, or photographic materials; one article of sports equipment or a used set of equipment that can be hand carried; books and magazines; 20 packages of cigarettes or 50 cigars or 250 grams of tobacco; 3 liters of wine, beer or liquor (adults only); medicines for personal use or with a doctor's prescription if it is a controlled substance, and the suitcases to carry baggage.

If you are a resident of a foreign country (USA, Canada, or other), in addition to the above you are allowed to take a set of binoculars, a photographic camera, a television, a radio or radio-cassette tape or disc player, up to 20 recording tapes or discs, a typewriter, a portable computer, a musical instrument that can be hand carried, a camping tent and camping equipment, a set of fishing equipment, a pair of skis, 5 used toys for minors, two tennis rackets, a motorless boat less than 5 1/2 meters long or surf board with or without a sail.

If you are inspected and are discovered with items of greater value than is permitted and you have not paid duty on them, you risk having to pay a high fine (of up to four times the value of each item). If weapons or ammunition are found, the penalty includes imprisonment.

The following are products you can take into Mexico without previous authorization: Dehydrated or canned foods, bamboo (dry), roasted coffee (packaged), fresh or dry meats (beef, sheep or goat from US or Canada), candy (not lactic), dried spices, dry herbal medicines, dry or preserved insects, canned jellies or fruit preserves, nuts, straw articles or artifacts, dried fish, cheese (processed in US or Canada), canned or processed sauces, soups without meat, canned or processed vegetables, dogs or cats (with a recent health certificate and vaccination record).

CAN I BRING IT BACK?

You are not allowed to bring back more than $10,000 in cash. If you bring back more than $500.00 in merchandise you must declare it, fill out importation documents and have it inspected at the customs house where the large trucks cross.

Declare all agricultural items. Failure to do so may result in delays and fines of $25.00 or more. Fruits, vegetables, meats and birds taken from the U. S., to Mexico may not be allowed to re-enter. Check in advance with U.S.D.A. inspectors. Also declare all medicines or prescription drugs bought in Mexico.

Prohibited Fruits and vegetables: Potatoes: cooked OK. Plants and seeds: Special permits are required and some are prohibited. Check in advance. (Except dried plant parts, such as for medicinal purposes, permitted) Meats and Game: Raw or cooked pork, including sausages, cold cuts, skins and pork tacos (except shelf-stable, canned pork and hard-cooked pork skin cracklings). Poultry: Raw meat from domesticated and game fowl (except well-cooked poultry). Game: Check in advance. Other meat: imports limited to 50 pounds per person. Eggs are prohibited (except boiled and cooked eggs). Live birds: Wild and domesticated birds, including poultry. To import personally owned pet birds, check in advance. Straw is generally prohibited including wheat straw, seeds and all other articles made from them including animal feed.

Permitted fruits and vegetables: Avocados without seeds, except in California, bananas, blackberries, cactus fruits, dates, dewberries, grapes, lycheés, melons, papayas, pineapples, and strawberries. Most vegetables permitted except those listed above. Okra, however, is subject to certain restrictions. Nuts: acorns, almonds, cocoa beans, chestnuts, coconuts (no husks or milk), peanuts, pecans, piñones (pinenuts), tamarind beans, walnuts and waternuts.

GAS AND GAS STATIONS

UNLEADED GAS and DIESEL are abundant everywhere in Mexico. Unleaded gas is called Magna Sin (87 octane). Also a higher octane (93) Premium unleaded gas is sold in most stations. Nova (leaded gas) has been phased out. There is only one brand, PEMEX, which stands for PEtroleos MEXicanos. Prices are the same throughout the interior. Diesel is also found at most stations. The diesel pumps are in a different part of the station and are red. The best diesel is *centrifugado*, or centrifuged. Diesel Sin has lower sulfur content.

It's still a good idea to make sure that the pump has reset to zero before the attendant starts pumping. Stay at the pump until the operation is finished. Don't just rush off to the bathroom. Although most stations still do not take credit cards, more and more are accepting MC and VI cards.

The bathrooms used to be filthy, but lately they have embarked on a cleanup effort. Often there will be an attendant. Tipping them is a nice thing to do. A personal supply of toilet paper is smart, though not always necessary.

Speaking of restrooms, in Mexico *his* will be called *Caballeros* and *hers* will be *Damas* (sometimes W.C. for water closet). In the bathrooms of many Mexican hotels, you'll notice the initials C on one faucet and F on the other. Bear in mind that C means *caliente* (hot) and F means *fría* (cold).

AUTO PARTS AND REPAIRS

You'll find lots of spare parts in Mexico, though not always the right ones. Fords, Chevys, Dodges and Nissans are all made there. Many of the parts are interchangeable. The best thing to do is to have a good, honest mechanic check out your car before you go and to pay particular attention to the brakes, tires, front end, U-joints, belts (carry spares) and any "computer" parts. Please do not even think about messing with your catalytic converter. Get a tune-up, including new spark plug wires etc. Your car is going to be your servant for the next few thousand miles. Don't let it be the other way around.

Goodyear is in every town and can do a good job with brakes, front ends, etc. You'll find shade tree mechanics, identified by a "*taller mecánico*" sign beside the road. Taller has nothing to do with his height. It means shop. If they don't have the brake pads you need, they will make them.

Carry: belts (all), fuel filters (4), air filters (2), a good set of tools, windshield washer fluid (lots), auto transmission fluid (1 qt.), fuel injector cleaner (5 bottles). Diesels should have (5) filters and any additive that might combat water and the buildup of sulfuric acid in your crankcase.

A spare gas can should only be necessary if you are going four wheeling. Carrying gas is too dangerous and smelly. Ninety-nine per cent of folks won't need it. Also make sure your tires (including spare) are in good shape. Mexican tires are excellent, but the sizes are slightly different.

RENTING A CAR

Over 3,000,000 people fly to Mexico, and then rent cars for all or part of their trip while 1,500,000 drive from the U.S. or Canada. These "more than average" tourists have realized that driving is the most practical way to get around, offering unlimited freedom. Renting a car in Mexico is similar to renting one anywhere in the world with a few caveats. You must have a major credit card. All the major rental car agencies are located at major airports. Their rates vary, so shop around. There are also some independent rental car agencies at many airports. Sometimes they offer a better deal and sometimes not. Again, shop around.

Please check the vehicle carefully! Any little ding not noted will be charged to you as if you damaged their car on purpose. Make sure all lights, signals and especially the horn work. Unlimited mileage is the exception rather than the rule, so be sure to ask if it is available. In Mexico City, all vehicles are prohibited from circulating one day a week, based on the last number of their license tag. This applies to rental cars, too. A good rental car company will swap cars so you don't lose a day's driving. We have heard that some rental companies will try to switch license tags and tell you it's okay. It's not. Make sure they agree to give you another legal car for that day. There should be a decal in the back window with the license tag number on it. Be sure they match or refuse the car. Renting in one city and then dropping off in another is expensive. The car rental company will charge you a per kilometer fee that may double you bill.

MONEY MATTERS

Pay with your credit card whenever possible to take advantage of the best exchange rate. Credit cards like Visa© and MasterCard© are accepted almost everywhere. Discover© is not accepted anywhere. American Express©, Diner's Club© and Carte Blanche© are accepted only at the finer establishments. You can get cash advances on the Visa© and MasterCard© at some ATMs. Pesos bills come in denominations of $10, $20, $50, $100, $200, $500 and probably bigger. Coins are 5¢, 10¢, 20¢, 50¢ (*centavos*) and $1,$2, $5, $10, and $20 pesos.

TRAVEL TIPS

If you wish to catch up on the news in the States, there is one daily English language newspapers published in Mexico City called *The News*. It carries all the latest U.S. and world news as well as sports columns, editorials and your favorite comics.

Many of the hotels in Mexico have self-operated elevators.Remember that the main floor or lobby is PB (*Planta Baja*), not the first (1) floor.

Topes or speed bumps, sometimes called *vibradores,* are the common speed control devices used in Mexico. All you really need to know about them is that you do not want to hit them going over five miles an hour. Both pilot and navigator should keep an eye out for them as you approach any small town. They will be at the entrance and somewhere in the middle. Don't be lulled into a false sense of security by the fact that some of them have signs marking their location. If traffic is slowing down for no apparent reason, you'll find out why when you get closer.

Most railroad crossings in Mexico have STOP signs. All trucks and busses must stop. It doesn't follow that you have to stop, but slow down and watch for tailgating traffic.

Commonly nicknamed "Moctezuma's Revenge," diarrhea is sometimes developed by tourists while visiting Mexico. One must realize that traveler's diarrhea can be caused by several factors and can occur anywhere in the world. Overeating, overdrinking and overexertion at high altitudes are typical causes. However, drinking impure water is the main cause for contracting the *turista*. Avoid tap water (even for brushing your teeth). Use purified water or agua *purificada* available in gas stations and small stores, just like in the States. In supermarkets, it can be purchased in one-gallon plastic containers. Mineral water, while perfectly safe, has the effect of a mild laxative on some individuals due to its mineral content. So be sure and ask for purified water at hotels, motels and restaurants. Avoid eating from street carts and sidewalk vendors.

NEED TO CALL HOME?

Calling home from Mexico has gotten easier. We recommend that you purchase international long distance phone cards available at most pharmacies and grocery stores. Pay phones that use phone cards are quite common. Simply dial: 001 + Area Code + Phone Number. You may also use you personal telephone calling card to call home from your hotel or a pay phone.

POLICE

You've probably heard nothing but bad stories about Mexican police. Most of them are helpful, polite and honest. While it's true that many years ago, *mordida* (a little bite, meaning a bribe) was a way of life, things have changed. The best advice is to approach each policeman with the attitude that he is honest and just doing his job. If, however, you encounter one from the old school who is looking for a bribe, ask for his badge number. Always carry a note pad and a pen.

MISSING LICENSE PLATES? — There is one sure way to know that your car is over parked or illegally parked – your license plate will be missing. There's a practical reason for this. Paper parking citations can be ignored and fines forgotten. However, when the police possess a license plate, drivers are compelled to go to the station and pay their fine to reclaim their plates (*placas*). Our Rita Meter maid carries a book of tickets. In Mexico, she carries a screw driver. Although fines are not usually costly and officials are courteous, it's better to avoid the problem.

Most policemen are honest. Some travelers have told us about policemen who went out of their way to help them or guide them out of town when they were lost. Should you encounter one who's not so liberated, don't panic. Get his badge number and insist you want to see his *jefe*. The phrase is "*Vamos a la comandancia.*" Another is, "*Hablemos con su jefe.*" Usually that will start a negotiating process. Stick to your guns, so to speak, as long as you are sure you didn't do anything wrong. If you insist on going to the police station, bogus infractions will vanish. However, if you have broken a law, he has every right to take your license plates. You must go to the station to pay your fine. If it's a weekend, you may have to wait until Monday. Although we do not recommend it, some old-timers prefer to pay the fine "on the spot" to save the aggravation. If a policemanc asks you for a bribe, report him. The government is very concerned about officers "on the take" and treat all reports seriously. You should report the officer's badge number and when and where the incident occurred. Send any complaints about policemen, other officials, hotels, restaurants, etc. (or praise for those who went out of their way to help you) to: Departamento de Quejas, Dirección General de Turismo, Presidente Masaryk #172, Mexico, DF. In Mexico City, call: (55) 5604-1240. The Policia Federal de Caminos are quite professional and honest. They can be your best friend in an emergency.

U.S. CONSULATES

CD. JUÁREZ, CHIH — López Mateos #924-N CP. 32000 Tel: (656) 613-4048 or 613-5050 Fax: (656) 616-9056 Duty Officer: (915) 526-6066 (in El Paso, TX) Office Hours: 08:00 to 15:45 Mailing Address: American Consulate Apdo. Postal #1681 32000 Cd. Juárez, Chih.

GUADALAJARA, JAL — Progreso 175, Col. Americana Guadalajara, Jalisco ZP C. 44100. Tel: (01-33) 3825-2700; Fax: (01-33) 3826-6549 Duty Officer and after hours calls: (33) 3626-5553.

HERMOSILLO, SON — Monterrey #141 entre las calles Rosales y Galeana, Col. Esqueda, Hermosillo, Sonora, México 83260 Ph: (662) 217-2575 Fax: (662) 217-2578.

MATAMOROS, TAM — Calle Primera #2002 y Azaleas, Matamoros, Tamaulipas 87330. Tel.: (868) 912-4402/03/08 Fax: (868) 912-2171 Office Hours: 08:00 to 12:00 and 13:00 to 17:00 Mailing Address: American Consulate Apdo. Postal #451, 87350 Matamoros, Tamps.

MÉRIDA, YUC — Paseo Montejo #453 por Avenida Colon, Merida, Yucatan, Mexico 97000. Ph: (999) 925-5011 Fax: (999) 925-6219.

MONTERREY, NL — Avenida Constitución #411 Pte. Monterrey, N.L. Mexico 64000. Tel.: (81) 8345-2120 Fax: (81) 8345-7748 Mailing Address: P.O. Box #3098 Laredo, TX 78044-3098.

NVO. LAREDO, COAH — Calle Allende #3330, Colonia Jardín, Nuevo Laredo, Tamps. Mexico 88260. Tel.: (867) 714-0696 or 714-0512 Fax: (867) 714-0696 Office Hours: 8:00 a.m. - 12:30 p.m. / 1:30 p.m. - 5:00 p.m. Principal Officer: Thomas Armbruster

TIJUANA, BCN — Tapachula 96, Colonia Hipodromo, Tijuana, Baja California, Mexico 22420. Tel.: (dialing from the U.S.) 011-52-(664) 622-7400 Fax: (dialing from the U.S.) 011-52-(664) 681-8016. U.S. Mailing Address: P.O. Box 439039, San Diego, CA 92143-9039.

U.S. CONSULAR AGENTS

ACAPULCO, GRO — Alexander Richards, Hotel Acapulco Continental, Costera M. Alemán 121 Local 14, Acapulco, Gro. 39670 Tel: (744) 469-0556, Tel./Fax: (744) 484-0300. Email: consular@prodigy.net.mx

CABO SAN LUCAS, BCS — Michael J. Houston, Blvd. Marian Local C-4, Plaza Nautica, Centro, Cabo Sal Lucas, B.C.S. 23410. Tel.: (624) 143-3566 Fax: (624) 143-6750. Email: usconsulcabo@hotmail.com

CANCÚN, Q ROO — Lynnette Belt, Segundo Nivel #320-3232, Plaza Caracol Dos, Blvd. Kukulcán, Zona Hotelera, Cancún, Q. R. 77500. Mailing Address: Apdo. Postal 862., Concun, Q.R. Tel.: (998) 883-0272, Fax: (998) 883-1373 Email: uscons@prodigy.net.mx, Lynnette@usconscancun.com

Cd. ACUNA/DEL RIO, COAHUILA — Elvira Morales, Ocampo No. 305 (corner with Morelos), Centro, Ciudad Acuña, Coahuila 26200. Tel.: (877) 772-8661, Fax: (877) 772-8179 Email: elviramz@msn.com

COZUMEL, QR — Anne R. Harris, Offices 8 & 9, "Villa Mar" Mall - Between Melgar and 5th. Ave., Cozumel, QR. 77600. Tel.:(987) 872-4574/872-4485 Fax: (987) 872-2339. Email: usgov@cozumel.net, usca@cozumel.net Mailing Address: Av. 35 Norte No. 650 (between 12 bis and 14 Norte), Cozumel, QR. 77622

IXTAPA / ZIHUATANEJO — Elizabeth Williams, Local 9, Plaza Ambiente, Ixtapa, Zihuatanejo. Tel.: (755) 553-2100 Fax: (755) 554-6276 Email: liz@lizwilliams.org, Lizpersonal@bigfoot.com Mailing Address: Apdo. Postal 169, Zihuatanejo, Gro. 40880

MAZATLÁN, SIN — Patti Fletcher, Hotel Playa Mazatlán, Playa Gaviotas No. 202, Zona Dorada, Mazatlán, Sinaloa 82110 Ph & Fax: (669) 916-5889 , Email: mazagent@mzt.megared.net.mx

OAXACA, OAX — Mark Arnold Leyes, Macedonia Alcala # 407, Office 20, Oaxaca, Oax. 68000. Tel.: (951)514-3054 or 516-2853. Fax: (951) 516-2701 Email: conagent@prodigy.net.mx.

PIEDRAS NEGRAS, COAHUILA — Dina L. O'Brien, Prol. General Cepeda No. 1900, Fraccionamiento Privada Blanca. Piedras Negras, Coahuila 26700. Tel.: (878) 795-1986, 795-1987, 795-1988. Off. U.S. (830) 773-9231. Email: obriendina@hotmail.com

PTO. VALLARTA, JAL — Kelly Anne Trainor, Plaza Zaragoza #160, Piso 2 Oficina18, Puerto Vallarta, Jal.48300 Tel.: (322) 223-0074. Fax: (322) 223-0074. Email: amconpv@prodigy.net.mx

REYNOSA, TAMPS. — Roberto Rodríguez, Calle Monterrey No. 390 (corner with Sinaloa), Col. Rodríguez, Reynosa, Tamps., 88630. Tel.: (899) 923-9331, 923-8878, 923-9245. Email: usconsularagent@hotmail.com

SAN LUIS POTOSÍ, SLP — Carolyn H. Lazaro,Edificio "Las Terrazas" Ave. Venustiano Carranza 2076-41, Col. Polanco, San Luis Potosi, S.L. P., 78220. Tel.: (444) 811-7802 Fax: (444) 811-7803 Email: usconsulslp@yahoo.com

GENERAL SOCIAL RULES

If someone invites you to dine with them or come to their house, they are sincere. To refuse without giving good reason is bad manners. In general, whenever a specific place and time are mentioned, the invitation is sincere. Their sense of time (except in business situations) is different than ours, so allow thirty minutes to an hour for acceptable tardiness.

Never make fun of someone's station in life or what they have or don't have. People are proud of themselves and their possessions, no matter how meager they may appear to your eyes.

Please, don't ask, "How much is it in real money?" Often people will quote you in dollars to be polite. Also, don't worry too much about being short changed. People are a lot more honest than you might suspect.

WAITING IN LINE — Chances are that someone will cut in. You politely say, "*Desculpe, la fila sigue atrás*," to tell them that the end of the line is somewhere behind you. Unfortunately, Mexicans are no different than people anywhere in the world. Some rude people will just ignore you, but most people are polite and will go farther back in the line and try again.

PARKING ATTENDANTS — In small towns there are still some guys who are wearing khaki clothing and official looking hats that are as old as they are and will direct you to a parking space. They are not police officers but will watch your car. Pay them the peso equivalent of fifty cents or so.

PARKING LOTS — Many hotels have underground lots that are narrow and have low ceilings. You will not be able to use them if you have a tall camper. If you have an extended cab pickup with a long bed, it will take some maneuvering to get in and out, but it can be done if you have the patience. Find another open-air lot if possible. At some parking lots you will get a time ticket. Make sure you know the price before leaving and don't lose the ticket.

TIPPING — It's customary to tip the gas pump attendant the peso equivalent of a quarter. Remember that your U.S. coins are useless to anyone in Mexico, so don't use them for tips. The kids who wash your windshield get a quarter and porters get fifty cents a bag. Maids should get a dollar a day. Waiters get 10-15% average and exceptional service, of course, gets up to 20%. Please use common sense and don't overtip like an ugly American or undertip like a cheapskate.

WOMEN TRAVELING ALONE

While many people enjoy their trips more with a companion, traveling alone in Mexico should be no more daunting than doing so anywhere in the U.S. Use common sense, dress conservatively, don't sleep in your car and you will find the Mexican people to be very hospitable. As in any country, how you are treated often depends on the signals you give out. Don't dress provocatively. Places to be careful are ruins and other tourist attractions close to closing time, bars, lonely beaches (Please don't camp on one) or anywhere you would not go back home. Use common sense and you'll have a good time.

DON'T DRIVE AT NIGHT!

Please don't drive at night — You are quite safe in terms of personal safety on Mexico's highways. A number of factors make night driving hazardous; On older, two lane roads, you could hit a chuckhole with no warning that could seriously damage your suspension. Shoulders are narrow or sometimes nonexistent. Drivers of broken down vehicles often place rocks on the road to "warn" you that they are taking up a lane ahead. Even if you see the rocks in time, it may be too late. Long after they are gone, the rocks often remain, despite signs telling you not to leave them. These rocks can tear up your car or send you careening off a mountain.

Mexico has a lot of open range. Cows, burros, goats and horses think they have the right of way. You can't see a black cow at night. Cows, burros etc. don't wear taillights. Outside of cities, some drivers may drive without headlights, thinking they can see better or that they will conserve their lights by not using them. Others may have only one (or no) taillights. There is often a high drop from the pavement to the shoulder that could cause you to roll over. The famous Green Angels don't drive at night.

Many people in Mexico have never or seldom been in a vehicle. They walk everywhere they go, usually in the brush very close to the edge of highway pavement. frequently, they suddenly step out of the brush onto the highway placing themselves in the immediate path of an automobile. Because they have no conception fo the speed and weight of a vehicle, they are unaware of the danger. Most of them have never owned a flashlight and trust thier instincts to walk and find their way in the dark. In the daytime, small children often sit on the very edge of highway pavement with their backs to passing traffic only inches away from trucks buses and cars passing at high speeds.

GREEN ANGELS

Green Angels are trained mechanics who roam all the major highways to assist disabled travelers. This is a free service provided by Mexico's Department of Tourism. You'll see their bright green panel trucks driving slowly down every major highway. They cover each route twice a day. If you break down, they will find you, or you can call them on your CB, channel 9. There are over 800 "Angels" covering 230 routes. If one of them helps you, his service is free, but he will have to charge you for any parts you need or gasoline. He can also provide emergency medical aid, so a tip is recommended and always well received. **If you need help and a phone is nearby, call the Green Angel Hot central radio room at 01-55-5250-8221.**

MORE DRIVING ADVICE

TOLL ROADS — Take the toll roads whenever possible as they can save a lot of time, although some are quite expensive especially if you're on a budget. We no longer post them in this Travelog because they go up so often. You can find the latest tariff rates on the internet at the following web site: http://www.capufe.gob.mx/tarifas.html

CUTTING IN — This is very common. If you are in a line of traffic and it doesn't seem to be moving and cars are passing you on the dirt on the right, chances are they are cutting in front of the line. In city traffic when someone wants to turn right or left (from any lane), one of the passengers (or driver) will stick an arm out and indicate with hand signals the direction of an intended turn. It's customary to let them. When you are in a traffic jam and someone acts like they are going to cut in but point their finger straight in front of them, they're indicating that they are crossing the line of traffic, not trying to cut in. They are usually telling the truth. Let them in.

BUSES — Passing a long distance bus (not the little local *colectivos* and *lecheros* or second class stop-and-go varieties) is usually an invitation to a duel. Do so at your own risk, or better yet, don't. They will always go faster than you. Bus drivers really seem to be bothered if you use high beams of even fog lights or drive during the day with your headlights on. They will flash you if they are feeling pleasant, but if not, they will blind you with their forty-seven running lights and two million candlepower sets of quad-headlights. It's an awesome sight on a lonely road. When passing buses discharging passengers, slow down and be prepared for them to dash in front of you. Non-drivers don't comprehend velocity.

FLAGMEN — You're bound to encounter a few sets of these. Sometimes the flagman may be only an inattentive young man with a faded red rag who is supposed to warn you about upcoming dangers. Whenever you see a guy on the side of the road with a red rag, assume you'd better slow down as there could be a myriad of dangers ahead.

TRAFFIC SIGNALS — When a light changes from green to yellow to red, sometimes the green will start flashing, turn yellow, then red. Mexicans tend to inch forward before the red changes to green. When there are four lights on a signal (and a left turn lane), one is probably a protected left turn signal. Be careful if there is no left turn lane because the fourth signal may indicate a right turn or just be an extra green.

RIGHT TURN ON RED — This is not universally allowed, unless there is a sign, usually a right arrow with the words *Continua con precaución.*

LEFT TURNS — There are at least 4 kinds.

The first is easy — When you are in a city, there will be a left turn lane (usually, not always) and a traffic signal with four lights. The far left one is a protected turn signal. You must wait for the left turn arrow. You cannot turn left when the coast is clear on only a green light. You must wait for the protected arrow.

Left turn type two — There is a sign with an arrow indicating you should exit, then it turns left in front of traffic. What on earth does that mean? You should exit right onto a lateral or access road on a divided street. Stay in the left lane. Go to a stoplight. Turn left across the street you were just on. It's easier to do than it sounds.

Left turn type three — You are on a two-lane open road. If there is traffic coming, do not put on your left turn blinker and stop in the middle of an intersection to turn left. Just before you get there, you'll see a paved shoulder to the right. You should exit right, pull around until you are heading in the direction you want to turn. When traffic is clear, scoot across the highway.

Left turn type four — This is easy and familiar. You are on a divided highway. There is a break in the median and a sign that says *retorno*. You guessed it — a turnaround.

Well, now you have had a good introduction to what it's really like to drive in Mexico. The bottom line is go and have a good time. The Mexican people are friendly and don't get all uptight if you make a few mistakes. Remember: "If you want to have friends you must be friendly."

SANBORN'S COMPANY BIOGRAPHY

Sanborn's Mexico Insurance traces its roots to 1948 when Dan Sanborn, a newspaperman from Kankakee, Illinois, began writing a unique highway guide to Mexico for his friends.

In the early 1950's, he opened a roadside stand to sell citrus juice, curios, Mexico insurance and "horned toads" (lizards that shoot blood from their eyes). With the insurance, each customer got a *Travelog*, Dan's mile-by-smile highway guide of Mexico, custom-made for the customer's itinerary.

Today, Sanborn's has more than 40 agencies located at major US-Mexico border crossings, and in Mexico. Customers can purchase insurance by using our Faxinsure or Phoneinsure service, in addition to our walk-in and mail order service. We also sell Central American insurance. It's a "family-style" business with old-fashioned values and courtesy. Each customer is "one of the family."

Tourists need Mexican insurance because neither U.S. nor Canadian insurance is recognized in Mexico. We sell Seguros del Centro insurance, underwritten by GE and sold on a daily or inexpensive six-month or annual basis. Claims are settled in the U.S., and we have adjusters throughout Mexico (Our U.S. claims service will pay to fix vehicles in the U.S.A.).

Today, the *Travelog* is a series of 9 guidebooks to all Mexico with incredibly detailed directions, history, customs and humor, which get people where they're going safely and helps them enjoy the historic routes they drive. Detailed maps of most tourist towns are included, as well as lists of hotels, restaurants and RV parks. All price ranges are covered.

TEMPERATURE CONVERSION TABLE

Fairenheit	100	95	85	80	75	70	65	60	55	50	45	40	35	32
Celcius	37.3	35	29.4	46.6	23.8	21.1	18.3	15.5	12.7	10	7.2	4.2	1.6	0

CONVERTING KILOGRAMS TO POUNDS: Simply double the kilogram figure, then add 10%. For example, if a man's weight is 80 kilos, double this (160) and add 10% (16). His weight would be 176 pounds.

CONVERSION OF METRIC WEIGHTS AND MEASURES

1 gram = 0.035 ounces
1 kilogram = 2.205 pounds
1 metric ton = 1.102 tons
1 milliliter = 0.033 fluid ounces
1 deciliter = 3.381 fluid ounces
1 liter = 1.056 quarts

1 millimeter = 0.039 inch
1 centimeter = 0.393 inch
1 decimeter = 3.937 inches
1 meter = 3.289 feet
1 kilometer = 0.621 miles

TIRE PRESSURE:

Kilos	2.1	2	1.9	1.8	1.7	1.6
Pounds	32	30	28	26	24	22

CONVERTING KILOMETERS TO MILES

Kilometers	1	5	10	20	30	40	50	60	70	80	90	100	120
Miles	0.62	3.1	6.2	12.4	19	25	31	37.5	44	50	56	62.5	75

CONVERTING LITERS TO GALLONS

Liters	1	4	10	15	20	30	40	50	60	70	80	90
Gallons	0.26	1.06	2.64	3.97	5.28	7.92	10.6	13.2	15.8	18.5	21.1	23.8

5How about the Ferries!

First of all, this changes with the wind, but we verified all of this info in July, 2001. You canvisit the Ferry website for latest itineraries and tariffs: www.ferrysematur.com.mx Take seasick preparations if you're inclined that way. It can get rough. Don't plan on sleeping in the "salon" unless you really like people and kids as it only has airplane type seats. Go for the "turista" with two to four beds (it varies from ship to ship), interior wash basin and exterior toilet and bath or "cabina" with bunks in a comfortable room for two with interior bathroom. "Especial" is a two-room suite with full bath and closet and includes TV, video player and servibar. Your rig stays below. You won't be able to return, so get anything you need out before you leave the bowels of the ship. Food is served on board. **NO PETS** are allowed to ride in the passenger compartments. Prices include tax. Fare is per person, one way, sharing the accommodation. Children under 11 years old pay half price. Children under 2 years old must be registered at no cost. Pregnant women are not allowed aboard. The maximum vehicle width is 2.6 meters. If a vehicle exceeds this width it will cost double the tariff, because it will occupy 2 lanes. Maximum height is 4 meters.

You need to reserve a minimum of 72 hours to a week in advance. The easiest thing to do is register on the internet or have a travel agent do it for you. You can do it by phone, but must pick up your ticket in person. In La Paz, you must pick up ticket at downtown office at G. Prieto #1495, not at the dock. **Hours change**, but try 8-noon. Plan on a long line. Then, you must show up at the dock the day you are to leave and register, about 8 AM (this will vary, so ask and then arrive an hour early). Then you hang around until they begin boarding. There's always a chance of a cancellation, so you can **try** showing up, waiting and asking for a ticket. You **might** get one. At other locations, you can get them at the ferry landing. The Peso exchange rate is about $10.95 Pesos to $1.00 Dollar (as of May, 2005).

FERRY PRICES (as of May, 2005) RATES ARE IN PESOS and are based on length:

PRICE LIST

Vehicle (Length)	Mazatlán	Topolobampo	Guaymas
Under 5 meters	$2,020.00	$2,200.00	$3,550.00
5.01 to 6.5 meters	$3,030.00	$2,830.00	$4,600.00
Motorhome	$4,545.00	$4,600.00	$6,050.00
Auto/w/trailer under 9 meters	$6,450.00	$3.890.00	$6,450.00
Auto/w/trailer 9.01 to 17 meters	$11,960.00	$7,300.00	$11,960.00
Buses	$6,050.00	$4,600.00	$6,050.00
Motorcycles	$850.00	$720.00	$850.00
Passenger Compartments	**Price Per Person** (One Way)		
Saló n	$660.01	$360.00	$460.00
Turista	$1,702.94	$810.00	$1,040.00
Cabina	$2,088.94	$1,040.00	$1,270.00
Especial	$2,220.94	$1,270.00	$1,500.00

It doesn't matter how long you are if your pockets are deep enough. Sometimes the ferry runs, but only for freight, so don't plan too strictly.

FERRY SCHEDULE

Route:	La Paz to Mazatlán	Mazatlán to La Paz	La Paz to Topolobampo	Topolobampo to La Paz	Sta. Rosalía to Guaymas	Guaymas to Sta. Rosalía
Frequency:	Daily except some Saturdays	Daily except some Saturdays	Daily except Sundays	Daily except Sundays	Tuesday and Friday	Monday and Thursday
Departure:	3:00 PM	3:00 PM	10:00 PM	10:00 PM	11:00 PM	11:00 AM
Arrival:	8:00 AM	8:00 AM	8:00 AM	8:00 AM	8:00 AM	6:30 PM

INFORMATION AND RESERVATIONS

The best way to make reservations is to do it on the internet at http://www.ferrysematur.com.mx They provide an easy bilingual application form to fill out. Just click on the reservation icon and enter your information. Or you can call one of the following numbers: 01-800-696-9600 (reservations).
LA PAZ, B.C.S — Guillermo Prieto & 5 de Mayo Ph: (612) 125-3833 & 125-4666 Pichilingue Terminal Ph: (612) 122-5005 Fax: (612) 125-5717. Ahome Travel Agency Ticket office in La Paz: (612) 125-2366, 125-2346.
MAZATLAN, SIN. — Ferry Terminal Ph: (669) 981-7021 Fax: (669) 981-7023.
TOPOLOBAMPO, SIN. — Muelle Fiscal Ph: (668) 862-0141 Fax: (668) 862-0035 **STA. ROSALIA, B.C.S.** — Muelle Fiscal Ph: (615) 152-0013 & 152-0014. **GUAYMAS, SON.** — Muelle Fiscal Ph: (622) 222-2324 Fax: (622) 222-3393 **MEXICO CITY** — Ph: (55) 5523-8696, 5523-4477 Ahome Travel Agency: (55) 5559-7206, 559-7135. **LOS MOCHIS, SIN** — Ahome Travel Agency, Ph: (668) 915-6120, 918-6382, 912-3922 Toll Free: 01-800-201-9383, e-mail: vahome@interaccess.com.mx

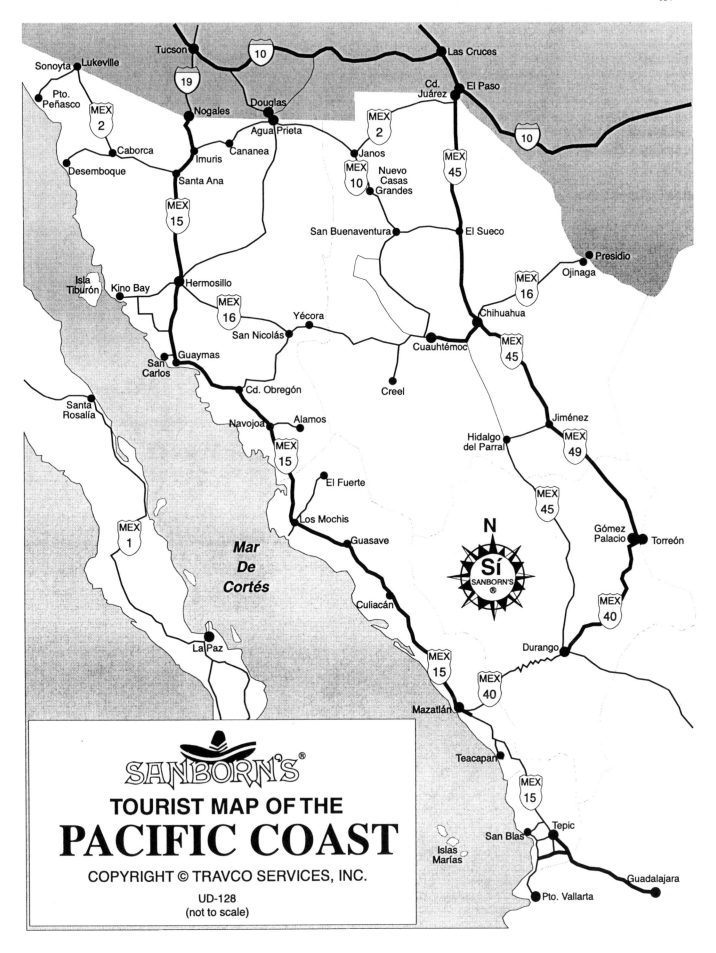

SANBORN'S®
TOURIST MAP OF THE
PACIFIC COAST
COPYRIGHT © TRAVCO SERVICES, INC.

UD-128
(not to scale)

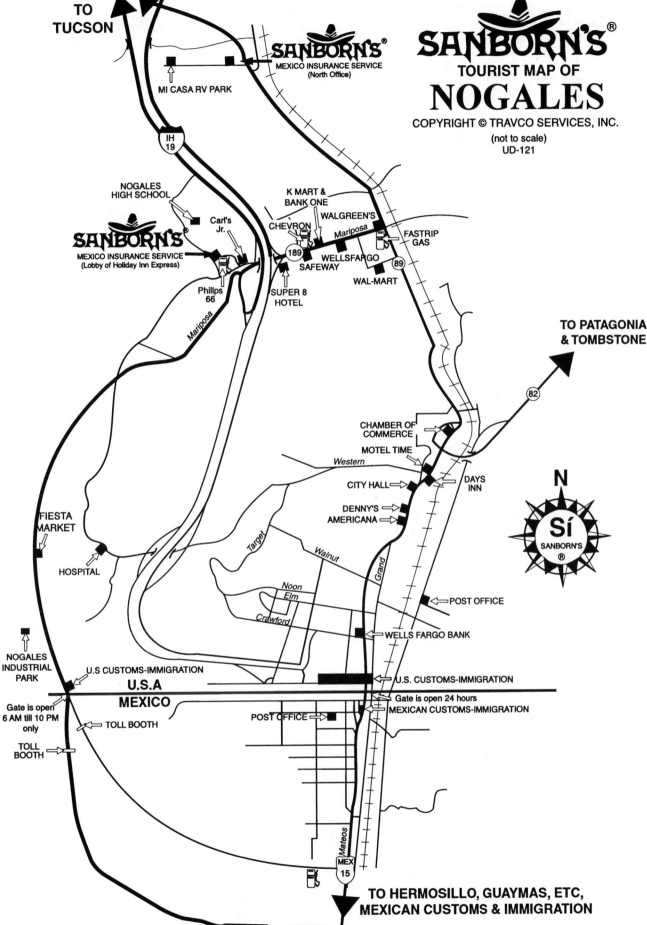

SANBORN'S®
TOURIST MAP OF
NOGALES
COPYRIGHT © TRAVCO SERVICES, INC.
(not to scale)
UD-121

TO TUCSON

SANBORN'S®
MEXICO INSURANCE SERVICE
(North Office)

MI CASA RV PARK

IH 19

NOGALES HIGH SCHOOL

Carl's Jr.

SANBORN'S®
MEXICO INSURANCE SERVICE
(Lobby of Holiday Inn Express)

Phillps 66

Mariposa

K MART & BANK ONE

CHEVRON

WALGREEN'S

Mariposa

189

SAFEWAY

WELLSFARGO

SUPER 8 HOTEL

WAL-MART

FASTRIP GAS

89

TO PATAGONIA & TOMBSTONE

82

CHAMBER OF COMMERCE

MOTEL TIME

Western

CITY HALL

DAYS INN

DENNY'S

AMERICANA

N

Sí
SANBORN'S®

FIESTA MARKET

HOSPITAL

Target

Walnut

Noon
Elm

Crawford

Grand

POST OFFICE

WELLS FARGO BANK

NOGALES INDUSTRIAL PARK

U.S CUSTOMS-IMMIGRATION

U.S.A
MEXICO

U.S. CUSTOMS-IMMIGRATION

Gate is open 6 AM till 10 PM only

TOLL BOOTH

TOLL BOOTH

POST OFFICE

Gate is open 24 hours
MEXICAN CUSTOMS-IMMIGRATION

Mateos

MEX 15

TO HERMOSILLO, GUAYMAS, ETC,
MEXICAN CUSTOMS & IMMIGRATION

LOG 1   *START:* Nogales, AZ   *END:* Imuris, Son

UD-019

If entering Mexico from Nogales, use this log. If entering from Douglas start Douglas - Imuris Log (page 3) or Douglas - Hermosillo Log (page 74).

48.0 MI or 76.8 KM
DRIVE TIME 50 MIN — 1 1/4 HOURS
SCENIC RATING - 2

NOTE: The newer border crossing via the "loop" is open from 6 AM till 10 PM only; otherwise, you have to cross at the "old" gateway via Hwy 89 downtown. Since you're not driving at night, it doesn't matter — right?

MI	KM	
0.0	0.0	Leave Sanborn's Mi Casa RV Travel Park and head south down U.S. #89 (Grand Ave.). Pass Nogales Service Center and Truck Stop on right.
1.6	2.6	TURN RIGHT onto U.S. Hwy #189 (Mariposa Road – it's the 4th light after leaving Sanborn's). Fast Trip **GAS** is on left.

IF TO: Old gateway thru downtown Nogales, Nogales Sonora and on to Imuris, continue straight ahead on US Hwy 89 (Grand Ave.). However, this route is not recommended, especially for trailers and RV's.

1.7	2.7	Having elected not to go thru downtown, continue ahead on Mariposa Rd.
2.0	3.2	Pass Safeway (on left) for last-minute items. There is a K-Mart, Bank One and Chevron **GAS** plus two other gas stations on right.
2.2	3.5	Pass Super 8 Hotel on left and under IH-19 overpass and continue west. Phillips 66 **GAS**, Carl's Jr., Holiday Inn Expres and Nogales High School on right. *Sanborn's Nogales South office located in Lobby of Holiday Inn.*
4.4	7.0	Shell gas station on left (last chance for US gas).
4.7	7.5	Straight to border gateway – you are entering Mexico. This is Nogales, Sonora. You'll get your tourist and vehicle permits farther down the pike at what is referred to as KM 21 (veinte y uno). "Bienvenidos a Mexico!" (Welcome to Mexico!)
4.8	7.7	As you have now entered Mexico, veer to the right if going to downtown Nogales, Sonora. Otherwise, go straight entering toll road following Hermosillo signs.
10.0	16.0	Come to tollhouse and pay toll (cars $50, trucks $78).
10.6	17.0	Come to "check" station – red light/green light – If red light comes up, stop for vehicle check; if green proceed ahead. KM 265.
12.1	19.4	Pass turnoff (right) to Nogales' airport. Sign says, "Santa Ana 94 KM. Hermosillo 260 KM." The "KM" numbers we put to the side are the Mexican highway markers which denote the distance to the next major town or highway junction. So now you'll see "KM 260" and realize it's 260 kilometers to Hermosillo or the next intersection with a major road or next major town. Got it? KM 260.
16.5	26.4	GAS, left.
16.6	26.6	Slow now! Pull off to right and STOP for MIGRACIÓN and ADUANA . This is where you get your tourist card and vehicle permit. Park your vehicle(s) in the parking lot and walk to the appropriate buildings.

If only going to Sonora, look for the "Sonora only" building. Enter building to get your tourist permit and "Sonora Only" vehicle permit. These permits are free. Note: You must surrender your "Sonora Only" vehicle permit upon leaving Mexico. If travelling beyond the state of Sonora, go to the second building to obtain a long term vehicle permit and tourist card. Both permits are good for 6 months. You can exit and enter Mexico as many times as you would like during the 6 month period. Note: the cost for the 6-month vehicle permit is about $17.00 (US), payable only by a credit card and must be surrendered prior to the expiration date on the permit.

27.0	43.2	Bear right thru Cibuta and slow thru school zone. Pedestrians. **KM 240.**
34.2	54.7	Curve left. Now up. Topped 3,500 feet. **KM 229.**
34.9	55.8	We have descended to 3,400 feet.
45.0	72.0	Up past Las Viguitas on right. Speed limit is 90 KMPH.
46.8	74.9	Imuris railroad depot at right. Then into fringe of hilltop town of Imuris (e-moo-rees).
48.0	76.8	Come now to junction left with Hwy #2 from Douglas, Arizona and Agua Prieta, Mexico. **GAS**, right. There is a VERY neat statue at left. Take a few minutes to stop and walk all the way around it. **KM 207.**

IF TO: Magdalena and Santa Ana, straight. Start Imuris — Santa Ana Log (page 6).

IF TO: Cananea, Agua Prieta and Douglas, left. Start Imuris — Douglas Log (page 67).

End of Log 1

LOG 2	**START: Douglas, AZ**	**END: Imuris, Son**

UD-019

104 MI OR 166.4 KM
DRIVE TIME 2 — 3 HOURS
SCENIC RATING — 4

If you want to take the alternate route that goes to Hermosillo via Nacozari, use Douglas - Hermosillo Log (page 74).

The most interesting place to stay in Douglas is the historic old Hotel Gadsden with the best restaurant in town. Motels are the Family Crest Bed and Breakfast, Motel 6 and Thriftlodge. If you wish to overnight in Agua Prieta and get an early start, there's the Hotel Hacienda. There are 2 RV parks.

None of our customers ever forget anything, but they might misplace some things, so please check now for: proof of your citizenship (or notarized affidavit) and proof of ownership of your vehicle (title or registration and driver's license plus an international credit card, AE, DI, MC, VI in the same name). You'll leave a photocopy of your credentials with Mexican officials. REMEMBER — The person whose name is on the car permit MUST be in car whenever it is driven. Your permit is good for multiple entries, but you MUST turn it in at any border crossing BEFORE it expires. Also, all minors need either both parents with them, or notarized permission from the absent parent.

MI	KM	
0.0	0.0	Starting at the corner of 10th St. and "F" Ave. in Douglas, Arizona, head west on (10th St.) Hwy #80.
0.1	0.2	Straight at light. Pass city hall at left.
0.3	0.5	After two long blocks, come to dead end. Cochise Vocational College ahead. TURN LEFT onto wide Pan American Ave. Ahead for about three-quarters of a mile.
1.0	1.6	Wave good-bye to U.S. Customs on your left (Don't stop). Cross border (There's no river to cross here.) on one-way bridge — you're now in Mexico.

Take far right slot and pull up to Mexican official and tell him you're going to Guadalajara or Guaymas or Kino or wherever you're going. He'll tell you to park diagonally just ahead at right. Then go into Mexican government building at right and head for the counter at MIGRACIÓN (immigration) on right side of building where your tourist cards will be written (or those that you have will be validated). There's a $17.00 fee per person. Then cut across the big room to ADUANA (Customs) where you'll get your car permit and pay another fee of $17.0. They'll put a sticker on your windshield and you're on your way.

Now back out of the diagonal parking spot and careful for incoming traffic. Then head straight down their main street. GAS, left on corner. You're now in Agua Prieta, Spanish for "dark water" or "dirty water."

1.1	1.8	Turn left at first corner. Then GAS at right. Pinheras Vildosa on left. Go 3 blocks. The 3 story building on right is Hacienda Hotel. Turn right onto Avenida 6.
1.3	2.1	Pass seafood restaurant "Gómez Hnos. (Brothers abbreviated)" and La Fogata at right, then El Mesquite. Continue ahead till you get to Hwy #2. Watch — several stoplights. Cross Porfirio Calles Street.
1.6	2.6	Goodyear at left. Then stoplight.
1.8	2.9	Past Motel Ruiz at right.
2.0	3.2	Cemetery at right. Industrial park at left. Then ball park at right. GAS and then Motel Arizona.
2.8	4.5	Come now to junction Hwy 2.

IF TO: CANANEA, Imuris, Nacozari and Hermosillo, TURN RIGHT here.

IF TO: Janos and on to Chihuahua, TURN LEFT and start Douglas - Janos Log (See Mexico's Central Route book, page 31).

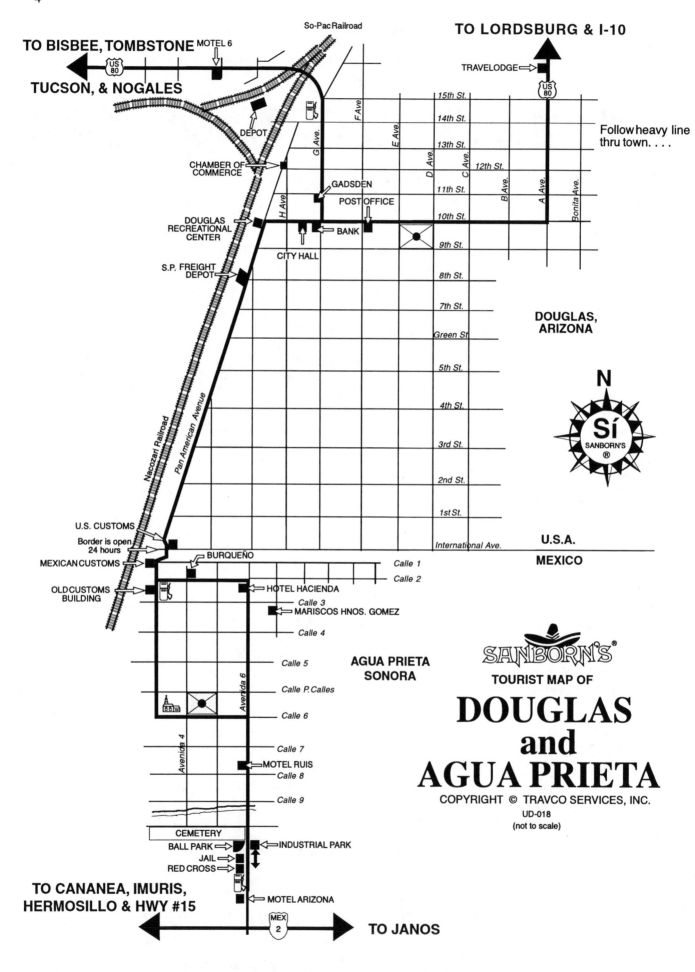

4

TO LORDSBURG & I-10

TO BISBEE, TOMBSTONE
MOTEL 6

TUCSON, & NOGALES

So-Pac Railroad

TRAVELODGE ⇒

Follow heavy line
thru town. . . .

15th St.
14th St.
13th St.
12th St.
11th St.
10th St.
9th St.
8th St.
7th St.
Green St
5th St.
4th St.
3rd St.
2nd St.
1st St.

DEPOT

CHAMBER OF
COMMERCE

GADSDEN

POST OFFICE

DOUGLAS
RECREATIONAL
CENTER

BANK

S.P. FREIGHT
DEPOT

CITY HALL

F Ave.
E Ave.
D Ave.
C Ave.
B Ave.
A Ave.
Bonita Ave.
G Ave.
H Ave.

DOUGLAS,
ARIZONA

N
Sí
SANBORN'S
®

Nacozari Railroad

Pan American Avenue

U.S. CUSTOMS

Border is open
24 hours

MEXICAN CUSTOMS

OLD CUSTOMS
BUILDING

International Ave.

U.S.A.

MEXICO

BURQUEÑO

Calle 1
Calle 2

HOTEL HACIENDA

Calle 3

MARISCOS HNOS. GOMEZ

Calle 4

Calle 5

AGUA PRIETA
SONORA

Calle P. Calles

Calle 6

Avenida 6

Avenida 4

Calle 7

MOTEL RUIS

Calle 8

Calle 9

CEMETERY

BALL PARK ⇒

JAIL ⇒

RED CROSS ⇒

INDUSTRIAL PARK

TO CANANEA, IMURIS,
HERMOSILLO & HWY #15

MOTEL ARIZONA

MEX
2

TO JANOS

SANBORN'S ®

TOURIST MAP OF

DOUGLAS
and
AGUA PRIETA

COPYRIGHT © TRAVCO SERVICES, INC.

UD-018
(not to scale)

MI	KM	
3.5	5.6	Over TWO railroad tracks — line runs to Nacozari, another copper town.
4.3	6.9	Come now to junction with Sonora Hwy #12 and road (left) to Hermosillo.

IF TO: Cananea and on to Imuris, STRAIGHT AHEAD and on to Imuris, 46 miles south of Nogales on Hwy 15.

IF TO: Hermosillo (thru Nacozari and Moctezuma), turn left and join Douglas - Hermosillo Special (page 74) at mile 4.3. Sign says "118 kilometers to Nacozari" or 73 miles.

13.5	21.6	Curve left and up a little and then wide right around foothills at right.
16.3	26.1	Curve left and over and down big hill on straight stretch. That big mountain ahead at one o'clock is MT. GRANIZO (which means hail or hailstorm).
19.0	30.4	Abandoned customs check at right.
22.0	35.2	Now left and nice straight stretch with good view of Mt. Granizo over at right.
27.8	44.5	Curve right at Kilometer 40 and start straight stretch.
29.5	47.2	Pass side road (right) up to Naco, Bisbee's border town. Stop there on way home.
30.8	49.3	Ejido Cuauhtémoc over to right.

Cuauhtémoc (1502-1525) was the 11th and last Aztec Emperor, the son of Emperor Ahuizotl and princess Tilalcaptl. He was educated in the Calmecac School for nobles. Cortés made him a prisoner on Aug. 13, 1521 and had him killed by hanging him by his feet like a common criminal on Feb. 28, 1525. He was 23. He was betrayed by Malinche, who acted as interpreter. To this day, a "Malinche" is a woman who cannot be trusted — that's the polite version.

31.0	49.6	Slow now and stop for immigration check station. Have your papers ready.
35.3	56.5	Now right curve and up and then thru long rock cut and wind thru hills.
38.0	60.8	Curve right and up thru cut onto mesa (plateau) — note Cananea in distance ahead.
38.8	62.1	Now a long downward stretch and over bridge over Arroyo Claro and up.
41.0	65.6	Ejido Ignacio Zaragoza over to right. Nice ranching country thru here.
43.8	70.1	Now curve right and down on another straight stretch practically to Cananea.
46.3	74.1	Ejido Emiliano Zapata to left. (Zapata was the hero of the land revolt.)
52.5	84.0	Pass Motel Valle de Cobre —MOD— 38 rooms, CATV, pool, Ph: (645) 332-2086 Fax: 332-3808. Also Motel and Restaurant Mesón, looks good, near Chrysler/Dodge dealership on right. Then pass side road (left) to Arizpe and airport at right.
53.0	84.8	On divided boulevard. Careful now!

IF TO: Bypass Cananea, take right fork (at IMURIS sign) and curve right.

54.0	85.4	Volkswagen agency at right. Monument at left honoring the strikers killed in 1906 during a labor dispute. GAS, right. Then over railroad (LOOK-&-LISTEN). Then curve left and wind down over arroyo and up.

If you have the time and wish to drive into Cananea, this is a pleasant little town with really nice folks. You can visit the old jail, view a museum and just soak up the atmosphere. Motel Zafari (into town 1 mile on left) — MOD— 36 A/C rooms, SATV. Ph: (645) 332-1308, 332-1528, 332-1108 Fax: 332-3739. Gives discount on weekends. Take left fork above.

56.0	89.6	Nice view over to left of famous Cananea copper mine. You can drive to front gate but no tours or visits.
58.5	93.6	Wind on thru Río San Miguel canyon.
60.5	96.8	Up on winding road. Then left horseshoe curve and on up.
61.5	98.4	Summit - 1840 meters (or 6,036 feet) elevation. Then start winding down.

REMEMBER: On downhill stretches, brake with your motor — not your brakes. A burning smell means you've used your brakes too much. If you can, pull over and let them cool for ten minutes or so.

67.5	108.0	Pretty trees at left. Then slow for sharp right curve.
69.5	111.2	Come now to scattered village of Cuitaca. Detour over Arroyo Cuitaca and start up.
71.0	113.6	Now over and down. Elevation now 4400 feet above sea level.
73.5	117.6	Curve left and down big hill on straight stretch and into green valley.
74.0	118.4	Slow now! Pull over to right and stop for customs check — have car permit ready.
76.3	122.1	Pass side road (right) to Santa Cruz up near Arizona line. Over another arroyo.
80.1	128.2	Note little church up at right next to ruins of older, bigger church.
85.3	136.5	Nice Rancho El Aribabi in pretty setting at left. Then curve right and wind up.

MI	KM	
89.5	143.2	Slow for sharp left horseshoe curve and down thru cuts.
91.3	146.1	Now sharp left horseshoe curve and start up on other side — and up and up.
94.0	150.4	Note pink color of rocks.
94.3	150.9	Start gradual winding decline from 4300-foot elevation (9 miles to go).
96.5	154.4	Majestic panorama to left. Watch for new twin enginge airplane in someone's yard!
97.3	155.7	Old road over at right. On down and careful on this deceptive grade.
98.8	158.1	Bottom. Now along past dry gulch at right.
104.0	166.4	Ahead into Imuris (pronounced "e-moo-rees"). Slow for dangerous right curve and take RIGHT FORK and THEN LEFT (follow SANTA ANA signs) and careful as you move slowly onto Highway #15. **GAS**, right.

IF TO: U.S.A. (Nogales) turn right and start Imuris - Nogales Log (page 175).

IF TO: Magdalena, Santa Ana, Hermosillo, Caborca, etc., turn left and start Imuris - Santa Ana Log (page 6). There are pretty good motels in Magdalena: Motel Ayabay, Saguaro and Kino Hotel and Trailer Park Ph: (632) 322-0983.

End of Log 2

LOG 3   START: Imuris, Son   END: Santa Ana, Son

UD-019

26.5 MI or 42.4 KM
DRIVE TIME 30 — 45 MINUTES
SCENIC RATING — 2

0.0	0.0	Proceed ahead at junction with Hwy #2 from Douglas, Arizona at statue of Father Kino. **GAS**, right. Then down and over bridge over Río de los Alisos. Careful for next 7 winding miles.
4.4	7.0	Careful for curves.
6.5	10.4	Careful for sharp right and left curves.
9.6	15.6	Pass side road (right) to San Ignacio, baseball field on right.
10.4	16.6	Over bridge over Río Tasicuri and under power line. **KM 171**.
12.1	19.4	Pass school at right. Then bypass Magdalena (pop. 41,000), famous as the place where the skeletal remains of the great PADRE KINO were discovered in 1966. (See our special report, page 7.) A magnificent job has been done beautifying the plaza where his bones are displayed — if you have an extra 20 minutes, don't miss this!

IF TO: Magdalena and Padre Kino's mausoleum, exit here. Left at first fork after Hermosillo sign. Pass VW dealer, right and school, left. **GAS**, left, then **GAS**, right. Fancy restaurant. After viewing remains, straight ahead to rejoin Hwy. Up and merge right.

IF TO: Santa Ana, straight ahead.

12.3	19.7	Sign says: Hermosillo, 186 KM. Thru series of cuts.
13.1	21.0	TOPES. CAREFUL!
13.4	21.4	Come to toll house and pay toll (cars $50, trucks $78) then ahead.
14.0	22.4	**GAS** at left. Then Conasupo grocery store at right.
14.3	22.9	**GAS**, right. Pass Red Cross office then school at left. Cross bridge over Río Magdalena. Motel Ayabay (best in town) and nice restaurant, left. Railroad at right. Turnoff to Kino Motel and Trailer Park to right. **KM 181**.
14.5	23.2	Slight curve to right. **KM 183**.
17.1	27.2	CAREFUL. Curve left! This is where Magdalena road rejoins highway.
18.2	29.1	Propane at right.
24.5	39.2	Now down and over bridge across Arroyo de las Calabazas and enter Santa Ana (Pop. 25,000). **GAS**, right just ahead (More ahead).
26.2	41.9	Still divided. Ahead on right is Hotel Elba —MOD— Restaurant (open 6 AM till 11 PM) with good food (serve 1/2 orders for those who have a small appetite, MC, VI, Ph: (641) 324-0361, 324-0777, or 324-0178. At left is Motel San Francisco, Ph: (641) 324-0322
26.5	42.4	Come now to junction Hwy #2 and end of log. Punta Vista RV Park with nice view at top of hill is ahead on

Hwy #15, 0.7 mile south of junction. Another nice RV campground is Rancho Betania about 3 miles ahead, see description in Santa Ana - Hermosillo Log at mile 2.5.

IF TO: Hermosillo, start Santa Ana — Hermosillo Log (page 8) and curve left and up. **GAS** at right.

IF TO: Caborca, Sonoyta, Mexicali, etc., turn right here at Hwy #2 junction and start Santa Ana — Sonoyta Log (page 95).

End of Log 3

PADRE KINO SPECIAL REPORT

One of the greatest men ever to come to Mexico was the Italian-born, German-educated Father Eusebio Francisco Kino, the Conquistador of the Desert, who came with the Spanish Jesuit order. One of the greatest archaeological discoveries of our modern times was right here in Magdalena in 1966 when Padre Kino's grave was uncovered.

TOURIST MAP OF
MAGDALENA
COPYRIGHT © TRAVCO SERVICES, INC.

You can drive to the magnificent new plaza where Kino's remains can be viewed — it's very interesting. You'll be stirred by emotion when you realize you are looking upon the skeletal remains of the man who brought Christianity and civilization to this whole area some 250 years ago.

How did they know the skeleton was Padre Kino's? Well, they knew that the mission church that he and the Indians built was in this immediate area. They also knew that he died here when he came to dedicate his new mission church (which has long since disintegrated), so it seemed reasonable to assume he was buried nearby.

Historic documents indicated that the good father was badly crippled with arthritis and the hands of the skeleton they found were badly crippled. There was also other evidence found which established beyond doubt that these bones are definitely those of Padre Kino, who founded at least 25 missions in Northern Mexico, Arizona and 'way up into California.

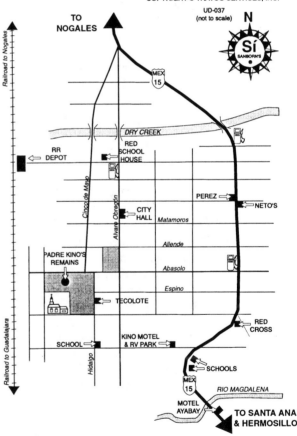

Padre Kino labored in this area for some 25 years from around 1687 until he died on March 15, 1711. Matter of fact, he didn't even come to Mexico until he was 50 years old.

He Christianized seven Indian tribes - the Apaches, Yumas, Seris, Maricopas, Papagos, Pimas and Cocopas. He built all his missions, which have long since disappeared, but the Franciscans who came 75 years later built new churches either nearby or on the very site of the old Kino missions. The church just next to the Kino remains is one of the Franciscan missions built around 1775.

Padre Kino brought new farming techniques to the Indians. Also, he proved that Baja California was not an island. The good padre was quite a mathematician, astronomer, architect and cartographer, in addition to being a rancher and economist. He wanted to become a Jesuit missionary in China because he knew the Chinese were interested in mathematics and astrology but instead ended up in Mexico and the Bishop of Mexico sent him way out here to the wild country. Really quite a guy, this great Padre Kino!

The plaza is easy to find and the streets are mostly paved. If it's late, you won't find a motel in these parts any better than the Motel Kino which is between Padre Kino Plaza and the south end of town.

LOG 4 *START:* Santa Ana, Son *END:* Hermosillo, Son

UD-019

107.1 MI or 171.4 KM
DRIVE TIME 1 1/2 — 2 HOURS
SCENIC RATING — 2

MI	KM	
0.0	0.0	Here in Santa Ana at junction Hwys #15 and #2, up past **GAS** (right) and proceed ahead.
0.1	0.2	Retorno Nogales/Magdalena — 6 lane divided for 1/2 mile, then 4 lane.
0.6	1.0	Uphill. Curve to right then school to right. At right is Hotel Elba, —MOD— restaurant (open 6 AM till 11 PM) with good food (serve 1/2 orders for those who have a small appetite), MC, VI, Ph: (641) 324-0316, 324-0777, 324-0178 and at left, San Francisco, Ph: (641) 324-0322. Over little bridge. Centro bus station. Turn left.
0.7	1.1	Punta Vista RV park, right. Run by nice folks, Ana and Edgar Osuña. Restaurant El Zarape and Corona sign. Nice view at top of hill.
2.0	3.2	Plaza Kennedy truck stop (RV parking, sometimes) and highway patrol, right. Short stretch of winding road.
2.5	4.0	Pass side road (left) to Rancho Betania, an economical church-sponsored campground, that offers 26 RV spaces with full hookups (E/W/S) plus showers and restrooms. English spoken. It's about a mile down the road. (For more info inquire at 543 W. Curtis Street, Nogales, AZ 86521.)
7.0	11.2	**GAS**, to right. **KM 159.**
8.0	12.8	Restaurant to right. **KM 157.**
13.0	20.8	Pass railroad town of Estación Llano at right. Cemetery with pearly gates at left. "Swing low, sweet chariot...."
15.0	24.0	**GAS** and restaurant on left under construction. Cross Río El Alamo (cottonwood).
15.3	24.5	**GAS**, at left, clean bathrooms. Expensive refreshments.
26.3	42.1	**GAS**, left. Then pass side road (right) that leads to railroad junction of Benjamín Hill. The town has an unusual name for a Mexican place especially since there's no "hill." It's named after a general in the Mexican Constitutionalist forces during the Mexican Revolution of 1910-1917. General Hill was the defender of the Mexican border town of Naco (south of Bisbee, Arizona) in 1914 and was of British descent.
27.1	43.4	The hand carved art works by the Seri Indians are done with *palo fierro* or iron wood. A non-Indian taught them the skill within the last 20 years. By the way, Libby Langdells of Yuba City, CA, tells us bargaining is no longer done with them. They've formed cooperatives and sell for fixed prices now. **KM 125.**
28.8	46.1	Now up and over railroad overpass. **KM 123.**
29.5	47.2	Restaurants at left and right.
34.5	55.2	Pass side road left to Querobabi on railroad. Hwy #82. **KM 113.**
41.9	67.0	The Pápago Indians are desert dwellers. Their pottery and wood carvings are sold in "trading posts" in Phoenix and Tucson, AZ. **KM 100.**
51.3	82.1	Over bridge over dry Río Apache. A Texas Aggie had to make an emergency landing with his plane around here. He banged it up pretty badly. When he was pulled from the wreckage, he asked, "Now why would somebody make a runway that's 100 miles long and only 20 feet wide?"
52.0	83.2	Water for radiator sign with place to left. Don't count on finding water though. **KM 84.**
54.3	86.9	Chapel at right and truck stop of "Los Chinos" (the Chinamen), then microwave tower at right.
55.5	88.8	*Parador turístico* to left.
61.3	98.1	Up into El Oasis. **GAS**, right. Emergency motel Oasis, also at right with bus station restaurant. Pass side road left to town of Carbo on railroad.
61.8	98.9	The Yaqui Indians are also natives here. Their "deer dance" is pretty neat. 'Course young folks of all tribes do "dear" dances. Like most Indians, they have a dance to celebrate the important passages in life and the seasons. It's also an excuse to socialize and relax. **KM 68.**
73.5	117.6	Mount Cuervos over to right.
84.0	134.4	Pass side road (left) to Pesqueíra, named after Ignacio Pesqueíra, a former governor of Sonora.
99.4	159.0	**GAS**, at right. Altitude 1,000 feet. **KM 10.**
99.6	159.4	Statue Capitán de Anza to right. ITESM Technical School to left.
100.0	160.0	Hermosillo straight, then side road, left, to old town of Ures (capital of state of Sonora from 1838-79) and on to Agua Prieta and border town of Douglas, AZ. This is where free road joins Hwy #15. **KM 9.**

IF TO: Douglas, Agua Prieta, turn left and start Hermosillo — Douglas Log (page 64).

| 101.8 | 162.9 | Note Rodríguez Lake off ahead, together with fertile valley. This is a rich farming area with a lot of allied industry. Pass icehouse at left. |

MI	KM	
102.2	163.5	Pass town of La Victoria on road over to left.
103.0	164.8	Enter Hermosillo (population: 750,000), capital of the state of Sonora. It's named for Colonel J. María González Hermosillo in 1828, a leader in the war for independence. **GAS**, left. **KM 4**.

For info on accommodations see Hermosillo Eat & Stray (page 102). If you get disoriented here look for the tallest building in town. It's on Hwy #15 in the middle of the hotel zone.

103.6	165.8	Ice plant to left. 60 KMPH. Motel Costa del Sol, left.
104.0	166.4	Café Combate plant at right. 5 horses in middle of road.
104.4	167.0	Mercedes Benz dealer at right.
104.5	167.2	Hotel Autoparador at left, nice. *Gruas* (tow trucks), right.
104.6	167.4	Under pedestrian crossing. Railroad station to left.
104.8	167.7	Come to traffic light and junction with bypass around town. Huge **GAS**, right (across intersection). Periférico south, left. "Periférico" means "bypass" or "loop."

IF TO: Bypass town and on to Guaymas or to Copper Canyon, turn LEFT and start bypass stublog below.

Stub Log: Bypass Hermosillo to Guaymas and Kino Bay.

0.0	0.0	Having turned left at junction with Hwy #15, thru town. **GAS**, on right. Following signs to Guaymas. Chevy dealer to right after Periférico Ote. sign. Protected left turn with arrow and pass ice house.
0.1	0.2	Chevy dealer with Fiesta Americana Hotel behind it and Mobile at right.
0.3	0.5	Firestone at left.
0.4	0.6	Pemex gasoline storage facilities at left and right. 50 KMPH.
0.5	0.8	Curve left at Y.
0.8	1.3	Over railroad crossing. Topes. Curve right under pedestrian crossing. Now on one-way heading SE. You are on Calle Sanalona. Careful for children.
1.4	2.2	At "T" turn left. Go one block. At another "T" turn right. **GAS** at left. School on right.
1.8	2.9	TURN RIGHT to airport and Kino Bay. Veer left then right. Then uphill.
2.2	3.5	Over canal and railroad bridge above you on left.
2.4	3.8	Lake Domínguez at left.
3.0	4.8	Railroad crossing.
4.5	7.2	Roll up your windows, cattle feed lot at left.
4.8	7.7	Junction (left) to Sahuaripa or Tecoripa. Right to Guaymas and Kino Bay. Veer right.

IF TO: Chihuahua or the Copper Canyon, turn left and start Hermosillo — La Junta Log (page 48).

5.0	8.0	**GAS**, left.
5.8	9.3	Goodyear at right. Come to junction with Hwy #15. Stoplight.

IF TO: Kino Bay, straight ahead and continue this stub log.

IF TO: Guaymas, turn left and start Hermosillo — Guaymas Log (page 12) at mile 3.3.

IF TO: DOWNTOWN, TURN RIGHT.

5.9	9.4	Pass Plaza Sur shopping center. You can get slide film from photo stores only.
6.8	10.9	Pass automatic transmission repair shop, right.
7.0	11.2	Pass **GAS** station, left. Stoplight. Cemento Campana, left just before light.
7.8	12.5	Amazing rock formation at left behind Las Palmas shopping center
9.2	14.7	Another shopping center, left.
9.5	15.2	Stoplight. Plaza Satélite, left just past light.
10.1	16.2	Pass big dry cleaner (*tintorería*) at left.

IF TO: Kino Bay, turn left and begin Hermosillo — Kino Bay Special at mile 2.0 (page 43).

End of Stub Log

104.9	167.8	Highrise Fiesta Americana Hotel and big Ariaza Hotel at left.
105.2	168.3	Well-known motel Gandara at left, 1000 Blvd. Kino. Pretty Bancomer at right.
105.3	168.5	Excellent restaurant Henry's, right. Motel Encanto at left. Ahead down wide divided parkway.
105.5	168.8	Hotel Petic Valle Grande, left. Motel Bugambilia Valle Grande, right.

MI	KM	
105.6	169.0	Señorial hotel at left. Motel Siesta, left. Ford dealer at right. Mannix Cafeteria at right (fast service). Laundromat at left. **GAS**, right.
105.8	169.3	La Fiesta restaurant at right. Chrysler dealer at left.
105.9	169.4	To the right is a grocery store, "Valle Petic." You should veer slightly right here. Do not get into "lateral" lane at far right. Then **GAS**, left.
106.2	169.9	Pass shopping center right. Left to downtown at the light. Chevy dealer and Ford clock tower to right. Sports Palace at left. STAY OUT OF EXTREME LEFT LANE AS YOU MIGHT BE FORCED TO TURN LEFT.
106.5	170.4	Come to monument, at left, to one-armed man — General Alvaro Obregón. He was president of Mexico from 1920-24, a native of Sonora state. His arm was shot off during a revolutionary battle with Pancho Villa at Celaya. Hertz Rent-a-Car, right. You are on Av. A.L. Rodríguez.
106.8	170.9	KFC, left. Then pass Av. Madrid.
107.0	171.2	STOPLIGHT. Japanese restaurant Mirikon, left.

IF TO: Kino Bay, take right fork just past next monument, but before stoplight. Start Hermosillo — Kino Bay Special (page 43).

107.1	171.4	Come to busy Yánez St. Take LEFT FORK past monument of mounted Capitán de Anza (a native of Sonora and founder of San Francisco, California). Come to STOPLIGHT. Rodríguez Museum and Library at left. Ahead and at your right is plaza of University of Sonora. Rodríguez Museum and Library, Rodríguez Dam and Lake and Rodríguez Boulevard you were just on, are all named for Abelardo Rodríguez, a Sonora boy who served as president from 1932-34.

IF TO: Guaymas, start Hermosillo — Guaymas Log.

End of Log 4.

LOG 5 *START:* Hermosillo, Son *END:* Guaymas, Son

UD-019

82.5 MI or 132.0 KM
DRIVE TIME 1 1/4 — 2 HOURS
SCENIC RATING — 3

0.0	0.0	Here at University Plaza, ahead down wide two-way Avenida Rosales.
0.5	0.8	Hotel Calinda, right. Hotel San Alberto, right. Civic center, right. Then Jo Wah Restaurant.
0.7	1.1	Hotel Kino, left
0.9	1.4	Under pedestrian walkway. Another turnoff to Kino Bay, right.
1.1	1.8	Go over old bypass around city. Up and over dry bed of Río de Sonora. Big Rodríguez Dam which feeds Lake Rodríguez behind it, is upstream to left.
1.5	2.4	Hotel Grenada at right. Note monument at right to *Los Tres Pueblos* in memory of three little villages on Río de Sonora that were washed away years ago by a big flood. **GAS**, left.
3.0	4.8	Large shopping plaza, right.
3.3	5.3	Come to **GAS**, left (watch them). Whenever you see "watch them" that means several of our customers have had bad experiences here. Then junction with Periférico or loop around town. Welcome to those folks joining us from Periférico.

IF TO: Santa Ana and El Novillo Dam (and lake), 95 miles (good bass fishing), turn LEFT.

IF TO: Kino Bay, turn right and start Kino Bay stub log below. Otherwise continue straight.

Stub Log: Kino Bay Via Bypass

0.0	0.0	Having turned onto Periférico heading west, pass Plaza Sur shopping center (you can get slide film from photo stores only).
0.4	0.6	Pass Palo Verde business park, left.
0.9	1.4	Pass automatic transmission repair shop, right.
1.1	1.8	Pass **GAS** station, left. Stoplight. Cemento Campana, left just before light.
1.9	3.0	Amazing rock formation at left behind Las Palmas shopping center

Periférico Norte (Bypass)

CONVENTION CENTER

TO
SANTA ANA
& NOGALES

STADIUM

G. Arriola

Blvd. Morelos

MEX 15

R.R. STATION

STADIUM

Quintana Roo
Tlaxcala
Aguascalientes

BUGAMBILIA
VALLE GRANDE
HENRY'S
EL ENCANTO
MANNIX
GANDARA

BLOCKY'O CLUB

Blvd. Quinta

LA SIESTA
PITIC
VALLE
GRANDE
VALLE GRANDE
HERMOSILLO
ARIAZA
FIESTA
AMERICANA

Blvd. Transversal

TO AIRPORT
& KINO BAY

MIYAKO

Veracruz
Tamaulipas
Zacatecas

VILLA FIESTA

MERENDERO
LA HUERTA

Yucatán

UNIVERSITY
STADIUM

HOSPITAL
MUSEUM & LIBRARY
UNIVERSITY
OF SONORA

RODEO

JUAREZ GARDEN

EL PALOMINO

REGIONAL HISTORY
MUSEUM

CALINDA HERMOSILLO
QUALITY INN
ART GALLERY

CHILDREN'S
PARK

(Bypass)

SAN ALBERTO
US CONSULATE
PLAZA ZARAGOZA

MARKET
KINO
POST OFFICE

BUS STATION

PRESA
RODRIGUEZ

CITY HALL
GOVERNMENT
PALACE

JO-WAH

MUSEO
COSTUMBRISTA

N

Sí
SANBORN'S
®

Blvd. Fco. Serna

CERRO
DE LA
CAMPANA

CASA DE
LA CULTURA

XOCHIMILCO

POPULATION: 500,000

ALTITUDE: 720 Feet

Blvd. Agustib de Vildosola

Periférico Sur (Bypass)

SANBORN'S®
TOURIST MAP OF
HERMOSILLO
COPYRIGHT © TRAVCO SERVICE INC.
(not to scale)
UD-017

FORD PLANT

Periférico Sur (Bypass)

INDUSTRIAL PARK

MEX 15

MEX 16

TO
GUAYMAS

TO
YECORA,
CHIHUAHUA
& CREEL

MI	KM	
2.1	3.4	Road goes over usually dry river and freeway to nowhere.
2.8	4.5	Fuel injection service, right.
3.3	5.3	Another shopping center, left.
3.6	5.8	Stoplight. Plaza Satélite, left just past light.
4.2	6.7	Pass big dry cleaner (tintorería) at left.

IF TO: Kino Bay, turn left and begin Hermosillo — Kino Bay Special (page 43) at mile 2.

End of Stub Log

3.4	5.4	Shopping plaza at right with store selling slide film.
3.9	6.2	Motel Cid at right. AA sign.
4.0	6.4	Conasupo at right. Tecate agency at left. Left to Hermosillo Ecological Park — a very worthwhile place. **KM 248.**
4.9	7.8	Police Institute, left. Mexico is working hard to modernize it's police forces and hires some consultants from the U.S. and other places.
13.2	21.1	Notice camel-hump hill over to left.
15.0	24.0	SHARP left and over bridge over little dry Río La Poza. **KM 233.**
22.4	35.8	Sierra Madre Mountains to right.
28.0	44.8	Those rugged mountains ahead to left are called *El Pilar* (The Pillar).
35.5	56.8	Whistle stop of La Pintada at left where there are supposed to be caves whose walls are carved with prehistoric hieroglyphics (though nobody seems to know about them, so look for them only if you are adventurous and speak Spanish). CAREFUL, there will be some fairly sharp curves ahead. Also, the smokeys have ears here, dear. Go the speed limit. Nice as we are, we won't pay your traffic tickets.
40.9	65.4	SHARP "S" CURVE. There's about a mile more of them.
44.3	70.9	Slow! Brown-and-white cow in middle of road. This is the original brown cow from Dan's day.
54.3	86.9	**GAS**, right. WELCOME TO THOSE JOINING US FROM KINO SHORTCUT. Pass side road right back to Kino Bay.
61.1	97.8	WATCH OUT for posts on left side of road. Dangerous.
71.6	114.6	Series of well-marked curves for a mile or two.
73.5	117.6	Wide spot of El Caballo (The Horse), left. Truck inspection station, left. **KM 141.**
74.5	119.2	**GAS** and diesel, right. Then careful as you come to junction with toll bypass around Guaymas. Get in left lane for toll bypass.

IF TO: San Carlos, straight ahead and skip stub log.

IF TO: Bypass of town, VEER LEFT following CD. OBREGÓN sign and follow stublog below. Otherwise skip down to mile 78.3. The free bypass is OK unless you're in a hurry.

Stub Log: Toll Bypass around Guaymas

0.0	0.0	Having veered left at OBREGÓN sign, continue ahead on 4-lane bypass around Guaymas. **KM 21.**
1.1	1.8	Come to toll house and pay toll (cars $22, trucks $42). Then under overpass. Sign says "Cd. Obregón 129 KM."
3.0	4.8	Truck-stop restaurant Los Faroles, left.
11.8	18.9	Restaurant in middle of road.
12.0	19.2	Pass big Fertimex plant at left. Then **GAS** at right and up and over railroad. Topes. Then come to junction with HWY #15.

IF TO: Downtown Guaymas, turn left.

IF TO: Navojoa, Mazatlán, continue straight and join Guaymas — Navojoa Log at Mile 10.5 (page 13).

End of Stub Log

78.3	125.3	Come to side road (right) to San Carlos.

IF TO: SAN CARLOS, exit RIGHT here and start Guaymas — San Carlos Special (page 59) — it's quite a nice place, sort of a Gringo oasis. It's about 5 miles straight ahead on a fine road — you won't get lost. Be CAREFUL, watch your speed. They really have traffic cops now.

MI	KM	
78.5	125.6	Come to overpass. **KM 132**.

IF TO: GUAYMAS, under overpass and ahead.

80.0	128.0	There's Guaymas airport over to left.
81.5	130.4	**GAS** at right.
82.0	131.2	Motel Flamingos at left. Tecate agency at right and enter city of Guaymas - a fish and shrimp processing town. You can tell by the smell.

For info on accommodations see Guaymas Eat & Stray (page 110)

82.5	132.0	Miramar exit, right to Bacochibampo Bay, Playa de Cortés Hotel and RV Park. This h otel is a wonderful old place with plenty of charm. Also down the road is economical Leo's Inn. Careful for big topes.

IF TO: Navojoa, Alamos, Los Mochis, Mazatlán, etc., STRAIGHT. Start Guaymas — Navojoa Log (page 15).

IF TO: Ferry Baja California, proceed ahead and then bear right onto main street a short mile ahead (see Guaymas map on page 14). You just keep going straight through town until you see ferry compound on your right. See "How About The Ferries!" in front section (page xiv) of your *Travelog*.

IF TO: Guaymas RV Parks, start Guaymas RV Stub Log below:

Stub Log: To Guaymas RV Parks

Note: They were building a new bypass when we were there. It will get you there and avoid the first two miles of this stub log. Otherwise, this log works well. Watch your speed.

0.0	0.0	Having veered right just past light, continue on past obelisk monument, left,
0.1	0.2	Modelo beer distributor, right.
0.2	0.3	Stoplight. VH shopping center on right just beyond light. TURN RIGHT onto Calle Diez (even though it looks like a one-way the other way).
0.5	0.8	IMSS hospital, left. Then stoplight and **GAS** at left.
0.6	1.0	Statue of Lázaro Cárdenas, left.
1.0	1.6	Veer right at second light, then take left fork at intersection with divided blvd. Go uphill with trees and small plaza at right.
1.2	1.9	Stoplight. You're now on Benito Juárez.
2.6	4.2	Veer left. Beer distributor on right.
2.7	4.3	Athletic stadium, right. Large stucco commercial building, right. Then cemetery on right. After cemetery turn right.
2.8	4.5	Bay at left. Watch speed thru here (20 kmph). Then veer left. Right goes to subdivision.
3.5	5.6	Bahía RV Park, left.
3.8	6.1	Industrial park, right.
3.9	6.2	Naval club, left.

End of Log 5

LOG 6   *START:* Guaymas, Son   *END:* Navojoa, Son

UD-019

121.7 MI or 194.7 KM
DRIVE TIME 2 — 2 1/2 HOURS
SCENIC RATING — 2

0.0	0.0	Having passed exit right for Bocachibampo Bay (Bay of the Sea Serpents) and neat Hotel Cortés, with large RV park, continue ahead under overpass on divided 4-lane.
0.4	0.6	"Ley" shopping plaza, left.
0.5	0.8	Las Villas Subdivision at right. Then Nissan and Ford dealers, right. Also VW and Chrysler/Dodge. Then **GAS**, right.
1.0	1.6	Hotel Armida, left. Under pedestrian crossing. Then traffic light. Stay left and veer left at obelisk.

IF TO: Cd. Obregón, Navojoa, VEER LEFT here.

IF TO: Guaymas, RV parks on bay, TURN RIGHT.

MI	KM	
1.1	1.8	HAVING DECIDED NOT TO GO TO DOWNTOWN GUAYMAS, STRAIGHT AHEAD. Monument at right to Héroes of Guaymas. Chevy dealer.
1.3	2.1	"Topes," General Tire, right. Coca Cola bottling plant, left.
1.5	2.4	Monument to Benito Juárez on hilltop to right. SLOW thru SCHOOL ZONE.
2.0	3.2	**GAS,** left. You're skirting edge of town. Another SCHOOL ZONE.
2.3	3.7	Careful for merging traffic. Then slow for school zone.
3.6	5.8	Veer left past junction with road to ferries. Mexico calls the Gulf of California *Mar de Cortés* (Sea of Cortés).
3.8	6.1	Power plant, right. LP gas, left and right. **KM 120.**
5.3	8.5	Onto causeway alongside railroad track, right. CAREFUL.
6.5	10.4	End of causeway — LOOK-&-LISTEN for DOUBLE railroad crossing. AHEAD on Hwy 15. Left fork is to railroad town of Empalme (population, 70,000) And there, left stands old engine 70 of the *Ferrocarril de Sonora* ("Sonora Railroad"), a monument to Empalme and its railroad industry. Then slow for another railroad crossing — LOOK-&-LISTEN.
6.7	10.7	Restaurant to left.
7.3	11.7	Topes! Then big Anderson-Clayton complex, also, right. And one more railroad switch line LOOK-&-LISTEN. Then white palm trees lining highway.
8.0	12.8	*Ferrocarril del Pacífico* station (Pacific Railroad station), left. Railroad crossing.
8.1	13.0	**GAS** (watch them), right. Highway patrol, left. **KM 11.**
10.5	16.8	Pass side road (right) to beachfront community of El Cochori, 2 miles (no accommodations) and careful for merging traffic from toll bypass, left.
13.0	20.8	Pass side road (left) to Ortiz. Down this road a short mile is where famous NASA space capsule tracking station was located (the place that a couple of the early astronauts referred to when they remarked as they passed over, "Hello, Guaymas! Send us up some enchiladas!"). This station is no longer used by NASA.
15.0	24.0	Pass side road (right) to Playa del Sol, a beachfront development.
15.5	24.8	Pass Cruz de Piedra (Cross of Stone) over to left on railroad. Note disabled and outdated railroad cars now used as homes. Here is where a big Yaqui Indian Reservation starts and runs for about 50 miles to the Yaqui River just north of Cd. Obregón. The Yaquis had a big uprising back in the late 1920's and Mexico gave them this territory for a reservation.
21.0	33.6	Thru rock cut of Boca Abierta (Open Mouth).
22.8	36.5	Livestock-shipping community of Las Guásimas.
27.3	43.7	Slow for sharp right curve.
36.7	58.7	Pass side road (left) to Pitahaya.
42.5	68.0	Pass side road (right) to Potam. Note irrigated countryside thru here — very fertile soil. Main crops — cotton, wheat soya, sunflower oil, sorghum. There's a drug check point at this junction.
48.0	76.8	Slow thru little town of Vicam. Red Cross, right. **GAS,** left.
52.5	84.0	Community of Cárdenas and site of the famous YAQUI INDIAN VOCATIONAL AND AGRICULTURAL SCHOOL, where "knowhow" is taught to Yaqui Indian kids. Emergency hotel "Yaqui Aggies"? (right) with long distance phone and laundry. "Ehwee" in Yaqui means "Yes."
54.1	86.6	Pass side road (right) to Torim.
57.0	91.2	Sign advising there will be a choice of either toll road or free (*libre*) road in 10 km. This log takes the toll road.
59.0	94.4	Truck weigh station. Yaqui masks are made of desiccated deer heads, wood and dried goat skin.
61.8	98.9	Come to junction (right) with free road.

IF TO: Cd. Obregón via toll road continue straight, but if via free road, veer right and you're on your own.

61.9	99.0	Having taken toll road continue ahead on 4-lane divided. **KM 26.**
62.9	100.6	Pass another road, left to Bacum.
68.0	108.8	Thru scattered settlement of Loma de Guamúchil.

Guamúchil is a tree, very common in this part of Mexico, with thorny leafstalks, hairy white globe-shaped flower clusters and black shiny seeds in spirally twisted pods from 5-6 inches long.

MI	KM	
69.8	111.7	CAREFUL! Settlement of Tajimaroa to right. Then pass side road (left) to Estación Corral, 3 km. Bend right and slow for *Salida de Camiones* (yield to trucks merging with highway traffic).
70.8	113.3	Cross over famous Río Yaqui whose course from the state of Chihuahua to the Sea of Cortés is 419 miles long. This is also where the Yaqui Indian Reservation ends.
72.8	116.5	Stop and pay toll (cars $50, trucks $78). **GAS**, left (has Diesel Sin). Careful for stoplights.
73.8	118.1	Skirt edge of Esperanza (Hope). Pass side road (right) to Cocorít, while side road (left) goes to Tezopaco de Rosario and to Presa (dam) Alvaro Obregón which has a reputation for the best bass fishing in North America. **GAS** (right) but there's a better one ahead in Cd. Obregón, 5 miles.
74.4	119.0	Military base, left.
75.8	121.3	Pemex tank farm, left.
77.5	124.0	Enter prosperous town of Cd. (abbreviation for *ciudad* "city") Obregón, the agricultural heart of the Yaqui Valley (known as the Bread Basket of Mexico) with a population of 450,000. This was formerly called Cájeme after the famous chief of the Yaqui Indians, but the name was later changed in honor of ex-President Obregón (O'Brien... His family, O'Brien, was originally of Irish lineage).
77.7	124.3	TURN LEFT onto bypass around Cd. Obregón just beyond statue of soldier and ahead on divided roadway.

IF TO: Cd. Obregón continue straight. There is a **GAS** station 1/2 mile towards town that takes credit cards (when manager is in), several new hotels, a Holiday Inn Ph: (644) 414-0936 Fax: (644) 413-4194, and a good restaurant, Mr. Steak, where they roll a cart of beef out and cut your steak to your request.

See Cd. Obregón Eat & Stray (page 111) for more info on accommodations.

78.3	125.3	Pass Mobile, right. Then Corona left.
78.8	126.1	VW agency on left.
79.3	126.9	Very nice Travelodge on right (70 rooms, pool, Ph and Fax: 14-5044).
79.5	127.2	**GAS**, right.
79.8	127.7	Over railroad crossing (LOOK-&-LISTEN).
80.6	129.0	Here is where the bypass rejoins highway. TURN LEFT at traffic lights. **GAS** on right after turn.
81.3	130.1	Ley shopping center, right.
81.5	130.4	Coca-Cola bottling plant, right. Then big Gamesa (Galletas Mexicanas, S.A.), left, one of Mexico's largest cookie producers - sort of like Nabisco in the States. SLOW, (LOOK-&-LISTEN) at bumpy railroad crossing. Many cotton grain-related industries here. Industrial park, right. **KM 222.**
82.0	131.2	Pass turnoff (right) to Villa Juárez.

If you have a generous and compassionate heart and would like to visit an orphanage, you will find Hogar de Refugio Infantil Villa Juárez by turning right onto side road to Villa Juárez, go 26 miles on paved road, turn right for another mile, then turn left following signs to the orphanage. Bob Mason, the director, welcomes visitors. They are able to accommodate motor homes, trailers etc. and have a crude dumping station as well as electrical hookups.

84.0	134.4	**GAS**, right (accept credit cards), but watch them. **KM 210.**
88.8	142.1	Pass side road (right) to airport.
90.0	144.0	Enormous shrine to the Virgin of Guadalupe over at left. **KM 203.**
95.5	152.8	**GAS**, right. Exit right to take free road bypass around Navojoa and follow stub log below, otherwise jump down to continuation of log (MI 97.9). Free road is OK. It takes 15 minutes longer.

Stub Log: Free Road To Navojoa

96.5	154.4	Having turned right at "V. Juárez/Navojoa" sign, continue ahead on 2-lane road.
105.5	168.8	Thru village of Jecopaco, store with phone. "Topes" and Texaco sign, left.
111.4	178.2	Come to "T." For Navojoa, TURN LEFT. Villa Juárez, is to the right. Suddenly you are at **KM 28.**
113.0	180.8	Village of Bacobampo and Calle 26 to right. Then over canals at **KM 26.**
113.5	181.6	Thru Agua Blanca and "topes." Farm equipment yard, left, then more "topes." **KM 24.**
116.6	186.6	Pass side road (right) to Buaysiacobe. **KM 20.**
122.4	195.8	Pass village of Bacame Nuevo to left.
128.9	206.2	Come to "T" and rejoin Hwy #15 at mile 119.1 below. TURN RIGHT and ahead to Navojoa.

End of Stub Log

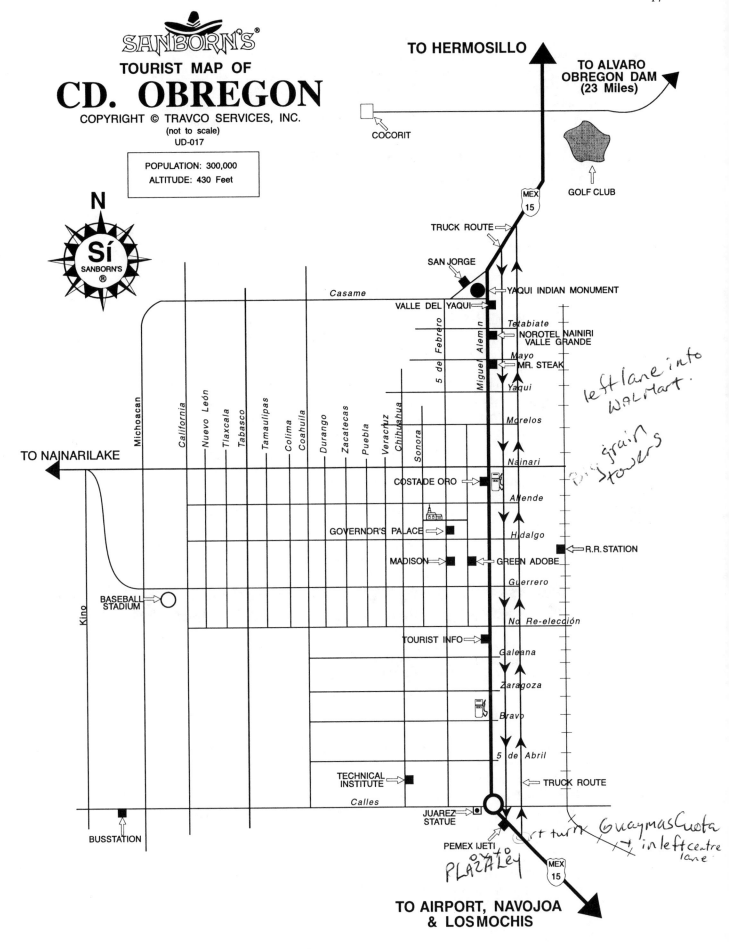

SANBORN'S®
TOURIST MAP OF
CD. OBREGON
COPYRIGHT © TRAVCO SERVICES, INC.
(not to scale)
UD-017

POPULATION: 300,000
ALTITUDE: 430 Feet

N

Sí
SANBORN'S
®

TO HERMOSILLO

TO ALVARO
OBREGON DAM
(23 Miles)

COCORIT

MEX 15

GOLF CLUB

TRUCK ROUTE

SAN JORGE

Casame

YAQUI INDIAN MONUMENT

VALLE DEL YAQUI

Tetabiate

NOROTEL NAINIRI
VALLE GRANDE

Mayo

MR. STEAK

Yaqui

Morelos

Nainari

Allende

Hidalgo

Guerrero

No Re-elección

Galeana

Zaragoza

Bravo

5 de Abril

5 de Febrero

Miguel Alemn

Michoacan

California

Nuevo León

Tlaxcala

Tabasco

Tamaulipas

Colima

Coahuila

Durango

Zacatecas

Puebla

Veracruz

Chihuahua

Sonora

TO NAINARILAKE

COSTADE ORO

GOVERNOR'S PALACE

MADISON

GREEN ADOBE

R.R. STATION

Kino

BASEBALL
STADIUM

TOURIST INFO

TECHNICAL
INSTITUTE

Calles

JUAREZ
STATUE

BUSSTATION

PEMEX IJETI

MEX 15

TO AIRPORT, NAVOJOA
& LOSMOCHIS

left lane into WALMart.

grain towers

rt turn Guaymas Cuota + in left centre lane

oxxo PLAZA Ley

MI	KM	
97.9	156.6	Tollbooth. Stop and pay toll (cars $50, trucks $78). **KM 195.**
110.8	177.3	Cotton community of Sibolibampo.
112.5	180.0	Pass side road (right) to Villa Juárez, 30 km. (18 miles).
118.0	188.8	**GAS**, right. If taking the free road to Los Mochis, turn right here.
119.1	190.6	Motel Rancho down at right. Then pass good bed and breakfast Hotel Cazadores —16 rooms. Pollo and Elsa Acosta, owners. Ph: (642) 422-9360. Then thru little community of Guaymitas. **KM 1.**
119.6	191.4	Over bridge.

IF TO: Alameda RV Park, exit right immediately after bridge.

119.9	191.8	Turn right into RV Alameda just after bridge. Motel Del Río at right. Restaurant Los Arcos at right. Tecate store at left. Corona distributor at right.
120.0	192.0	The bypass is not worth taking, go thru town. Enter Navojoa (Population: 122,390), a clean agricultural boom town and birthplace of LA Dodgers' pitcher, Fernando Valenzuela. Straight on thru on nice wide main street. Very good **GAS**, left. This has SELF-SERVICE lanes! What's Mexico coming to? Neat little coffee shop Alamos, next door with packaged ice, etc. Then Asadero Restaurant (tasty "*carne asada*"), left. Friends of Bill W. in town (Spanish only) Tel: (642) 422-5953. AA at Pesqueíra #105 Nte.

Navojoa means "place among the tunas" in Mayo Indian, tuna being a prickly pear.

120.6	193.0	**GAS**, left. Restaurant/bar Los Coporales at left. 2 smiling elephants at right. Goodyear left. Nissan right. Chevy left. General tire at right. Restaurant Jo Wah to right. ISSTE clinic at right.
120.9	193.4	Uniroyal at left and Firestone at right.
121.2	193.9	Pass side road (right) to San Ignacio and Tetanchopo.
121.4	194.2	Several photo supply stores at right.
121.5	194.4	Pass Nissan dealer right. Funeral parlor and General Tire at left. Stoplight.
121.7	194.7	V H shopping center at left. Come to junction with road to Alamos. Semi-Llantas on right just past light. Ahead on right is a highly recommended Dodge dealer.

For info on accommodations, see Navojoa Eat & Stray (page 112).

IF TO: Los Mochis, start Navojoa — Los Mochis Log.

IF TO: Alamos, one of the neatest old mining towns in Mexico, start Navojoa — Alamos Special (page 59).

End of Log 6

LOG 7   *START:* Navojoa, Son   *END:* Los Mochis, Sin

UD-019

98.0 MI or 156.8 KM
DRIVE TIME — 2 HOURS
SCENIC RATING — 2

0.0	0.0	In Navojoa at STOPLIGHT and junction (left) with side road to Alamos, head south/southeast on Hwy 15. Tips' Restaurant, left. On right, Goodrich, VW dealer and Chrysler/Dodge. Pass **GAS**, left..
0.3	0.5	Over railroad tracks. Social security hospital (ISSTE) at right. Curve right. Big flour mill (Conasupo) also at right. Motel Colonial at right. Then over Canal Las Pilas, **KM 155**, and take leave of Navojoa as you pass industrial park on left. Then pass Navojoa Medical Center.
1.0	1.6	**GAS**, right. Exit for free road, right. Free road is 15 km longer than toll road. If you want to avoid tolls, follow "Libre" signs. You may prefer the toll road if you can afford it. Ask locals regarding the condition of the free road. **KM 153.**
5.2	8.3	Pass airfield at left.
6.0	9.6	Railroad tracks follow road at left.
10.0	16.0	Rest area El Abajeno at right, restaurant — popular with truck drivers. Then small shrine at right. **KM 139.**
16.5	26.4	Slow for tollbooth. Stop and pay toll (cars $50, trucks $78).

MI	KM	
17.0	27.2	Pass side road (right) to Huatabampo "Willow Tree in the Water," a nice little city located in a large, prosperous irrigated district. Four miles south of town is Huatabampito, a little resort on the Gulf of California with miles and miles of inviting sandy beach. Then at left is Ejido Luis Echeverría, named after one of Mexico's ex-presidents (1970-1976).
26.3	42.1	Pass another side road (left) to Masiaca, 6 miles and (right) to Las Bocas, 7.5 miles, a beach resort on the Sea of Cortés. **KM 118**.
30.3	48.5	Truck stop restaurant Carmelita, right.
39.0	62.4	Railroad station community of Estación Luis at left. Then pass side road (left) to Ejido Tierra y Libertad (Land and Liberty).

"Tierra y Libertad" was Emiliano Zapata's cry as he seized and burned the haciendas in his home state of Morelos and divided the land among his white—clad Indian followers, paving the way for Article 27 of the Mexican Constitution, upon which all subsequent land reform laws have been based.

44.9	71.8	Big Ejido Francisco Sarabia at right. Bumpy railroad crossing! Watch for animals and bicycles along highway. Then huge Conasupo farmers' co-op at right. **GAS** (right) with clean restrooms. **KM 93**.
47.4	75.8	Note pig farm at right, the smell is hard to miss.
52.0	83.2	Thru village of Estación Don. **KM 72**.
54.0	86.4	**GAS**, left and agricultural inspection station. **KM 70**.
54.5	87.2	Come now to state line. Leave state of Sonora and enter state of Sinaloa.

You've been traveling in the state of Sonora, which must be the longest state in Mexico. It's 433 miles from Nogales down to this point; and if you came by way of San Luis Río Colorado, you've been in Sonora for the last 665 miles. Sinaloa is also pretty lengthy — 397 miles. Please be aware that, seat belts are required by law in Sinaloa.

54.6	87.4	Veer right and slow down for agricultural station to left.
56.0	89.6	SLOW and pull over to right. Be ready to stop for truck agricultural inspection station. There is also a drug inspection checkpoint here.
59.0	94.4	Big Ejido Talamantes at right. Pass side road (left) to San Francisco microwave tower.
63.7	101.9	Ejido El Carrizo at right, headquarters town for irrigation district of huge El Fuerte irrigation project. Red Cross. **GAS**, left. **KM 55**.
65.6	105.0	Pass Restaurant La Posta, left. **KM 52**.
65.8	105.3	Pass side road (left) to El Fuerte and Chiox, but there's another shorter route at Los Mochis.
79.5	127.2	Curve left and start winding thru Cerro Prieto. Pass carefully. Devil's Canyon over at right.
85.4	136.6	Prepare to pay toll (cars $18, trucks $35) at "caseta puente San Miguel." **KM 20**.
87.3	139.7	Pass side road (right) to nice, pleasant Río Fuerte RV Park and Hacienda de Zamora. Bumpy bridge over Río Fuerte, the principal river in these parts.
88.1	141.0	Now thru edge of little town of San Miguel Zapotitlán. **KM 16**. **GAS**, left sometimes they try to charge more for it, so watch them. Over main irrigation canal. *Vibradores* (speed bumps). **KM 15**.
91.0	145.6	Cavalry's 18th regiment barracks at right. If you go through on leave day, don't be alarmed. There will be hundreds of soldiers hitchhiking.
98.0	156.8	Come now to Los Mochis interchange. **GAS**, left but watch them.

For accommodations see Los Mochis Eat & Stray (page 115). If it's lunch or dinner time, don't miss Restaurant El Farallón on the corner of Calle Obregón and Flores.

IF TO: Los Mochis, take right turnoff and head into town. See map (page 21).

IF TO: Culiacán or Mazatlán, start Los Mochis — Culiacán Log. Go under 2 overpasses.

IF TO: El Fuerte and nearby lakes of Hidalgo and Domínguez (plentiful black bass and catfish and hunting) take right turnoff and start Los Mochis — El Fuerte Special (page 63). The twin lakes are about 40 miles NE of Los Mochis, via a paved road, a few miles from the town of El Fuerte. The two lakes are about 5 miles apart. They have some of the best fishing south of the border.

Incidentally, the Chihuahua-Pacific (Copper Canyon) Railroad passes near El Fuerte — you might wish to combine a little fishing with this very scenic train ride through the Sierra Madre Occidental.

End of Log 7

LOG 8 *START:* Los Mochis, Sin *END:* Culiacán, Sin

UD-019

135.5 MI or 216.8 KM
DRIVE TIME 2 — 2 1/2 HOURS
SCENIC RATING — 1

MI	KM	
0.0	0.0	Starting here in Los Mochis at junction with highway to El Fuerte, proceed ahead on Hwy 15, a nice divided four-lane highway. If you want to take the old *libre* routes and aren't in a hurry, just follow the *Libre* signs. Some folks prefer them. On this route, though, you're better off paying your way.
1.0	1.6	**GAS**, on right. Mountain at right is called *Cerro de la Memoria*. Turnoff, left, is to nice Hotel Colinas and RV Park, left, on hilltop (67 spaces EWS, 30 AMP, Ph: (668) 812-0101, 812-0134)). It was formerly a Holiday Inn. *Lienzo del Charro* arena at right where the Mexican "charro" (cowboy) performs in the rodeo, usually on Sunday. Turnoff to Topolobampo, right.
2.0	3.2	Curve right around hill, then up and over Chihuahua-Pacífico Railroad overpass which is the same line that goes up into the Sierra Madres thru scenic Copper Canyon.
5.5	8.8	Northrup-King seed plant at right. Then rice factory at right. Then pass entrance to industrial park at right.
9.5	15.2	Cross Río Estero, curve right and pass *Ejido Las Vacas* (The Cows) at right. Heading due east.
11.0	17.6	Big town of Juan José Ríos, the largest *ejido* in Mexico at right. **GAS**, right. Then agricultural experiment school (Ciapan), left. **KM 186.**
14.1	22.6	Careful at crossroads (right) to Bachoco. Occasional farm equipment and bicycles on road.
17.1	27.4	**GAS**, to left. Unfriendly (watch them)
18.0	28.8	Little town of Ruiz Cortines, at right, named for a past president of Mexico (1952-58).
25.0	40.0	Pass side road (right) to Huitusi over on Bahía de San Ignacio. Pass LP **GAS** to left.
28.3	45.3	Pass side road (right) to Las Barritas.
30.3	40.0	Road left to Estación Naranjo. **GAS** on road to Estación Naranjo.
32.5	52.0	Pass Trébol Park Motel, left.
35.0	56.0	Curve left and pass baseball park at right. Guasave belongs to the powerful Mexican Pacific Baseball League.
36.1	57.7	Now thru edge of boom town of Guasave, founded in 1595 (population, 258,000). Shopping center to left. Then ahead over Río Petatlán. **KM 145.**

GUASAVE has three hotels and a great mechanic, Taller Bojórquez (see map inset). The best hotel is El Sembrador at Guerrero and Zapata. It has 85 nice quiet rooms, 10 suites, restaurant, bar, parking and is very reasonably priced. SATV (English and weather channel, HBO, CNN, etc). Ph: (687) 822-4062, 822-3141, Fax: 822-3131.

GUASAVE, SINALOA

44.0	70.4	**GAS**, right.
45.0	72.0	Come to tollhouse and pay toll ($15, $8 extra axle).
51.0	81.6	Veer left (follow CUOTA sign). Exit (right) is old two-lane "libre" highway which goes thru Guamúchil. Veer left for Culiacán.
56.7	90.7	Under overpass. **KM 119.**
62.0	99.2	Come to tollhouse and pay toll ($15, $8 extra axle). Pass side road (right) to Angostura and left Guamúchil. **GAS**, right. **KM 110.**
70.0	112.0	Thru rich farmland with mountains on horizon. Excellent road thru here.
84.6	135.4	**GAS** at right. **KM 75.**
91.1	145.8	Pass side road (right) to La Reforma and Zapatillo. Then under overpass. **KM 63.**
91.7	146.7	Pass Restaurant El Bacatete, left.
103.5	165.6	Curve left and cross bridge over Río Pericos. Nice cattle farm over to left on Hwy #259.
110.5	176.8	Exit right to La Palma and Vitaruto a couple of miles over to left.
111.5	178.4	Tollbooth if you exit.
115.5	184.8	Under overpass. Then **GAS** at left.
122.5	196.0	Over bridge and exit right to San Pedro and La Curva. **KM 13.**

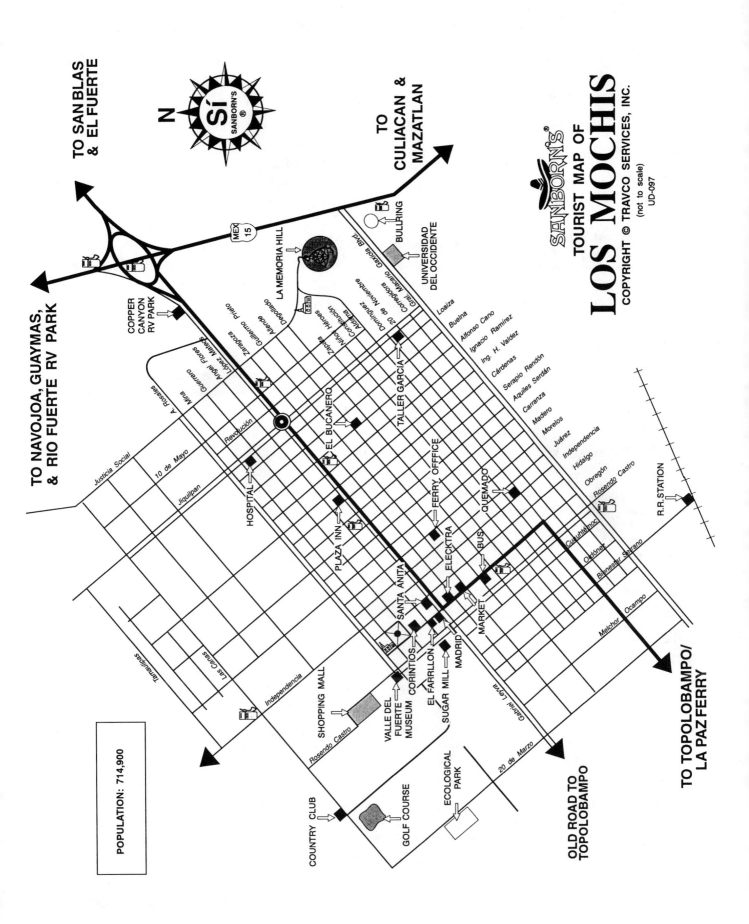

TO SAN BLAS & EL FUERTE

N

Sí
SANBORN'S ®

TO CULIACAN & MAZATLAN

SANBORN'S ®
TOURIST MAP OF
LOS MOCHIS
COPYRIGHT © TRAVCO SERVICES, INC.
(not to scale)
UD-097

TO NAVOJOA, GUAYMAS, & RIO FUERTE RV PARK

POPULATION: 714,900

COPPER CANYON RV PARK

LA MEMORIA HILL

MEX 15

BULLRING

UNIVERSIDAD DEL OCCIDENTE

Gaxiola Blvd
Gral. Macario
Corregidora
20 de Noviembre
Domínguez
Aldama
Constitución
Niños Héroes
Degollado
Allende
Zaragoza
Guillermo Prieto
López Mateas
Angel Flores
Guerrero
Mina
A. Postales

Justicia Social
10 de Mayo
Jiquilpan
Tamaulipas
Las Cañas

Revolución

HOSPITAL

EL BUCANERO

TALLER GARCIA

PLAZA INN

FERRY OFFICE

ELECKTRA

BUS

QUEMADO

SANTA ANITA

CORINTIOS

EL FARRILLON

SUGAR MILL

MADRID

MARKET

VALLE DEL FUERTE MUSEUM

SHOPPING MALL

Independencia

Rosendo Castro

Loaiza
Buelna
Alfonso Cano
Ignacio Ramírez
Ing. H. Valdez
Cárdenas
Serapio Rendón
Aquiles Serdán
Carranza
Madero
Morelos
Juárez
Independencia
Hidalgo
Obregón
Rosendo Castro

R.R. STATION

Cuauhtémoc
Obdónez
Bienestar Serrano
Melchor Ocampo

Gabriel Leyva

20 de Marzo

OLD ROAD TO TOPOLOBAMPO

TO TOPOLOBAMPO/ LA PAZ FERRY

COUNTRY CLUB

GOLF COURSE

ECOLOGICAL PARK

MI   KM

127.5 204.0   Come to tollhouse ($19, $10 extra axle) and pay it again, Sam. **GAS** at left and restaurant with good food, nice rest area with swings for kids. Then proceed ahead.

129.5 207.2   Come to junction with Hwy 15 "Libre" from downtown Culiacán (population: 602,000), whose only real tourist attraction is the Sinaloa art museum.

For accommodations see Culiacán Eat & Stray (page 117).

IF TO: Culiacán, turn left and follow map to hotels.

IF TO: Mazatlán, toll road, turn right just after **GAS** station.

IF TO: Mazatlán, free road, start Culiacán — Mazatlán Log, continuing straight just past **GAS** station.

End of Log 8.

LOG 9 *START:* Culiacán, Sin   *END:* Mazatlán, Sin

UD-019

136.8 MI or 218.9 KM
DRIVE TIME 3 — 3 1/2 HOURS
SCENIC RATING — 2

Note: This log covers the free road and the toll. The toll road is rather expensive. There are 2 toll booths, one at KM 22 and the other at exit to Mazatlán. Some say it's worth it (if you're in a hurry) saving at least an hour of driving time and is safer although the free road is more scenic.

0.0   0.0   Here at the junction of Hwy #15 and the toll road, with Pemex **GAS** on left.

IF TO: Toll road, exit right, after bridge (also to Culiacán) and follow stub log below:

Culiacán — Mazatlán Toll Road

0.0   0.0   Having veered right just past tollhouse and **GAS** station, proceed ahead.

0.7   1.1   Go under overpass.

2.8   4.5   Los Comales restaurant, right. If you want to go there, get in lateral lane well before.

4.5   7.2   Pass chicken processing plant at right. **GAS**, right. Then pass exit (right) to Villa Juárez.

6.5   10.4   **GAS**, left.

7.1   11.4   Agriculture Experimental School, left. You are now passing thru rolling hills and farm country.

9.6   15.4   Veer right, following Mazatlán El Dorado sign. Straight ahead for Costa Rica. At top of overpass stay in left lane. Then down, following Mazatlán - La Cruz sign.

10.5   16.8   **GAS**, right. **KM 180**.

MI   KM

11.3   18.1   Come to tollhouse and pay toll (Car - $85, extra axle - $43). They accept AE, MC, VI. **KM 179**.

25.1   40.2   Pass exit (right) to Quila and El Dorado.

There is a nice pastoral spot 4.1 miles west of here on highway #19. It's Los Cascabeles, on the lake of the same name. 20 fenced acres with 10 cabins, boats, pool, hunting and fishing. RV section (MOD) with 44 spaces, electricity and water. Dump station. Medical services. Palapa. BBQ pits. Security. Store. Laundry. Restaurant. Fax: (671) 713-6418 or in Culiacán, Ph: (667) 673-6418, 673-6822.

71.1   113.8 Pass exit (right) to La Cruz and Cueta. This is also the exit to take if you want to go to Cosalá.

Cosalá, founded in 1516, is a small Spanish colonial town with cobblestone roads and churches over 250 years old. There are two OK (two Mexican star) hotels and some restaurants. The Sabinal River feeds the *Vado Hondo* Spa (not reviewed) with clear water. 20 km north is Lake Comedero chock-full of largemouth bass. There is also a Museum of the History of Mining. The Balneario and waterfall are 8 km off the highway on a dirt road. Do not attempt this road when it has been raining. It is 6.5 miles before town, on the left.

PRESA LÓPEZ PORTILLO (LAKE COMEDERO) — One of Mexico's most popular lakes, Comedero was opened to fishermen only since 1987. Comedero has fast become a legend in the number of fish caught per man per day. With catches from 100 to 200 bass per day common, it is easy to see why this remote lake has become a prime destination for the traveling angler. Turn east on the Cosalá turnoff to the town of Cosalá (50 miles). The lake is 30 miles from town on a dirt road that winds up in the steep mountains to the village of Higueras de Urea.

The San Lorenzo River is the source of Lake Comedero and the lake is one of the prettiest in the northern hemisphere. Towering mountains surround the lake with lush subtropical jungle right up to the water's edge. Comedero's banks are lined with some brush and cover, however the lake is large and very open and it's also very, very deep. With depths approaching 300 feet in places, Comedero's fish tend to school up and suspend sometimes in water as deep as 60 feet. At present there's only one full time camp on the lake. Full packages are available as well as room and board. Contact: Ron Speeds S and W Tours, 1013 Country Lane, Malakoff, TX, 875148 (903) 489-1656.

MI	KM	
104.0	166.4	Come to tollhouse and pay toll ($75, extra axle $50). There are restrooms and tourist information. **KM 27**.
106,7	170.7	Over Río Quilete.
116.7	186.7	Pass exit (right) to North Beach (Playas). This is the exit for north end RV parks and Zona Dorada hotels.
121.0	193.6	Exit right for Mazatlán. This is junction with free road. After exit, Quaker State to left. Ahead on two-lane road.
122.0	195.2	**GAS**, right. Monterrey Tech. to left. Veer right for Mazatlán, left for airport, Durango and Tepic. There is a stoplight just beyond where you veer right. Motel Relax on right.

IF TO: Downtown Mazatlán, see stub log at end of free road log (page 28).

End Culiacán — Mazatlán Toll Road

2.0	3.2	Motel Cabañas del Rey.
5.3	8.5	Pass little town of El Ranchito.
6.3	10.1	Come to "T." Mazatlán to right, Culiacán to left.
6.8	10.8	Pass a truck and bus wrecking yard, right. **KM 208.**
7.5	12.0	Huge field of wrecked car, left ("used auto parts"). **KM 206.**
8.5	13.5	Pass restaurant Los Caminantes, left.
12.3	19.7	Laguna Colorada at left.
16.1	25.8	Seafood restaurant. Pass side road (right) to Costa Rica. Careful for slow-moving farm traffic.

There is a nice pastoral spot 4.1 miles west of here on highway #19. It's Los Cascabeles, on the lake of the same name. 20 fenced acres with 10 cabins, boats, pool, hunting and fishing. RV section (MOD) with 44 spaces, electricity and water. Dump station. Medical services. Palapa. BBQ pits. Security. Store. Laundry. Restaurant. FAX: (671) 713-6418 or in Culiacán (667) 673-6418, 673-6822.

16.4	26.2	Restaurant Centro Recreativo Los Cascabeles. **GAS**, both sides of the road.
17.3	27.7	Thru San Miguel. Cattle ranches thru here (also, careful for people on bicycles on road).
27.0	43.2	El Dorado to the right. To right is also another entrance to toll road if you want to take it.
27.5	44.0	Topes! Up thru town of El Salado and over couple of bridges over Río Salado.
33.8	54.1	Now curve right and over Río San Lorenzo and thru Tabala. Note ruins of ancient church at left with burial tombs. Cactus growing out of spiral on church. **KM 165.**
38.9	62.2	Pass side road (right) to Oso (bear).
40.6	65.0	Thru village of Las Flores. Then curve right and over north fork of Río Obispo.
43.3	69.3	Pass side road (right) to Obispo (bishop).
46.5	74.4	Curve right and cross south fork of Río Obispo and pass village of Higueras de Abuya.
55.4	88.6	Thru settlement of El Avión. **KM 130.**
61.7	98.7	Pass Las Tinas at left. **KM 121.**
63.1	101.0	Thru El Espinal. More "topes." **KM 118.**
66.8	106.9	Thru El Aguaje and curve right. Pass Glass House Resort hotel — MOD — 36 rooms, Restaurant, Pool, English spoken; looks brand new and very nice. **KM 112.**
69.7	111.5	Pass side road (left) to picturesque ex-mining town of Cosalá (see description in the toll road stub log on page 24), 33 miles, on Hwy #D-1.
71.2	113.9	Pass side road (right) to La Cruz. Red Cross. **KM 105.**
79.7	127.5	Pass side road (left) to nearby town of Elota. Cross Río Elota.
80.0	128.0	Slow for sharp right curve and pass so-so-restaurant-bus stop. Then right and wind up.

24

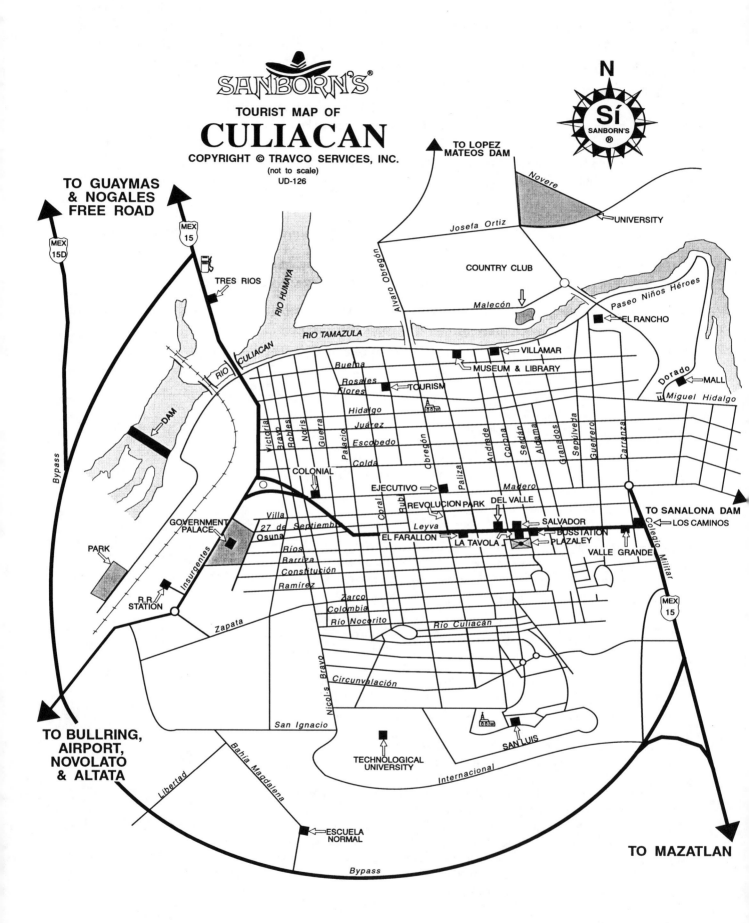

SANBORN'S ®

TOURIST MAP OF
CULIACAN
COPYRIGHT © TRAVCO SERVICES, INC.
(not to scale)
UD-126

N

Sí
SANBORN'S
®

TO LOPEZ
MATEOS DAM

TO GUAYMAS
& NOGALES
FREE ROAD

MEX 15D

MEX 15

Novere

Josefa Ortiz

UNIVERSITY

COUNTRY CLUB

TRES RIOS

RIO HUMAYA

Alvaro Obregón

Malecón

Paseo Niños Héroes

EL RANCHO

RIO TAMAZULA

RIO CULIACAN

Buelna

VILLAMAR

MUSEUM & LIBRARY

Dorado

MALL

RIO

Rosales
Flores

TOURISM

Miguel Hidalgo

DAM

Hidalgo

Juárez

Escobedo

Colda

Victoria

Bravo

Robles

Norís

Guerra

Palacio

Obregón

Andrade

Corona

Seldán

Aldama

Granados

Sepúlveda

Guerrero

Carranza

COLONIAL

Bypass

EJECUTIVO

Paliza

Madero

TO SANALONA DAM

REVOLUCION PARK

DEL VALLE

LOS CAMINOS

Cbral

Rubí

GOVERNMENT
PALACE

Villa
27 de Septiembre

Osuna

Leyva

SALVADOR

BUSSTATION

EL FARALLON

LA TAVOLA

PLAZALEY

Colegio Militar

PARK

Ríos

Barriya

VALLE GRANDE

Constitución

Ramírez

MEX 15

R.R.
STATION

Insurgentes

Zarco

Colombia

Río Nocorito

Río Culiacán

Zapata

Nicolás Bravo

Circunvalación

TO BULLRING,
AIRPORT,
NOVOLATO
& ALTATA

Bahía Magdalena

Libertad

San Ignacio

TECHNOLOGICAL
UNIVERSITY

SAN LUIS

Internacional

TO MAZATLAN

ESCUELA
NORMAL

Bypass

MI	KM	
84.4	135.0	La Minita (The Little Mine) up at left. The mill here grinds ore in from Mexico's interior, separating zinc, copper and lead.
86.8	138.9	Village of Piaxtla off to left.
88.3	141.3	Cross Río Piaxtla and right and up.
90.6	145.0	Settlement of Crucero de Piaxtla. Then side road right to Hacienda Piaxtla.
95.2	152.3	Pass side road (left) to San Ignacio, 32 KM. San Ignacio is a very picturesque town. Founded in 1582 as San Ignacio de Loyola.
95.6	153.0	**GAS** left. Diesel, but be ready for lots of kids here.
97.7	156.3	Pull off to right. Over bridge, then start winding with sharp curves.
99.1	158.6	Pass side road (left) to El Limón.
99.4	159.0	Pull off for view watching to right.
111.5	178.4	El Moral off to left and then a straight stretch for a change.
116.6	186.6	Come to crossroads. Mazatlán, straight. Left is to Quelite.
117.0	187.2	Curve right past side road (right) to Mármol (marble) and over Río Quelite. Wonder if there's any marble?
122.6	196.2	Los Zapotes off to left and El Recreo off to right.
123.5	197.6	Come now to TROPIC OF CANCER — note marker at right.
127.0	203.2	Pass side road (right) to El Potrero. Note bust of General Juan Carrasco at right.
127.1	203.4	Pass side road (left) to La Palma.
130.0	208.0	Come to junction.

IF TO: Beach. Take side road (right) to Playa Cerritos and shortcut beach road to Mazatlán. (If heading to North Beach hotels, RV parks, etc., go ahead and turn here. When you come to ocean, turn left and head toward town.)

IF TO: Downtown Mazatlán, Tepic, Durango, straight.

132.6	212.2	Hilltop restaurant at left. **KM 7.**
134.6	215.4	Big mango grove at right. Then highway police station at right.
134.8	215.7	Begin 4-lane divided roadway (Toll road to Culiacán, exit right here), then under bridge. Toll road from Culiacán rejoins Hwy #15 here.
135.0	216.0	Be ready to turn left soon, if bypassing Mazatlán, going south.
136.1	217.8	**GAS**, right. Then at left is Ciudad de los Niños ("boys' town" or "orphanage," not to be confused with the "red-light district"). Centro de Bodegas at left. Gamesa Plant at left.
136.8	218.9	Careful now as you approach bypass left around Mazatlán. Get into left lane for left turn for bypass if continuing on Hwy #15. **GAS**, right. Restaurant La Palmita, left.

IF TO: Durango, veer left just before stoplight and start Mazatlán — Durango Log (See Mexico's Central Route book, page 102).

IF TO: Tepic, Guadalajara, Airport, etc., veer left just before stoplight and start Mazatlán — Tepic Log (page 26).

IF TO: Beachfront, downtown Mazatlán, follow stub log below:

STUB LOG TO DOWNTOWN MAZATLÁN

0.0	0.0	Continue straight with Motel Relax at right and Pacific beer at left.
0.4	0.7	Up and over railroad.
0.6	1.0	Come to intersection and turn right just past bus station at right.
1.1	1.8	Bullring at right. Then Gigante at right.
1.2	1.9	Sharp hospital at left. Then **GAS** that takes credit cards at left.
1.4	2.2	La Posta Trailer Park, left.
1.5	2.4	Hotel San Diego on left, McDonald's on right and come to ocean-side boulevard (see map). Don't bypass Mazatlán if you have the time — it's well worth a look-see. If you check out Mamucas Restaurant on Calle Simón Bolívar, you'll see a picture of Dan Sanborn receiving the key to the city. You can buy the pottery, fish-shaped charcoal braziers, just like the one your fish is sizzling on at your table (while it singes your eyebows). For info on accommodations, see Mazatlán Eat & Stray (page 118).

End of Log 9

LOG 10 *START:* Mazatlán, Sin *END:* Tepic, Nay

UD-019

173.5 MI or 277.6 KM
DRIVE TIME 4 1/2 — 5 HOURS
SCENIC RATING — 2

Some divided, mostly two lane. Heavy truck traffic. Although it has been vastly imporved this route still has stretches of poor surface. The last 70 miles are thrilling enough to recall the carnival ride you'd like to get off but can't till it's over. Imagine dueling semis racing, passing at top speed on a narrow two lane blacktop road. Be prepared, drive in daylight, don't run out of gas or have a flat tire. There is no way to stop and no place to pull off. When it's behind you, you feel an exhilerating appreciation for wellbeing!

MI	KM	
0.0	0.0	Having turned left off Hwy #15, (following Tepic, *Aeropuerto* signs) ahead on nice divided bypass around Mazatlán. Gamesa plant and Corona distributor, right. Basketball field, left. Divided, six lanes. Palm tree lined. There will be a stoplight here in the future.
0.3	0.5	Pass up motel Real, a motel *del paso* (rents by the hour).
0.5	0.8	Cemetery at right. Pass multicolored Colonia (subdivision) Lic. Mario A. Arroyo.
1.3	2.1	Community of Colonia Echeverría at right. Over bridge. Then thru Colonia S. Allende. Parque Industrial. Stoplight. Church ahead on left.
1.8	2.9	General Tire, left.
2.5	4.0	ISESM Campas Mazatán, subdivision, left. Farmer's market (Central de Abastos), left. Pass Café Marino plant left. Up and over overpass. Then right and down. Road narrows to four lanes divided. Thru suburb of Rincón de Urias. Then curve right and pass school at left.
3.0	4.8	End of bypass. Come to intersection. Stop sign. LEFT, following "Tepic, Aeropuerto" signs. In front of you is Corona distributor. Ahead and right is Pepsi agency, "Bebidas Purificadas." AFTER turning, John Deere, left and Goodyear, right. Then Aga plant, left. Sign says: "Aeropuerto 14 KM, Tepic 286 KM."
3.2	5.1	Under overpass. **GAS**, right. LP gas, left. Overhead sign says "Durango and Tepic straight ahead."
3.3	5.3	Tractores de Occidente, left. Golf course, left. Divided 4 lane.
3.5	5.6	LP gas.
4.0	6.4	Under *Buen Viaje* arch. Follow "Tepic, Aeropuerto" signs, straight.
5.5	8.8	Colonia La Sirena, right. Salt flats, right.
6.3	10.1	Begin long curve, right. Big power plant, right. Then side road (right) to El Castillo. Speed limit **70 KM**.
8.5	13.6	Large penitentiary, left. Speed limit 80 KMPH. Then over bridge. **KM 272.**
10.9	17.4	Experimental farm station at right.
11.3	18.1	Pass side road (right) to Mazatlán's airport. **KM 275.**
13.4	20.8	Divided ends. Then El Pozole, right. **KM 271.**
14.0	22.4	Cross Río Presidio. Slow thru town of Villa Unión. Hotel El Kino, right. Slow thru town. TOPES. SPEED 30 KMPH.
15.3	24.5	End of town. Curve left and out.
15.5	24.8	Motel El Pino, left, OK. **GAS**, right.

IF TO: Hwy #40 to Durango, Torreón, Saltillo, Monterrey etc., left here. Start Mazatlán — Durango Log. (See Mexico's Central Route book, page 103.)

IF TO: Tepic, ahead on Hwy #15 for you.

26.5	42.4	Village of El Huajote, at right, with its baseball field.
29.0	46.4	Ejido El Tablón, mostly at right.
29.5	47.2	Thru Tablón #1.
31.0	49.6	Village of Potrerillos down at right. Then experimental fruit station.
32.5	52.0	Pass side road (left) to Presa (dam) Las Higueras and then cross *río* and pass village of Las Higueras off to left.
36.5	58.4	Over bridge and then settlement of Los Otates (The Bamboos), left.
38.6	61.8	Mango orchard to left.
41.5	66.4	That's Mount Yauco dead ahead. Begin new blacktop toll road here.

(Continued on page 29)

27

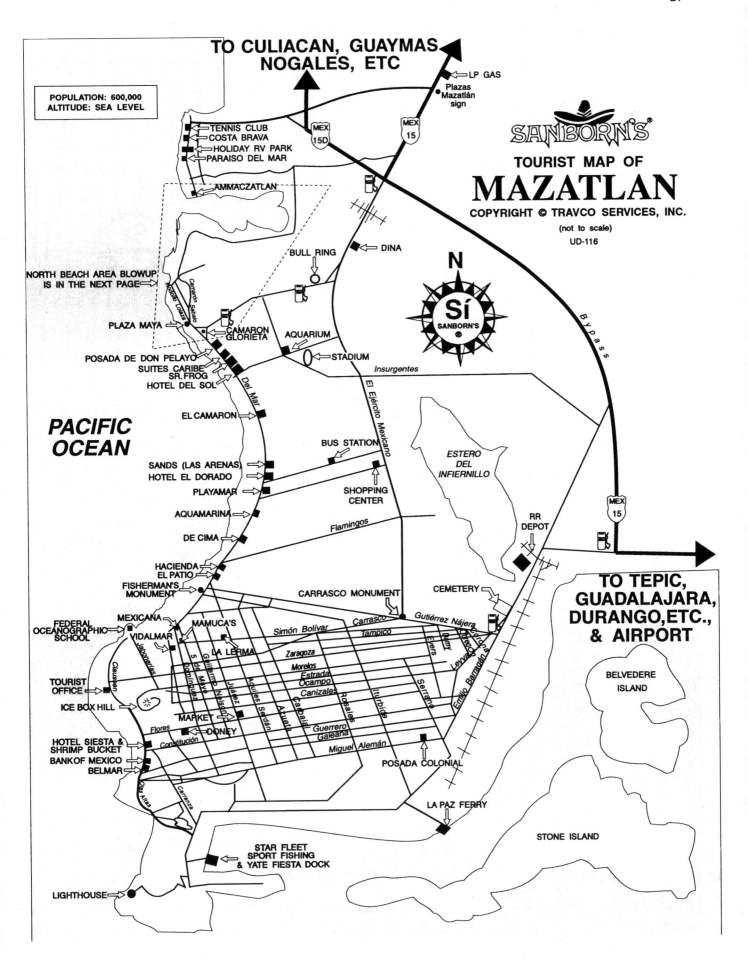

28

SANBORN'S®
TOURIST MAP OF
MAZATLAN
NORTH BEACH AREA
COPYRIGHT © TRAVCO SERVICES, INC.
(not to scale)
UD-041

GINGER'S HORSE RANCH

TO CULIACAN

MARINA MAZATLAN

EL CID MEGA RESORT

MEX 15D

PUNTA DEL SABALO

CAMINO REAL

N
Sí
SANBORN'S®

PUEBLO BONITO

POSADA LA MISION

LUNA PALACE
EL PARAJE
OCEANO PALACE
SAN BARTOLO RV PARK

DOUBLE TREE

FIESTA INN
SOLARMAR INN

EL QUIJOTE INN
CASA COUNTRY
MAR ROSA RV PARK
ISLAS DEL SOL
EL PARADOR ESPAÑOL
HOLIDAY INN
EL CID GOLF
HYATT
COURSE & HOTEL
PUESTA DEL SOL
INN AT MAZATLAN
POSADA SANTA FE
Camarón
COSTA DE ORO
DAIRY QUEEN
BALBOA TOWERS
BALBOA CLUB
CASA LOMA
COCINA DE ALMA
LONG DISTANCE & FAX

PACIFIC
OCEAN

SHANGRI-LA
GUADALAJARA GRILL
TEQUILA CHARLIE'S
LAS PALMAS MOTEL & RV PARK
Rodolfo Loaiza
SUITES LINDAMAR
TACOS EL TROMPO & AA
MARLEY
SUITES LOS ARROYOS
LOS ARCOS
AHA TORO
NO NAME CAFE
SUITES LAS FLORES
CINEMA

SHRIMP FACTORY
LA CASA CONTENTA
AZTECA INN

Sábalo

TONY'S PLAZA
PLAYA MAZATLAN
PLAZA GAVIOTAS
CANADIAN CONSULATE
GIGANTE
LOS SABALOS
TROPICANA ARISTOS
RIVIERA MAZATLAN
NISSAN
POINT SOUTH RV PARK
McDONALD'S
SHARP
HOSPITAL
CAMARON GLORIETA
(Traffic Circle)
LA POSTA RV PARK

VALENTINO'S DISCO
DAMY'S BUNGALOWS

MI	KM	
42.5	68.8	Pass LP gas (left) and skirt town Rosario (50,000 population). Hotel Los Morales at left. **GAS**, left. Nice snack stands with soft drinks etc. Icehouse, right and down, then cross Río Baluarte on half-mile-long bridge. Up past village of Chilillos and onto particularly bad stretch of road. Goodyear on left.
48.5	77.6	Pass side road (right) to Chametla. Very long bridge
50.6	81.0	Cross south fork of Río Baluarte.
53.3	85.3	Rest area. San José restaurant on right.
54.0	86.4	Mango orchard to right. Restaurant to left. If you want a snack, you can eat at a bus stop restaurant without fear. Then **GAS** at right.
54.5	87.2	Good enough Motel Virginia on left. **KM 202**.
55.6	89.0	Over bridge and enter town of Escuinapa (population 60,000). Try lunch at El Rodeo Restaurant (shrimp and Quesadillas). Then careful and at the stoplight, turn right (follow TEPIC signs) onto one-way street. At end of two blocks, turn left and ahead thru Escuinapa on one-way street. **GAS**. Come to junction with road (right) to Teacapan.

IF TO: Teacapan, turn right.

TEACAPAN, Sinaloa is a little off the beaten track, 26 miles away, a sleepy tropical village with nice white beaches. This is a birder's paradise area. Efforts are underway to have the government declare it a sanctuary and park. A great place to go if you have a spirit of adventure and you are tired of the party atmosphere of Mazatlán. Naturalists will enjoy the place and the (so far) unspoiled beaches. You can fish, go birding and loaf. Wildlife includes white and pink heron and pichihuila and deer. This is a small town with friendly folks and beautiful scenery. There are two good hotels: In town on plaza is Hotel Denisse, which is small (5 rooms) and inexpensive; farther out is the Rancho Los Angeles (after 15.8 miles, turn right at mini-Super Los Angeles sign; use gate entrance to right of arch; enter and veer right, follow dirt road 1.5 miles to hotel) with the best restaurant (excellent Bar-B-Q fish) in town, perhaps in Mexico. It is for a more affluent crowd with private bungalows and a swimming pool. The only RV park is The Oregon, on the beach, near Señor Wayne's Restaurant. Hotel Palmeras (under construction) will be a nice place once it's finished. Jejenes (no-see-ems, or sand fleas) do exist here but are not as bad as in San Blas. They only come out for about an hour in the morning and an hour at dusk.

		Back on one-way Hwy #15.
56.5	90.4	Parador Turístico just on the other side of the village to the left. Clean restrooms and shower.
57.0	91.2	Turn right as one-way street comes to end and merges with Hwy #15. **GAS**, left. Empacadora (packing company) de Escuinapa, right.
58.5	93.6	Loma Linda Restaurant at left and chapel across street. Thru long mango grove. At end, LP gas, left.
61.0	97.6	Santa Anita fumigation station at right.
63.0	100.8	Village of Tecualilla , off to right, behind trees. Toll road ends here.
70.0	112.0	Big Ejido La Campaña, left. Pick up railroad on right.
75.0	120.0	Thru village of Palmillas.
78.1	125.0	Up alongside mountain with salt marshes on right. Then slow for sharp left curve.
79.1	126.6	Community of Las Mulas (The Mules). Careful for couple of sharp curves ahead.
83.4	133.4	Pass railroad village of Copales.
88.0	140.8	Inspección de Sanidad Fitopecuaria Y Forestal. No pigs allowed!
87.5	140.0	Thru village of La Concha. Then curve right and slow past truck inspection, right. Over Río Cañas and cross state line — leave Sinaloa and enter Nayarit. **KM 143**.
92.3	147.7	Up and over bridge over railroad.
92.8	148.5	Pass side road (left) to Acaponeta, founded in 1584 by the Franciscans (about 1.3 miles away where there's OK motel Cadenales at entrance to town). **GAS**, right. Then paved side road (right) to Tecuala and on to Novillero (22 miles), a rather solitary village on the Pacific coast with miles and miles of open beaches known as "Playas de Novillero."

You'll find the accommodations somewhat inadequate and primitive — Margarita 2-story, 33-room hotel within walking distance of beach; ceiling fans, restaurant, covered parking and Bungalows Paraíso 12 kitchenette units on beach, space for few RV's with no hookups, tenting permitted.

| 95.0 | 152.0 | Pass side road (right) to Sayulita. Then slow for sharp left curve and over steel bridge. Limit of 50 tons, strictly enforced. |

MI	KM	
96.4	154.2	Over Río Acaponeta and thru San Francisco.
103.4	165.4	Village of San Miguel, mostly to left. **KM 113**.
107.7	172.3	Up thru village of Tierra Generosa (Generous Land). TOPES. TOPES. **KM 110.**
120.0	192.0	**GAS**, right. Truck stop of El Mil (1000) at right. Then couple of bridges and railroad at left. Tobacco field, on right, just past **GAS**. New 4 lane road ahead 57 KM.
121.2	193.9	Cross Río Rosamorada. Railroad bridge, left and railroad town of Rosamorada (Purple Rose), left.
132.5	212.0	Pass side road (right) to Chilapa. Then cross bridge over Río El Bejuco. Road improves.
132.0	211.2	Come now to side road (right) to little island town of Mexcaltitán, Mexico's mini-Venice. Helo's 24 hour on right. You can get purified water there for RV's.

If you insist on visiting Mexcaltitán, go approximately 29 miles over a rough gravel road to a place called "*El Embarcadero*," where you'll park, then hire a dugout canoe for the 15-minute trip to the island town of about 3,500 inhabitants, many of whom have never left the island. This side-sortie is suggested only for the adventuresome as Mexcaltitán isn't ready yet for the normal course of tourist traffic, but the shrimp is fresh, jumbo-size and delicious.

MI	KM	
133.0	212.8	Cross Río San Pedro and thru roadside market community of Peñitas. Careful for side road (right) to Tuxpan. **GAS**, left.
138.0	220.8	Community of Heróico Batallón de San Blas up road, left.
141.1	225.8	Pass side road (right) to Santiago Ixcuintla and on to Los Corchos (The Corks) on beach. **GAS**, in town. **KM 55.**

If you're interested in the Huichol Indians' weaving and bead work, this is the place where the Huichol Center for Cultural Survival and Traditional Arts is located. Susana Valadez, who helps organize things will be glad to arrange classes for interested groups. She runs a hospital and cultural center there, so please be considerate. She's not ready for troops of tourists to drop by and visit, but if you have a sincere interest, or a fledgling importer who wants to buy some really unique art, please call and make an appointment to see her. She's usually gone in late June-July. She'll put on demonstrations for tour groups also. The hotel Bugamvillas is the best, just on the outskirts of town. There is an OK hotel, Casino, in town, basic, but clean. You can call her at (323) 235-1171 Fax: 235-1006, or write: 20 de Noviembre #452, Santiago Ixcuintla, Nay.

When you get back, if you want to buy some of their art work, they have a U.S. outlet: 801 2nd Ave., Suite 1400, Seattle, WA 98104. Ph: (206) 622-4067 Fax: (206) 622-0646. The Huichols are shy, artistic people who are becoming extinct due to TB and other diseases. They have a 50% infant mortality rate. If you want to help with medical supplies or donations, they are tax-exempt: IRS # 95-3012063.

MI	KM	
143.0	228.8	Thru village of Capomal. Cemetery on left. **KM 52**.
143.5	229.6	Pass side road (left) to Estación Yago on railroad. **GAS**, right.
144.0	230.4	Cross Río Grande de Santiago on big steel bridge. This is a bad-acting river. Large tobacco fields on right. **KM 50**.
145.5	232.8	Wind past tobacco town of Valle de Lerma at left. Note tobacco fields thru here.
152.0	243.2	Pass side road (right) to another tobacco town of Villa Hidalgo.
151.3	242.1	El Paraíso at right. Note big stand selling freshly squeezed fruit juices.
154.6	247.4	Careful now! **GAS**, right and come to junction (right) with side road down to famed old-time seaside town of San Blas. If you have a couple of hours to spare, run down for a quick look-see at this tropical historic place. Friends of Bill W. sometimes in town.

IF TO: San Blas, See Jct Hwy #15 - San Blas Special (page 68).

MI	KM	
154.7	247.5	Four-lane highway after San Blas turnoff, pass restaurant Amalia at left at TOME FANTA sign — cold cokes, package snacks, plus a zoo of sorts including jaguars, parrots, etc. Veer right onto divided, then straight ahead and start climbing.
157.2	251.5	Tepic (Quota) Toll road to right. Tepic Libre (free road) to left. Altitude 1,600 feet. Now divided 4 lane. Road gets much better at this point.
162.3	259.7	Community of Trapichillo to left. Then Summit at 2,600 feet.
166.1	265.8	Toll gate 2,300 feet. PAY TOLL (car — $30; 2 (rear) axles — $45; extra axle — $15). Free highway still to the left.
169.1	270.5	Divided ends.
169.3	270.8	Under overpass. Come now to nice Periférico (loop) around Tepic. For accommodations see Tepic Eat & Stray (page 129).

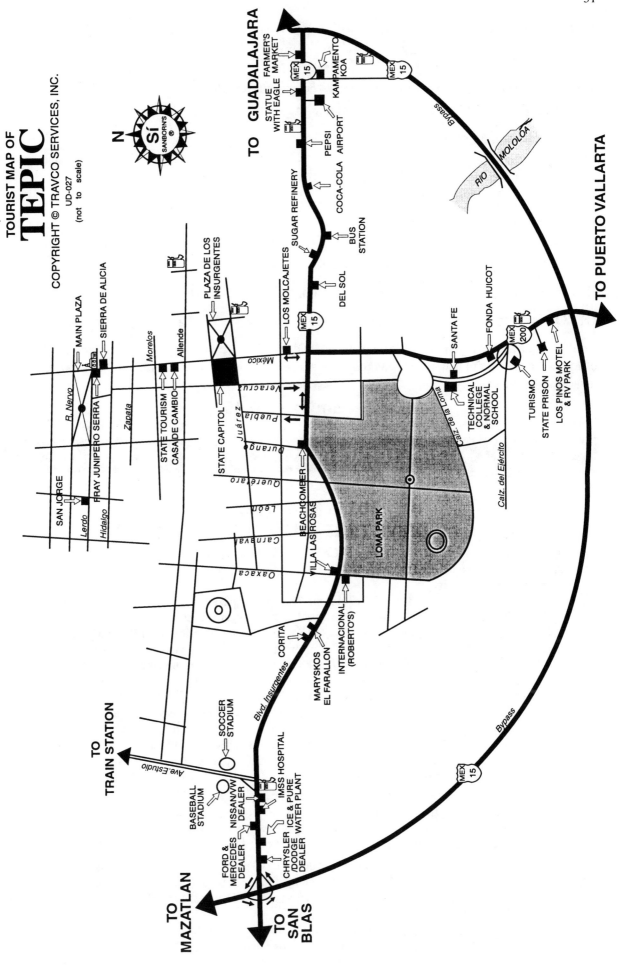

SANBORN'S®

TOURIST MAP OF

TEPIC

COPYRIGHT © TRAVCO SERVICES, INC.

UD-027

(not to scale)

N

Sí
SANBORN'S®

TO GUADALAJARA

TO PUERTO VALLARTA

TO MAZATLAN

TO SAN BLAS

TO TRAIN STATION

STATUE WITH EAGLE

FARMER'S MARKET

MEX 15

KAMPAMENTO KOA

MEX 15

Bypass

RIO MOLOLOA

PEPSI

COCA-COLA AIRPORT

SUGAR REFINERY

BUS STATION

MEX 15

LOS MOLCAJETES

DEL SOL

MAIN PLAZA

SIERRA DE ALICIA

B. Nervo

Morelos

Zapata

Allende

PLAZA DE LOS INSURGENTES

FRAY JUNIPERO SERRA

SAN JORGE

Lerdo

Hidalgo

STATE TOURISM

CASA DE CAMBIO

STATE CAPITOL

México

Veracruz

Puebla

Juárez

Durango

Querétaro

León

Carnaval

Oaxaca

BEACHCOMBER

VILLA LAS ROSAS

LOMA PARK

Calz. de la Loma

SANTA FE

FONDA HUICOT

TECHNICAL COLLEGE & NORMAL SCHOOL

Calz. del Ejército

MEX 200

TURISMO

STATE PRISON

LOS PINOS MOTEL & RV PARK

Bypass

MEX 15

Blvd. Insurgentes

CORITA

MARYSKOS EL FARALLON

INTERNACIONAL (ROBERTO'S)

SOCCER STADIUM

Ave. Estudio

BASEBALL STADIUM

FORD & MERCEDES DEALER

NISSAN/VW DEALER

IMSS HOSPITAL

CHRYSLER /DODGE DEALER

ICE & PURE WATER PLANT

IF TO: Downtown Tepic, on old Hwy #15, exit at right (follow TEPIC signs). If you need gas, there's a big station down old highway.

MI   KM

169.8 271.7   Housing project to right. Suburb and school to left. **KM 12**.

IF TO: Downtown Tepic (Centro, Miramar sign), exit right.

IF TO: Vallarta, go straight.

170.0	272.0	Note Tepic at left.
172.0	275.2	Curve right. Col. del Bosque to left. **KM 8**.
172.1	275.4	Cement block factory to left.
172.4	275.8	Cuauhtémoc suburb to right.
173.1	277.0	Thru rock cut. **KM 6**.
173.5	277.6	Come now to junction with Hwy #200. Radiator distributor "Sanher" at right. **KM 5**.

IF TO: Guadalajara, straight ahead and start Tepic - Guadalajara Log (page 34).

IF TO: Puerto Vallarta, turn right and start Tepic - Puerto Vallarta Log.

IF TO: Downtown Tepic (and to Los Pinos and Linda Vista RV Parks), turn left here.

Don't hesitate to stop if you've a little time to spare and visit Tepic, capital of the state of Nayarit, a very nice town of 150,000 at the foot of inactive Sanguey Volcano. Of interest are its cathedral (built in 1750) and its regional museum of anthropology.

End of Log 10

LOG 11   *START:* **Tepic, Nay**   *END:* **Pto. Vallarta, Jal**

UD-019

103.5 MI or 165.6 KM
DRIVE TIME 3 1/2 – 4 1/2 HOURS
SCENIC RATING – 3

0.0	0.0	Having taken PUERTO VALLARTA exit at right, proceed ahead and up. Slow as you merge with traffic coming from Tepic.
1.5	2.4	Thru little town of Xalisco. **GAS** at right. Then pretty plaza at right.
4.5	7.2	Thru settlement of El Testerazo, mostly at left. Thru sugarcane country.
15.1	24.2	Pass side road (left) to coffee-growing El Refilión. Then over bridge over Río Refilión.
19.8	31.7	Take RIGHT FORK here and curve right thru cut for bypass around town of Compostela (10,000 population), biggest place between Tepic and "PV" with a couple of emergency hotels on plaza. Of interest here is the old church built with red "tezontle" (volcanic rock) in 1539.
21.8	34.9	Pass Autonomous University of Nayarit branch at right.
32.3	51.7	Thru village of Mesillas and then thru redlands. It's becoming more tropical now.
38.8	62.1	Thru village of Las Piedras (The Stones). Then over Río Las Piedras.
40.5	64.8	Thru little settlement of La Cuata (The Female Twin) and over Río Viejo.
41.8	66.9	Now thru little town of Las Varas. Pretty fruit stands and charming shoppers cause fender benders, so be attentive to slow traffic. Pass side road (right) to Zacualpan. **GAS**, at right. Then come to junction left with Hwy #68-D toll road that cuts across east to Chapalilla on Hwy #15.

IF TO: San Blas, turn right and start Las Varas - San Blas Special (page 72).

IF TO: Guadalajara, Start Las Varas - Chapalilla Special (page 73).

43.5	69.6	Pass side road (right) to Chacala and over Río Las Varas. This used to be magnificent jungle.
49.0	78.4	Pass side road (right) to Lima de Abajo and Puesta de la Lima. Then over Río de la Lima.
54.3	86.9	**GAS**, at right. Then pass side trail (right) to La Peñita RV Park (274-0996), a nice cliffside layout overlooking the Pacific.
54.5	87.2	Slow for topes and into seaside brick-making village of La Peñita de Jaltemba (simply known as "La Peñita"). Pass divided boulevard to right to downtown La Peñita.

IF TO: Russell Motel and RV Park, go to end of boulevard and then a block north (or right).

MI	KM	
55.0	88.0	Over Río La Peñita. Icehouse a few blocks off to left. Then over Río de Jaquey.
56.5	90.4	Come to side road (right) to Rincón de Guayabitos (see Eat & Stray, page 133), a popular resort development.
59.8	95.7	Pass edge of village of El Monteón at right.
62.0	99.2	Thru settlement of Chula Vista.
64.5	103.2	Pass side road (right) to Lo de Marcos and to nice El Caracol RV Park.
70.8	113.3	Settlement of San Francisco at right with its own hospital and vocational fishing school. Also Hotel Costa Azul sport resort. Adriana's Bed and Breakfast is one block from plaza. Then thru banana plantations.
73.5	117.6	Pass side road (right) to Playa Sayulita and Sayula RV Park on beach, 1.5 miles (not recommended for large RV's because of rough entrance road).
83.3	133.3	Begin divided highway. Pass side road (right) to La Cruz de Huanacaxtle and to its nautical institute. There is also a Japanese resort Pinta Mitaketmar.
84.3	134.9	Bungalows Vista del Bahía at right on beach. 8 nice kitchenettes. Pool. Pets OK. Portable fans only. 5 RV spaces, all hookups, shower, toilet. Bungalows Los Picos, also at right on beach. Complex of 6 buildings, each with two 3-bedroom, 2-bath apartments. Portable fans only. Pets allowed.
84.5	135.2	Thru seaside village of Bucerias and over Río de Bucerias. Slow for topes. Mirador Restaurant, right.
86.0	137.6	Pass side road (right) to Hotel Playa de Bucerias and to Bucerias RV Park. 25 spaces with hookups, 30 more with electricity and water, showers, toilets, laundromat, rec room.
88.0	140.8	Nice Club de Golf and Hotel Los Flamingos at right. Restaurant-bar. Pool. Pro shop. Sauna. Massage. Green fee. Electric cart fee. Caddy fee.
90.5	144.8	Pass side road (right) to Nuevo Vallarta, a resort city development.
91.0	145.6	Motel Marina del Sol, right.
91.5	146.4	Now past side road (right) to Jarretaderas. Then up and over big, long toll bridge over Río Ameca. This is also state line – leave Nayarit and enter Jalisco. Likewise, this also marks a time zone - leave Mountain Time and enter Central Time. You loose an hour – set your watches and dashboard clock FORWARD an hour. Come to tollhouse and pay toll. Then pass Policia Federal de Caminos.
92.0	147.2	Continue on 4-lane divided road into Puerto Vallerta. Near KM 139 on left is a new KOA campground for RV's.
93.8	150.1	Pass side road (left) to Las Juntas, 2 kilometers.
95.5	152.8	Pass Puerto Vallarta's international airport at right. LP gas and Sam's Club at left.
97.5	156.0	Bumpy side road (left) to Tacho's RV Park. Car-passenger ferry terminal at right. **GAS** down at right. Then Hacienda del Lobo Hotel and Tennis Club at right. Pass side street (right) to big Posada Vallarta Hotel and Village, Hotel Playa de Oro and Miller Travel Service, across from Posada Vallarta and Hotel Kristal.
98.5	157.6	Highrise Ramada Inn, Fiesta Americana (outstanding) and Los Tules Resort, all at right. La Onda Disco at right and side road (right) to economic Hotel Los Pelícanos and Hotel Las Palmas. Side road left to Puerto Vallarta RV Park. Careful for stoplight. *"Libramiento"* under construction at left, a bypass around Vallarta.
98.8	158.1	Sports field at left. Then excellent Sheraton Hotel at right.
100.3	164.5	Over bridge over Arroyo Camarones (shrimp) and start one-way cobblestone street. Enter Puerto Vallarta and pass big gas station at left. For accommodations see Puerto Vallarta Eat & Stray (page 134).
100.5	160.8	Bend right slightly past little plaza at left. Hotel Rosita at right and ahead on waterfront boulevard, known locally as the "malecón."
101.0	161.6	Jog left and right and pass little lighthouse at left. Post office at left – and many shops.
101.1	161.8	Waterfront boulevard ends. Puerto Vallarta's main plaza and city hall at left and straight ahead for you. Turismo (tourist office in Banamex building) at left. Then Hotel Río, another of Puerto Vallarta's old-timers.
101.5	162.4	Up over bridge over Río Cuale. Then note houses back at left built up alongside river. That's famous "Gringo Gulch," a colony of expatriate Americans and plush homes.
101.5	162.4	Turn left 5 blocks after bridge. Move right and after 2 blocks, turn right onto Insurgentes. Now after Hotel El Mesón de los Arcos at right, start winding up and thru residential area alongside Pacific. **GAS**, at right. Periférico (loop) at left around PV.
103.5	165.6	Pass El Set Restaurant. Then fabulous Hotel Camino Real at right. To get there, turn off left and slow just ahead for topes.

IF TO: Barra de Navidad or Manzanillo, start Pto Vallarta - Melaque Jct. Log. (See Mexico's South Pacific book, page 2.)

End of Log 11

TO AIRPORT,
NUEVO VALLARTA
& TEPIC

MEX 200

TO
LA MOJONERA

SANBORN'S®
TOURIST MAP OF
PUERTO VALLARTA
COPYRIGHT © TRAVCO SERVICES, INC.
UD-039
(not to scale)

N
SÍ
SANBORN'S
®

SIERRA PLAZA
PTO. VALLARTA
PLAZA
IGUANA
MELIA

TACHO'S
RV PARK

PLAYA
DE ORO

TENNIS CLUB
VALLARTA

KRYSTAL
VALLARTA

CASA GRANDE
VALLARTA

RAMADA PLAZA
(HOLIDAY INN)

FIESTA
AMERICANA

LOS TULES

PTO. VALLARTA
RV PARK

PELICANOS
LAS PALMAS

PLAZA LAS GLORIAS
CONTINENTAL PLAZA
JOHN NEWCOMB

EL CONQUISTADOR

COSTA
DEL SOL

BUGAVILIAS
SHERATON

BAHIA BANDERAS

Brasilia
Guatemala
San Salvador
Nicaragua
Honduras
Panama
Uraguay
Venezuela

Av. México

BUENAVENTURA

SUITES EL PESCADOR

ROSITA

Argentina
31 de Octubre
Allende
Abila

Morelos
Argentina

Lázaro Cárdenas

Olas Altas

LOS CUATRO VIENTOS

Río Cuale

Francisco Villa
Viena

Bypass

EL SET

MEX 200

TO
BARRA DE NAVIDAD
& MANZANILLO

MOBY
DICK

ROSITA
EL JARDIN
SHOPPING CENTER
CEBOLLA ROJA
CARLOS O'BRIAN'S

31 de Octubre
Allende
Pipila

MOCAMBO

Morelos
Leona Vicario
Dominguez
Abasolo
Aldama
Corona
Mina
Matamoros
Miramar

ZAPATA
CASA DEL ALMENDRO

LA SIESTA

BRAZZ
POST OFFICE
CITY HALL

Díaz Ordaz
Galeana
Iturbide

LOS CUATRO
VIENTOS

CHEF ROGER'S

Juárez
Hidalgo
Morelos
Zaragoza
Cadena
Guerrero
Libertad
A. Rodríguez

MUSEUM

Isla Cuale

Río Cuale

MOLINA DE AGUA
POSADA RIO CUALE

3 de Febrero

LE BISTRO

THEATER

A. Serdán
Fco. Madero
Lázaro Cárdenas

Vallarta
Constitución

LA LAGUNA

Carranza

Insurgentes
Aguacate

DAIQUIRI
DICK'S
PLAYA
LOS ARCOS
FONTANA
DEL MAR
COSTA ALEGRE

Olas Altas
Ola Badillo
Pino Suárez

PIZZA JOE'S

POSADA ROGER

ROBERTO'S

LAS
CAZUELAS

M. Diéguez

Fco. Rodríguez

Rodolfo Gómez

TROPICANA

Amapas
Pulpito
Pilitas

SEÑOR CHICO'S

LOG 12   *START:* Tepic, Nay   *END:* Guadalajara, Jal

147.3 MI or 235.7 KM
DRIVE TIME 4 – 5 1/2 HOURS
SCENIC RATING – 3

MI	KM	
0.0	0.0	Here at junction with Hwy #200, proceed ahead on Hwy #15.
0.6	1.0	Under railroad overpass. Just past overpass is side road (left) to downtown Tepic.
1.8	2.9	Los Sauces suburb on left. Left here to KOA RV Park. Paradise motel and **GAS**, left.
2.8	4.5	Over Río Mololoa (also known as Río de Tepic). Under overpass. **KM 1**.
3.1	5.0	Straight ahead is old congested Hwy #15 thru town. Take right fork.
6.2	9.9	Thru village of San Cayetano. Pass side road (right) to Pantanal.
9.3	14.9	Pass El Refugio at right. Mechanic to left.
14.3	22.9	Pass little town of La Labor over to right. **KM 200**.
18.8	30.1	Pass side road (left) to Santa María del Oro and La Laguna, with neat motel and trailer park Koala.

Koala Bungalows and trailer park is 52 KM SE from Tepic and 20 KM from Tepic/Guadalajara Hwy on Laguna de Santa Maria near Crater Lake (730 M above sea level and 2 KM in diameter). High entrance. 15 spaces with all hookups. Showers. Swimming. Boat ramp. Boating. Fishing. Ph: (327) 272-3772 or (311) 214-0509 (in Tepic).

25.8	41.3	Pass village of El Ocotillo. Altitude 4,250 feet.
26.1	41.8	Careful now! Here's the turnoff for Puerto Vallarta.

IF TO: Puerto Vallarta take "PUERTO VALLARTA CUOTA and COMPOSTELA CUOTA" slot. Start Chapalilla – Las Varas Special (page 73).

27.1	43.4	Come to junction with toll road Free road stay in right lane. For toll road, veer to left at confusing circle and stop sign. Then turn left and ahead. Follow stub log below.

Toll Road to Guadalajara

27.2	43.5	Having turned left onto toll road proceed ahead.
29.0	46.4	Wind up. Leave lush farmland and enter drier, poorer soil, mountain sides.
32.0	51.2	For Guadalajara, curve sharply to right straight goes back to Tepic). Come to toll house and pay toll (cars, $35, with extra axle, $17). Now begin 4-lane.
38.0	60.8	Cross bridge over gully of black lava rock down below and covering the mountain side.
45.0	72.0	Pass exit (right) to Jala and Ahuacatlán. Then ahead thru dry, treeless mountains with a few cacti.
49.0	78.4	Mirador pull-off with a view of the town of Ixtlán del Río.
52.0	83.2	Pass exit (right) to Ixtlán del Río.
57.0	91.2	Under overpass of Hwy #15 free road. **GAS** across over to left (inaccessible from this side).
58.0	92.8	Over puente Ocote. Ocote is a strip of pine wood, dripping with sap, used as a catalyst to start a fire.
59.0	94.4	Pass monument dedicating this toll road. Cross state line. Leave state of Nayarit and enter state of Jalisco. Also come to a new TIME ZONE – leave Mountain Standard Time and start Central Standard Time, so set your watches and dash clock AHEAD one hour. Mountains are now covered with deciduous trees.
63.0	100.8	Slow and curve over puente Platamar.
69.0	110.8	Come to tollhouse and pay toll (cars $90, extra axle $45). 24-hour emergency medical service, cafeteria and clean restrooms.
81.0	129.6	Town of Magdalena over to left with pretty church dome and Hacienda Sta. Teresa.
83.0	132.0	Pass exit (right) to Magdalena. Sign says, Guadalajara, 75 km.
88.0	140.8	Down over puente Gorgorrones.
91.0	145.6	Over puente Tequila. Sorry folks, that doesn't mean that tequila flows in the stream below. Sign says, Guadalajara, 57 km.
96.0	153.6	To the right are fields of Blue Agave, the plant from which the finest tequilas are distilled. The Guadalajara area produces most of Mexico's tequila.
99.0	158.4	Come to last tollhouse (cars $69, with extra axle $87). There's a snack shop, restrooms and a mechanic shop.
101.0	161.6	Pass exit (right) to Ameca and now toll road joins free road. It's 4-lane but slow down. Join free road log at mile 124.3.

End Toll Road

MI	KM	
30.0	48.0	**GAS**, left. Then thru Chapalilla. Emergency Motel La Cumbre and Restaurant at left. Pass village of El Torreón on right. **KM 175**.
33.3	53.3	Into little town of Santa Isabel. Pass a sugar mill on left.
36.8	58.9	Pass side road (right) to Estación Tetitlán and Balneario Acatique Springs.

IF TO: Springs – Turn left at Balneario sign just beyond school. Over bumpy railroad tracks, 3/4 mile on right. It has fresh water, but not hot. Large pools. Balneario Acatique. Proprietor J. Trinidad Dueñas A., a former taxi driver in Tijuana and former owner of a KFC in Phoenix. Space for self-contained RV's and trailers. Nice flat parking. They'll run a water hose for you. Very nice folks and a nice restful place.

37.3	59.7	Uzeta off to right. **KM 167**.
38.8	62.1	Parador Turístico to left. **KM 160**. In 3 miles, you're in for a treat!

Now here's Something Special – Have you ever wondered what it's like on another planet? Well, here's your chance to be a spaceman (or space lady) and land on Mars or Jupiter or somewhere. Now you go thru a short mile of the famous LAVA-BEDS-OF-CEBORUCO caused by the eruption of Ceboruco Volcano in 1885. Sort of eerie, no? Like something out of this world – but bear in mind that it's against the law to pick up the little green one-eyed men or to stop and swipe lava samples.

42.3	67.7	Settlement of Copales.
45.3	74.5	Altitude 3,200 feet. Alongside railroad at right. **GAS**, right and town of Ahuacatlán over to right. There's a road to a nearby volcano. You can drive within 2 km of top, then walk. It's an active volcano. **KM 152**.
47.3	75.7	Pass side road (left) to Jala. From now on you'll spot patches of maguey (pronounced "muy-gay," the cactus from which the juice that is distilled into tequila is derived). Railroad runs along right side of road.
48.3	77.3	Pass side road (right) to Amequita and La Ciénega (The Swamp).
49.5	79.2	Over narrow bridge over railroad. Note at the left where the train comes out of the tunnel.
50.3	80.5	Note railroad tunnel ahead at left. Thru village of Mexpan. Straw weaving furniture etc.

When it rains, this road has invisible puddles that will give you an unpleasant surprise. Please slow down.

52.3	83.7	Ixtlán del Río's railroad station at left. Highway patrol station. 3,400 feet. **GAS**, left. Slow thru town of Ixtlán del Río (population 15,000). Ixtlán International Airport. School on left. Then questionable hotel Calle Real to right. Motel-restaurant Santa Rita to right. Looks like the nicest in town. Topes. Careful for crosswalk for children in front of church. Hotel-restaurant Colón, left as you leave town. It has clean restrooms and good food. If it's late, consider staying here. **KM 138**.
53.8	86.1	Up high on yonder mountain ahead you'll see the famed huge statue of CRISTO REY or "Christ the King." There's a side road up to it but don't tackle it – it's in very poor shape and we can't recommend it.
55.0	88.0	To left is IXTLÁN Archeological RUINS, on which very little is known (except that they are post-Classic, 900 A.D. and later). If you wish to drive over tracks and into compound, hop to it. (Admission is charged and zone is open from 9 AM – 4 PM daily.) Slow now. Railroad crossing.
57.3	91.7	Hotel Hacienda, left.
58.0	92.8	La Sidia restaurant to right. Spa Casida, for home folks. **KM 134**.
59.8	95.7	Village of Ranchos de Arriba off to left with church that stands out. Toll road crosses to left. **KM 129**.
62.5	100.0	For free road VEER LEFT. Toll road veer right. "Plan de Barrancas," Altitude 4,000 feet. Under overpass. Emergency telephone on right. **KM 117**. Magnificent view to left. Over railroad bridge.
63.3	101.3	Come to state line – leave state of Nayarit (pronounced "nye-a-reet") and enter state of Jalisco. Also come to a new TIME ZONE – leave Mountain Standard Time and start Central Standard Time, so set your watches and dash clock AHEAD one hour. Top. Cross bridge over the railroad. Careful for rocks on road.
65.8	105.3	Downhill view of El Zapote to left.
74.5	119.2	Santo Tomás to right. Under bridge and thru cut rock.
80.7	129.1	Hostotipaquillo to left.
82.0	131.2	Village of La Quemada, right.
87.1	139.4	**GAS**, left. Sometimes kids directing traffic around town on unofficial bypass. Take it.
91.3	146.1	TURN LEFT at stop sign and proceed on down thru town of Magdalena, an opal town. Plan on taking it easy through here; congestion is amazing. After turn, you will see two opal shops ahead. Airport, right. **GAS** at far end of town.

By the way, "La Única," the largest opal mine in the area, is located 7 miles from town atop Ocatera Mountain.

92.8	148.5	Quinta Minas hotel on south edge of town. Ph: (386) 864-0560.

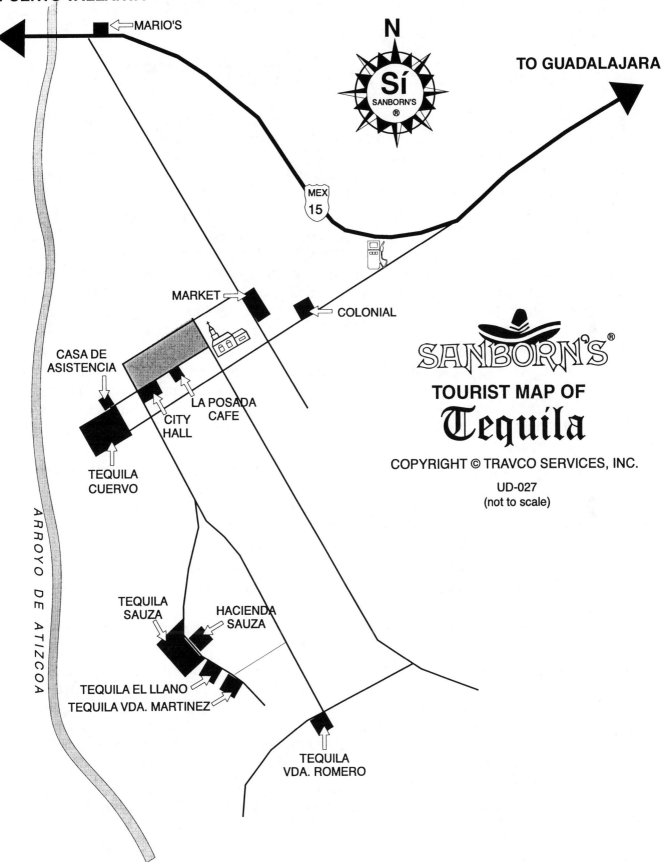

Sanborn's Special Reports

SPECIAL REPORT ON THE TOWN OF TEQUILA

TEQUILA, Founded in 1530 by Spanish Captain Cristóbal de Oñate, is quite a place! There are about 24 distilleries all busy turning out Mexico's number one liquor, tequila, which technically means the rock that cuts. Now, this doesn't refer to what it'll do when it hits the gullet — the town came first, then the drink. It got its name from the shiny black glass-like razor sharp obsidian that's found in the nearby hills.

Tequila liquor was first distilled here in 1600. The oldest and largest tequila distillery is called La Perseverancia (Endurance), operated continuously since 1875 by the Sauza family. Another old and large distillery is La Rojeña, operated continuously since 1888 by the Cuervo family. Both are very interesting plants so please feel free to visit them — tourist are most welcome. Across from the Sauza plant is the old Sauza family hacienda which was built in 1833 — you're also welcome to visit this fascinating old place. *Don't visit the distilleries between 1 and 2 PM — that's lunch and siesta time and almost everything shuts down tight.*

If you'd like a guide to show you the town and take you through the two main aforementioned tequila distilleries, we recommend Mario Sanchez who runs a restaurant and tequila shop on the highway. Mario speaks enough English to be helpful and will take you on a half to one hour tour. He knows the folks at each distillery and they sort of let him have the run of the place.

Tequila is made from the juice of the heart of the Agave cactus, better known as *maguey*. The heart is cooked and the juice is extracted from this pulp. It is then fermented, distilled, and bottled. Cuervo bottles its products at the distillery, whereas Sauza ships its tequila in big glass-lined tank trucks to Guadalajara where it is bottled at the big plant on the highway a few blocks toward town after the Camino Real Motel.

An interesting by-product of the tequila process are the shreds from the ground-up heart of the cactus. These brown shreds are purchased by Guadalajara brick makers who mix them with clay to produce a stronger brick.

There are two little emergency second-rate hotels in Tequila, Casa de Asistencia across the street from the Cuervo plant and Colonial on the main stem above the bus station.

There are a lot of smaller tequila factories located further through town. It seems as though too many of the old-time tequila distillery owners imbibed too freely their own products (sort of like the saying we had in our own Prohibition days that it was a no-account bootlegger who wouldn't drink his own hooch!) and so they all had big funerals and wealthy widows. Several of the distilleries are named for widows, like Vda. (abbreviation for *viuda* or widow) de Martínez and Vda. de Romero which would mean Widow of Martínez and Widow of Romero.

You'll have an enjoyable half hour or so here in TEQUILA — if you don't mind the smell.

MI	KM	
96.5	154.4	Along in here you'll spot some jet-black rocky stuff called OBSIDIAN. You'll descend about 800 feet in the next 7 miles.
100.3	160.5	Climbing lane for oncoming traffic! Then down hill. CAREFUL! DANGEROUS, ALMOST HORSESHOE CURVE.
102.4	163.8	Down hill. CAREFUL! DANGEROUS, ALMOST HORSESHOE CURVE.
103.0	164.8	Village of Teresa down at left. **GAS**, right.
103.5	165.6	Nice panorama with deep Barranca de Santiago off to left. Burlap and carton factory on right.

If your windows are open, you'll know that you're coming into the famous Tequila-distilling town by the same name – TEQUILA (mostly off to right). Can you catch a whiff of the tequila smell in the air? On left just ahead is Mario's Restaurant and Tequila Shoppe (Mario sells all kinds from grade A on down at competitive prices.) If you'd like a tour of this interesting town, Mario will take you on one – he's on a first-name basis with just about everybody at the SAUZA and CUERVO tequila distilleries and speaks enough English to get by (see SPECIAL REPORT ON TEQUILA on page 38 and map on page 37). **GAS** at right. Curve left at the fountain (right fork to downtown). Leave Tequila.

109.0	174.4	Cross the railroad again.
111.5	178.4	Pass bullring on left. **GAS**, left and at far end. Skirt town of Amatitán, right. Pass cemetery, left.
116.8	186.9	Over fancy bridge. Careful for this railroad crossing!
117.5	188.0	Sharp right curve. Little tequila distillery town of Arenal, right – note the cone-shaped grain silos.
119.6	191.4	Note the maguey ("muh-gay") growing on the hillsides hereabouts – it's the heart or core of the maguey cactus that is used to make tequila.
121.5	194.4	Thru village of Santa Cruz del Astillero.
124.3	198.9	Slow a little for bumpy railroad crossing – Ameca branch line. Curve left (take left fork) past side road (right) to town of Ameca. This is where toll road joins the free road again.
125.3	200.5	Over railroad crossing. **KM 25**.
125.5	200.8	Note deep arroyo (gulch) over to the right. Don't you agree that "arroyo" is a much prettier word than our English "gulch"?

IF TO: Río Caliente Spa, a vegetarian health spa, turn off to the right just ahead at town of Primavera and follow stub log below (see map). These folks frown on drop-in guests. Although they probably won't shoot you, it is best to call ahead and make a reservation, U.S.: 1-800-200-2927, Fax: (415) 615-0601.

RÍO CALIENTE SPA

0.0	0.0	After right turn, go thru village of Primavera. When road dead ends, turn right. At "T," turn left and cross bridge. Continue straight at "Y" take middle fork with gate and sign that says "Las Tinajitas 2.2 km."
2.8	4.5	Come to another fork. Do not take right fork which goes to Al Río del Valle. Take the left fork. Go over cattle guard.
3.0	4.8	Pass road (right) to Balneario La Primavera and (left) to Hogar Betania. This is where nuns give mud baths and iridology readings.
3.1	5.0	Come to gate and a bridge over steamy river. If gate is locked don't despair. There is a little opening to left. Park and walk up hill to office. If you look respectable, they will let you in. Ask for Dr. Ricardo Heredia or Javier Contreras.
3.2	5.1	Cross bridge over steamy river into Río Caliente Spa.

END STUB LOG

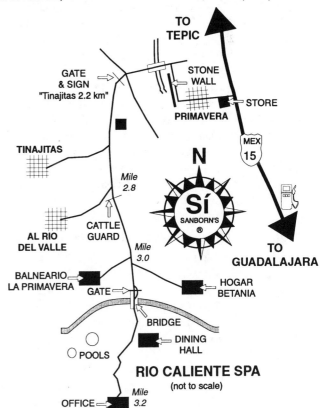

MI	KM	
127.0	203.2	Wind past village of Primavera "Spring" (the season) in Spanish.
128.3	205.3	**GAS**, left. Careful for farm machinery. Thru village of La Venta del Astillero.
130.3	208.5	Hunting club of Jalisco, left.
131.5	210.4	Turnoff for botanical institute. Alongside the railroad. Slow a little for a sharp left-right "S" curve.
132.5	212.0	"Rancho Contento" at right – nice retirement condominium deal for Americans – has its own golf course.
134.7	215.5	Gamesa plant, left. Good cookies and crackers.
135.0	216.0	Still divided. Often cops here, so obey traffic laws. **GAS**, left. Pass side road left to Ocotán Air Force Base – also called "Zapopan" Air Force Base – one of Mexico's largest.
135.3	216.5	Intersection with Periférico. Stoplight. Straight. Hospital Dr. Angel Leano, left. Divided ends. Conasupo warehouses.

IF TO: Chapala, Morelia, Mexico City, etc., TURN RIGHT and join Guadalajara Bypass Counterclockwise Log at mile 8.3 (page 78).

IF TO: Zacatecas, TURN LEFT and join Guadalajara Bypass Clockwise Log (page 76) at mile 16.5.

136.0	217.6	Pass nice cemetery, right.
136.3	218.1	Traffic light. Nissan dealer, right. Overhead sign, "TRAILER-PARK-HACIENDA."
136.5	218.4	Corona Vallarta left. Right is to Hacienda Trailer Park. Protected right turn, but better turn ahead.
138.0	220.8	Chevy left. El Gallo Pope left. Divided begins again. Road widens. Car dealership, right. **GAS**, left. Hotel Nuevo Real Vallarta, left. Coca Cola dealer left.
139.3	222.9	Goodyear left. Left to U. Autónomo de Guadalajara. Banco Atlántico, left. Road widens. Interesting townhouses, left. Volks Vallarta, right. Mayoral Restaurant on left. Block sculpture in middle of street.
139.5	223.2	Pass electrical generating station, left. Pretty brick. Street changes name. Down and under overpass. Left lane for local traffic. Veer a little to right. Chrysler dealer on left.
139.7	223.5	Cross Av. Niño del Obrero.
139.9	223.8	General Tires on right. Tutankhamen bar and restaurant, left.
140.1	224.2	Hotel Malibu, way over to left.
140.5	224.8	Soccer field in middle of street!
140.8	225.3	Banco del Atlántico. Teléfonos de México, right.
140.9	225.4	"*Todo Fácil*" – a neat superstore, left. Renault dealer, right. Cross divided López Mateos.
141.4	226.2	**GAS**, left.
141.5	226.4	Ahead on wide divided Av. Cárdenas. Valencia Restaurant and La Mansión, a cabrito restaurant, left. Straight. Come to small glorieta. Go 3/4 around and veer left. Stop sign.
141.7	226.7	Under overpass. Road narrows. Left LANE DISAPPEARS!
142.0	227.2	Pass farmer's market "Centro de Abastos," left.
142.5	228.0	MANZANILLO EXIT.
142.8	228.5	Pass Calzada del Sur exit.
143.8	230.1	Cárdenas is a six lane divided parkway.
144.2	230.7	Pass LP gas tank and satellite dish vendor. Pass exit from Periférico. Get ready for left turn. Then turn left.
144.9	231.8	4 lane divided street. Banco Nacional, right. PPG Industrias de México left. DANGEROUS INTERSECTION. Up, then cross railroad crossing (LOOK-&-LISTEN).
145.3	232.5	Under railroad bridge. Train station, left.
145.5	232.8	Plaza, left. Market, right. Straight. Federal Express on right.
145.7	233.1	Left 3 lanes MUST go around glorieta. Railroad station dead ahead. Beautiful park, right. Follow signs for train. Pass Biblioteca Nacional. Right 2 lanes can turn right. Cross wide González Gallo. **GAS** right.

Right lane MUST turn right onto González Gallo – don't do that. You'll dead end into Curiel.

146.3	234.1	Hotel 13,000 – not for you. STAY OUT OF RIGHT LANE. Airport, Bomberos signs. **GAS** right. Around little circle. Av. La Paz, left. **GAS** left. Cross divided 2-way Calz. Revolución. Next one-way left.
146.5	234.4	Go around and straight ahead. Street left 2 way. Come to circle with angel on top.
146.7	234.7	Streets crossing or dead-ending into Independencia will alternate one-way right, left. Cine Avenida, right. Pass Hotel Los Reyes, left.
146.9	235.0	Light. Cross Juárez left. Go under park. Left ONTO INDEPENDENCIA. 4 lanes each way.
147.0	235.2	MEXICO, SALTILLO, right. Pizza Express, right. 1 lane.
147.3	235.7	Cross Carranza. Road widens. Stay left. Degollado Theatre to your left. Cross Pino Suárez left, Belén, right. Turn Left off Hidalgo, one-way, left. Parking lot, left. Cross Morelos, one-way your right. Ahead down Av Corona. Come to cathedral at your left.

IF TO: Mexico City via Morelia, turn right and start Guadalajara – Morelia Log; Via La Piedad, Irapuato-Querétaro, start Guadalajara – Querétaro Log. (See Mexico's Colonial Heart book, page 2.)

IF TO: San Luis Potosí direct, start Guadalajara – San Luis Potosí Log. (See Mexico's Huasteca Potosina book, page 199.)

IF TO: Zacatecas and Saltillo, start Guadalajara — Zacatecas Log. (See Mexico's Huasteca Potosina book, page 204.)

IF TO: Chapala and Ajijic, start Guadalajara —Jocotepec Log (page 79).

IF TO: Manzanillo via Barra de Navidad, start Guadalajara — Melaque Jct. Log (See Mexico's South Pacific book, page 50); or via Colima start Guadalajara — Tecomán Jct. Log. (See Mexico's South Pacific book, page 7.)

IF TO: Downtown, go 3/4 way around circle, take Zacatecas exit, immediately pull onto service road and turn right at Calle Hidalgo which will take you straight to downtown.

For accommodations see Guadalajara Eat & Stray (page 142).

End of Log 12

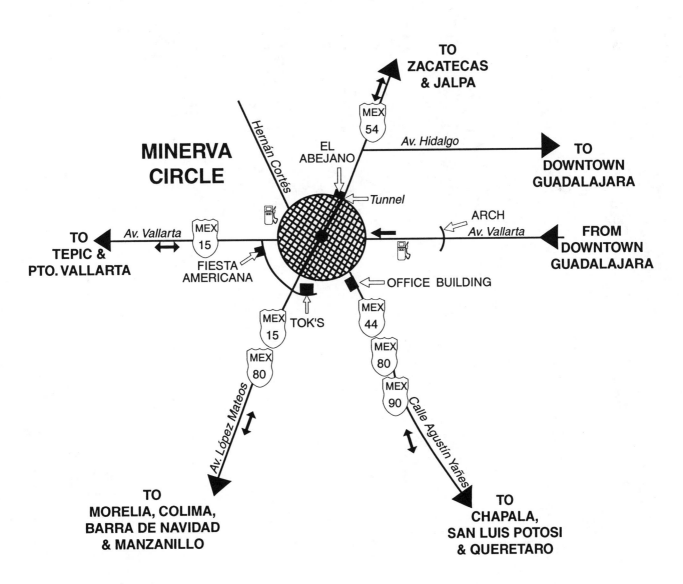

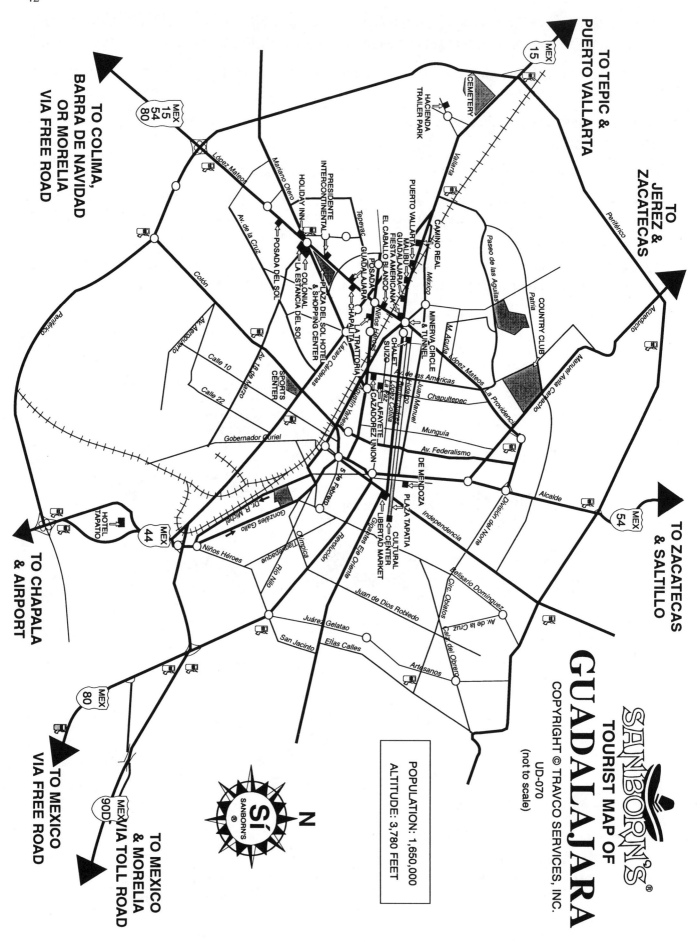

SPECIAL A *START:* Hermosillo, Son *END:* Kino Bay, Son

UD-019

73.0 MI or 116.8 KM
DRIVE TIME 1 1/2 — 2 HOURS
SCENIC RATING — 2

MI	KM	
0.0	0.0	Here in Hermosillo at the University of Sonora Plaza, having turned off Hwy #15, proceed ahead on nice divided Luis Encias Blvd. Stick to middle lane — it's easier going. University campus at left.
0.2	0.3	Pass IMSS Hospital, right.
0.3	0.5	Denny's at right. Sanborn's store and restaurant, left.
0.9	1.4	STAY IN LEFT 2 LANES, or you'll be forced to turn right. Then under pedestrian crossover.
1.0	1.6	Now down under overpass.
1.5	2.4	**GAS** at right.
1.6	2.6	Miyako Restaurant and Jardines — very nice Japanese restaurant.
2.0	3.2	Sports center at right and careful here at stoplight and junction with Periférico (bypass). Here's very good El Sahuaro **GAS** at right. This is where folks from the bypass stub log join us.
2.1	3.4	John Deere and Bancomer at right.
3.7	5.9	Cemetery to left.
4.2	6.7	Pass Mariscos Mateo, left.
4.5	7.2	Buho's Motel Suites (has jacuzzi) a motel *del paso* (sometimes won't rent to *Gringos*), left.
5.5	8.8	Pass Hermosillo's airport at right.
6.5	10.4	Chinos Eventos Restaurant, left. **KM 11.**
7.0	11.2	Pass Casa Pedro Domecq winery at left (of Brandy Presidente fame). Then a short mile later pass Vinícola Vergel winery at right (makers of Viejo Vergel brandy).
8.6	13.8	Road narrows to 2 lanes.
12.8	20.5	University of Sonora experimental farm at left. There are quite a few flash-flood dips (*vados*) on this road, but you can engage them easily and safely at 55-60 m.p.h.
18.0	28.8	Road narrows to its regular width. Note grape vineyards thru here.
21.0	33.6	Pass side road (right) to Monte Carlo. A little later pass grape vineyards on right.
29.0	46.4	Pass roadside community of Costa Rica at right. Then cotton gin at left. Strange stand of tall sahuaro cactus at right.
33.0	52.8	Take RIGHT FORK. Left fork takes you to Guaymas. The road's good and it's only 54 miles to Hwy #15 plus another 24 miles to Guaymas. It's a time-saver and beats driving back thru Hermosillo, especially if you're heading to Guaymas on your return. If you take this shortcut, pick up Hermosillo — Guaymas Log at Mile 54.3 when you reach Hwy #15.
35.0	56.0	Lots of *ejidos* in this area. There's Ejido El Triunfo at right.
37.0	59.2	Cotton gin at left. Thru village of Miguel Alemán. Careful for topes. **GAS** at left. Then pass IMSS clinic at left. Palm oasis, left. Watch for topes.
41.5	66.4	Pass farm workers' campo of San Francisco at left. Veterano winery and vineyards at left.
42.8	68.5	Come to junction with road to Plan de Ayala.

IF TO: San Carlos and Guaymas, here to left is another shortcut. It's a great time saver. Start Kino Bay — Hwy #15 Shortcut Special (page 47).

43.0	68.8	Thru community of Santa Isabel.
44.0	70.4	Pass side road (right) to La Choya and left to Sahuaripa.
46.5	74.4	Power plant at left and pass settlement of Orebalma at left.
48.0	76.8	Farm workers' campo of San Isidro at left. **KM 79.**
54.0	86.4	Note fields of "nopal" cactus on right and then "saguaro."
64.0	102.4	Interesting Rancho Monte Cristo at left.
66.0	105.6	Pass side road (left) to Kino del Mar.
67.3	107.7	Come now to "El Desierto" **GAS** station. Ice plant at right. Stop sign and herd of goats out for a roadside ramble. Side road (left) goes to Islandia RV Park in OLD KINO, but remember that the action is all at NEW KINO. Continue ahead on highway to New Kino. Then Misión del Sol over to left.

MI	KM	
68.0	108.8	Now alongside bay. This is a very clean beach. Pass public camping area down at left. Then on right is Posada del Mar. For info on accommodations see Kino Bay Eat & Stray (page 104).
70.5	112.8	Posada Santa Gemma at left.
71.0	113.6	Saguaro RV Park at right.
72.5	116.0	Pingüino Restaurant and little Padre Kino Plaza at right.
73.0	116.8	Come now to Motel/RV Park Kino Bay.

IF TO: Caverna del Seri RV and Trailer Park, continue ahead for half-mile to end of pavement.

End of Special A

SPECIAL B *START:* Kino Bay, Son *END:* Hermosillo, Son

UD-019

73.0 MI or 116.8 KM
DRIVE TIME 1 1/2 — 2 HOURS
SCENIC RATING — 2

0.0	0.0	Starting here in Kino Bay at entrance to Kino Bay Motel/RV Park, continue ahead.
0.5	0.8	Pass Pingüino Restaurant and little Padre Kino Plaza at left.
2.0	3.2	Pass Saguaro RV Park at left.
2.5	4.0	Pass Posada Santa German at right.
5.0	8.0	Pass Posada del Mar, left. Pass public camping area down at right. This is a very clean beach.
5.7	9.1	Pass Misión del Sol over to right. Pass side road (right) to Islandia RV Park in Old Kino. Ice plant at right. Then "El Desierto" **GAS** station (accepts credit cards).
7.0	11.2	Pass side road (right) to Kino del Mar.
9.0	14.4	Interesting Rancho Monte Cristo at right.
27.3	43.7	Pass small new reservoir surrounded by newly planted trees and palapa stands, left.
29.5	47.2	Thru village of Santa Isabel.
29.8	47.7	Now come to junction with road to Plan de Ayala. Continue straight ahead. **KM 69**.

IF TO: Guaymas, turn right. This takes you through Plan de Ayala to Hwy 15 and on to Guaymas. You can also go straight and take next right if this road is in bad shape. All roads lead you to where you want to go, but be careful for turns. Start Kino Bay — Hwy #15 Shortcut Special (page 47).

IF TO: Hermosillo, straight ahead.

36.0	57.6	Watch for topes. Palm oasis, right. Then IMSS clinic, right. Thru village of Miguel Alemán, **GAS** right. More topes. Then cotton gin at right.
40.0	64.0	Pass another road (right) that takes you to Hwy #15 and to Guaymas. The road's good and it's only 54 miles to Hwy #15 plus another 24 miles to Guaymas. It's a time-saver and beats driving back thru Hermosillo, especially if you're heading to Guaymas on your return. If you take this shortcut, pick up Hermosillo — Guaymas Log at Mile 54.3 when you reach Hwy #15.
44.0	70.4	Strange stand of tall sahuaro cactus at left. Then cotton gin at right and past roadside community of Costa Rica, at left.
52.0	83.2	Pass side road (right) to Monte Carlo. Note grape vineyards through here.
60.2	96.3	Watch for flash flood dips (*vados*) on this road. University of Sonora experimental farm at right.
65.0	104.0	Pass Vinicola Vergel winery at left (makers of Viejo Vergel brandy). Then a short mile later pass Casa Domecq winery (makers of famous Brandy Presidente) at right. Road widens.
66.5	106.4	Pass Chinos Eventos Restaurant, right.
67.5	108.0	Pass Hermosillo's airport, left.
68.5	109.6	Buho's Motel Suites (has jacuzzi) a motel *del paso* (sometimes won't rent to *Gringos*), right.
68.8	100.1	Pass Mariscos Mateo, right.
70.5	112.8	Bancomer and John Deere, left.
70.6	113.0	Here's very good El Saguaro **GAS** station, **GAS** and ice shop at left. Careful here at stoplight and junction with Periférico (bypass). Then sports center at left.

IF TO: Guaymas or Nogales via bypass around Hermosillo, turn right and start stub log below,

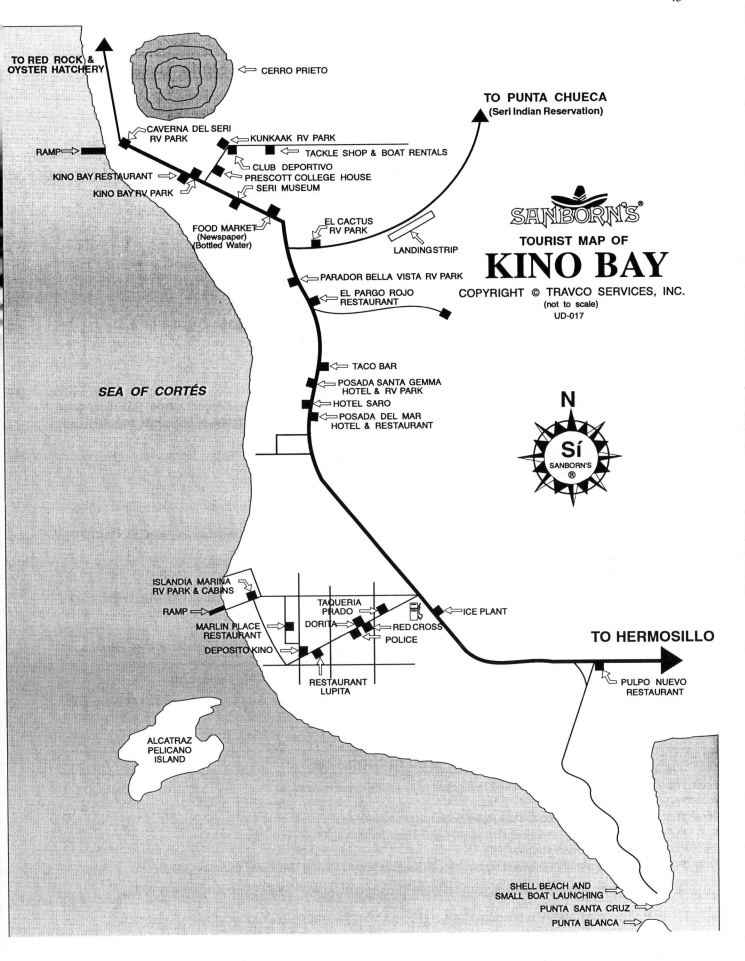

TO RED ROCK &
OYSTER HATCHERY

CERRO PRIETO

TO PUNTA CHUECA
(Seri Indian Reservation)

CAVERNA DEL SERI
RV PARK

KUNKAAK RV PARK

TACKLE SHOP & BOAT RENTALS

RAMP

CLUB DEPORTIVO
PRESCOTT COLLEGE HOUSE

KINO BAY RESTAURANT

SERI MUSEUM

KINO BAY RV PARK

EL CACTUS
RV PARK

FOOD MARKET
(Newspaper)
(Bottled Water)

LANDING STRIP

SANBORN'S®

TOURIST MAP OF

KINO BAY

COPYRIGHT © TRAVCO SERVICES, INC.
(not to scale)
UD-017

PARADOR BELLA VISTA RV PARK

EL PARGO ROJO
RESTAURANT

SEA OF CORTÉS

TACO BAR

POSADA SANTA GEMMA
HOTEL & RV PARK

HOTEL SARO

POSADA DEL MAR
HOTEL & RESTAURANT

N

Sí
SANBORN'S
®

ISLANDIA MARINA
RV PARK & CABINS

TAQUERIA
PRADO

ICE PLANT

RAMP

DORITA

RED CROSS

TO HERMOSILLO

MARLIN PLACE
RESTAURANT

POLICE

DEPOSITO KINO

PULPO NUEVO
RESTAURANT

RESTAURANT
LUPITA

ALCATRAZ
PELICANO
ISLAND

SHELL BEACH AND
SMALL BOAT LAUNCHING

PUNTA SANTA CRUZ

PUNTA BLANCA

otherwise jump down to mile 71.0.

Stub Log: Hermosillo bypass From Kino Bay Jct. to Santa Ana Jct.

MI	KM	
0.0	0.0	Having turned right onto bypass, pass big dry cleaner at right.
0.3	0.5	Pass thatched mariscos palapa, left.
0.7	1.1	Plaza Satélite, right. Then stoplight.
1.0	1.6	Another shopping center, right.
1.8	2.9	Another stoplight. Long distance fax office on right just past light.
2.2	3.5	Road goes over usually dry river and freeway to nowhere.
2.4	3.8	Amazing rock formation at right behind Las Palmas shopping center.
3.1	5.0	Under pedestrian overpass, then pass Calle Lázaro Cárdenas, right.
3.2	5.1	Cemento Campana, right. Then stoplight and **GAS** station, right.
3.4	5.4	Pass automatic transmission repair shop, left.
3.9	6.2	Pass Palo Verde business park, right.
4.3	6.9	Pass Plaza Sur shopping center. You can get slide film from photo stores only.
4.4	7.0	Come to junction with Hwy #15. Goodyear at left.

IF TO: Guaymas, turn right and pick up Hermosillo — Guaymas Log (page 10) at mile 3.3.

IF TO: Downtown, turn left.

4.6	7.4	Uniroyal at right.
5.2	8.3	**GAS** at right.
5.4	8.6	VEER LEFT at Santa Ana sign. Straight ahead is to Yécora and Hwy 16 to Copper Canyon. Take food, water and extra gas on this 13-hour trek if going all the way to the Canyon. Right is to Sahuaripa. Industrial park at right. Then pass street left to downtown Hermosillo. Ahead for you.
5.7	9.1	**GAS** at right. Cattle feed lot at right. Roll up your windows.
6.2	9.9	Prison at left. Then Lake Domínguez at right.
6.4	10.2	Careful thru school zone and over railroad tracks.
7.2	11.5	Railroad crossing. Curve right.
7.4	11.8	Cement plant to left.
8.0	12.8	Dangerous curve and over bridge. Railroad bridge overhead to right, then dangerous curve to left. CAREFUL.
8.4	13.4	Get in right lane. Left lane turns to the bus station.
8.7	13.9	Baseball field at right. Soccer field at left. Careful for school zone.
8.9	14.2	**GAS**, at right.
9.0	14.4	Veer right onto one-way street, "Las Vírgenes." Farmacia, left. AA (Spanish) *Buenos Amigos* at right, Alanon meetings — 4:30 till 6:00 PM, Mon. and Wed.
9.4	15.0	Over railroad crossing. Curve right.
9.9	15.8	Pemex gasoline storage facilities at left and right. Ahead, to left, is highrise Fiesta Americana Hotel.
10.0	16.0	Firestone at right. Goodrich, left.
10.1	16.2	Come to junction with Hwy #15. Mobile and Chevy dealer at left. **GAS**, ahead at left.

IF TO: Nogales, turn right onto Hwy #15. Start Hermosillo - Santa Ana Log (page 172) at mile 2.2.

IF TO: Downtown, turn left.

End of Stub Log

71.0	113.6	Miyako Restaurant and Jardines – very nice Japanese restaurant.
71.2	113.9	**GAS** at left.
71.8	114.9	Under overpass. Then under pedestrian crossover.
72.5	116.0	Sanborn's store and restaurant, right. Then Denny's at left.
72.7	116.3	Pass IMSS Hospital, left.
73.0	116.8	University campus at right. Come to junction Hwy 15 at the University of Sonora Plaza.

IF TO: Nogales and Santa Ana, turn left and start Hermosillo - Santa Ana Log (page 172).

IF TO: Guaymas and points south, turn right and start Hermosillo - Guaymas Log (page 10).

End of Special B

SPECIAL C   *START:* Kino Bay, Son   *END:* Jct Hwy #15

UD-019

63.8 MI OR 102.1 KM
DRIVE TIME 1 – 1 1/4 HOURS
SCENIC RATING – 2

This log is a shortcut to go to San Carlos and Guaymas without going back to Hermosillo. Inquire locally as to the condition of this road before taking it.

MI	KM	
0.0	0.0	Having turned onto road to Plan de Ayala, continue ahead.
2.7	4.3	Pass cornfields, left and right.
6.2	9.9	Pass campo La Tercera at right.
6.8	10.9	Pass orange groves on right.
7.2	11.5	Slow! "*Vados*" (dips) thru here.
18.2	29.1	Thru village of Plan de Ayala. Pass general store at left, then TURN LEFT at crossroads. If you pass this turn, road will end about 2 miles ahead. You're now heading east.
19.2	30.7	Road roughens.
23.3	37.3	Under power lines, just before electric generator station on right. Stop sign.
26.4	42.2	Watch for "*vados.*" Then San Fernando and Lourdes to left.
28.5	45.6	TURN RIGHT, regular gas on left after turn.
37.8	60.5	Pass Puerto Arturo to right.
40.0	64.0	Deep vado.
44.7	71.5	Deeper vado.
46.2	73.9	Pass San Agustín and Colorado to right.
55.2	88.3	Very impressive view of desert with mountains at edges.
63.8	102.1	Come to junction with Hwy #15. Restaurant Los Arrieros at left across highway; strange looking shrine across highway. **GAS** at left on freeway.

IF TO: Guaymas or San Carlos, turn right and pick up Hermosillo - Guaymas Log (page 10) at mile 54.3.

IF TO: Hermosillo, turn left and pick up Guaymas - Hermosillo Log (page 170) at mile 28.2.

End of Special C

SPECIAL D   *START:* Jct. Hwy #15   *END:* Kino Bay, Son

UD-019

63.8 MI or 102.1 KM
DRIVE TIME 1 – 1 1/4 HOURS
SCENIC RATING – 2

This log is a shortcut to Kino Bay without going to Hermosillo. Inquire locally as to the condition of this road before taking it.

MI	KM	
0.0	0.0	Starting here at junction with Hwy #15 and with Restaurant Los Arrieros behind you at your right, continue ahead on 2 lane road.
8.6	13.8	Very impressive view of desert with mountains at edges.
17.6	28.2	Pass San Agustín and Colorado to left.
19.1	30.6	Watch for deep *"vados"* ("dips").
23.8	38.1	Another *"Vado."*
26.0	41.6	Pass Puerto Arturo, left.
35.3	56.5	Regular gas on right. TURN LEFT here.
37.4	59.8	Pass San Fernando and Lourdes to right. Then watch for *"vados."*
40.5	64.8	Come to stop sign. Then under power lines just past electric generator station. Road roughens.
45.6	73.0	Come to crossroads and TURN RIGHT. Then thru village of Plan de Ayala. Pass general store at right.
56.6	90.6	Slow! More *"vados"* thru here.
57.0	91.2	Pass orange grove on left.
57.6	92.2	Pass campo La Tercera at left.
61.1	97.8	Pass cornfields left and right.
63.8	102.1	Come to junction with road between Hermosillo and Kino bay.

IF TO: Kino Bay, turn left and pick up Hermosillo — Kino Bay Special (page 43) at mile 42.8.

IF TO: Hermosillo, turn right and pick up Kino bay – Hermosillo Special (page 44) at mile 29.8.

End of Special D

SPECIAL E *START:* Hermosillo, Son *END:* La Junta, Chih

UD-019

335.0 MI or 536.0 KM
DRIVE TIME 8 – 13 HOURS
SCENIC RATING – 3

NOTE: Watch for rocks on pavement along this route. Also, be sure to check your rearview mirror before attempting to pass. Take food, water and extra gas on this 13-hour trek if going all the way to the Canyon.

0.0	0.0	Starting here in Hermosillo at junction of Periférico Sur bypass with Hwy #16 (see map on page 11), proceed ahead on divided highway, heading southeast.
1.2	1.9	Pass new Hermosillo subdivision, right.
2.0	3.2	**GAS** at left. Better fill up to top here while you can. Sometimes gas is scarce on this route.
2.1	3.4	Pass Ford plant and industrial park, left.
3.0	4.8	T.I.F plant, left. Divided highway ends.
7.8	12.5	Over bumpy railroad crossing.
11.0	17.6	Majestic Cemento del Yaqui plant, right.
29.0	46.4	Over bridge and thru El Colorado. Two "topes." Pretty plaza with Bougainvilleas and palms, right. Then more topes.
46.0	73.6	Over puente San José Pimas. Road curves left and thru San José de Pimas. Topes. Green trees and pretty plaza to right.
51.0	81.6	Note mountains at left, with a strange plateau top.

MI	KM	
74.0	118.4	Thru town of Tecoripa. Topes. Altitude 1,300 ft. Good turkey hunting here.
81.0	129.6	Flat straight road. Enjoy!
88.0	140.8	Pass San Xavier, left.
96.0	153.6	Going down now about 2,000 ft.
105.0	168.0	Cross El Yaqui Bridge over Río Yaqui.
123.0	196.8	A variety of fowl thru here: Hawks, blue jays, roadrunners, etc.
135.0	216.0	Rough road. Thru town of Tepoca and over bridge.
136.0	217.6	Road has potholes. Watch for rocks on road.
139.0	222.4	Pass side road (left) to San Garipa.
140.0	224.0	Come to junction (right) with Hwy #117. Then pass town of San Nicolás on left.

IF TO: Esperanza, Cd. Obregón, turn left and start San Nicolás — Cd. Obregón Log (page 86).

IF TO: Chihuahua, straight ahead and continue this log.

143.0	228.8	Cactus begin to disappear. Altitude 2,800 ft.
145.3	232.5	Come to crossroads. Santa Ana, left. Santa Rosa, right. Straight ahead for you.
158.0	252.8	Up very steep ascent. Come to summit. Altitude 6,000 ft.

REMEMBER: On downhill stretches, brake with your motor — not your brakes. A burning smell means you've used your brakes too much. If you can, pull over and let them cool for ten minutes or so.

159.0	254.4	Magnificent mountains to left.
160.0	256.0	Pass big white house and restaurant on left.
167.1	267.4	Enter town of Yécora. Population 3,000. **GAS**, regular only, left. RV's can park at ball park across from **GAS** station. You'll find a restaurant and a grocery store. There is also Motel Las Brisas (emergency only).
180.0	288.0	Handsome steep rocks at left.
184.0	294.4	Pass farm buildings at left.
185.0	296.0	Start descent. Rock sculpture at right.
185.5	296.8	Down and over bridge. Then hairpin curve and up. More rock formations.
188.8	302.1	Descend again and cross bridge over river.
192.0	307.2	Ascend out of flatlands.
195.0	312.0	Wide open vistas to left.
201.5	322.4	Thru village of Maycoba.
206.0	329.6	Over Kipor Creek and thru village of Kipor.
209.7	335.5	Pass restaurant El Venadito, cute log cabin at left.
212.1	339.4	View of dramatic rock formations and thru red rock cuts.
212.3	339.7	Thru village of Arroyo Hondo. **KM 245**. Then steep climb.
213.1	341.0	Now another long climb.
218.0	348.8	Cross state line. Leave Sonora and enter Chihuahua. Also entering the Central Time Zone, so turn your clock forward an hour. Altitude 4,800 feet.
218.4	349.4	Begin a long ascent. Altitude 5,000 feet.
223.0	356.8	Thru red rock landscape with scrub trees. Curves and another ascent.
229.0	366.4	Thru lumber-mill town of Yepachic. Tire repair shop and restaurant Los Pinos. Altitude: 5,500 feet.
231.6	370.6	Thru village of Piedras Azules. A botanist would have a field day here with all this plant variety.
236.3	378.1	Thru community of El Potrero.
237.6	380.2	Descend to bottom and up again.
239.1	382.6	Over bridge. Careful now on twisting, curving climb.
249.0	398.4	Thru village of Pinos Altos.
253.2	405.1	Pass **GAS** station. **KM 282**.
255.2	408.3	Thru Baguiriachic. Tire repair shop on left.
256.2	409.9	Pass doctor's office at left.
256.3	410.1	Come to junction (right) with road that leads to Basaseachic National Park Cascade Fall 3 km). Hotel Alma Rosa —ECON— very nice, but ask for the rooms in back, front rooms are basic. Restaurant. Overnight dry parking for RV's. Ph: (Chihuahua) (614) 142-3698.

IF TO: Basaseachic National Park, turn right and follow stublog below. The parking lot is about 2 miles down the road. The falls are then a 20 minute up and down walk from there. However, you can't see much because you will be on the "back side" and will only be able to see the water go over the edge and

50

not see it actually fall to the bottom. It's a beautifully scenic spot. Plans are being made to open up a new KOA Campground here.

IF TO: Creel, Cuauhtémoc, Chihuahua, continue straight ahead.

257.1	411.4	Thru village of El Tocolote.
259.3	414.9	Pass state judicial police check point. Then pass side road (right) to San Juanito. It will be a great short cut to Creel when it is paved.
264.2	422.7	Thru village of Tonachic.
264.6	423.4	Pass Motel Villa Alpina at right.
265.6	425.0	Pass Tonachic airport at left. **KM 261**.
269.0	430.4	Thru village of El Perico (The Parrot).
269.8	431.7	Come to a summit. Altitude 7,300 feet.
276.0	441.6	Note colossal cliffs, caves and rock formations to left.
277.0	443.2	Pretty river down below at left.
279.7	447.5	Thru village of La Ahumada. Note that the roofs are wider than the houses, forming an overhang so you don't get wet when you open the front door.
280.7	449.1	Thru village of Agua Caliente. Checked out *ojo de agua* here — nothing doing (hole in farmer's yard).
281.8	450.9	Thru scattered community with no name. **KM 235**.
285.5	456.8	Careful for sharp curves right and left.
286.2	457.9	Over bridge and curve right.
292.0	467.2	Pass Cabaña Negra (Black Cabin), right.
293.0	468.8	Watch for unmarked topes. Then **GAS** at right.
293.4	469.4	Careful for topes (6 sets thru town) as you enter Tomochic. Watch for burro in middle of street.
301.4	482.2	Farm buildings at right. Then over bridge.
303.0	484.8	Careful on steep climb up hill. Top and down.
305.0	488.0	Steep downgrade. Brake with your motor. Then pass Cieneguita (Little Swamp).
306.8	490.9	Over bridge and climb again. Altitude 6,500 feet. Watch for "S" curves ahead.
313.0	500.8	Come to another summit. Altitude 7,400 feet. Thru pine forest and down another downgrade.
321.6	514.6	Thru thick young apple orchards, right and left.
323.1	517.0	Pass Parrahuirachic to left.
323.9	518.2	Up long hill with double S curve.
324.7	519.5	Come to junction of Hwy #16 and #137. Four years ago this junction was marked by a dilapidated old shack. Now it's replaced by two log cabins. Prosperity has struck!

IF TO: Creel, Batopilas, Divisadero, turn right and join Cuauhtémoc — Creel Special (page 51) at mile 27.0.

IF TO: Cuauhtémoc, Chihuahua, continue ahead.

325.2	520.3	Sharp curve left. Then over bridge.
327.2	523.5	Slow for sharp curve left and up over hill.
334.2	534.7	Over bridge. **KM 52**.
335.0	536.0	Come to La Junta with Winn's Restaurant at left and **GAS**, left.

IF TO: Cuauhtémoc, Chihuahua, pick up Creel — Cuauhtémoc Special (page 57) at mile 68.4.

End of Special E

SPECIAL F *START:* Cuauhtémoc, Chih *END:* Creel, Chih

92.0 MI or 147.2 KM
DRIVE TIME 3 — 3 1/2 HOURS
SCENIC RATING — 3
This is a beautiful scenic drive. There are several series of curves and lots of livestock .

Rv'ers: There is a gravel road from Creel to Divisadero. The Hotel LA MANSIÓN TARAHUMARA is our favorite spot. The owner is friendly, and she will let RV's park there (if you want to drive the gravel road). Go about 3 1/2 miles past the first hotel, the Cabañas Divisadero (which is pricey). Maria's hotel is on the left. Be careful of the railroad track in front, as it's sometimes uneven. Take food, water and extra gas if going all the way to the Canyon.

MI	KM	
0.0	0.0	Starting at junction (right) with road to Alvaro Obregón, Gómez Farías and Buenaventura, proceed ahead on 2 lane road.

By the way, up the road (right) to Alvaro Obregón there is a Motel Del Camino, Loewen's RV Park and Rancho La Estancia. See the Cuauhtémoc section of Creel Eat & Stray (page 126) for details.

0.4	0.6	Pass huge LP gas plant at right. **GAS** at left. **KM 108.**
1.8	2.9	Pass big barn at right. That's the famous Copper Canyon railroad at right. You'll go thru pretty orchards. Careful for livestock and farm equipment!!
8.8	14.1	Local industry, Latin American Minerals (sulfur), at right.
10.8	17.3	Las Haciendas orchard, right (note fruit trees covered with hair nets). The Copper Canyon is 1 1/2 times as deep as the Grand Canyon and 4 times the area.
12.5	22.0	Rancho Las Glorias, left. Altitude 7,400 feet.
13.1	21.0	Thru village of Pedernales. Look at the old choo-choo, right! Then a straight stretch thru agricultural valley.
13.6	21.7	Log cabins and logging mills. That and orchards are the main industries around here.
18.6	29.8	Apple orchard, right. Although we say "the" Copper Canyon (*Barranca del Cobre*), there are actually 6 important canyons which form the network.
23.2	37.1	Pass Huerta Los Rosales at left. Careful for black spotted cow on road.
26.1	41.8	Careful! Crossroads sneak up on you! TURN LEFT (Hwy #16) beyond sign toward Basaseachic, Hermosillo or Tomochic. Straight goes to Madera on state Hwy #37. Don't go straight toward Matachic or Madera! You're now in La Junta. **GAS** at right, regular and diesel. Winn's restaurant next to **GAS** station at right.

IF TO: Hermosillo, Cd. Obregón, Basaseachic, start La Junta — Hermosillo Log (page 84).

26.9	43.0	Over bridge. The highway you're on has a name — *Gran Visión*.
27.6	44.2	Miñaca to right. Thru hills and over streams. Curves.
29.2	46.7	Thru cut. Down and up and over stream. **KM 165.**
31.5	50.4	Curve left and down. Creel, incidentally, was named for a former governor who helped build the highway. Remind you of Huey Long in Louisiana?
32.3	51.7	Settlement of Baquiachic, left. Be careful and watch for lumbering lumber trucks. Toot your horn when coming around a blind curve.
34.3	54.8	Sharp curve right then left. Birds commonly seen thru here are roadrunners, ravens, broadtail blue jays, hawks and grackles.
35.5	55.8	Cross railroad tracks. LOOK DOWN into canyon (if you're not driving!). Railroad now on left. **KM 166.**
36.0	57.6	Pay attention! At crossroads, TURN LEFT (south) for Creel towards San Juanito on Hwy #127. Straight goes to Hermosillo or Cd. Obregón (Hwy #16). There may be a sign saying "Tomochic straight, 51 KM and Basaseachic 110 KM." There are log cabins at the crossroads. It's the only turnoff recently, so you probably won't miss it.
36.1	67.8	Having turned left at crossroads, there may be a sign saying "Creel 90 KM." **KM 0.**
37.2	59.5	Rancho San Marcos to right. Panchera to left. Notice mountains ahead. That's where you're heading. Enjoy the next few miles of beautiful, peaceful scenery thru cattle country.
44.8	71.7	Sorry to break into your reverie, but sharp curves coming up. Left and down and over bridge and up. Then begin pine and juniper forest. *Bienvenidos al Bosque* (welcome to the woods).
47.1	75.4	Nice picture spot with some room to pull off.

REMEMBER: On downhill stretches, brake with your motor — not your brakes. A burning smell means you've used your brakes too much. If you can, pull over and let them cool for ten minutes or so.

MI	KM	
47.9	76.6	Nice view of canyon. There are 85 railroad bridges in the canyon.
48.0	76.8	Sharp right, left, down, right. Then comes the curvy part. **KM 19**.
48.2	77.1	Over Arroyo "Ancho" (wide) and up. Two cows in middle of road.
48.8	78.1	Can this be the summit? Now down and more curves.
52.7	84.3	It's like you stepped back in time! Log cabins to the left of me, log cabins to the right. Nice mountain stream flowing alongside. Watch for goats crossing with black herd dog.
54.9	87.8	Down thru Cebollas ("Onions"). Watch for horses on road. **KM 32**.
57.4	91.8	Thru cut. Cross bridge over Río Alamillo and past El Alamito at right. The railroad was the dream of a young American engineer, Albert Kinsey Owens, who settled in Los Mochis, Sinaloa in 1872.
65.1	104.2	Thru Sehuerachic, altitude 8,000 feet! Okay, so it wasn't really the top back at mile 48.8 — but it sure felt like it. Aren't you glad you brought Sanborn's with you?
68.8	110.1	Pass lumber mill at left.
69.5	111.2	School at right. Then cross railroad tracks. Railroad became a reality in 1961, when President Adolfo López Mateos inaugurated the "Chihuahua al Pacífico" railroad. Town of San Juanito (population 6,693). "Topes." Very rough railroad crossing.
70.3	112.5	Cobblestone begins. Bumpety-bumpety! Railroad now at left. Careful for logging trucks in town.
70.8	113.3	Very nice motel Posada del Cobre at right. Eight heated rooms. Restaurant attached. Long-distance telephone at the drug store.
71.0	113.6	There is **GAS** one block to right, to get there, turn right just before church.
71.4	114.2	You'll see railroad on your left. Pass Carta Blanca sign, barber shop (*peluquería* or *barbería*), right. Turn RIGHT at stop sign (end of main street). There may be a sign saying "Creel and Basaseachic, to right."
71.9	115.0	Crossroads! TURN LEFT to Creel — 36 km. Basaseachic to right. Topes.
72.5	116.0	CAREFUL! SHARP CURVES! In winter, patchy ice as the sun doesn't hit the road until late in the day. Church at left. Two "topes." **KM 77**.
75.3	120.5	Over railroad crossing. Log storage at right.
79.8	127.7	Downhill. Brake with engine.
84.5	135.2	Downhill to valley and thru settlement of Chocquita and over bridge.
85.0	136.0	Now climb to 8,000 foot pass. Sharp curves. Watch for melting ice and snow in winter.
87.2	139.5	Down into town of Creel (population, 3,063). Topes. Pass Pensión Creel Bed and Breakfast.
90.0	144.0	Pass Hotel Nuevo Barrancas del Cobre at left. Then cross bridge and down.

IF TO: Downtown hotels, turn left onto Av. Cristo Rey. Go down steep hill to end. Turn right just before railroad tracks. Go 1/2 block, then cross tracks. CAREFUL, they're high and uneven! For accommodations see Creel and Copper Canyon Eat & Stray (page 126).

90.8	145.3	Over railroad crossing. Then **GAS** at right.
92.0	147.2	Sign says Guachoci straight ahead 157 km. Then another sign: Batopilas 140 km (Hwy #129), Cusarare 22 km (Hwy #127), Basihuare 43 km (Hwy #127).

IF TO: Hotel Copper Canyon Lodge, straight ahead, 13.7 miles.

IF TO: Divisadero, turn right and start Creel — Divisadero Special (page 53).

IF TO: Batopilas, straight ahead and start Creel —Batopilas Special (page 55).

IF TO: Tejabán, turn right and start Creel — Tejabán Special (page 53).

End of Special F

SPECIAL G *START:* Creel, Chih   *END:* Divisadero, Chih

UD-019

29.0 MI or 46.4 KM
DRIVE TIME 1 HOUR
SCENIC RATING — 4

This is a good paved road.

MI	KM	
0.0	0.0	Starting here in Creel at junction with road to Batopilas.
0.2	0.3	Uphill and curve left.
0.6	1.0	Railroad tracks on right, road parallels track. Thru cornfields.
5.0	8.0	Curve down thru chalk-white rocks lining road surrounded by pine forests.
7.9	12.6	Take right fork and down long steep incline.
10.6	17.0	Up steep hill and thru sandstone cut walls .
12.0	19.2	Cross bumpy railroad.
13.0	20.8	Slow as you cross bumpy railroad again.
18.7	29.2	Another railroad crossing. Very rough road and uphill.
26.4	42.2	Enter town of Divisadero. Then hotel Cabañas Divisadero, right, in front of artisan market at left.
28.5	45.6	Long downhill. Then Motel Posada Barrancas —UPPER— (35 rooms Ph: (Los Mochis) (668) 815-7040 Fax: 812-0046, lovely gardens) at right immediately after railroad crossing.
28.7	45.9	Thru community at right. Place to buy oil and auto parts.
29.0	46.4	Pass pretty church at right. Take very sharp left, uphill past railroad crossing to Hotel Mansión Tarahumara —MOD— 45 rooms, looks like castle or chalet up on hill. Family style dining. Feels more like a guest house than a hotel. Fireplace in big hall. Jacuzzi. Horseback riding. Tours. RV parking. Ph: (Chihuahua) (614) 415-4721 Fax: 416-5444). Turn left into gate.

End of Special G

SPECIAL H   *START:* Creel, Chih   *END:* Tejabán, Chih

UD-019

28.5 MI or 45.6 KM
DRIVE TIME 2 HOURS
SCENIC RATING — 4

The first 14 miles of this log is the same as to Batopilas. Two miles past the Copper Canyon Lodge exit, you turn right to go to Tejabán. This is a very rough drive suitable only for pickups and 4-wheel-drive vehicles. The hotel and views are spectacular.

0.0	0.0	Starting at junction with road to Divisadero at right.
1.8	2.9	Pass side road (right) to Arecho and Urique Canyon.
4.9	7.8	Pass side road (right) to Recohuata Hot Springs.
5.8	9.3	Sharp curves and down.
11.8	18.9	Pass side road (left) to Cusarare. Then curves. Exit to Copper Canyon Lodge is next dirt road to right.
12.1	19.4	CASCADA sign and road to Copper Canyon Lodge at right.
14.0	22.4	Turn right onto dirt road. Straight is to Batopilas. Cross creek and curve left and up. Ford Cusarare River (more like a stream) and up, curving left.
14.7	23.5	Pass rock fountain at right. Road is straight for a while.
15.0	24.0	Road divides. Take right fork. Very bumpy.
17.0	27.2	First steep hill. Then down.
17.5	28.0	Pass log cabin at left. Then up. Altitude 8,000 feet.
18.5	29.6	Sometimes there are washouts here. Slow!
18.9	30.2	Really rough road and downhill.
19.2	30.7	Pass Tarahumara settlement and school, Bajío Largo, at left. Altitude 7800 feet. Then down and curve left. Take right fork and up.

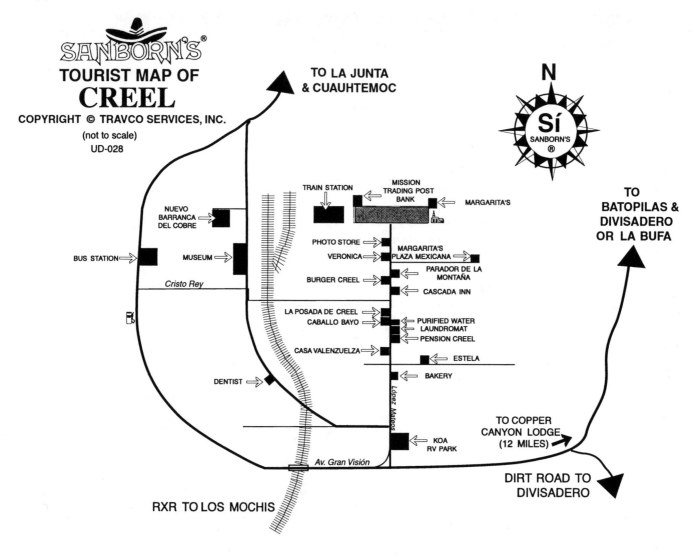

SANBORN'S®
TOURIST MAP OF
CREEL
COPYRIGHT © TRAVCO SERVICES, INC.
(not to scale)
UD-028

TO LA JUNTA
& CUAUHTEMOC

N
Sí
SANBORN'S
®

TO
BATOPILAS &
DIVISADERO
OR LA BUFA

TRAIN STATION

MISSION
TRADING POST
BANK

MARGARITA'S

NUEVO
BARRANCA
DEL COBRE

BUS STATION

MUSEUM

Cristo Rey

PHOTO STORE
VERONICA

MARGARITA'S
PLAZA MEXICANA

BURGER CREEL

PARADOR DE LA
MONTAÑA

CASCADA INN

LA POSADA DE CREEL
CABALLO BAYO

PURIFIED WATER
LAUNDROMAT
PENSION CREEL

CASA VALENZUELZA

ESTELA

DENTIST

BAKERY

López Mateos

TO COPPER
CANYON LODGE
(12 MILES)

KOA
RV PARK

Av. Gran Visión

DIRT ROAD TO
DIVISADERO

RXR TO LOS MOCHIS

MI	KM	
20.2	32.3	Note cold water spring down to right.
20.5	32.8	Take right fork.
26.3	42.1	Take left fork. Now open rock area.
26.9	43.0	Rough white rock washing area.
27.0	43.2	Cross large landing strip. This area is La Mesa Colorada.
28.5	45.6	Come to Hotel Tejabán. Altitude 7,200 feet.

TEJABÁN — MOD — Isolated with stupendous view on the rim of canyon. Difficult to get to, you must have a vehicle with high clearance. 12 rooms with fireplaces and small tubs that have jacuzzi jets. Excellent restaurant. Pool. 2 *casas* with tub and jacuzzi. Own generating plant. Also has dormitory rooms with bunk bed space for 40 people. Altitude 7,200 feet. Great view.

Stub Log: Return to Creel

0.0	0.0	Having enjoyed your stay in El Tejabán, proceed ahead on road back to Creel. Take left fork.
1.9	3.0	Take right fork.
4.7	7.5	Sharp curves and up and up. Altitude 7,600 feet.
9.1	14.6	Curve right at settlement, heading east.
11.0	17.6	Take left fork.
13.7	21.9	Curve left and down.
14.5	23.2	Ford stream. Then turn left onto highway.
16.3	26.1	Pass entrance (left) to Copper Canyon Lodge.
20.4	32.6	Pass side road (right) to Cusarare (2 km away). **KM 112**.

MI	KM	
29.2	46.7	Pass beautiful lake, right. Picnic area with BBQ pits.
29.5	47.2	Camping area, right. Sites on lake, port-a-potties, showers, hiking trails (costs $10 per person).
32.2	51.5	Pass turnoff (left) to San Rafael and Divisadero.
32.9	52.6	Cross bridge over railroad tracks.
33.2	53.1	Enter Creel. **GAS** at right.

End of Special H

SPECIAL I *START:* Creel, Chih   *END:* Batopilas, Chih

UD-019

85.0 MI or 136.0 KM
DRIVE TIME 13 HOURS
SCENIC RATING — 4

Mostly unpaved — it is only for the adventurous or foolhardy — pickup, suburban or 4-wheel drive is needed. This road is practically vertical at many points and has more curves than Dolly Parton. There's no **GAS**. There are no accommodations until Batopilas, so you may have to camp out. Still it is spectacular. An alternative is to take a local bus or let the Copper Canyon Lodge drive you and set you up on a package for the Hacienda Batopilas.

REMEMBER: On downhill stretches, brake with your motor — not your brakes. A burning smell means you've used your brakes too much. If you can, pull over and let them cool for ten minutes or so.

0.0	0.0	Starting here in Creel with **GAS** station and Licores "RJ" at right.
0.3	0.5	Cross bridge over railroad tracks and down hill.
1.0	1.6	Pass turnoff to San Rafael and Divisadero.
1.4	2.2	Sign says: *No hay mañana, debe ser hoy mismo* (There is no tomorrow; it must be today).
4.1	6.6	Camping area, left with sites on lake, port-a-potties, showers, hiking trails (costs $10 per person).
4.3	6.9	Pass beautiful lake. BBQ pits and picnic tables, left. Little girl selling woven belts and bags. Now road curves up hill till you reach the altitude of 8,000 feet. Then down.
8.3	13.3	Altitude 7,200 feet.
10.5	16.8	Over bridge and curve right.
13.5	21.6	Pass side road (left) to Cusarare (2 km away). **KM 112**.
13.7	21.9	Pass Copper Canyon Lodge, right, a short distance down road. Careful. Turnoff is next dirt road to right. Now begin a multitude of curves and exquisite scenery.
15.8	25.3	Pass road (right) to El Tejabán, an interesting side trip to the rim of the canyon.
24.3	38.9	Sharp right curve past "god" house on right.
26.2	41.9	Thru village of Basihuapa. Then uphill for a little while.
28.0	44.8	Hairpin turns. Very fancy scenery.
31.1	49.8	Downhill now.
31.8	50.9	Thru community of Humira. Altitude 6,000 ft. Then roadwork.
33.9	54.2	Pavement ends. Downhill on rough road.
36.1	57.8	Over bridge, then pass little shrine at left. **KM 60**.
42.8	68.5	At right is a large detailed map of area. Be sure to look at both sides of map at roadside.
44.6	71.4	Sign at right. Straight is road to Samachic and continues on to Hidalgo del Parral. Right is to Batopilas. SHARP RIGHT TURN.
46.4	74.2	Very sharp curve left and then up.
47.1	75.4	You're now on a red dirt road, very twisting, rough and steep, thru beautiful pine forest.
50.9	81.4	Very wide spot here in case you need to pull off.
51.7	82.7	You have achieved Basigochi. Elevation 7,500 feet.
53.0	84.8	Thru woods with stream to left.
53.6	85.7	Go very slow — sharp deep curve to left thru magnificent pine and live oak forest.
57.0	91.2	Wide pullout to right.
59.5	95.2	Another wide pullout to right. Then spectacular view.
59.9	95.8	Thru settlement of Kirare also spelled Quirare. Note shingle-roofed houses at right. Altitude 6,600 feet. School at left.

MI	KM	
58.7	93.9	Over bridge and leave Kirare. Bank of century plants, right.

NOTE: From this point on you have a very treacherous, steep, unpaved road and no turning around. So decide now. Watch for burros.

59.7	95.5	Steep descent beyond belief (and views as well). Break with motor and anything else you've got. Thru oak woodland.
60.0	96.0	Great photo opportunity. Altitude 6,000 feet. Then down thru narrow cut.
60.5	96.8	Flank of mountains in front of you is staggering. Altitude 5,000 ft. Serpentine road thru cuts and graffiti — *Dios los lleve* (May God carry you).
61.2	97.9	Careful for 180° turn.
63.3	101.3	Small pond to right (to admire only).
63.5	101.6	Tiny cemetery at left. Altitude 4,100 ft.
64.1	102.6	Above at right are large projecting rocks.
64.5	103.2	Over vado (ford).
65.7	105.1	Lookout for falling rocks. Hairpin bizarre curve.
65.9	105.4	Cross bridge. Altitude 3,100 feet.
66.3	106.1	Sign says La Bufa, but not much of a town. Just a one-handed Indian in corn patch on side of road is it. Careful over wooden bridge. **KM 38**.
67.9	108.6	Note cave up over at right.
68.3	109.3	View pullout to right. See road on other side of canyon.
68.9	110.2	Little cemetery at right. Very pretty with mountains behind.
69.3	110.9	Slow for sharp right turn around tree.
72.2	115.5	Thru cut. Altitude 3,000 feet.
72.9	116.6	Last steep descent. Altitude 2,500 ft.
73.0	116.8	Sign to M. Yerba Buena (Peppermint).
74.6	119.4	Over bridge. Altitude 2,200 feet.
77.9	124.6	A. de Santiago — thinning metropolis at left. Very desert scenery — tall cactus in bloom (late June).
80.1	128.2	Aqueduct at right on other side of river. Then another ford. Watch for bikes.
81.5	130.4	Cross white bridge to right and come into river town of Batopilas — a very pretty town.

WELCOME VISITORS — You are entering a hidden town of Mexico, full of history and friendly people. Founded in 1711. Population 500, altitude 1,823 feet (556 meters), and subtropical climate. We hope you enjoy our hospitality, natural scenery, beautiful edifices and ecological environment. Please help keep the town clean. Don't run in the streets. If you drink, don't drive.

85.0	136.0	Topes. Hotel Palmera at right — best inexpensive hotel in town. A short stretch farther is Hotel Chula Vista at right. Then the Hacienda Batopilas, one of the nicest in Mexico. Go to dead end and turn left. Hotel Mary, to right on Calle Juárez.

End of Special I

SPECIAL J *START:* Batopilas, Chih   *END:* Creel, Chih

UD-019

85.0 MI or 136.0 KM
DRIVE TIME 13 HOURS
SCENIC RATING — 4

0.0	0.0	Starting here in Batopilas take left fork up past Hotel Palmera, cross white bridge and curve left.
3.0	4.8	Downhill for a stretch.
3.4	5.4	Desert scenery — tall saguaro cactus in bloom (late June). Quite green in December.
4.2	6.7	A. de Santiago, right. Altitude 2,000 feet.
4.5	7.2	Careful, if raining, for series of fords.
6.7	10.7	Steep downgrade. Then pullout at left.
9.0	14.4	Turnoff to M. Yerba Buena (Peppermint). Begin steep ascent. Altitude 2,300 ft.
11.7	18.7	Thru cut and continue uphill. Altitude 3,000 feet. Then cave on right.
12.0	19.2	Slow over rough ford.

MI	KM	
13.2	21.1	Pretty little cemetery to left.
14.7	23.5	Magnificent stucco-colored land formation, immediate left. Atop a small farm is a one-handed farmer. Historic town of La Bufa, 1/2 mile walk to right. Altitude 3,100 feet.
15.4	24.6	Over another ford.
15.9	25.4	Begin descent, cross wooden plank bridge. Altitude 3,000 ft. **KM 38**.
16.6	26.6	Cross another bridge and then begin major ascent.
18.7	29.9	Tiny cemetery at right. Altitude 4,100 ft.
21.1	33.8	Little homes at right. Sometimes little girls selling dolls in front. Pullout at right.
21.7	34.7	Sharp curves thru cuts. Great photo opportunity.
22.5	36.0	Road straightens out — end of crisis.
23.7	37.9	Thru settlement of Kirare, also spelled Quirare. Altitude 6,100 feet.
24.5	39.2	Ilaka artisan store (stop if open) and school at right.
26.0	41.6	Thru magnificent forest. Sharp curve to right.
28.8	46.1	Slow curve right thru rough ford. Altitude 6,000 feet.
30.4	48.6	Thru town of Basigochi. Altitude 6,200 feet.
32.3	51.7	Slow around boulder in road. 7,100 feet.
33.3	53.3	Slow. Cross bridge then curve left uphill to 7,300 feet. Then downhill.
34.4	55.0	Very sharp curve right.
36.6	58.6	Pass side road (right) to Samachic which continues on to Hidalgo de Parral (Pancho Villa's home). TURN LEFT, then wind down hill.
39.7	63.5	Come to halfway point and map of area on left. Road widens.
42.5	68.0	Notable downgrade for several miles.
44.6	71.4	Slow for series of crankcase crackers — very rough road.
49.8	79.7	Thru community of Humira. Altitude 6,000 ft. Begin uphill curvy road.
55.1	88.2	Hairpin turns. Then downhill. Very fancy scenery.
64.0	102.4	Pass side road (left) to El Tejabán.
66.2	105.9	Pass Copper Canyon Lodge at left, a short distance up road.
70.2	112.3	Pass side road (right) to Cusarare (2 km away). **KM 112**.
79.0	126.4	Pass beautiful lake, right. Picnic area with BBQ pits.
79.3	126.9	Camping area, right with sites on lake, port-a-potties, showers, hiking trails (costs $10 per person).
82.0	131.2	Pass turnoff (left) to San Rafael and Divisadero.
82.7	132.3	Cross bridge over railroad tracks.
83.0	132.8	Enter Creel. Come to **GAS** station.

IF TO: Cuauhtémoc, start Creel — Cuauhtémoc Special.

End of Special J

SPECIAL K *START:* Creel, Chih *END:* Cuauhtémoc, Chih

UD-019

94.5 MI or 151.2 KM
DRIVE TIME 3 — 3 1/2 HOURS
SCENIC RATING — 3

This is called *Gran Visión* Highway and is a beautiful scenic drive. There are several series of curves, lots of livestock and a few towns. Take food, water and extra gas.

0.0	0.0	Starting here in Creel at junction to Divisadero and San Rafael, turn left onto highway.
0.3	0.5	Exit at right goes into Creel but is a longer cobblestone route. Then up over bridge.
1.9	3.0	Over railroad crossing. Then another road right into town. Topes. Hotel Nuevo Barrancas del Cobre. Also Pensión Creel Bed and Breakfast (see Creel Eat & Stray, page 126). **KM 90**.
3.8	6.1	Sharp Curves. Watch for melting snow and ice in winter.
7.0	11.2	Over bridge and thru settlement of Chocquita. Then wind uphill.
10.3	16.5	Topes. Over long bridge and more topes as you go thru Bocoyna. **KM 77**.
14.5	23.2	Pass side road (right) to Baharuchic (4 km away).

MI	KM	
17.1	27.4	"Cuesta Prieta" lumber yard at left. Slow over railroad crossing.
19.9	32.0	Estación San Juanito (population 6,933) turn to right. Straight on partly unpaved road goes to Basaseachic falls. Topes. Begin cobblestone road.
20.8	33.3	Come to stop sign. TURN LEFT to La Junta just before tracks. There is **GAS** one block to left; to get there turn left just past church. Super Nelson store at left. Named for owner's son Nelson named after a singer named "Nelson." Long distance and f ax for pay at left. Then very nice Hotel Posada del Cobre at left.
21.2	33.9	Over rough railroad crossing. Then curve left. **KM 57**.
21.4	34.2	Pass village of Tayalotes, right.
27.4	43.8	Thru Sehuerachic. Altitude 7,900 feet. Then **KM 49**.
34.4	55.0	Pass El Alamito to left. Then cross bridge over Río Alamillo.
36.2	57.9	Thru Cebollas ("Onions"). Watch for horses on road. Then **KM 33**.
37.6	60.2	Thru stretched out community of Rancho Blanco ("White Ranch"). **KM 31**.
39.3	62.9	It's like you stepped back in time! Log cabins to the left of me, log cabins to the right. Nice mountain stream flowing alongside. Watch for goats crossing with black herd dog.
43.8	70.1	Over Arroyo "Ancho" (wide) and up. Cows in middle of road. Careful on upcoming sharp curves.
44.9	71.8	Nice picture spot with some room to pull off.
56.0	89.6	Come to junction with Hwy #16.

IF TO: Hermosillo, Cd. Obregón, turn left and start La Junta — Hermosillo Log at mile 10.3 (page 84).
If you need **GAS** continue on to La Junta.

IF TO: La Junta, Cuauhtémoc, Chihuahua, turn right, cross bridge and continue this log.

60.0	96.0	Settlement of Baquiachic, right. Be careful and watch for lumbering lumber trucks.
64.4	103.0	Pass side road (left) to Miñaca. Toot your horn when coming around a blind curve.
65.9	105.4	Come to La Junta junction. **GAS** at left. Winn's Restaurant (truck stop) next to **GAS** station. Matachic and Madera to left. Cuauhtémoc TURN RIGHT.
66.6	106.6	Having turned right toward Cuauhtémoc, continue ahead thru cornfields.
68.8	110.1	Fruit orchard Huerta Los Rosales at right. Careful for black spotted cow on road.
78.3	125.3	Lumber yard at left. Apple packing plant at right. **KM 147**.
78.9	126.2	Thru village of Pedernales. Look at the old choo-choo, left!
79.5	127.2	Rancho Las Glorias, right. Altitude 7,400 feet.
81.9	131.0	Pass side road (right) to Santiago (11 km away). **KM 129**.
82.7	132.2	Dangerous curves. Slow!
83.2	133.1	Local industry, Latin American Minerals (sulfur), at left.
85.0	136.0	LP **GAS** at left.
91.2	145.9	**GAS** at right. **KM 108**.
91.6	146.6	Come to junction (left) with road to Alvaro Obregón, Gómez Farías and Buenaventura.

By the way, up the road (left) to Alvaro Obregón there is a Motel Del Camino, Loewen's RV Park and Rancho La Estancia. See the Cuauhtémoc section of Creel Eat & Stray (page 126) for details.

92.0	147.2	Enter city of Cuauhtémoc (population 68,985). Búfalo Grill looks nice.
93.0	148.8	Begin one-way at bridge. Uniroyal, left. **GAS** at right. Come to stop light and TURN RIGHT.
93.1	149.0	Come to stop sign on Calle 16. Go two blocks and TURN LEFT at next stop sign onto López Rayón. Dólar store at left. Now two-way traffic.
93.3	149.3	AA meeting (Spanish) place on right.
93.9	150.2	Central Clinic at left. Argosa Pharmacy left. Then stoplight.
94.2	150.7	Mr. Burger restaurant, left. Goodyear, left. Then Equis Restaurant, downhill to left.
94.5	151.2	Come to stoplight at Calzada 16 de Septiembre, turn right. Chrysler/Dodge dealer at left. One block up is VW, right and Futurama on left.

IF TO: Chihuahua, start Cuauhtémoc — Chihuahua Log. (See Mexico's Central Route book, page 60.)

End of Special K

SPECIAL L *START:* Guaymas, Son *END:* San Carlos, Son

UD-019

7.6 MI or 12.2 KM
DRIVE TIME — 20 MINUTES
SCENIC RATING — 2

MI	KM	
0.0	0.0	Having turned west toward San Carlos continue ahead.
0.5	0.8	Camel humps of Teta de Cabra Mountains in distance.
4.8	7.7	Pass Hotel Posada San Carlos at right — little horses in the garden.
5.0	8.0	Condominios Triana, left.
5.2	8.3	Hotel Fiesta San Carlos, left.
5.3	8.5	Tecali Trailer Park, right.
5.4	8.6	Neptuno Restaurant-Disco at left. Totonaca RV Park (w/laundry) at right.
5.5	8.8	La Roca Restaurant-Bar, left on beach.
5.6	9.0	Hacienda Tetakawi Hotel and RV park (Best Western), right.
5.7	9.1	Pappa Tappas Restaurant, right.
5.9	9.4	Police station and post office, right. Laundry, left.
6.0	9.6	Rosa's Cantina Restaurant, left.
6.1	9.8	"El Mar" diving center, left. Terraza Restaurant, right.
6.3	10.1	Gary's boat trips, fishing and diving, left. Hotel Creston, left. Then a doctor's office, and **GAS**, right.
6.5	10.4	Mar Rosa Suites, left. Then San Carlos Country Club, right.
6.7	10.7	Loma Bonita Condo Hotel, right.
6.9	11.0	Hotel La Posada de San Carlos driveway to left.
7.3	11.7	Veer left at circle. Right goes to San Carlos Plaza Hotel, and Club Med. Straight ahead to Marina.
7.6	12.2	Plaza Las Glorias, right. For info on accommodations see San Carlos Eat & Stray (page 106).

End of Special L

SPECIAL M *START:* Navojoa, Son *END:* Alamos, Son

UD-019

33.5 MI or 52.6 KM
DRIVE TIME 45 MIN — 1 1/2 HOURS
SCENIC RATING — 4

Driving over to Alamos is an absolute "must" — very worthwhile. If driving an RV, it's recommended that you put up at El Caracol RV Park (9 miles before town, city bus stops at front gate) or at Dolisa RV Park at entrance to town. The streets of Alamos are just too narrow and are quite a chore (next to impossible) to negotiate with large vehicles.

0.0	0.0	Having turned off Hwy #15 here at Zarci Shopping Center in Navojoa at stoplight, proceed ahead and cross industrial railroad switch and then LOOK-&-LISTEN as you cross very bumpy double mainline railroad. Then over Francisco Sarabia (a famous pioneer Mexican aviator) Bridge.
0.5	0.8	Past statue in middle of divided road. School at left.
1.0	1.6	Pass road (left) to airport. **GAS**, right.
1.7	2.7	Basketball courts and ball field, right. Mountains straight ahead in the distance.
3.0	4.8	Large San Carlos chicken farm at left. Then curve right and left and over bridge and up and right.
4.3	6.9	Pass Río Mayo Gun Club firing range at left.
9.0	14.4	Pass side road (left) up to top of Cerro Prieto (Dark Hill) where a microwave station is located. Curve left and around base of hill.
16.3	26.1	Lime Plant (Productos Calcareos) off to left.
17.8	28.5	Come now to side road (left) that goes to Presa (Dam) Ruiz Cortines, known locally as Presa Mocuzari — excellent bass fishing.

continued on page 63

60

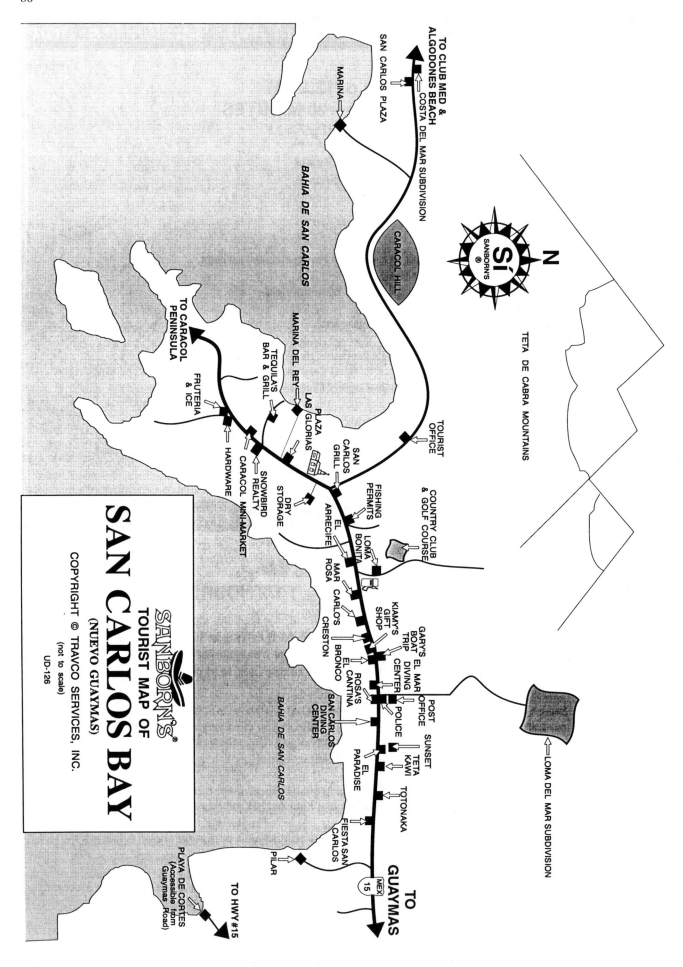

TOURIST MAP OF
SAN CARLOS BAY
(NUEVO GUAYMAS)

COPYRIGHT © TRAVCO SERVICES, INC.

(not to scale)

UD-126

N

TETA DE CABRA MOUNTAINS

TO CLUB MED &
ALGODONES BEACH

COSTA DEL MAR SUBDIVISION

SAN CARLOS PLAZA

MARINA

BAHIA DE SAN CARLOS

CARACOL HILL

TO CARACOL
PENINSULA

FRUTERIA
& ICE

TEQUILA'S
BAR & GRILL

MARINA DEL REY

PLAZA
LAS GLORIAS

HARDWARE

CARACOL MINI-MARKET

SNOWBIRD
REALTY

DRY
STORAGE

EL
ARRECIFE

SAN
CARLOS
GRILL

TOURIST
OFFICE

FISHING
PERMITS

LOMA
BONITA

COUNTRY CLUB
& GOLF COURSE

MAR
ROSA

CARLOS
CRESTON

KIAMY'S
GIFT
SHOP

BRONCO

EL
CANTINA

ROSA'S

GARY'S
BOAT
TRIP

EL MAR
OFFICE

DIVING
CENTER

POST

POLICE

SUNSET

TETA
KAWI

SAN CARLOS
DIVING CENTER

EL
PARADISE

TOTONAKA

BAHIA DE SAN CARLOS

FIESTA SAN
CARLOS

PILAR

LOMA DEL MAR SUBDIVISION

TO
GUAYMAS

MEX 15

PLAYA DE CORTES
(Accessible from
Guaymas Road)

TO HWY #15

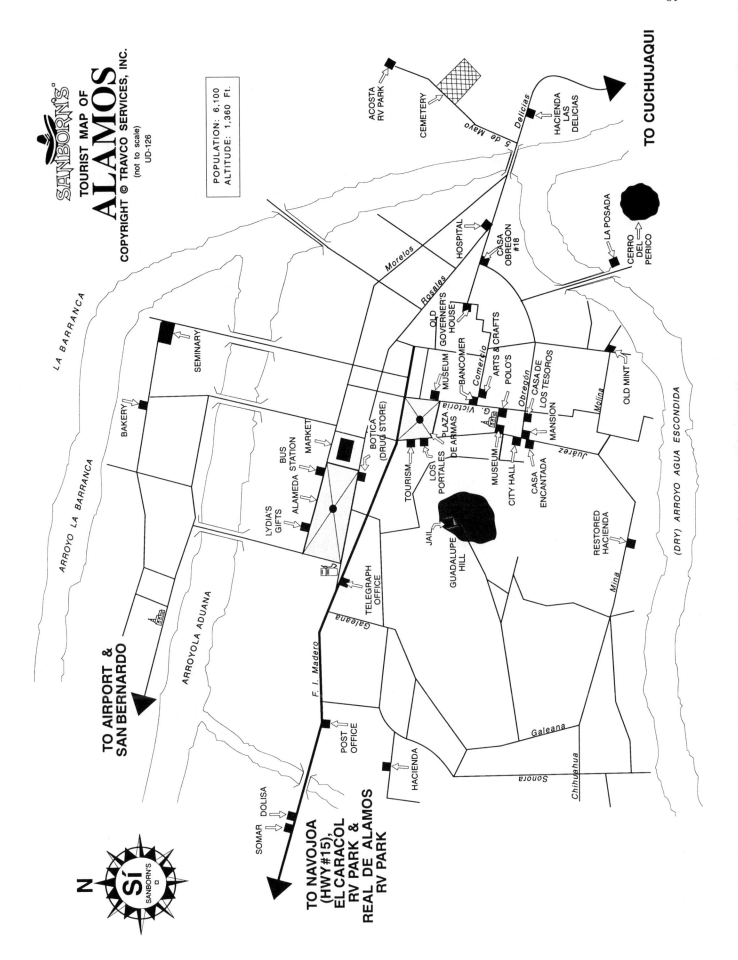

SANBORN'S"
TOURIST MAP OF
ALAMOS
COPYRIGHT © TRAVCO SERVICES, INC.
(not to scale)
UD-126

POPULATION: 6,100
ALTITUDE: 1,360 Ft.

N
Sí
SANBORN'S

TO AIRPORT &
SAN BERNARDO

TO NAVOJOA
(HWY #15),
EL CARACOL
RV PARK &
REAL DE ALAMOS
RV PARK

TO CUCHUJAQUI

LA BARRANCA

ARROYO LA BARRANCA

ARROYOLA ADUANA

ARROYO AGUA ESCONDIDA (DRY)

SEMINARY

BAKERY

LYDIA'S GIFTS

BUS STATION

ALAMEDA

MARKET

BOTICA (DRUG STORE)

TELEGRAPH OFFICE

POST OFFICE

SOMAR

DOLISA

F. I. Madero

Galeana

HACIENDA

Sonora

Chihuahua

Galeana

Mina

TOURISM

LOS PORTALES

PLAZA DE ARMAS

Victoria

MUSEUM

CITY HALL

CASA ENCANTADA

Juárez

JAIL

GUADALUPE HILL

RESTORED HACIENDA

Molina

OLD MINT

CASA DE LOS TESOROS

CASA DE MANSION

POLO'S

ARTS & CRAFTS

Comercio

BANCOMER

MUSEUM

Obregón

OLD GOVERNER'S HOUSE

Rosales

Morelos

HOSPITAL

CASA OBREGON #18

S de Mayo

Delicias

HACIENDA LAS DELICIAS

CEMETERY

ACOSTA RV PARK

LA POSADA

CERRO DEL PERICO

61

MI	KM	
18.5	29.6	Pass school "La Argentina" and tiny community of Las Lomas. Then start up.
20.7	33.1	An "S" curve to right.
23.0	36.8	El Caracól (The Snail) RV Park at right. That rugged peak at right is called "Cacharamba" (pierced ear in Yaqui, and it has, indeed, not visible from this side, a hole close to the top).
24.4	39.0	Horse rental sign at right. Road begins to climb and curve. **KM 40**.
27.5	44.0	Now thru village of Minas Nuevas (New Mines). Note a reopened silver mine off to right. School at right. Pass side road (right) to La Aduana, 3 km, once a smelter where silver from Alamos was cast into ingots. Today it's the site of an interesting religious pilgrimage which takes place on November 20th and attracts the Mayo Indians living in the surrounding area. Visit the indian shop to the left of the church, it features native crafts & some entiques. Across from the church is a good restaurant that has been opened by an American couple inside La Aduana's hacienda. **KM 45**.
31.5	50.4	There's another mine over to left, but it's a gypsum mine. Thru cut and over little Río La Aduana.
32.0	51.2	Real de Los Alamos RV Park (w/swimming pool) at right.
32.5	52.0	Shrine to San Bernardo, left; hospital sign, Red Cross, right. Still at left is Hotel Somar and then Dolisa Motel and RV Park. Enter old historic town of Alamos.
33.0	52.8	Telegraph office at right. **GAS** at left. Benito Juárez bust in center. Traffic goes right, thru street lined with white stucco buildings.
33.0	53.3	Come to Plaza, TURN RIGHT. Hotel Los Portales at right. Cathedral at left.
33.4	53.4	Posada Casa Encantada at right. TURN LEFT to go to Hotel Mansión.
33.5	52.6	Hotel Casa de los Tesoros at right.

IF TO: Hotel La Posada, take first right, cross dry arroyo, and up little hill. Posada straight ahead at end of road. For info on accommodations, see Alamos Eat & Stray (page 113).

Stub Log: Return From Alamos To Navojoa

0.0	0.0	Starting at Casa Encantada go straight on street in front.
0.3	0.5	Curve with street gently to right.
0.4	0.6	With store gate in front of you, turn right.
0.5	0.8	Come to Sonora Street. Turn left. Follow street between brick adobe walls.
0.8	1.3	Come to stop sign. Turn left and merge onto road out, with Dolisa Motel at right.
5.5	8.8	Pass Minas Nuevas. **KM 45**.
6.4	10.2	Sharp curve to right, then left. Pass La Luna, right. **KM 43**.
10.0	16.0	Pass El Caracol RV Park, left.
14.3	22.9	Pass Escuela Argentina and tiny community of Las Lomas.
15.5	24.8	Pass side road (right) that goes to Presa (Dam) Ruiz Cortines.
29.5	47.2	Storage silos, left. Road curves left, over bridge, then right.
30.0	48.0	Granite and marble quarry, right.
32.5	52.0	**GAS** left, begin divided (by trees) 4-lane.
33.0	52.8	Statue of Benito Juárez in center. End divided.
33.3	53.3	Over bridge (Francisco Sarabia), then over double railroad tracks.
33.5	53.6	Zarci Shopping Center, right and end of log.

IF TO: Los Mochis and points south, TURN LEFT and start Navojoa — Los Mochis Log (page 18).

IF TO: Guaymas and points north, TURN RIGHT and start Navojoa — Guaymas Log (page 166).

End of Special M

SPECIAL N *START:* Los Mochis, Sin *END:* El Fuerte, Sin

UD-019

47.8 MI or 76.5 KM
DRIVE TIME 1 — 2 HOURS

MI	KM	
0.0	0.0	Here at highway interchange into city of Los Mochis, take El Fuerte (Hwy #32) exit. Wrecking yards on both sides.
1.5	2.4	Spread out Ejido 5 de Mayo and soccer field at right.
6.4	10.1	Thru village of 2 de Abril with topes.
8.8	14.1	Little town of Mochicahui. Pass cemetery at right. Topes.
9.3	14.9	Watch for dip!
9.8	15.7	Nice mango orchard at right. Then thru Constancia with unmarked topes.
13.4	21.4	Rough road with dips.
15.8	25.2	Continue straight at fork.
17.1	27.3	Curve left past cemetery on left.
19.0	30.4	Centuries-old alamos (cottonwood trees) lining highway. Over irrigation canal and thru Ejido Lázaro Cárdenas.
20.3	32.5	SLOW-LOOK-&-LISTEN as you cross bumpy mainline of Nogales-Guadalajara Railroad. Big railroad station of El Sufragio at right.
21.1	33.8	Take RIGHT FORK. Left fork is to railroad town of San Blas.
22.3	35.7	Careful for low water crossing (vado).
22.6	36.1	Careful (LOOK-&-LISTEN) as you cross railroad again. Big power plant at right. **GAS** at right.
24.3	38.8	Settlement of Cuesta Blanca at right and Río Fuerte meandering at left.
28.0	44.8	Settlement of Sibajahui. Curve left, then slow for vados.
29.5	47.2	Rough riverbed road.
31.3	50.1	Large cemetery on left.
36.6	58.6	LOOK-&-LISTEN as you cross Chihuahua-Pacífico Railroad that runs thru famous Copper Canyon.
47.6	76.1	Social security clinic at left, and come to Av. Alvaro Obregón, at left thru El Fuerte. **GAS** at left.
47.8	76.5	Pass side road (right) to El Fuerte's airport and on to railroad station. Turn left into town. For info on accommodations see El Fuerte Eat & Stray (page 116).

End of Special N

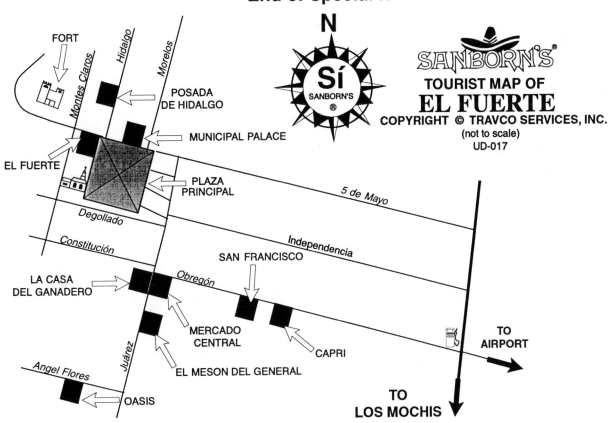

N

Sí SANBORN'S ®

SANBORN'S®
TOURIST MAP OF
EL FUERTE
COPYRIGHT © TRAVCO SERVICES, INC.
(not to scale)
UD-017

FORT
Hidalgo
Morelos
Montes Claros
POSADA DE HIDALGO
MUNICIPAL PALACE
EL FUERTE
PLAZA PRINCIPAL
5 de Mayo
Degollado
Constitución
Independencia
SAN FRANCISCO
LA CASA DEL GANADERO
Obregón
MERCADO CENTRAL
CAPRI
Juárez
TO AIRPORT
Angel Flores
EL MESON DEL GENERAL
OASIS
TO LOS MOCHIS

SPECIAL O START: Cd. Obregón END: San Nicolás, Son

UD-019

100.4 MI or 160.6 KM
DRIVE TIME 2 — 2 1/2 HOURS
SCENIC RATING — 3

This is a great road in good condition with virtually no traffic and no garbage! And almost no crosses signifying accidents. It winds thru beautiful hills with various kinds of cacti and mesquite.

MI	KM	
0.0	0.0	Starting here in Esperanza, just north of Cd. Obregón, at junction with Hwy #15, pass golf course on right, then TURN RIGHT at sign to TESOPACO.
9.0	14.4	Pass sign to El Coyote to right.
10.0	16.0	Enter town of Los Hornos. Slow for topes. Baseball field on right.
11.0	17.6	Turn right at intersection at sign to TESOPACO.
12.5	20.0	Curve to right over bridge (dam).
21.3	34.1	Curve left.
33.3	53.3	Sharp curve right, then left and over Arroyo Santana.
35.0	56.0	Wide curve left then, right.
39.7	63.5	Curve left.
44.5	71.2	Passing thru hills into a pretty view of mountains.
47.2	75.5	Topes. Entering Rosario de Tesopaco. Colegio Juárez at left. **GAS** on left. Come to intersection. Turn left, following sign to Yécora, San Nicolás. Topes.
54.9	87.8	Pass side trail (right) to Paredones.
60.0	96.0	Start climbing.
61.5	98.4	Beautiful view to right, like a natural park. Begin descent.
64.3	102.9	Fabulous large painting on cliff and shrine, left.
69.6	111.4	Pass side road (left) to Nurí.
70.0	112.0	At left you will see a large white church in Nurí with stone "thumb" on top of mountain behind it.
76.2	121.9	Thru town of El Palmarito.
85.3	136.5	Thru town of Curea.
96.4	154.2	Cut thru red rock.
100.4	160.6	Come to junction with Hwy #16 at San Nicolás.

IF TO: Yécora, Creel, Chihuahua, turn right and join Hermosillo — La Junta Log (page 48) at mile 140.0.

IF TO: Hermosillo, turn left and join La Junta — Hermosillo Log (page 84) at mile 195.0.

End of Special O

SPECIAL P START: Hermosillo, Son END: Douglas, AZ

UD-019

229.5 MI or 367.2 KM
DRIVE TIME 5 — 5 1/2 HOURS
SCENIC RATING — 3

0.0	0.0	Here at junction with Hwy #15, proceed northeast.
1.8	2.9	Pass Restaurant Jardines San Pedro, right. Come to junction. TURN RIGHT. Left is to Santa Ana via Hwy #15 free road.
2.4	3.8	Pass cemetery, left. Then curve right and over bumpy railroad crossing (Nogales — Guaymas line). **GAS** at left. Then thru San Pedro and down thru "vado" over Río San Miguel.
3.0	4.8	Curve to left. Note fruit stands at left.
4.5	7.2	Thru little village of San Miguel de Horcasita.
15.3	24.5	Pass San Francisco del Batuc at right.

MI	KM	
19.8	31.7	Pass village of Topahue with its technological and agricultural school at right.
22.3	35.7	Pass settlement of San José at right.
27.5	44.0	Note ruins at right. Then El Gavilán at right, an ideal spot for a picnic with its natural setting. Then cross bridge over Río Gavilán.
34.5	55.2	Pass side road (left) to San Rafael and (right) to Santa Rosalia. Then thru village of Las Lomas. Icehouse and **GAS** at left. Then Cemetery at left and thru settlement of El Sauz at left.
39.5	63.2	Enter old town of Ures, founded in 1644 and once the capital of the state of Sonora from 1838-79. Park at left. **GAS**, also at left. Then social security clinic at right. Now curve right and leave Ures. Cemetery at right.
48.0	76.8	Pass village La Puerta del Sol at left. Then curve right and road gradually begins to climb.
51.0	81.6	Río Sonora at left. The mountain you're now traveling on is locally known as *El Monstruo de Plomo* (Lead Monster) and also nicknamed "The Road of 700 Curves."
61.8	98.9	Thru village of Mazocahui (Indian for "The Hill of the Deer") which began as a ranch during the second half of the 17th century.
62.5	100.0	Slow now and TURN RIGHT. Follow Nacozari and Moctezuma signs. Straight ahead goes up to historical Arizpe (whose Indian name means "The Place of the Brave Ants") and on to copper mining town of Cananea.
68.0	108.8	Curve to left and on up. Then pass side road (right) to Mariscal.
72.0	115.2	Altitude now 3700 feet.
83.3	133.3	Pass side road (left) to Rancho El Calador.
98.5	157.6	Careful now for steep descent and several poorly banked curves.
100.3	160.5	Curve to left and over bridge. Note ancient Indian dwellings high in mesa (plateau) at right.
102.5	164.0	Cross bridge over Río Moctezuma. Now take LEFT FORK (right is to downtown Moctezuma). Skirt edge of Moctezuma, a town of 4,500 inhabitants founded in 1644 by the Jesuit Father Marcos Del Río.

While a sleeping pace seems to hover over the town, Moctezuma is an active agricultural center. It boasts an old plaza, where its early 18th-century church still preserves its original structure and colonial style. The town is also known for its leather industry which produces high-quality handmade embossed saddles. There are several leather shops in town. The best known is *Monturas La Industrial,* a block from the Plaza and across from Hotel Martha, where you can see the artisans at work.

103.5	265.0	Merge with side road (right) coming out from Moctezuma and TURN LEFT. **GAS** at right. You are now on Sonora Hwy #12.
114.8	183.7	Thru Vado and then two more just ahead.
117.3	187.7	Pass side road (left) to Jecori.
121.0	193.6	Pass town of Cumpas at left, founded by the Jesuit Father Egido de Montefrío in 1643 as Misión de Nuestra Señora de la Asunción (Mission of Our Lady of the Assumption). There are 2 **GAS** stations in town.
121.8	194.9	Pass side road (right) to Cumpas' airport.
123.0	196.8	Pass village of Ojo de Agua at left. Then cemetery with centuries-old tombstones.
127.8	204.5	Thru El Valle.
130.0	208.0	Thru little village of Los Hoyos (The Holes).
135.3	216.5	Restaurant La Carretera at right.
140.5	224.8	Thru Bella Esperanza (Beautiful Hope) and over bridge. Cinder block factory at right. Slow for dangerous curve to left. Careful for rocks on road. Then into canyon with river at right and mountains to left.
150.3	240.5	Note piles of metal residue. Come to side road (right) to Nacozari de García, where one of Mexico's largest mines, "La Caridad," is located. There are a couple of strictly emergency hotels in town, the Andrade and Nacozari (by the way, "Nacozari" means, "bad prickly pear" in Indian language).

Once named Placeritos de Nacozari, this copper mining town changed its name to Nacozari de García in honor of its hero, Jesús García. On November 7, 1907 at around 2 o'clock in the afternoon, siesta time, a gondola rail car loaded with dry hay caught fire at the railroad station located in the heart of town. The fire spread quickly and ignited two cars loaded with "Hércules" dynamite.

Jesús García, a 26-year-old railroad engineer of the Moctezuma Copper Mine, realized the potential disaster and quickly jumped into Engine #501, backed it up, and coupled the two smoldering cars. At full steam he sped toward the outskirts of town and, minutes later, in an area where there were only a few scattered houses, the dynamite exploded, blowing the rail cars to pieces along with García's body. Thirteen people perished in the mishap, but García's heroism saved 5,000 lives. The United States declared him a "Hero of Humanity" and posthumously awarded him with the "American Royal Cross of Honor." In the town plaza there is a replica of the famous Engine #501, immortalized in many "corridos" of folk songs.

66

MI	KM	
151.5	242.4	Merge with road at right from Nacozari. Then sports center for mine workers at right.
153.3	245.3	Slow for dangerous curve to right. There's another one about a mile ahead.
155.3	248.5	Over Agua Prieta-Nacozari main railroad line (LOOK-&-LISTEN).
158.0	252.8	LOOK-&-LISTEN as you cross railroad again.
164.8	263.7	Pass side road (right) to Nacozari's airport, La Caridad, and to Presa ("Dam") La Angostura, 34 miles from here on dirt road. The dam, built on the Río Bavispe, is famous for its catches of black bass, striped bass and catfish.
173.8	278.1	Settlement of La Pera at left. Then over vado and cross railroad once again.
176.5	282.4	Thru village of Turacachi.
180.8	289.3	Thru Esqueda, named after Enrique Esqueda, civil martyr of the revolution. Careful again as you cross railroad and curve right. Railroad station at right and over vado.
186.3	298.1	Curve right and over railroad (LOOK-&-LISTEN). Then curve left.
191.8	206.9	Slow now for vado.
193.3	309.3	Thru little town of Estación Fronteras, where Juan Bautista de Anza was born in 1734 — a soldier and explorer as well as founder of San Francisco, California and later governor of New Mexico Province.
197.3	315.7	Curve left and cross railroad line (LOOK-&-LISTEN). Slow for vado. Then thru Ejido 47.
208.5	333.6	Sharp right curve, railroad crossing (LOOK-&-LISTEN). Then over bridge and curve left.
213.3	341.3	Curve left and down long vado over Río Cabullona. Then thru village of Cabullona. Cross railroad again (LOOK-&-LISTEN). Custom inspection station at left — outbound motorists don't need to stop.
221.0	353.6	Pass side road (left) to Agua Prieta's airport and to lime plant (*planta de cal*).
225.3	360.5	Come now to "T" junction with Hwy #2. TURN RIGHT and ahead. Left is to copper mining town of Cananea and on to Imuris, 46 miles south of Nogales on Hwy #15.
226.0	361.6	Over a pair of bumpy railroad tracks and bridge.
226.8	362.9	SLOW now and TURN LEFT and head into Agua Prieta (population 70,000), which, incidentally, means "dark water." Ahead is to Janos and on to Chihuahua.
227.1	363.4	Pass Red Cross and **GAS** station left. Then ball park and big cemetery beyond on left.
227.3	363.7	Careful for stoplights. Continue straight ahead thru town.
227.5	364.0	Very nice Hotel Hacienda at left on corner (good dining room). Then TURN LEFT and ahead.
228.0	364.8	Come to stop-street. TURN RIGHT and proceed up to Mexican Customs official and turn in your tourist documents and head for U.S. Customs.

REMEMBER: Your vehicle permit is good for multiple entries into Mexico. However you MUST turn it in at the border BEFORE it expires. To turn in your papers, you'll have to park BEFORE you get to the bridge and walk into the customs building, unless there is a small building that says "BANJERCITO" or "HACIENDA"

| 228.1 | 365.0 | Pull up to U.S. Customs and the officer will ask you questions regarding your nationality, etc. — and will probably ask you to unload your gear onto the table. Then ahead on wide two-way Pan American Street into very nice town of Douglas, Arizona. |
| 229.3 | 366.9 | In front of Cochise vocational college, TURN RIGHT onto Tenth Street past ultramodern city hall on right. Then Phelps-Dodge Mercantile department store on corner at left, which is a far cry from the old-time mining company stores of the past. |

IF TO: Desert Inn or El Coronado Motel next door (or to Tombstone or Bisbee), turn left onto this Avenue "G" which is their main stem — motels are at far west end of town (refer to map page 4).

IF TO: Lordsburg and IH-10, continue ahead.

End of Special P

SPECIAL Q   *START:* Imuris, Son   *END:* Douglas, AZ

UD-019

104.0 MI or 166.4 KM
DRIVE TIME 2 — 3 HOURS
SCENIC RATING — 3

Note: If you were planning to head eastward (or northeastward) after you got to the border, like to New Mexico, Colorado, El Paso, etc., you'll find this Hwy #2 to Douglas, Arizona, quite a time-and-mileage saver with some mountainous winding and light traffic. It has some uphill and downhill mountainous winding but light traffic. It goes past the famous Mexican copper town of Cananea.

MI	KM	
0.0	0.0	In Imuris, at the top of the hill, take the right fork at the (#2) CANANEA sign.
2.0	3.2	Curve left and start easy winding stretch.
4.5	7.2	Down thru cut. Elevation 2,200 ft.
5.5	8.8	Pass side trail (left) to Rancho San Martin. Then start winding up thru mountains.
11.1	17.8	Top (4,400 feet). Now wind down.

REMEMBER: On downhill stretches, brake with your motor — not your brakes. A burning smell means you've used your brakes too much. If you can, pull over and let them cool for ten minutes or so.

24.0	38.4	Note newer church up at left next to ruins of old mission built by the great Padre Kino.
28.0	44.8	Pass village of San Antonio, then over bigger bridge and pass side road left to Santa Cruz up near Arizona border.
28.4	45.4	Pass customs inspection station for southbound traffic — Don't stop.
34.8	55.7	Cross bridge over Río Cuitaca and thru scattered village of Vicente Guerrero.
43.1	69.0	Top — 6,036 feet (or 1840 meters above sea level). Then down.
47.0	75.2	There's the Cananea copper mine over to right.
48.3	77.3	Pass road to the mine (no tours). Good view of the valley from here.
50.5	80.8	Sharp curve right at top and over railroad (LOOK-&-LISTEN). Pass OK **GAS** at left. Then take left fork — right fork would take you into Cananea. Volkswagen agency at left. Note monument at right in memory of the strikers killed in 1906 during a labor dispute.

If you have the time and wish to drive into Cananea, this is a nice little town with really nice folks. You can visit the old jail, now a museum and just soak up the atmosphere. Take right fork above. Motel Zafari (into town 1 mile on left) —MOD— 36 A/C rooms, SATV. Ph: (645) 332-1308, 332-1528, 332-1108 Fax: 332-3739.

51.5	82.4	Pass side road (right) down to old town of Arizpe. Past Motel Valle de Cobre —MOD— 38 rooms, CATV, pool, PH: (645) 332-2086 Fax: 332-3808. Also Motel and Restaurant Mesón, looks good, near Chrysler/Dodge dealership on left. Then some nice straight stretches.
63.3	101.3	Pass customs check (closed) at left. Then settlement of Ignacio Zaragoza to left.
67.1	107.4	Over pass (elevation 5,200 ft.). Then down hill on straight stretch.
73.3	117.3	Pass immigration check station at left (also not for you).
73.8	118.1	Pass Ejido Cuauhtémoc.

Cuauhtémoc (1502-1525) was the 11th and last Aztec Emperor. The son of Emperor Ahuizotl and Princess Tilalcaptl, he was educated in the Calmecac school for nobles. Cortés made him a prisoner on Aug. 13, 1521 and executed him, hanging him by his feet like a common criminal, on Feb. 28, 1525. He was 23. He was betrayed by Malinche, who acted as interpreter. To this day, a "Malinche" is a woman who cannot be trusted — that's the polite version.

76.5	122.4	Pass side road (left) that runs up to Naco, which is the Mexican border town opposite the American border town of Naco, approximately 12 miles from Bisbee.

If you would like to go to Bisbee and visit the Lavender Queen Pit Mine and on to famed old Wild West town of Tombstone, hop to it as the road is good blacktop all the way. You'll find a bed and breakfast Inn at Castle Rock in Bisbee.

91.3	146.1	There's Douglas and Agua Prieta ahead. The twin smoke stacks are at the big Phelps-Dodge copper smelter, which is the number one industry in these parts.

MI	KM	
100.3	160.5	Pass junction right down to another copper town of Nacozari, 95 miles. This nice road (Sonora Hwy #12) takes you thru Nacozari, and Ures to Hermosillo where it connects with Hwy #15.
101.0	161.6	Over a pair of bumpy railroad tracks and bridge.
101.8	162.9	SLOW now and TURN LEFT and head into Agua Prieta (population 70,000), which, incidentally, means "dark water." Ahead is to Janos and on to Chihuahua.
102.1	163.4	Pass Red Cross and **GAS**, left. Then ball park at left and big cemetery beyond, also on left.
102.5	164.0	Very nice Hotel Hacienda at left on corner (good dining room). Then TURN LEFT and ahead.
103.0	164.8	Come to stop-street. TURN RIGHT and proceed up to Mexican Customs official and turn in your tourist documents and head for U.S. Customs. The border is open 24 hours.

REMEMBER: Your vehicle permit is good for multiple entries into Mexico. However you MUST turn it in at the border BEFORE it expires. To turn in your papers, you'll have to park BEFORE you get to the bridge and walk into the customs building, unless there is a small building that says "BANJERCITO" or "HACIENDA."

103.1	165.0	Pull up to U.S. Customs and the officer will ask you questions regarding your nationality, etc. — and will probably ask you to unload your gear onto the table. Then ahead on wide two-way Pan American Street into very nice town of Douglas, Arizona.
104.3	166.9	In front of Cochise vocational college, TURN RIGHT onto Tenth Street past the ultramodern city hall on right. Then Phelps-Dodge Mercantile department store on corner at left, which is a far cry from the old-time mining company stores of the past.

IF TO: Desert Inn or El Coronado Motel next door (or to Tombstone or Bisbee), turn left onto this Avenue "G" which is their main stem — motels are at far west end of town (refer to map).

IF TO: Lordsburg and IH-10, continue ahead.

Folks, it's been a real pleasure to get you to Mexico and back, all in one piece, and we hope you've had a marvelous time. Please come see us again next time you go South of the Border, Down Mexico Way. We'd like to hear from you about your trip — use the "Comments" sheet at the end of the log book. And do drive carefully the rest of the way home.

End of Special Q

SPECIAL R START: Jct. Hwy #15 END: San Blas, Nay

UD-019

22.6 MILES or 36.2 KM
DRIVE TIME 30 MINUTES.
SCENIC RATING — 3

This special log will take you from Hwy #15 down to the ancient tropical Pacific port of San Blas, the starting point of the colonization expeditions of Coronado (military) and Padre Kino (religious — to Arizona) and Fray Junípero Serra (religious — to California). The road is good blacktop and you'll wind thru some beautiful tropical palm country. The little old town of San Blas is interesting, the beach is rather nice, and accommodations adequate. Don't hesitate to run down as you can see everything with time for a soft drink or lunch and still be back here at the junction in about 3 1/2 hours, or you might decide to stay the night or even longer if you enjoy the peaceful atmosphere.

0.0	0.0	Having turned off Hwy #15 at San Blas junction, proceed west on blacktop Hwy #11. **GAS**, right. Then wind down easy-like.
2.5	4.0	Down and left thru Ejido Cinco de Mayo and over little Río Ciruelo (plum) and left and up and wind up steep mountain ahead.
6.0	9.6	Thru village of Navarrete. Then pass side road (right) to Sauta and La Presa (dam). And over little Río Navarrete and up and down on straight stretch. Careful for 4 sets of "topes."
8.0	12.8	Pass side road (right) to Huaristemba.
8.3	13.3	Avocado and mango nursery at left. Then left thru El Palillo (the toothpick or little shack) and careful and down over low bridge over Río Palillo. Then left and up and wind.

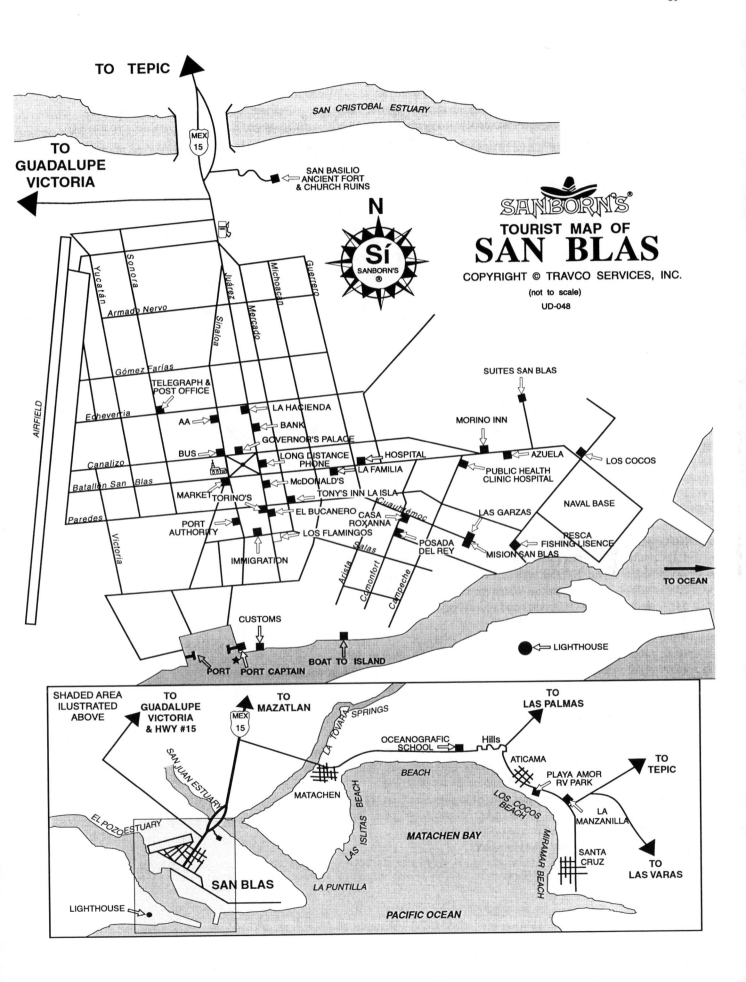

TO TEPIC

SAN CRISTOBAL ESTUARY

TO
GUADALUPE
VICTORIA

MEX 15

SAN BASILIO
ANCIENT FORT
& CHURCH RUINS

N
SÍ
SANBORN'S ®

SANBORN'S®
TOURIST MAP OF
SAN BLAS
COPYRIGHT © TRAVCO SERVICES, INC.
(not to scale)
UD-048

AIRFIELD

Yucatán
Sonora
Armado Nervo
Gómez Farías
Echeverría
Canalizo
Batallón San Blas
Paredes
Victoria

Juárez
Sinaloa
Michoacán
Mercado
Guerrero

TELEGRAPH &
POST OFFICE
AA
BUS
LA HACIENDA
BANK
GOVERNOR'S PALACE
LONG DISTANCE
PHONE
HOSPITAL
LA FAMILIA
McDONALD'S
MARKET
TORINO'S
TONY'S INN LA ISLA
EL BUCANERO
CASA
ROXANNA
PORT
AUTHORITY
LOS FLAMINGOS
IMMIGRATION

Cuauhtémoc
Salas
Arista
Camonfort
Campeche

SUITES SAN BLAS

MORINO INN
AZUELA
LOS COCOS
PUBLIC HEALTH
CLINIC HOSPITAL
LAS GARZAS
NAVAL BASE
PESCA
FISHING LISENCE
POSADA
DEL REY
MISION SAN BLAS

TO OCEAN

CUSTOMS

LIGHTHOUSE

PORT   PORT CAPTAIN
BOAT TO ISLAND

SHADED AREA
ILUSTRATED
ABOVE

TO
GUADALUPE
VICTORIA
& HWY #15

TO
MAZATLAN

MEX 15

LA TOVARA SPRINGS

OCEANOGRAFIC
SCHOOL
Hills

TO
LAS PALMAS

ATICAMA
PLAYA AMOR
RV PARK

TO
TEPIC

SAN JUAN ESTUARY

EL POZO ESTUARY

MATACHEN

BEACH

LAS ISLITAS BEACH

LOS COCOS BEACH

LA
MANZANILLA

TO
LAS VARAS

SAN BLAS

MATACHEN BAY

MIRAMAR BEACH

SANTA
CRUZ

LIGHTHOUSE

LA PUNTILLA

PACIFIC OCEAN

MI	KM	
10.7	17.1	Left and up on straight stretch. Village of Las Palmas at left. Maguey field at right.
11.6	18.6	Thru village of Guadalupe. Fields of papaya and mangos in this area.
13.0	20.8	Pass side road (left) to La Libertad. Then a short mile later, wind down.
16.0	25.6	Now wind down thru tropical forest of royal palms. Watch for cattle in road thru here.
17.5	28.0	Down and over little bridge and thru Singayta. Then more palms and jungles.
19.6	31.4	Come to junction with shortcut to Puerto Vallarta. Now paved. Sign says: "Santa Cruz, Los Cocos, Matanchén."

IF TO: Matanchén Beach (2 miles), Playa Amor RV Park (8.8 miles, look for "papelia" tree at entrance, on right), Casa Mañana (9.7 miles), Sta. Cruz, Aticama, or Las Varas turn left here and start San Blas - Las Varas Log (page 72).

22.3	35.7	Cross bridge over Estuary El Conchal. This is embarkation point for long jungle boat trips. Careful for "topes" and ahead on divided for spell. Note old fort atop hill at left. Before you attempt to drive it, be aware it's a long, hard climb. Then up a little and into historic old San Blas.
22.4	35.8	Under welcome arch and ahead down main street (Juárez) with town's only **GAS** station at left. Street now becomes one-way. **GAS** is also available at dock next to ice house in port.
22.6	36.2	Come to main plaza, at right, and end of log. For accommodations see San Blas Eat & Stray (page 130).

IF TO: Suites San Blas, Los Cocos RV Park, and El Dorado Motel, turn left at end of plaza and follow map (page 69). Los Flamingos Hotel, Restaurant Torino's, etc., straight ahead.

San Blas is famous for "jejene" (blood-thirsty gnats), so be sure to bring your "OFF" if you plan to stay.

End of Special R

SPECIAL S   *START:* Tepic, Nay   *END:* San Blas, Nay

UD-019

42.0 MI or 67.2 KM
DRIVE TIME 1 HOUR
SCENIC RATING – 3

MI	KM	
0.0	0.0	Starting here at Junction Hwy #15 at Miramar exit, proceed ahead due west. Go west, young man, go west!
1.1	1.8	El Ahuacate. Road winds somewhat. Altitude 3,200 feet.
2.6	4.2	Thru El Izote with topes. Note flower garden to right.
3.0	4.8	Thru Platanitos. Watch for school crossing.
5.0	8.0	Thru V. Carranza and more topes
7.3	11.7	Thru La Libertad.
9.5	15.2	Spectacular view to right.
10.1	16.2	Thru La Yerba. Topes with no signs but easy to find.
11.8	18.9	Beautiful view of Pacific. All sorts of tropical fruits growing along the road.
14.9	23.8	Watch for brown horse in middle of the road.
15.4	24.6	Thru Jalcolotán with a long rather rough main drag – a busy place.
15.7	25.1	Sharp dip at intersection.
15.9	25.4	Plaza on right. Then topes.
16.2	25.9	Bend right. Watch for more topes. Then curve left and right and out of town.
21.8	34.9	Thru Tecuitata. Kind of wind through town. Watch for school crossings.
26.4	42.2	Road straightens out and heads for the coast.
27.1	43.4	Come to Hwy junction. Sign says San Blas, Los Cocos, Matanchén. TURN RIGHT. Straight is to Santa Cruz. Left is to Las Varas. Follow along coast. Note coconut palms and jungle foliage.
28.8	46.1	Careful for a couple of sharp curves.
29.1	46.6	Now you are next to water.
29.3	46.9	Motel Casa Mañana at right is very clean and is owned by an Austrian couple. Opened in '93. 14 rooms. Small pool. No A/C.
29.7	47.5	Tire shop on right
30.3	48.5	Playa Amor Trailer Park.
30.9	49.4	Thru Atacama with many little seafood restaurants on left that serve fine oyster and shrimp cocktails.

MI	KM	
32.0	51.2	Pass Rincón de Matanchén restaurant on left, then Oceanographic school on right.
36.8	58.9	Coming up on Matanchén and topes
37.1	59.4	Jungle boat docks on right.
39.0	62.4	Come to "T" intersection. Turn left into San Blas. Right goes to Hwy #15.
41.7	66.7	Cross bridge over Estuary El Conchal. This is embarkation point for long jungle boat trips. Careful for "topes" and ahead on divided for spell. Note old fort atop hill at left. Before you attempt to drive it, be aware it's a long, hard climb. Then up a little and into historic old San Blas.
41.8	66.9	Under welcome arch and ahead down main street (Juárez) with town's only **GAS** station at left. Street now becomes one-way. **GAS** is also available at dock next to ice house in port.
42.0	67.2	Come to main plaza, at right, and end of log. For accommodations see San Blas Eat & Stray (page 130).

IF TO: Suites San Blas, Los Cocos RV Park, and El Dorado Motel, turn left at end of plaza and follow map (page 69). Los Flamingos Hotel, Restaurant Torino's, etc., straight ahead.

San Blas is famous for "jejene" (blood-thirsty gnats), so be sure to bring your "OFF" if you plan to stay.

End of Special S

SPECIAL T *START:* Las Varas, Nay *END:* San Blas, Nay

UD-019

55.0 MI or 89.6 KM
DRIVE TIME 1/2 HOUR
SCENIC RATING – 3

MI	KM	
0.0	0.0	Heading northbound on Hwy#20, turn left toward Zaqualpan, one block north of Pemex in town of Las Varas. Follow divided street through town.
0.3	0.5	Pass school and divided ends. Take leave of Las Varas. Pass stockyard on left.
1.1	1.8	Sign advises to watch for livestock, also remember this is a farming area with lots of machinery on the road.
3.2	5.1	Cross narrow bridge without railings.
4.8	7.7	Enter town of Zaqualpan with many topes.
5.4	8.6	**GAS** and diesel, right.
5.7	9.1	Just past plaza turn left and continue straight past church in right. Go down hill, bend right across a narrow bridge and leave Zaqualpan.
7.0	11.2	Thru community of San Ysidro. Watch for topes.
9.4	15.0	Curve left at Ixtapa/San Blas sign.
9.9	15.8	School on left. Very rough pavement.
10.5	16.8	Cemetery on right.
17.2	27.5	School zone and thru village of Platanitos and a great view of the Pacific Ocean. Pass restaurant and bar, El Mirador.
30.0	48.0	Over Río Jolotemba bridge.
32.0	51.2	Top another hill about 450 feet altitude and behold another spectacular view. Road becomes steep and curving.
33.4	53.4	Thru town of El Llano with 6 decorated BIG topes. Turn left to Santa Cruz.
34.0	54.4	Cross Río El Llano.
34.5	55.2	Come to "T" junction with Tepic, Santa Cruz highway.

IF TO: San Blas, turn left toward Santa Cruz.

IF TO: Tepic, continue ahead.

MI	KM	
40.5	64.8	Turn right at intersection with sign to Los Cocos, Matanchén, San Blas. Straight is to Santa Cruz.
41.5	66.4	Pass side trail (left) to Paraíso Miramar, a small immaculate, absolutely delightful motel-style resort and trailerpark with a great little restaurant.
44.0	70.4	Playa Amor Trailer Park on left.
45.0	72.0	Pass village of Aticama with its many seafood restaurants.
46.0	73.6	Pass Rincón de Matanchén restaurant on left, then Oceanographic school on right.
50.8	81.3	Coming up on Matanchén and topes.

MI	KM	
51.1	81.8	Jungle boat docks on right.
53.0	84.8	Come to "T" intersection. Turn left into San Blas. Right goes to Hwy #15.
55.7	89.1	Cross bridge over Estuary El Conchal. This is embarkation point for long jungle boat trips. Careful for "topes" and ahead on divided for spell. Note old fort atop hill at left. Before you attempt to drive it, be aware it's a long, hard climb. Then up a little and into historic old San Blas.
55.8	89.3	Under welcome arch and ahead down main street (Juárez) with town's only **GAS** station at left. Street now becomes one-way. **GAS** is also available at dock next to ice house in port.
56.0	89.6	Come to main plaza, at right, and end of log. For accommodations see San Blas Eat & Stray (page 130).

IF TO: Suites San Blas, Los Cocos RV Park, and El Dorado Motel, turn left at end of plaza and follow map (page 69). Los Flamingos Hotel, Restaurant Torino's, etc., straight ahead.

San Blas is famous for "jejene" (blood-thirsty gnats), so be sure to bring your "OFF" if you plan to stay.

End of SPECIAL T

SPECIAL U *START:* Santa Cruz, Nay *END:* Las Varas, Nay

UD-019

26.0 MI or 41.6 KM
DRIVE TIME 1/2 HOUR
SCENIC RATING –3

0.0	0.0	Start at corner of Tepic, Santa Cruz and Los Cocos, Matanchén road toward Tepic.
0.4	0.6	Come to intersection at right. Turn right to El Llano, Platanitos. Straight is to Tepic.
0.7	1.1	Enter little town of El Llano with at least 6 big topes. After El Llano start winding through very pretty banana plantations. Uphill a little.
3.7	5.9	Top hill. Now start winding down.
4.2	6.7	Cross bridge over Río Jolotemba.
6.3	10.2	Great view of the Pacific to right just before topping this little hill.
8.2	13.1	Sharp left right curve right after twin bridges.
10.0	16.0	Leaving coast, heading inland through some mangrove swamps.
14.5	23.2	Over Puente Arenoso with high crown.
16.0	25.6	Over Puente Jazmines a curved bridge with pretty view. Then thru community of Ixtapa de la Concepción with repair shops, and then bend left at junction and watch for traffic from right.
18.5	29.6	Pass village of San Ysidro. Topes.
19.0	30.4	Leave San Ysidro, bend left and cross a rather narrow bridge.
20.2	32.3	Curve left and enter Zaqualpan. Cross bridge and up into town. Cobblestones begin with topes too. Pass main square on left.
20.6	33.0	At end of plaza turn right, cobblestone for a block, then pavement starts and more topes.
21.1	33.8	Bull ring on left.
22.8	36.5	Sharp left turn and cross narrow bridge.
23.4	37.4	Watch for big green combines on road. Seriously – lots of farming here with machinery on roads.
25.6	41.0	Entering outskirts of Las Varas. Pass bullring on right and street divides with topes.
26.0	41.6	Come to junction with highway #200.

IF TO: Tepic, turn left and join Pto. Vallarta - Tepic (page 155) Log at mile 60.5.

IF TO: Puerto Vallarta, turn right and join Tepic - Pto Vallarta Log (page 32) at mile 41.8. There's **GAS** one block to right.

End of Special U

SPECIAL V START: Las Varas, Nay END: Chapalilla, Nay

UD-019

44.0 MI or 70.4 KM
DRIVING TIME: 2 HOURS
SCENIC RATING — 2

This log takes you on the toll road between Pto. Vallarta and Guadalajara that begins at the Compostela junction on the road between PV and Tepic.

MI	KM	
0.0	0.0	Heading north on Hwy #200, turn right at Guadalajara Cuota Sign. Town of Las Varas is off to left. Sign says, Guadalajara 213 km.
23.0	36.8	Pass an exit right to Mazatlán and Compostela. Ahead for you.
25.5	40.8	Come to toll house and pay toll (Cars $23, extra axle, $12). Then ahead on nice 2-lane road.
28.0	44.8	Slow for series of curves.
29.2	46.7	Pass exit (right) to Milpillas and continue winding.
34.0	54.4	Pass side road (left) to San Pedro Lagunillas. Then nice straight stretch. Note lake over to left.
37.0	59.2	Another side road (left) to San Pedro Lagunillas. Careful for slow-moving farm traffic.
39.0	62.4	Careful for sharp curves. A scenic photo pull-off. Then a sharp descent — brake with engine.
41.0	65.6	Community of Las Guásimas at right.
42.0	67.2	Striking view of green valley down to left.
44.0	70.4	Come to junction with Hwy #15. Tepic, straight. Guadalajara, veer right.

IF TO: Tepic, continue straight and join Guadalajara - Tepic Log (page 151) at mile 97.

IF TO: Guadalajara, veer right and join toll stub log of the Tepic - Guadalajara Log (page 35).

End Special V

SPECIAL W START: Chapalilla, Nay END: Las Varas, Nay

UD-019

21.5 MI OR 34.0 KM
DRIVE TIME 1/2 HOUR
SCENIC RATING – 2

This is a toll shortcut highway for motorist traveling between Guadalajara and Puerto Vallarta or Rincón de Guayabitos, saving 35 miles over former route by way of Tepic. Don't hesitate to take this route – unless there's a reason why you prefer to go via Tepic, like maybe it's growing dark and you need a place to stay for the night. It's 97 miles from here to Puerto Vallarta, which we folks- in-the-know refer to as "PV."

0.0	0.0	Having turned left onto toll road proceed ahead on nice divided roadway.
3.0	4.8	Pass exit (right) to Las Guásimas
8.0	12.8	Wind up past pretty Lake Lagunillas at right.
10.0	16.0	Bend left past exit right to San Pedro de las Lagunillas and under overpass.
15.0	24.0	Pass side road (left) to Milpillas.
18.5	29.6	Up over bridge over main line of Mexicali-Nogales-Guadalajara railroad line.
19.0	30.4	Slow as you come to tollhouse. Pay toll (cars $23, extra axle $12).
20.0	32.0	**GAS**, at left. Also neat hole-in-the-wall restaurant. It's clean, friendly and economical.
44.0	70.4	Come now to junction with Hwy #200 and town of Las Varas.

IF TO: Puerto Vallarta, turn left and join Tepic – Puerto Vallarta Log (page 32) at mile 41.8.

IF TO: Tepic, turn right and join Puerto Vallarta – Tepic Log (page 155) at mile 60.5.

IF TO: San Blas, continue ahead into Las Varas and start Las Varas - San Blas Special (page 71).

End of Special W

SPECIAL X *START:* Douglas, AZ *END:* Hermosillo, Son

UD-019

229.3 MI or 366.9 KM
DRIVE TIME 5 TO 5 1/2 HOURS
SCENIC RATING— 3

The most interesting place to stay in Douglas is the historic old Hotel Gadsden with the best restaurant in town. Motels are the Family Crest Bed and Breakfast, Motel 6 and Thriftlodge. If you wish to overnight in Agua Prieta and get an early start, there's the Hacienda Motor Inn. There are 2 RV parks. An hour away is Bisbee, AZ, an old mining town. The bed and breakfast Inn at Castle Rock is a "center for expanding consciousness," with *mucho* appeal for those on a journey of discovery. A New Age, 60's kind of place.

This highway is only a mile longer than the Douglas-Cananea-Imuris-Hermosillo route but is much more scenic. Mostly desert and foothill country, there are a couple of winding stretches crossing the Sierras - 37 miles between Moctezuma and Mazocahui and 20 miles between Mazocahui and Ures which climbs over a mountain known as El Monstruo de Plomo (Lead Monster).

MI	KM	
0.0	0.0	Starting on 10th street between "G" and "F" Ave. in Douglas, Arizona, head west on 10th St. (Hwy #80).
0.1	0.2	Straight at light. Pass city hall at left.
0.3	4.5	After two long blocks, come to dead end. Cochise vocational college ahead. Turn LEFT onto wide two-way Pan American Ave. Ahead for about three-quarters of a mile.
1.0	1.6	Wave good-bye to U.S. Customs on your left (don't stop). Cross border (there's no river to cross here) on one-way bridge - you're now in Mexico.

Take far right slot and pull up to Mexican official and tell him you're going to Guadalajara or Guaymas or Kino or wherever you're going. He'll tell you to park diagonally just ahead at right. Then go into the Mexican government building at right and head for the counter at MIGRACION (immigration) on right side of building where your tourist cards will be written (or those that you have will be validated). Then cut across the big room to ADUANA "BANJERCITO" where you'll get your car permit. They will put a decal on your windshield, and you're free to be on your way.

Now back out of the diagonal parking spot and watch carefully for incoming traffic. Then head straight down their main street. **GAS**, left on corner. You're now in Agua Prieta, Spanish for "dark water."

1.1	1.8	Slow for dip ("vado") and cross 3rd St. Continue straight ahead. Then **GAS** at left.
1.3	2.1	STRAIGHT 3 blocks. There will be a fence on your left. STOP SIGN and church on left. Turn **LEFT** onto Sixth Street. Then pass plaza at left.
1.5	2.4	Straight for 2 BLOCKS. Stoplight. Turn **RIGHT** onto Sixth Avenue and straight on down.
2.0	3.2	Cemetery at right. Industrial park at left. Then ball park at right. Then **GAS**. Then Hotel Las Palmas.
2.8	4.5	Come now to junction Hwy 2 and turn right here for Cananea, Imuris, Nacozari, and Hermosillo. (Left here takes you to Janos and on to Chihuahua.)
3.5	5.6	CAREFUL! There are sometimes policemen here making sure you stop at ALTO sign. As we mention in our cover, you should always be careful at railroad tracks and watch the guy behind you, as not all people stop at them. Here, plan on stopping. Over two railroad tracks - line runs to Nacozari, another copper town.
4.3	6.9	Come now to junction with Sonora Hwy #12 and TURN LEFT to Hermosillo (thru Nacozari and Moctezuma). Straight ahead is to Cananea and on to Imuris, 46 miles south of Nogales on Hwy 15. Sign says "118 kilometers to Nacozari" or 73 miles.
7.5	12.5	Easy now for "vado" or dip.
9.0	14.4	Pass side road (right) to Agua Prieta's airport and to lime plant ("planta de cal").
16.3	26.1	Slow now and STOP for customs inspection. Then thru village of Cabullona and cross Agua Prieta-Nacozari railroad line (LOOK-&-LISTEN). Down long "vado" over Río Cabullona.
21.3	34.1	Slow for *curva peligrosa* (dangerous curve) to right. Then over bridge and cross railroad line again (LOOK-&-LISTEN). Curve to left.
32.5	52.0	Thru Ejido 47. Slow for "vado" and cross railroad line one more time (LOOK-&-LISTEN). Bend to right and out.

MI	KM	
36.0	57.6	Thru town of Estación Fronteras where Juan Bautista de Anza was born in 1734, a soldier; explorer; founder of San Francisco, California; later governor of New Mexico Province.
38.0	60.8	Slow for "vado."
42.5	68.0	Ejido Adolfo Ruiz Cortines at right, named after an ex-president (1952-1958).
43.5	69.6	Curve to right and over railroad (LOOK-&-LISTEN). Then curve left.
48.5	77.6	Thru Esqueda. Railroad station at left. Incidentally, this town was named after Enrique Esqueda, a civil martyr of the revolution. Curve left and over railroad (LOOK- &-LISTEN) and curve right and out.
53.5	85.6	Thru village of Turicachi.
55.0	88.0	Slow for right curve and then for a left and another railroad crossing in-between (LOOK-&-LISTEN). Then over "vado." Settlement of La Pera at right. Río Nacozari at left.
57.8	92.5	Rancho El Vigia at right.
65.3	104.5	Pass side road (left) to Nacozari's airport of La Caridad and to Presa ("Dam") La Angostura, 34 miles from here. The dam, famous for its good catches of black bass, striped bass, and catfish, is built on Río Bavispe.
71.8	114.9	Slow for railroad crossing (LOOK-&-LISTEN).
74.0	118.4	Slow now for sharp curves ahead. . Then LOOK-&-LISTEN as you cross railroad again.
76.3	122.1	Thru rock cut and down.
78.3	125.3	Cemetery at left. Then thru long rock cut. Skirt edge of Nacozari de García, where one of Mexico's biggest copper mines, La Caridad, is located. Note mine workers' houses up at right. Pass side road (left) to Nacozari proper. There are a couple of strictly emergency hotels in town, the Andrade and the Nacozari. (Nacozari, by the way, means "bad prickly pear" in Indian language.) **GAS** in town.

Once named PLACERITOS DE NACOZARI, this copper mining town changed its name to NACOZARI DE GARCIA in honor of its hero, Jesus García. On November 7, 1907 around 2 o'clock in the afternoon, siesta time, a gondola car loaded with dried hay caught fire at the railroad station located in the heart of town. The fire spread quickly and ignited two cars loaded with Hercules dynamite.

Jesús García, a 26 year old railroad engineer of the Moctezuma Copper Company, realized the potential disaster and quickly jumped in Engine 501, backed it up, and coupled the two cars. At full steam he sped away from town. A few minutes later in the outskirts of town where there were only a few scattered houses, the dynamite exploded. It blew the railroad cars to pieces along with García's body. Thirteen people perished in the mishap, but García's heroism saved 5000 lives. The United States declared him a Hero of Humanity and posthumously awarded him the American Royal Cross of Honor. In the town's square there is a replica of famous Engine 501, immortalized in many *corridos* or folk songs.

79.5	127.2	Merge at left with road from Nacozari.
80.0	128.0	Note piles of metal residue. Río Nacozari at left.
88.3	141.3	Slow now for **dangerous right curve.** Then cinder block factory at left and over bridge. Thru village of Bella Esperanza.
94.8	151.7	Restaurant La Carretera at left.
96.8	154.9	Rancho La Noria at left.
99.3	158.9	Thru little village of Los Hoyos ("The Holes").
102.0	163.2	Thru El Valle.
106.3	170.1	Cemetery at right with centuries-old tombstones. Village of Ojo de Agua, also at right. Then thru rock cut.
108.5	173.6	Pass side road (left) to Cumpas airport.
109.3	174.9	Town of Cumpas at right, founded by Jesuit Father Egidio de Montefrío in 1643 as Misión de Nuestra Señora de la Asunción ("Mission of Our Lady of the Assumption"). There are 2 **GAS** stations in town.
112.5	180.0	Bend left and over vado and pass side road (right) to Jecori.
119.8	181.7	Thru left cut.
125.8	201.3	Slow now and **TURN RIGHT.** Straight ahead is to Moctezuma proper, and to **GAS**. Skirt edge of Moctezuma, founded in 1644 by the Jesuit Father Marcos del Río.

MOCTEZUMA is an active agricultural center. It boasts an old plaza, where its large 18th-century church still preserves its original colonial-style structure. The town is also well known for its leather industry which produces high-quality handmade embossed saddles. There are several leather shops in town - and you can visit Monturas La Industrial and see the artisans at work, a block from the square and across from Hotel Martha.

126.3	202.1	Merge with side road (left) coming from Moctezuma, and out. Over Río Moctezuma.
128.3	205.3	Note ancient Indian dwellings at left high in mesa.

MI	KM	
129.8	207.7	Over another bridge and up.
135.5	216.8	You are now 3578 feet above sea level. **Careful for sharp curves ahead.**
140.0	224.0	Cafe Chuyen at left, a whistle truck stop.
147.0	235.2	Pass side road to Rancho El Calador, a little over a mile off to right.
151.0	241.6	Over bridge with Rancho El Rodeo at left.
158.5	253.6	Altitude now 3700 feet.
162.0	259.2	Pass side road (left) to Mariscal.
167.5	268.0	Come to "T" and TURN LEFT. Right takes you to historical Arizpe (which means "The Place of the Brave Ants" in Indian language) and to copper town of Cananea. Then thru village of Mazocahui (Indian for "The Hill of the Deer") which started as a ranch in the second half of the 17th century. There's **GAS** in village. That's Río Sonora at right whose bed was once the old road between here and Ures.
170.5	272.8	Over bridge La Junta and up, climbing a mountain locally known as "El Monstruo De Plomo" ("Lead Monster") or "Road of 700 Curves."
182.0	291.2	Village of La Puerta del Sol at right.
187.8	300.5	Thru San Pedro.
189.0	302.4	Cemetery at left. Then curve left and enter old town of Ures. Ures, founded in 1644, was once the capital of the state of Sonora from 1838-1879. Pass social security clinic at left. Then **GAS**, right. Pass park at right and take leave of Ures.
194.5	311.2	Little village of Las Lomas. **GAS** at right. Ice house at right. Pass side road (right) to San Rafael and (left) to Santa Rosalía.
202.1	323.4	Bridge over Río Gavilán. Then El Gavilán at left.
208.0	332.8	Settlement of San José at left.
210.8	337.3	Village of Topahue with its technological and agricultural school at left.
214.8	343.7	Pass San Francisco del Batuc at left.
225.5	360.8	Thru little village of San Miguel de Horcasita. Outside village note fruit stands.
227.0	363.2	Curve right and cross "vado" of Río San Miguel. Thru San Pedro with **GAS**, right. Then over railroad crossing (Nogales-Guaymas line).
229.3	366.9	Pass military university up at left, sort of a West Point. Come to junction Hwy #15.

IF TO: Hermosillo, TURN LEFT to Hermosillo and join Santa Ana — Hermosillo Log (page 8) at mile 100.0.

IF TO: Santa Ana, Nogales, and Mexicali turn right and join Hermosillo — Santa Ana Log (page 172) at mile 7.2.

End of Special X

SPECIAL Y   Guadalajara Bypass   Clockwise

UD-019

25 MI or 40 KM
DRIVE TIME 45 MIN – 1 HOUR

This loop around the southern and western two-thirds of Guadalajara is a big time saver (although Lázaro Cárdenas Boulevard is quite suitable to get across the southern part of town). This log takes you from the southeastern corner of town south on Hwy #44 to the junction with the Periférico and then swings around the west side of town to the north end where it terminates at the junction with Hwy #54. Slow and congested, but safer than city traffic for RV's and cars with no power. Careful for potholes and trucks. See Guadalajara map (page 42)

0.0	0.0	Here at 90-D toll road from Zapotlanejo, proceed ahead. Take SECOND LEFT FORK (careful) and around and merge with road coming from right. Curve right and take leave of Hwy #44, now heading south. Traffic lights ahead.
1.0	1.6	Come to another traffic light at entrance to Hotel El Tapatio left. Over railroad overpass.
2.5	4.0	Slow now! Get into right lane and then TURN RIGHT under overpass onto Periférico. Pemex right.

MI	KM	
5.0	8.0	Pass fertilizer factory at right. Then SLOW for dangerous railroad crossing.
5.3	8.5	Villages of Toluquilla and López Cotilla to left.
6.0	9.6	Periférico Pte straight ahead, Chapala airport exit left. Vista hermosa, La Pinta to left. Las Juntas right. Electrical generating station and potable water plant on left. Rodeo stadium to left. Curve right.
6.2	9.9	Bumpy double railroad crossing. Curve right. Muelles Sandoval to left.
9.0	14.4	José Cuervo Tequila on right.
10.0	16.0	Over little bridge. Downtown exit left. Over overpass. Road widens. Casa de Huéspedes at left. Average speed should be about 25 MPH. San Sebatianito sign at left. Restaurant to left. Gas left. Subway station right. Down town left. Stoplight. Shizusa electronics on right. AT & T on left. **KM 15**.
13.0	20.8	Downtown right. Stoplight. Pass Coca-Cola plant at right. Over little bridge. Colonia El Briseño sign to left. Stoplight. Puebla Restaurant at left. Downtown right. 15 MI. Le Cistena sign at left.

IF TO: Holiday Inn, Plaza del Sol, Posada Guadalajara Hotels, etc., TURN RIGHT here and follow Guadalajara map (page 42).

IF TO: San José del Tajo RV Park, Manzanillo, Colima, TURN LEFT here and join Guadalajara - Tecomán Jct. Log. (See Mexico's South Pacific Coast book, page 7) at mile 5.

15.0	24.0	Centro Para Menores sign on left. Park at left. Hacienda Hotel and trailer park on right
16.0	25.6	Downtown right. Stoplight. Continuing ahead on Periférico southbound. Pemex left and right. Church on right. Curve right
16.7	26.7	SLOW as you approach another stoplight at junction Hwy #15-West. LOOK-&-LISTEN at railroad crossing. This is main Pacific line with lots of traffic and pretty bumpy so be careful!

IF TO: Tequila, Tepic, Mazatlán, Puerto Vallarta, etc., TURN LEFT here and pick up Guadalajara - Tepic Log (page 151) at mile 4.5 (Av. Vallarta).

IF TO: Hacienda RV Park, Hotel Camino Real, and Malibu and other motels, TURN RIGHT here and follow Guadalajara map (page 42).

17.8	28.5	Pass side road (left) to village of San Juan de Ocotán. Radio tower dead ahead. Pemex refinery at left. Nice view of Guadalajara ahead.
20.0	32.0	Church-like cluster of buildings at right. Exit right for AV. Acueducto, downtown. Stoplight. Road widens. Under overpass. Road narrows again. Nogales and Zapopan straight ahead.
21.5	34.4	Road narrows to two lane again. Cross overpass. Gigante at right. Now have median strip and 6 lanes. Hospital at left. Goodyear dealer, Gas at right. San Isidro and Club de Golf to left.
23.2	37.1	"Topes" Under arch Universidad de Guadalajara on left. Traffic light. Factory at right. Pass school at left. Restaurant Vallarta, left. Stoplight. Little market at right. Stoplight.
25.0	40.0	Caballo Negro (Black Horse) Restaurant, left. Corona distributor at right. Subway station at right and stoplight. Hotel Playboy at left. Big civic auditorium and convention center over to left. Then come to junction Hwy #54.

IF TO: Jalpa, Zacatecas, or Saltillo, TURN LEFT onto Hwy #54 and pick up Guadalajara - Zacatecas Log. (See Mexico's Huasteca Potosina book, page 204) at mile 5.5.

End of Special Y

SPECIAL Z Guadalajara Bypass Counterclockwise

UD-019

25 MI or 40 KM
DRIVE TIME 45 MIN – 1 HOUR

This loop around the northwest, west, southwest, and south parts of Guadalajara is a big time saver (although Lázaro Cárdenas Boulevard is quite suitable to get across the south part of town). This log takes you from the junction with Hwy #54 at the far north end of the city around to the junction with Hwy #90D toll road near Tlaquepaque at the southeast corner of Guadalajara. Slow and congested, but safer than city traffic for RV's and cars with no power. Careful for potholes and trucks. See Guadalajara map (page 42).

MI	KM	
0.0	0.0	Here at intersection with big civic auditorium and Zacatecas Hwy heading north, proceed ahead. Hotel Playboy at right. Subway station at left and stoplight. Sign says Tabachines, Nogales. Corona distributor at left. Caballo Negro (Black Horse) restaurant, right.
1.8	2.9	Stoplight. Little market at left. Stoplight. Restaurant Vallarta, right. Pass school at right Factory at left. Traffic light. Universidad de Guadalajara on right. Under arch. "Topes."
3.5	5.6	San Isidro and Club de Golf to right. Gas at left. Goodyear dealer. Hospital at right. Now have median strip and 6 lanes. Gigante at left. Cross overpass. Road narrows to 2 lanes again.
5.0	8.0	Under overpass. Nogales and Zapopan straight ahead. Road widens again. Now heading NW. Road narrows. Stoplight. Exit left for Av. Acueducto, downtown. Church like cluster of buildings at left.
7.2	11.5	Pemex refinery at right. Radio tower dead ahead. Pass side road (right) to village of San Juan de Ocotán.
8.3	13.3	LOOK-&-LISTEN at railroad crossing just ahead. This is main Pacific line with lots of traffic, pretty bumpy so be careful! SLOW as you approach stoplight at junction Hwy #15-West.

IF TO: Tequila, Tepic, Mazatlán, Puerto Vallarta, etc., TURN RIGHT here and pick up Guadalajara - Tepic Log (page 151) at mile 4.5.

IF TO: Hacienda RV Park, Hotel Camino Real, and Malibu and other motels, TURN LEFT here and follow Guadalajara map (page 42).

8.4	13.4	Continuing ahead on Periférico southbound. Stoplight. Downtown, left.
9.0	14.4	Curve left Church on left. Now heading NE. Pemex right and left. Guadalajara in distance.
10.0	16.0	Hacienda Hotel and trailer park on left. Park at right. Centro Para Menores sign on right.
12.0	19.2	Le Cistena sign at right. Sign says Colima straight ahead. Down town left. 15 MI. Puebla restaurant at right. Stoplight. Colonia El Briseño sign to right. Over little bridge. Pass Coca-Cola plant at left.

IF TO: Holiday Inn, Plaza del Sol, Posada Guadalajara Hotels, etc., TURN LEFT here and follow Guadalajara map (page 42).

IF TO: San José del Tajo RV Park, Melaque, Barra de Navidad, Manzanillo, Morelia, Mexico City, Tepic, Colima, Jiquilpan, etc., TURN RIGHT here and pick up Guadalajara - Tecomán Jct. Log (See Mexico's South Pacific Coast book, page 7) at mile 5.

IF TO: Chapala, Guadalajara straight.

12.5	20.0	Road widens. Cross overpass. Downtown exit right. Over little bridge. **KM 15.**
15.0	24.0	AT & T on right. Shizusa electronics on left. Stoplight. Downtown right. Chapala, airport straight ahead. Subway station left. Gas right. Restaurant to right. San Sebastianito sign at right. Casa de Huéspedes at right. Average speed should be about 25 MPH.
16.0	25.6	José Cuervo Tequila on left.
18.8	30.1	Muelles Sandoval to right. Curve left. Heading E now. Las Juntas to left. Bumpy railroad crossing.
19.0	30.4	Curve left. Rodeo Stadium to right. Electrical generating station and potable water plant on right. Las Juntas left. Vista Hermosa, La Pinta to right. Chapala airport exit right. Periférico Ote. straight ahead.
19.7	31.5	Villages of Toluquilla and López Cotilla to right.
20.0	32.0	SLOW for dangerous railroad crossing. Pass fertilizer factory at left.
22.5	36.0	Pemex left. Slow now! Get into right lane, then exit RIGHT, then under overpass off Periférico.

IF TO: Lake Chapala, continue ahead on Hwy #44 past gas at right and join Guadalajara – Jocotepec Log (page 79) at mile 7.

IF TO: Downtown, exit right. Go Over overpass and Curve around to your left.

MI	KM	
24.0	38.4	Over railroad overpass. Come to traffic light at entrance to Hotel El Tapatio right.
25.0	40.0	Traffic lights ahead. Curve left and merge with Hwy #44, now heading north. Take SECOND RIGHT FORK (careful) and around and merge with road coming from left. Come to 90-D toll road to Zapotlanejo.

IF TO: Lagos de Moreno, San Luis Potosí, etc., follow MEXICO CUOTA SIGNS and join Guadalajara – San Luis Potosí Log (See Mexico's Huasteca Potosina book, page 199) at mile 6.3.

IF TO: Irapuato, Querétaro, follow MEXICO CUOTA SIGNS and join Guadalajara – Querétaro Log (See Mexico's Colonial Heart book, page 2) at mile 4.0.

IF TO: Morelia via toll road, join Guadalajara – Morelia Toll Log (See Mexico's Colonial Heart book, page 33) at mile 4.0.

End of Special Z

SPECIAL AA *START:* Guadalajara, Jal *END:* Jocotepec, Jal

UD-019

49.8 MI or 79.7 KM
DRIVE TIME 1 – 1 1/4 HOURS
SCENIC RATING – 3

If you wish to run down to Lake Chapala and to the lakeside towns of Chapala, Chula Vista, Ajijic, San Juan Cosalá, and Jocotepec, and maybe on to junction Hwy #15, use this log; also if heading for Zamora-Pátzcuaro-Morelia via Ocotlán-La Barca.

0.0	0.0	Starting at Minerva Glorieta in west end of Guadalajara, turn right off circle just beyond tall office building at right and onto Agustín Yañez. Follow "Chapala – Mexico" sign. Stay in right lane.
0.5	0.8	Pass Hotel Diana at left.
0.6	1.0	Veer right onto Av. De Los Arcos, a divided road.
0.8	1.3	Cross bumpy railroad crossing. Wide modernistic sculpture at left. Frankfurt Restaurant, right.
1.0	1.6	Tizic Restaurant, left.
1.5	2.4	Sendai Restaurant, left. Thru Glorieta de Abastos. You cross over Lázaro Cárdenas. Go 3/4 way around. Follow "Mexico" sign. Aim for Chevy dealer.
1.6	2.6	Pass Chevy dealer on right. Stay on lateral street. Pass Mercado de Abastos, right. Continue straight. Lázaro Cárdenas is at your left. You'll enter it soon. Bancomer, right. Stay in left lane.
2.2	3.5	Veer left onto divided.
2.5	4.0	Cross overpass. Electric generating station, right.
3.5	5.6	Gigante, then IMSS hospital, both at left. Chrysler, right.
3.8	6.1	Pass exit for railroad station.
5.2	8.3	Detroit Diesel Allison, right. Follow signs that say "Chapala, Aeropuerto."
5.3	8.5	Cummins dealer, right. Then over railroad crossing.

IF TO: Chapala, Aeropuerto, EXIT RIGHT.

IF TO: Mexico, Zapotlanejo, Central de Autobuses, straight.

5.4	8.6	Curve right onto multi-lane divided. Get into left lane. Enter Hwy #44.
5.7	9.1	Pass "restaurant row," right. Hotel Tapatío exit at left. Las Juntas, right. Go up hill. Still one way. **KM 2**.
6.0	9.6	Las Juntas exit, right. Lomas de Tapatío, left.
6.5	10.4	Down and curve left. Cement factory, right. **KM 3**.
7.0	11.2	Pass **GAS** at right and left. Restaurant La Mason del Mariachi on right. Sign to Chapala airport on right. Then careful for entrance to "Periférico" overpass and continue ahead.

IF TO: Tepic, exit right and start Guadalajara Periférico clockwise (page 76).

MI	KM	
8.9	14.3	**GAS** at left.
9.3	14.9	La Capilla restaurant right.
10.0	16.0	Atlas Golf Club to left. Las Pintas to right. Exit for industrial park of Guadalajara. Restaurant Mi Ranchito on left. Las Pesites on left. Road narrows at turn to airport.
13.0	20.8	Airport turnoff at right but ahead for you onto overpass. **GAS** at right.
18.5	29.6	Pass **GAS** at right.
19.5	31.2	Pass side road right to Cajititlán. Then old Hacienda La Celera at right.
22.5	36.0	Come now to junction left with Hwy #92 to Ocotlán, La Barca, and Zamora – this is called "Entronque Santa Cruz" junction. End 4-lane divided.

IF TO: Ocotlán, La Barca, Zamora, Pátzcuaro, Morelia, Mexico City, etc., TURN LEFT here onto Hwy #35 and start Santa Cruz – Zamora Log (See Mexico's Colonial Heart book, page 58).

25.9	41.4	Pass town of Buenavista at left. Mostly farmland thru here – corn and wheat.
27.9	44.6	Village of Ixtlahuacan over at right. Then wind on up.
29.9	47.8	Summit. Now down thru cut with Lake Chapala ahead. See Chapala map (page 81) and Chapala Eat & Stray (page 148) for accommodations.
30.9	49.4	Pass Brisas de Chapala subdivision at left with Best Western Hotel Brisas de Chapala at right offering a 9-hole golf course.
31.6	50.6	Motel Chapala Haciendas at left. Come to bypass ("Libramiento") around Chapala.

IF TO: Chula Vista, Ajijic, El Manglarcito RV Park, Jocotepec, etc. TAKE RIGHT FORK.

IF TO: Chapala, STRAIGHT AHEAD.

31.8	50.9	On bypass, wind easily around base of mountains. Nice view of Lake Chapala at left.
33.5	56.8	Come now to end of bypass and junction with lakeside Hwy #94. Careful for topes at intersection.
35.9	57.4	Pass Hotel Real de Chapala on left and La Floresta Hotel on right.

IF TO: Chula Vista, turn left.

IF TO: Ajijic, Jocotepec, etc., turn right and continue on log.

36.2	57.9	**GAS** at right.
36.5	58.4	Hotel Real de Chapala at left (4 blocks on Paseo del Lago and a block left).
36.8	58.9	**GAS** at right. Thru edge of famed little lakeside town of Ajijic ("ah-hee-heek"). Don't hesitate to exit off left to go down and look over town as there are several interesting shops and restaurants.
37.0	59.2	Posada Las Calandrias at left. Las Casitas apartment complex next door.
37.5	60.0	Hacienda del Oro subdivision at right with terrific Danza del Sol Hotel.
40.5	64.8	Now alongside pretty Lake Chapala for spell. That's Mount García across lake.
41.5	66.4	Balneario (spa) San Juan Cosalá over at left on lake. Then skirt edge of San Juan Cosalá (population 4,000). El Palomar Apartments in town on lakeside.
46.8	74.9	Settlement of El Chante. Posada del Pescador at right.
48.0	76.8	Now into fishing village of Jocotepec, founded in 1528 and famous for its hand-loomed serapes. Sunday is market day.
48.3	77.3	Here's a really good little serape shop at left on corner with some very attractive designs at reasonable prices.
48.5	77.6	El Mesón de Los Naranjitos Restaurant and arts-and-crafts shop at right on corner. Then ahead to plaza and turn left at dead end. Go 3 blocks, turn right, and out.
49.8	79.7	Slow now. Come to junction Hwy #15. **GAS** at left.

IF TO: Morelia, etc., TURN LEFT and join Guadalajara – Jiquilpan Log (See Mexico's Colonial Heart book, page 39) at mile 35.5.

IF TO: Guadalajara, TURN RIGHT and join Jiquilpan – Guadalajara Log (See Mexico's Colonial Heart book, page 198) at mile 61.0.

End of Special AA

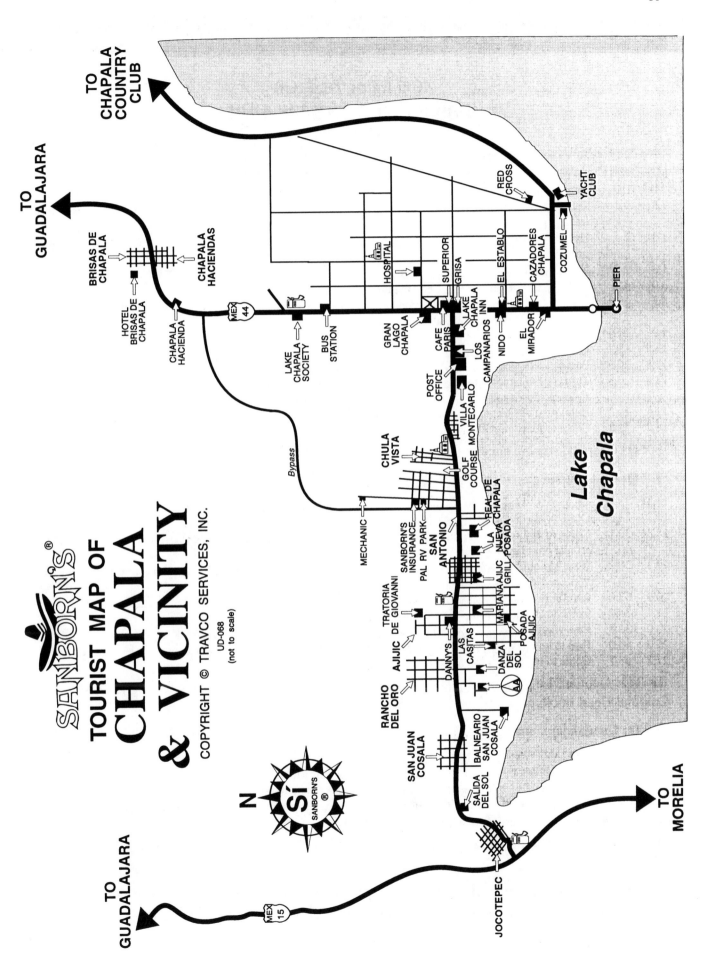

SPECIAL BB *START:* Jocotepec, Jal *END:* Guadalajara, Jal

49.0 MI or 78.4 KM
DRIVE TIME 1 – 1 1/4 HOURS
SCENIC RATING – 3

See Chapala & Vicinity map (page 81) and Chapala Eat & Stray (page 148) for accommodations.

MI	KM	
0.0	0.0	Here at junction with Hwy #15, proceed ahead. **GAS**, right. Slow now.
1.3	2.1	Turn left. Go 3 blocks. Turn right at plaza. El Mesón de Los Naranjitos restaurant and arts-and-crafts shop at left on corner.
1.5	2.4	Here's a really good little serape shop at right on corner with some very attractive designs at reasonable prices.
1.8	2.9	Now into fishing village of Jocotepec, founded in 1528 and famous for its hand-loomed serapes.
3.0	4.8	Posada del Pescador at left. Settlement of El Chante.
8.3	13.3	Skirt edge of San Juan Cosalá (population 4,000). El Palomar apartments in town on lakeside. Balneario (spa) San Juan Cosalá over at right on lake.
9.3	14.9	Now alongside pretty Lake Chapala for spell. That's Mount García across lake.
12.3	19.7	Hacienda del Oro subdivision at left with terrific Danza del Sol Hotel.
12.8	20.5	Posada Las Calandrias at right. Las Casitas apartment complex next door.
13.0	20.8	Thru edge of famed little lakeside town of Ajijic ("ah-hee-heek"). Don't hesitate to exit off right onto narrow street, go down and look over town as there are several interesting shops and restaurants. **GAS**, left.
13.5	21.3	Hotel Real de Chapala at right (4 blocks on Paseo del Lago and a block right).
14.7	22.4	Come to junction with bypass around Chapala. Careful for topes at intersection

IF TO: Chapala, straight ahead.

IF TO: Guadalajara etc., turn left onto bypass and continue on log.

14.8	23.7	On bypass, wind easily around base of mountains. Nice view of Lake Chapala at right.
15.3	24.5	Oso Dorado Golf driving range at right. Gently wind up on bumpy pavement.
18.8	30.1	Come to end of bypass ("Libramiento") around Chapala. Straight thru underpass and curve right, up and around onto Hwy #44.
19.3	30.9	Note Motel Chapala Haciendas up at right. Then pass Brisas de Chapala subdivision at right with Best Western Hotel Brisas de Chapala at left offering a 9-hole golf course.
20.6	33.0	Careful for series of sharp-banked curves at highway winds up.
21.4	34.2	Come to summit. Then begin windy descent.
23.0	36.8	Pass village of Ixtlahuacan (population 5,000 – where are they?) over at left.
25.0	40.0	Pass town of Buenavista at right. Mostly farmland thru here – corn and wheat.
27.3	43.7	Come to junction right with Hwy #35 (formerly #92) here at Santa Cruz community.

IF TO: Ocotlán, La Barca, Zamora, turn right and start Santa Cruz – Zamora Log (See Mexico's Colonial Heart book, page 58).

IF TO: Guadalajara, continue ahead.

27.8	44.5	Pass Eddy's motel at right.
31.5	50.4	Over to left is Ranch of Vicente Fernández, a famous Mexico Ranchero singer.
33.1	53.0	Pass exit to El Salto, right. Don't bother going, it's only a trickle these days.
36.4	58.2	Pass exit right for airport. Careful for traffic merging from right. Now 6 lanes and intense traffic.
41.0	65.6	Pass exit to Periférico to Colima, right. **GAS**, left.

IF TO: Colima, Puerto Vallarta, exit right, then left under overpass and start Guadalajara Bypass Clockwise (page 76).

IF TO: Guadalajara, Mexico, straight, curve right and up over overpass and ahead, winding up.

42.5	68.0	Get in left lane for Tapatío Hotel (up on hill at left), center lane for Guadalajara, right lane for Morelia or Mexico.

MI	KM	
43.0	68.8	Exit RIGHT for L. Cárdenas at "Mexico, L. Cárdenas, S.L.P." exit, curving to right. Straight will take you downtown on González Gallo. CAREFUL NOW! After 1/4 mile L. Cárdenas will exit LEFT, then curve around left and join divided. Mexico, Zapotlanejo, Tlaquepaque will veer right.

IF TO: Tlaquepaque follow stub log below

IF TO: Morelia, Mexico via toll road, veer right and follow Mexico, Zapotlanejo signs and join Guadalajara – Morelia Toll Log (See Mexico's Colonial Heart book, page 33) at mile 4.0.

IF TO: Querétaro, veer right, follow Mexico, Zapotlanejo signs and join Guadalajara – Querétaro Log (See Mexico's Colonial Heart book, page 2) at mile 4.0.

IF TO: San Luis Potosí or Aguascalientes, veer right, follow Mexico, Zapotlanejo signs and join Guadalajara – San Luis Potosí Log (Mexico's Huasteca Potosina book, page 199) at mile 4.0.

IF TO: Minerva circle, skip down to continuation of this log.

STUB LOG TO TLAQUEPAQUE

0.0	0.0	Having veered right at L. Cárdenas/Zapotlanejo split, proceed ahead.
0.2	0.3	Downhill merge onto L. Cárdenas west. **GAS**, left. 2-lane divided.
1.0	1.6	Ignore first Tlaquepaque exit. Cross Glendale. Stoplight.
2.0	3.2	Exit RIGHT for Tonolá. For Mexico toll and bus depot, continue straight ahead. Having exited right, curve right and GET INTO LEFT LANE. Exit left at retorno. Go straight for Tlaquepaque.
2.5	4.0	Pension trucks and trailers at right. Mi Pueblo Grill, right. Arizona Grill, left.
3.0	4.8	Pass arches of Tlaquepaque, left.
3.5	5.6	**GAS**, right. Get into left lane.
3.7	5.9	Monument to Toltecas, left. At light, TURN LEFT protected with arrow onto one way Hidalgo.
3.9	6.2	Pass school at right. Watch for topes into town.
4.5	7.2	Come to Plaza Tlaquepaque. TURN RIGHT and go 2 blocks, then LEFT and 2 blocks to Plaza. Turn Left on Monela. Parking 1/2 block on right at market. The Parian is one block to right. In front of church at Matamoros is a lady who will ship anything anywhere.

End of Stub Log

Continuation of main log:

45.0	72.0	Firestone at left. **GAS**, left.
46.0	73.6	Bimbo Bread at left. TURN Left at stoplight. Continue ahead for 3 blocks until you come to another stoplight and TURN Right. Come to stoplight.
46.5	74.4	Pass railroad depot at left. Come now to stoplight.
47.0	75.2	Railroad freight depot at left. Continue ahead on divided.
48.0	76.8	Proceed ahead alongside walled railroad yard at left. Stay in middle as traffic flows easier. Railroad workers' hospital at right. Bear left.
48.5	77.6	Pass Hotel Diana at right.
49.0	78.4	Turn right onto circle just after tall office building at left and onto Agustín Yañez. Come to Minerva Glorieta in west end of Guadalajara. For accommodations see Guadalajara Eat & Stray (page 142).

IF TO: Morelia, Colima, or Manzanillo, turn left and go 1/4-way around circle and turn left on Av. L Mateos. Start Guadalajara – Morelia Toll Log (page 33) or Guadalajara - Tecomán Jct. Log. (See Mexico's South Pacific Coast book, page 7).

IF TO: Tepic or Puerto Vallarta, turn left and go 2/3-way around circle and turn left at Av. Vallarta and start Guadalajara – Tepic Log (page 151).

IF TO: Downtown Guadalajara, turn right and go 1/4-way around circle and turn right at Av. Vallarta.

IF TO: Zacatecas, turn right and go 1/2-way around circle and turn right onto Hwy #54. Start Guadalajara – Zacatecas Log (Mexico's Huasteca Potosina book, page 204).

End of Special BB

SPECIAL CC *START:* La Junta, Chih *END:* Hermosillo, Son

335.0 MI or 536.0 KM
DRIVE TIME 8 – 13 HOURS
SCENIC RATING – 3

NOTE: Watch for rocks on pavement along this route. And be sure to check your rear-view mirror before attempting to pass. Take food, water and extra gas on this 13-hour trek.

MI	KM	
0.0	0.0	Starting here in La Junta with GAS at right (This is your next to last gas; fill it to the top here and at next station too). Then Winn's Restaurant at right, continue ahead on Hwy #16.
0.8	1.3	Over bridge. **KM 52**.
7.8	12.5	Over hill and slow at bottom for a sharp curve right, then left.
9.8	15.7	Over bridge, then sharp curve right. Note ruins of old bridge below at right.
10.3	16.5	Come to intersection of Hwys #16 and #137, sign says "Hermosillo and Tomachic straight. Creel, left." Four years ago this junction was marked by a tumbledown shack. Now it's replaced by 2 log cabins. Prosperity has struck!
11.1	17.8	Down long hill with double S curve.
11.9	19.0	Past Parrahuirachic to right.
13.4	21.4	Thick young apple orchard on right and left. Mountains in view ahead also on right and left.
19.5	31.2	Leave flatland and start uphill thru thick woods.
22.0	35.2	Climb another very steep hill. Now thru pine forest. Come to summit. Altitude 7,400 feet. **KM 184**.

REMEMBER: On downhill stretches, brake with your motor – not your brakes. A burning smell means you've used your brakes too much. If you can, pull over and let them cool for ten minutes or so.

MI	KM	
26.8	42.9	Steep drop down into canyon. Watch for S curves.
28.2	45.1	Over bridge and end of descent. Altitude 6,500 feet.
30.0	48.0	Past Cieneguita (Little Swamp). Then up steep curves left and more!
32.0	51.2	Top another hill and start winding down. Careful on steep downhill grade.
33.6	53.8	Over bridge. Farm buildings to left.
36.0	57.6	This part of road not as recently paved as previous 35 miles.
41.6	66.6	Careful for "topes" (6 sets thru town) as you enter Tomochic. Watch for burro in middle of street.
42.0	67.2	Pass GAS station left (Diesel). Watch for unmarked "topes."
43.0	68.8	Pass Cabaña Negra (Black Cabin), left.
48.8	78.1	Curve left and over bridge.
49.5	79.2	Sharp curve left, then right, and continues to curve.
53.2	85.1	Thru scattered community with no name. **KM 235**.
54.3	86.9	Thru village of Agua Caliente. Checked out ojo de agua here –nothing doing (hole in farmer's yard). **KM 237**.
55.3	88.5	Thru village of La Ahumada. Note that the roofs are wider than the houses, forming an overhang so you don't get wet while you open the front door.
58.0	92.8	Pretty river down below to right.
59.0	94.4	Note colossal cliffs, caves and rock formations to right.
61.0	97.6	Thru nice farming area.
65.2	104.3	Come to another summit at 7,300 feet altitude.
66.0	105.6	Thru village of El Perico ("The Parrot").
69.4	111.0	Past Tonachic airport at right. **KM 261**.
70.4	112.6	Past Motel Villa Alpina on left.
70.8	113.3	Thru village of Tonachic.
72.8	116.5	River to left.
75.7	121.1	Pass side road (left) to San Juanito. It will be a great shortcut to Creel when it is paved. State judicial police check point.
77.9	124.6	Thru village of El Tocolote.
78.7	125.9	Come to junction (left) with road that leads to Basaseachic National Park (Cascade falls 3 km). Hotel Alma Rosa –ECON– very nice, but ask for rooms in back, front rooms are basic. Restaurant. Overnight dry parking for RV's. Ph: (Chihuahua) (614) 142-3698.

IF TO: Basaseachic National Park, turn left. The parking lot is about 2 miles down the road. The falls are then a 20 minute up and down walk from there (each way). However, you can't see much because you will be on the "back side" and will only be able to see the water go over the edge and not see it actually fall to the bottom. It's a beautifully scenic spot. Plans are being made to open up a new KOA Campground here.

IF TO: Esperanza and Hermosillo, continue straight ahead.

MI	KM	
78.7	125.9	Sign says "Chihuahua's Door to the Sea," Hermosillo 416 KM.
78.8	126.1	Pass doctor's office at right.
79.8	111.4	Thru Baguiriachic. Tire repair shop on right.
81.8	130.9	Pass GAS station, right. **KM 282**.
86.0	137.6	Thru village of Pinos Altos.
95.9	153.4	Careful on twisty, turny downgrade! Over bridge.
97.4	155.8	Reach bottom, then start up again.
97.8	156.5	See the arch in the rock ahead at 11 o'clock high.
98.7	157.9	Thru community of El Potrero.
103.4	165.4	Thru village of Piedras Azules. A Botanist would have a field day here with all this plant variety.
106.0	169.6	Thru lumbermill town of Yepachic. Altitude 5,500 feet. Restaurant Los Pinos and another tire repair shop.
112.0	179.2	Begin long descent. Curves. Red rock landscape with scrub trees.
116.6	186.6	End long descent. Altitude 5,000 feet.
117.0	187.2	Cross state line. Leave state of Chihuahua and enter state of Sonora. Also enter the Mountain time zone, so turn your clock back an hour. Sign says 302 KM to Cd. Obregón. Altitude 4,800 feet.
121.9	195.0	Begin another long descent. Brake with your engine.
122.7	196.3	Careful for steep downgrade into village of Arroyo Hondo. **KM 245**.
122.9	196.6	Thru red rock cut at sides and continuing dramatic rock formations.
125.3	200.5	Pass Restaurant El Venadito, cute log cabin at right.
129.0	206.4	Thru village of Kipor and over Kipor creek.
133.5	213.6	Thru village of Maycoba.
134.2	214.7	Sign says Yécora 47 km.
140.0	224.0	Wide open vistas to right.
146.2	233.9	Cross bridge over river then climb again.
149.5	239.2	More rock formations. Descend to hairpin curve at bottom, cross bridge and up.
150.0	240.0	Rock sculpture at left. Start to climb and then flat.
151.0	241.6	Farm buildings at right.
155.0	248.0	Handsome steep rocks at right.
167.1	267.4	Enter town of Yécora. Population 3,000. **GAS**, at right. RV's can park here at the ball park across from gas station. You'll find a restaurant and a grocery store. There is also Motel Las Brisas (emergency only).
175.0	280.0	Pass big white house and restaurant on right.
176.0	281.6	Magnificent mountains to right.
177.0	283.2	Come to summit. Altitude 6,000 feet. Down very steep descent, open to right.
183.0	292.8	Spectacular view down to right.
189.7	303.5	Crossroads. Santa Ana, right, Santa Rosa, left and San Nicolás, straight. Follow San Nicolás sign.
192.0	307.2	Cactus appear. Altitude 2,800 feet.
195.0	312.0	Pass town of San Nicolás on right, continue ahead. Come to junction (left) with Hwy #117.

IF TO: Esperanza, Cd. Obregón, turn left and start San Nicolás – Cd. Obregón Log (page 86).

IF TO: Hermosillo, continue straight on Hwy #16 using this log.

195.5	312.8	Over bridge.
196.0	313.6	Pass side road (right) to San Garipa.
199.0	318.4	Road has potholes. Watch for rocks on road.
200.0	320.0	Over bridge and thru town of Tepoca. Rough road. A variety of fowl thru here: Hawks, bluejays, roadrunners, etc.
212.0	339.2	Palm trees in view. Can the ocean be far? Congratulations you made it this far.
216.0	345.6	Road flattens out thru scrub trees.
230.0	368.0	Cross El Yaqui bridge over Río Yaqui.

MI	KM	
239.0	382.4	Going up again – about 2,000 feet.
247.0	395.2	Pass San Xavier at right. House with Tecate sign.
254.0	406.4	Flat and straight road. Enjoy!
262.0	419.2	Gas station at left, Nova only. Enter town of Tecoripa. Topes. Altitude 1,300 feet. Good turkey hunting here. Patty's restaurant at left – looks dead.
264.0	422.4	Looks like a straight 78 mile run into Hermosillo, boring but be grateful for it.
284.0	454.4	Note mountains at right, that strange tilted top plateau affair.
289.0	462.4	Thru San José de Pimas. Topes. Green trees, pretty plaza to left. road curves to right (more "topes") and out. Then over puente San José Pimas.
306.0	489.6	Thru El Colorado. Topes. Pretty plaza with Bugambilias and palms, left. Two more topes. over bridge and you're out of here.
324.0	518.4	Majestic Cemento del Yaqui plant, left.
327.2	523.5	Over bumpy RR crossing.
332.0	531.2	Begin divided highway. T.I.F. Plant, right. Industrial Park to right. **KM 4**.
332.9	532.6	Ford plant, right.
333.0	532.8	GAS at right.
333.8	534.1	New Hermosillo subdivision, left.
335.0	536.0	Come to junction with Hermosillo bypass.

IF TO: Nogales and north side hotels, turn right and pick up Hermosillo – Santa Ana Log (page 172) at mile 1.0 of stub from Guaymas highway to Nogales.

IF TO: Guaymas, turn left and pick up Hermosillo – Guaymas Log (page 10) at mile 4.8 of Bypass Hermosillo to Guaymas and Kino Bay stub log.

IF TO: Hermosillo, straight ahead.

End of Special CC

SPECIAL DD START: S. Nicolás, Son END: Cd Obregón

UD-019

98.6 MI or 157.8 KM
DRIVE TIME 2 – 2 1/2 HOURS
SCENIC RATING – 3

0.0	0.0	Having turned onto Hwy #117 here at San Nicolás, continue ahead following Obregón sign.
5.0	8.0	Slow on rough pavement!
10.4	16.6	Cross bridge over arroyo Santana.
12.0	19.2	Road improves a little.
15.0	24.0	Thru town of Curea.
18.5	29.6	Thru town of Tacupeto.
23.4	37.4	Thru town of Palmarita.
27.6	44.2	Very scenic view to right and ahead.
30.2	48.3	Pass side road (right) to Nuri.
43.0	68.8	Pass pink roadside shrine at right.
51.4	82.2	Enter Rosario de Tezopaco, slow for "topes." Turn right at "T" intersection following Esperanza/Obregón signs.
65.4	104.6	Cross over arroyo Santana again. Then a sharp left curve.
86.0	137.6	CAREFUL HERE – A VERY SHARP LEFT TURN after crossing irrigation canal.
87.2	139.5	Enter Hornos and turn left at intersection toward Esperanza.
92.1	147.4	Careful for unmarked "topes" and more traffic.
97.5	156.0	Entering Esperanza. Watch for intersection with Hwy #15.
98.6	157.8	Come to junction with Hwy #15 and end of log.

IF TO: Cd. Obregón and Navojoa, turn left and pick up Guaymas – Navojoa Log (page 13) at mile 72.8.

IF TO: Guaymas and Hermosillo, turn right and pick up Navojoa – Guaymas Log (page 166) at mile 48.0.

End of Special DD

SPECIAL EE *START:* Sonoyta, Son *END:* Pto. Peñasco, Son

UD-019

61.3 MI OR 98.1 KM
DRIVE TIME 1.1 1/2 HOURS
SCENIC RATING — 2

The U.S.-Mexico border is closed here at Sonoyta from midnight to 6 AM daily. There are no **GAS** stations between Sonoyta and Puerto Peñasco; however, there are several **GAS** stations at Puerto Peñasco, and some good hotels and cafes. Remember, too, that this popular Gulf resort is absolutely loaded over Easter weekend with Arizonan fishermen and college kids. No vehicle permit papers are necessary to go to Puerto Peñasco (If entering from Lukeville or Baja California).

Incidentally, the road from Lukeville, the border town in Arizona facing Sonoyta, to Puerto Peñasco was paved in early 1942 by the U.S. Army Corps of Engineers following the Japanese attack on Pearl Harbor. Thinking that similar action might be taken on California's oil deposits and storage, Puerto Peñasco was chosen as an emergency escape route to the sea.

MI	KM	
0.0	0.0	In Sonoyta (population,15,000), after passing customs and immigration, right, proceed ahead.
1.3	2.1	Curve right uphill past a basketball court on left then wind down hill.
1.9	3.0	Left to statue of Plutotarco Calles, educator.
2.1	3.4	Over bridge and pass **GAS** station (they accept US $) on left.
2.2	3.5	Then veer right onto Hwy #8 (straight, Hwy #2, goes to Caborca) past Motel San Antonio at right.
2.3	3.7	Pass Motel Sol del Desierto (clean, color TV) at left.
2.6	4.2	Pass telegraph office on right.
2.8	4.5	Pass new Palacio Municipal (City Hall). **KM 1**.
3.7	5.9	Over a vado (dip). Then fairly sharp curve left and over another vado. You'll go over lots of vados on this road, but you can easily take them at 55-60 mph.
8.2	13.1	Slow a little for poorly banked right curve. Ditto for a left curve.
10.1	16.2	Pass side road (left) to Rojillo microwave station.
11.8	18.9	Note rugged El Encantado (The Haunted) Mountain up at left.
14.0	22.4	Watch for precaution sign.
15.6	25.0	Slow for poorly banked right curve.
16.2	25.9	Begin long straight stretch of 6 miles.
23.1	37.0	Curve right.
24.3	38.9	Pass side road (right) to rancho El Pich.
25.7	41.1	Rest area, no restrooms, only a table and BBQ pit.
25.8	41.3	Slow for bump in road.
26.6	42.6	End vado zone.
28.1	45.0	Note microwave tower of San Pedro off to right on mountaintop.
30.0	48.0	Curve right. **KM 44**.
30.4	48.6	Pass Ejido Puerto Peñasco.

By the way, an ejido is a government-sponsored community agriculture project — you'll pass many of these on your Mexico motor trip. They usually have fancy names, like famous revolutionary heroes, ex-presidents or historical dates. There are about 30,000 ejidos throughout Mexico. The concept of some land for every Mexican was one of the tenets of the Revolutionary struggle in Mexico. The ejido system has been eliminated in modern times, but the names and signs live on.

34.4	55.0	Over a couple of bridges over usually bone-dry Rio Sonoyta. Then thru Ejido Nayarit and pass trail right to El Pinacate Natural Park.

31.8	50.9	Rest area (no restrooms).

31.8 50.9 Rest area (no restrooms).

41.5 66.4 How would you like to be stranded on top of those mountains over to your right?

47.5 76.0 Ah, trees — and wide spot of El Oasis.

55.6 89.0 Thru Ejido Las Lágrimas.

59.6 95.4 Propane, right.

59.9 95.8 Public storage, right.

61.5 98.4 Airport at right. Then Motel Mar y Sol at left.

62.0 99.2 1 KM to **GAS**.

62.6 100.2 Pass side road (right) to Cholla Bay where there's a fishing club whose membership is mostly from Phoenix and Tucson. Then enter Puerto Peñasco, also known as Rocky Point to residents of Arizona. School at right and athletic field at left.

62.7 100.3 Pass Motel Parada del Leon on left.

62.8 100.5 Pass **GAS** station at left. Then pass little plaza at left.

63.1 101.0 Then more **GAS** at right, then stoplight

63.4 101.4 **GAS** on left. Pick up railroad at right (Mexicali branch line). Then come to side street left that leads to Motel Villa Granada, two short blocks.

63.6 101.8 Now, one long block past power station, turn right on paved street, and over railroad and ahead toward beach.

63.8 102.1 Stoplight. Right is to beach hotel, Playa Bonita.

63.9 102.2 Motel Señorial at left. Then a block later is Posada Colonial at left.

64.1 102.6 Turn left at Gulf waterfront onto grounds of Playa Hermosa Resort Hotel and RV Park.

64.2 102.7 Come to Freemont road, also known as Las Conchas road. Palacio Municipal ahead on left. A left turn here goes to Las Conchas development. Then to the left are several RV parks and hotels (see map on page 89).

64.5 103.2 Curve right, then left, to go to hotels Costa Brava and Viña del Mar. See Pto. Peñasco Eat and Stray (page 100) for accommodations.

End of Special EE

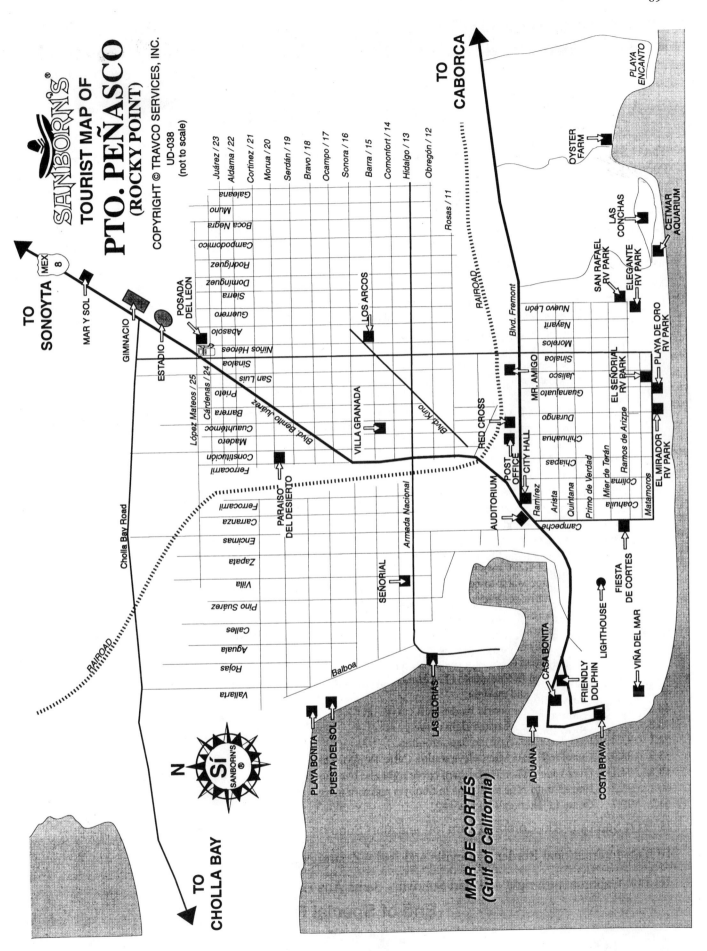

SANBORN'S®
TOURIST MAP OF
PTO. PEÑASCO
(ROCKY POINT)

COPYRIGHT © TRAVCO SERVICES, INC.

UD-038
(not to scale)

SPECIAL FF *START:* Pto. Peñasco, Son *END:* Sonoyta, Son

UD-019

61.3 MI or 98.1 KM
DRIVE TIME 1 1/2 HOURS
SCENIC RATING — 2

The U.S.-Mexico border is closed at Sonoyta from midnight to 8 AM daily. There are no gas stations between Puerto Peñasco and Sonoyta; however, there are several gas stations at Puerto Peñasco, so fill up here. Remember, too, that this popular Gulf resort is absolutely loaded over Easter weekend with Arizonan fishermen and college kids. Incidentally, the road from Lukeville, the border town in Arizona facing Sonoyta, to Puerto Peñasco was paved in early 1942 by the U.S. Army Corps of Engineers following the Japanese attack on Pearl Harbor. Thinking that similar action might be taken on California's oil deposits and storage, Puerto Peñasco was chosen as an emergency escape route to the sea.

MI	KM	
0.0	0.0	Starting at junction of Hwy #8 and Freemont road (that goes to Caborca and Desemboque) with Municipal building behind you at right, proceed ahead on Benito Juárez Blvd.
0.3	0.5	Now, one long block past power station.
0.7	1.1	**GAS** at right.
0.9	1.4	Pass side street (right) that leads to Motel Villa Granada, two short blocks away. Pick up railroad at left (Mexicali branch line). Then more **GAS** at left and again on right. Then pass little plaza at right. Pass **GAS** station at right.
1.5	2.9	Athletic field at right and school at left. Road narrows. Then leave Puerto Peñasco, also known as Rocky Point to Arizonans. Pass side road left to Cholla Bay where there's a fishing club whose membership is mostly from Phoenix and Tucson.
2.5	4.0	Motel Mar y Sol at right.
3.4	5.4	Airport at left.
4.2	6.7	Pass Peñasco Security Storage, left.
4.5	7.2	Lp gas. left. Now begin 28 miles of mostly straight road.
13.1	21.0	Ah, trees — and wide spot of El Oasis.
14.0	22.4	Pass side road (right) to Ejido Fco. Zarco. Look for hawks, eagles, ravens, doves, coyotes etc.
16.2	25.9	How would you like to be stranded on top of those mountains over to your left? Pinacate mountain reaches a height of 1,206 meters.
29.4	47.0	Pass orange water tower and trail (left) to El Pinacate Natural Park. Then thru Ejido Nayarit and over a couple of bridges over usually bone-dry Río Sonoyta.
32.3	51.7	Roadside rest area. No restrooms.
33.4	53.4	Note microwave tower of San Pedro off to left on mountaintop. **KM 45.**
37.5	60.0	Begin series of vados (dips).
40.0	64.0	Pass side road (right) to Rancho El Pich.
45.6	73.0	Note rugged El Encantado (The Haunted) Mountain up at right.
46.5	74.4	Pass curio stand on right.
48.7	77.9	Slow a little for poorly banked left curve.
48.8	78.1	Slow for poorly banked right curve.
52.1	83.4	Pass side road (right) to San Jerónimo.
53.7	85.9	Curve left. Pass Microwave station Cerro Rojillo. Then vados, curve right and more vados.
58.8	94.1	Over vados. Then fairly sharp curve right and over another vado.
60.1	96.2	End of vado zone and come to Sonoyta and thru town.
61.7	98.7	Come to junction with Hwy #2.

IF TO: San Luis Río Colorado, turn left and start Sonoyta - San Luis Río Colorado Log (page 98).

IF TO: International Border, Lukeville and Ajo AZ, straight ahead.

IF TO: Caborca, turn right and start Sonoyta - Santa Ana Log.

End of Special FF

SPECIAL GG START: Sonoyta, Son END: Santa Ana, Son

UD-019

161.1 MI or 257.8 KM
DRIVE TIME 3 1/2 TO 4 HOURS
SCENIC RATING — 2

This is a very scenic drive in the spring after rains. It has a 50-mile stretch of washboard road. All rest areas are without restrooms unless otherwise noted, but they do have tables and BBQ pits.

MI	KM	
0.0	0.0	At U.S.- MEXICO border at Sonoyta (sometimes spelled Sonoita), having obtained and/or validated
1.3	2.1	Cross bridge over dry Rio Sonoyta.
2.0	3.2	Take LEFT FORK here at junction; right would take you back to San Luis Rio Colorado. **GAS** (diesel, too) and convenience store at left (clean restrooms).
2.3	3.7	Pass Excelsior Motel and Restaurant at right. Best in town (100 a/c rooms). Then Motel San Antonio next door (26 fairly nice units; pool).
2.4	3.8	Ahead is Motel Nora on Hwy #2. Then take LEFT FORK and continue ahead on Hwy #2. Right fork is Hwy #8 down to Puerto Peñasco ("Rocky Point").

IF TO: Puerto Peñasco, start Sonoyta - Pto. Peñasco Special (page 87).

2.5	4.0	Just beyond the junction, pass Motel Desert Sun and Restaurant at right - 50 a/c units. **GAS**, at right. Then Motel Nora - 23 a/c units; pool; restaurant; MC, VI.
2.8	4.5	Sharp curve left and uphill. **KM 255.**
4.3	6.9	Another curve left winding uphill. **KM 250.**
6.5	10.4	Pass side road (left) to Club Venadelo.
10.0	16.0	Those are the Cubabi Mountains off to left.
14.7	23.5	Pass Ejido Lázaro Cárdenas. Then Ejido Patria Mexicana.
16.4	26.2	Roadside rest area and little shrine at left. Interesting rock formations.
18.2	29.1	End of "free zone." Slow for customs inspection station ahead.
19.2	30.7	Come now to San Emeterio check station. Pull over to right and stop for customs and immigration check. That's Mt. Quitovac off to right ahead.
20.5	32.8	Microwave station Cerro La Silla at right, and also roadside park at right. Continue downhill straight road for a while.

REMEMBER: On downhill stretches, brake with your motor — not your brakes. A burning smell means you've used your brakes too much. If you can, pull over and let them cool for ten minutes or so.

22.5	36.0	Down thru cut. Then bend left and a long straight stretch.
25.1	40.2	Side road (right) to Rancho San Antonio. Rancho Los Torritos at left. Thru Villa Hermosa.
28.6	45.8	Pass Restaurant San Jorge on right. More straight road, some rough patches.
36.0	57.6	Down thru dip over dry Río El Sahuaro.
38.5	61.6	Pass trail (left) to Rancho Viet Nam. Then Ejido Río Escondido at right.
47.0	75.2	Over dry Río El Cozón ("The Kick"). El Cozón Mountains to right.
51.8	82.9	Side trail (left) to microwave station Cerro Gamo ("Buck Hill").
55.5	88.8	Truck stop restaurant and settlement of San Luisito ("Little San Luis").
65.5	104.8	El Coyote Mountains 'way off to left.
68.2	109.1	Pass Rancho San Pedro Restaurant, right.
69.8	111.7	Rest area at right.
80.6	129.0	Past Cerro Basura (Garbage Hill) microwave tower.
91.5	146.4	There's Caborca in the distance. Pemex **GAS** station to right
92.3	147.7	Ignore abandoned customs check station.
94.3	150.9	Come now to side road (right) into Caborca (population 90,000), discovered in 1693 by Padre Kino who built a mission known as La Concepción de Nuestra Señora de Caborca. The Magdalena River has, thru time, destroyed the rear part of the mission but it has been restored.

Back in 1857, a free-booter from the States by the name of Henry A. Crabb tried to take over the town, but his men were beaten off by the Caborca people with some timely assistance from the Sonora State Troopers plus the folks from the Altar area. Every year on April 6th, they celebrate the Big Day here in Caborca. In Mexico, any town that beats off invaders gets to call itself "heroica" which of course means "heroic." So if you see Caborca written with an "H" in front of it you'll know that stands for *Heroica*. Today Caborca (whose Pima name means "small hill") is a prosperous agricultural and livestock center with many vast vineyards in the surrounding area. The town's Grape Fair and Fat-stock Show takes place during the first half of July.

IF TO: Desemboque, turn right and start Caborca - Desemboque Special.

MI	KM	
94.5	151.2	Asadero Ruffo Restaurant, clean, Gringo style, (Open 7 AM till 1 AM), across street from Beep-Beep Hamburgers with playground for children. Then good 2-story Motel El Camino at right, 90 A/C units; pool; central heat; AE, MC, VI; restaurant-bar; best place in area) PH: (637) 372-0455 Fax: 372-0627. If to OK Motel Posada Caborca (70 A/C units, heat, pool, big dining room, MC, VI PH: 372-1993), turn right beyond El Camino onto wide street leading into town - it's just ahead on right beyond bumpy railroad. Caborca is a rather nice town - drive down their main street and have a look. On side road into town, there is **GAS** over at right.
95.0	152.0	Pass cemetery on right and curve right.
95.2	152.3	Over railroad (STOP-LOOK-LISTEN). Then pass a couple more roads at right into town.
95.4	152.6	Pass Motel Los Arcos, clean, MOD, on highway.
96.0	153.6	Slow! School zone.
96.5	154.4	Cross Río Magdalena and take leave of Caborca.
98.3	157.3	Monument marker at left commemorating building of this highway.
98.5	157.6	Vineyards on left and right.
101.0	161.6	Little town of Pitiquito at right. **GAS** at right. Here is Misión San Diego del Pitiquito built by Padre Kino in 1706 and rebuilt by the Franciscans between 1768 and 1778.
101.1	161.8	Pitiquito leather factory, right. For factory prices visit sales room. Uphill curve right and over into nice farming valley.
103.0	164.8	Road at left takes you back to Caborca.
103.2	165.1	Over bumpy railroad crossing then long curve right and then straight. The next 50 miles is washboard road.
105.5	168.8	Slow for dangerous right curve.
105.8	169.3	Pass side road (right) to Llano Blanco.
110.0	176.0	Pass Ejido 16 de Septiembre on left. Note blue plastic killer bee traps on trees.
115.0	184.0	Enter little town of Altar (population 10,000). Careful for *topes* in and out of town. Motel Maria Elena at right (fair; 17 A/C units). Then **GAS** at right. Pass side road (left) to adobe village of Tubutama where there's another of Padre Kino's missions (Mision San Pedro y San Pablo Tubutama). Then pass church (dating back to 1880's) at left with nice little plaza just beyond. Over bridge over Río Altar. More *topes*.
115.7	185.1	Pass side road (right) to Los Chacuales.
116.8	186.9	Obligatory sanitation inspection stop for all vehicles.
118.0	188.8	Cerro Altar microwave station at right.
121.1	193.8	Pass Telemex substation on left.
130.5	208.8	Pass side road (right) to Rancho El Prieto.
133.3	213.3	Pass trail (right) to Estación Trincheras.
134.1	214.6	Cross bridge over Río de las Pedradas.
134.5	215.2	Molino Del Viento microwave station on right.
138.9	222.2	From elevation of 2,100 ft, begin downhill run.
141.3	226.1	Thru settlement of El Ocuca. (elevation 2,000 ft.)
147.9	236.6	Pass Rancho San José de Purira, right.
152.6	244.2	Pass side road (right) to Rancho El Socorro.
154.4	247.0	Ranch on right sells quarter horses and alfalfa.
155.4	248.6	Curve right then left uphill. Then over another bridge.
157.4	251.8	Curve left uphill, then right downhill.
157.5	252.0	There's Santa Ana ahead in distance.
158.8	254.1	Pass **GAS** and centrifugal diesel. Restaurant.
159.5	255.2	Ejido Santa Marta at left and Santa Ana Viejo at right.
160.3	256.5	Enter little city of Santa Ana (population 18,000). Then cross Río Magdalena. Gas at left. Then over railroad crossing (STOP-LOOK-LISTEN). AA Grupo Santa Ana (8 PM on M-W-F-Sat).
161.1	257.8	Come now to junction Hwy #15 (locally known as "Carretera Internacional"). **GAS** station at right and end of log. San Francisco Motel Ph: (641) 234-0322 and Restaurant ahead at left and Motel Elba —MOD— and Restaurnt (open 6 AM till 11 PM, serve 1/2 order for those with small appitites) MC, VI, Ph: (641) 324-0316, 324-0777, or 324-0178, to right on Hwy #15. For Punta Vista RV Park, Av Juárez #300, run by nice

folks, Ana and Edgar Osuña, turn right onto Hwy #15 go 0.7 miles south; it's on top of hill. It's humble, but clean. Then Motel San Carlos (50 rooms and less expensive than El Camino across the Hwy. Ph: (641) 322-1300 or 322-3698.)

IF TO: Hermosillo, Guaymas, etc., turn right and start Santa Ana - Hermosillo Log (page 8).

IF TO: Nogales, Agua Prieta, Douglas, etc., turn left at junction and start Santa Ana - Imuris Log (page 174).

End of Special GG

SPECIAL HH START: Caborca, Son END: Desemboque, Son

UD-019

63.1 MI OR 101.0 KM
DRIVE TIME 1 1/2 HOURS
SCENIC RATING – 3

This is a completely undeveloped area with no facilities, but a nice beach. It is of interest mainly to fishermen. The drive is pretty, though. Desemboque was the original home of the Seri Indians, but there's little to recommend the town. The comercial fishing has played out and there's an air of decay about the place.

MI	KM	
0.0	0.0	Having turned onto AV. Obregón, continue westward.
0.1	0.2	Pass **GAS** on left. Fill up here as there is no gas in Desemboque.
0.2	0.3	Another **GAS** on left.
0.9	1.4	Past Caborca Chrysler dealership, continue staight ahead at signal with Nissan dealership left.
1.8	2.9	Sign says 98 KM (60 MI) to Desemboque.
2.9	4.6	Watch for cattle. Olive Pedro Domeq distillery on left, then Pasamex, a raisin processing plant on right.
4.1	6.6	Pass Planta Viticultura de Caborca (winery), right.
4.6	7.4	Airport on right. Airtaxi? or aerial spraying?
5.4	8.6	Thru a series of *vados* ("dips").
6.5	10.4	Virgen of Guadalupe shrine on left. Curve left, then right.
8.1	13.0	Thru another series of *vados*.
9.3	14.9	Another winery at right (Wine Society of Caborca).
10.8	17.3	Pass side road (Hwy #29) to airport. Then past Domeq Vineyards on left for several miles.
12.7	20.3	CIANO agricultural experimental farm on left.
13.3	21.3	Sign says Desemboque 80 KM (48 MI).
15.2	24.3	Past Ejido Jesús García on right, an emergency gas stop.
15.7	25.1	Bizani II road, left.
16.7	26.7	Winery (VEPCAI) Co-op – vinyards on both sides of roadway.
17.2	27.5	Pass side road (right) to San Ysidro.
17.4	17.8	Olive orchards on both sides now.
18.6	29.8	EJEL MEXICO, then slow for vado.
20.4	32.6	Pass side road to Los Angeles. Then past Campo El Samurai and more vinyards on left and right.
26.2	41.9	Ejido San Pedro on right.
28.5	45.6	Pass rancho "You name it" packing house and vineyard on left.
30.1	48.2	Pass village El Coyote, on left. Vinyard on right, also olive tree grove.
35.0	56.0	CFE – Electrical substation on left and ice factory.

IF TO: PUERTO PEÑASCO, via only partly paved road (it's passable, but really rough), turn right.

IF TO: Desemboque, straight.

37.3	59.7	Careful for killer *topes*.
40.0	64.0	Rancho El Pino. **KM 66**.
41.2	65.9	Pass side road (right) to Rancho Delicias.
44.1	70.6	Pass rancho Santo Niño, then rancho Los Hermanos.
51.0	81.6	Pass side road (left) to El Cerrito.

MI	KM	
53.1	85.0	Rancho Vides del Desierto, right – quite a spread.
55.8	89.3	Pass side road (right) to El Oasis, then curve left and uphill.
58.1	93.0	Begin green fields (in April) some with wheat.
62.5	100.0	Uphill curve left and enter Desemboque.
62.6	100.2	"Soon" to be RV park, Horizonte Azul.
62.9	100.6	Over series of killer *topes*.
63.0	100.8	End pavement and onto beach.
63.1	101.0	Lighthouse of the Virgin of Guadalupe on hill at left.

RETURN LOG: DESEMBOQUE TO CABORCA

0.0	0.0	Starting here in Desemboque at beach with lighthouse on hill at left, proceed ahead.
0.2	3.2	Over series of killer *topes*.
0.5	0.8	"Soon" to be RV park, Horizonte Azul. Downhill curve to right as you leave Desemboque.
4.9	7.8	Note green fields (in April) some with wheat.
7.2	11.5	Downhill and curve right. Then pass side road (left) to El Oasis.
9.9	15.8	Rancho Vides del Desierto, left – quite a spread.
12.0	19.2	Pass side road (right) to El Cerrito.
18.9	30.2	Pass rancho Santo Niño, then rancho Los Hermanos.
21.8	34.9	Pass side road (left) to Rancho Delicias.
23.0	36.8	Rancho El Pino. **KM 66**.
25.7	41.1	Careful for killer *topes*.

IF TO: Puerto Peñasco, via only partly paved road (it's passable, but really rough), turn left.

IF TO: Caborca, straight.

28.0	44.8	CFE – Electrical substation on right and ice factory.
33.0	52.8	Pass village El Coyote, on right. Vinyard on left, also olive tree grove.
34.5	55.2	Pass rancho "You name it" packing house and vineyard on right.
36.8	58.9	Ejido San Pedro on left.
42.6	68.2	Pass Campo El Samurai and more vinyards on left and right. Then pass side road to Los Angeles.
44.4	71.0	Slow for vado. Then EJEL MEXICO.
45.6	73.0	Olive orchards on both sides now.
45.8	73.3	Pass side road (left) to San Ysidro.
46.3	74.1	Winery (VEPCAI) Co-op – vinyards on both sides of roadway.
47.3	75.7	Bizani II road, right.
47.8	76.5	Pass Ejido Jesús García on left.
50.3	80.5	CIANO agricultural experimental farm on right.
52.2	83.5	Domeq Vineyards on left. Then pass side road, right, (Hwy #29) to airport and on to Puerto Lobos.
53.7	85.9	Another winery at left (Wine Society of Caborca).
55.0	88.0	Thru a series of *vados* ("dips").
56.5	90.4	Curve right, then left. Virgen of Guadalupe shrine on right.
57.6	92.2	Thru another series of *vados*.
58.4	93.4	Airport on left. Airtaxi? or aerial spraying?
59.0	94.4	Past Planta Viticultura de Caborca (winery), left.
60.1	96.2	Watch for cattle. Pasamex, a raisin processing plant on left, then Olive Pedro Domeq distillery on right.
62.1	99.4	Enter Caborca. Continue staight ahead at signal with Nissan dealership right. Pass Caborca Chrysler, left.
62.8	100.5	Pass Pemex **GAS** on left.
63.0	100.8	Come to junction with Hwy #2.

IF TO: Sonoyta, turn left and join Santa Ana - Sonoyta Log at mile 68.8.

IF TO: Santa Ana, turn right and join Sonoyta - Santa Ana Log (page 91) at mile 94.3.

End of Special HH

SPECIAL II *START:* Santa Ana, Son *END:* Sonoyta, Son

UD-019

159.6 MI or 255.4 KM
DRIVE TIME 3 – 4 HOURS
SCENIC RATING – 2

NOTE: This highway sort of parallels the border - it gets a bit lonesome. It also has a 50-mile stretch of washboard road.

MI	KM	
0.0	0.0	Having turned off Hwy #15 here at junction in Santa Ana, proceed up street. Cafe Tecolote ("Owl") at left. Then LOOK-&-LISTEN as you cross main line of railroad. **GAS** station at right.
0.5	0.8	Cross Río Magdalena and leave Santa Ana. Curve left, and road becomes fairly straight.
1.5	2.4	Santa Ana Viejo ("Old Santa Ana") at left and Ejido Santa Martha at right.
2.4	3.8	Pass **GAS** and centrifugal diesel and restaurant.
3.8	6.1	Curve left uphill then right downhill.
5.1	8.2	Curve right and cross bridge over Arroyo del Coyotillo ("Little Coyote's Stream") and curve left.
6.6	10.6	Ranch at left sells alfalfa and quarter horses.
8.4	13.4	Pass side road (left) to Rancho El Socorro. Caution: Washboard road for the next 50 miles.
13.1	21.0	Pass Rancho San José de Purira, left.
20.0	32.0	Thru village of El Ocuca. Altitude 2,000 ft.
25.8	41.3	Molino Del Viento microwave station up at left and cross little Río de las Pedradas. Altitude 2,350 feet.
30.0	48.0	Pass side road (left) to Estación Trincheras down on railroad.
32.8	52.5	Pass side road (left) to Rancho El Prieto.
42.2	67.5	Past Telemex substation on right.
45.3	72.5	Past Cerro Altar microwave station up at left.
47.6	76.2	Pass side road (left) to Los Chacuales.
48.0	76.8	Careful for "topes"and over Río Altar which is a fork of Río Magdalena and thru little oasis of Altar (population 6,000). Pass church (dating back to 1880's) at right with nice little plaza just beyond. Then pass side road (right) to adobe village of Tubutama where there's "Mision San Pedro y San Pablo Tubutama" built by Padre Kino. Mgas at left. Motel Maria Elena at left (17 fair a/c units). Note La Cuchilla ("The Knife") Mountains over to right ahead. Brick factory to right.
53.0	84.8	Pass Ejido 16 de Septiembre at right. Note blue plastic killer-bee traps on trees.
57.2	91.5	Pass side road (left) to Llano Blanco. Then slow for dangerous left curve.
60.1	96.2	Curve left and over railroad (LOOK-&-LISTEN) – this line runs to Mexicali.
62.3	99.7	Curve right past little town of Pitiquito on left. (In this town is "Mision San Diego del Pitiquito" built by Padre Kino in 1706 and later rebuilt by the Franciscans between 1768 and 1778.) **GAS** at left (but there's a bigger station 6 miles ahead at Caborca). Then out past cemetery at left.
65.0	104.0	Monument marker at right commemorating the building of this highway. This is good farm country.
66.8	106.9	Cross Río Magdalena. Then enter outskirts of booming city of Caborca (population 70,000), founded in 1688 by Padre Kino who built Misión La Concepción de Nuestra Señora de Caborca. (The Magdalena River has thru time destroyed the rear part of the mission, but it has been restored and is still in use.) Skip first paved entrance into town at left ahead as there's a better one a mile farther on.
68.1	109.0	Cross railroad (LOOK-&-LISTEN). Pass cemetery on left.
68.8	110.1	Come now to wide street (left) into town. **GAS** at left (next gas at Sonoyta, 91 miles) and then good 2-story Motel El Camino at right, 90 a/c units; pool; central heat; AE, MC, VI; restaurant-bar; best place in area) Ph: (637) 372-0455 Fax: 372-0627. If to OK Motel Posada Caborca (70 a/c units, heat, pool, big dining room, MC, VI, Ph: (637) 372-1993), turn right beyond El Camino onto wide street leading into town - it's just ahead on right beyond bumpy railroad. Caborca is a rather nice town - drive down their main stem and have a look.

Back in 1857, a free-booter from the States by the name of Henry A. Crabb tried to take over the town, but his men were beaten off by the Caborca people with some timely assistance from the Sonora State Troopers plus the folks from the Altar area. Every year on April 6th, they celebrate the Big Day here in Caborca. In Mexico, any town that beats off invaders gets to call itself "heroica" which of course means "heroic." So if you see Caborca written with an "H" in front of it you'll know that stands for "Heroica." Today Caborca (whose Pima name means "small hill") is a prosperous agricultural and livestock center with many vast vineyards in the surrounding area. The town's Grape Fair and Fat-stock Show takes place during the first half of July.

IF TO: Desemboque, turn left and start Caborca - Desemboque Log.

MI	KM	
71.8	114.9	Pass **GAS** at left.
82.7	132.3	Note Cerro Basura (Garbage Hill) microwave station at right.
90.0	144.0	Curve left and cross Río El Coyote and thru wide spot of Tajitos.
93.5	149.6	Rest area at left.
95.1	152.2	Past Rancho San Pedro Restaurant, left.
97.8	156.5	El Coyote Mountains off to right.
107.8	172.5	Truck stop settlement of San Luisito ("Little San Luis").
111.5	178.4	Pass side trail (right) to Cerro Gamo (Buck Hill) microwave station.
116.3	186.1	El Cozón Mountains to left and over dry Río El Cozón.
120.0	192.0	Pass Ejido Río Escondido at left.
124.8	199.7	Pass trail (right) to Rancho Viet Nam.
127.3	203.7	Down thru dip over dry Río El Sahuaro.
134.6	214.9	Thru little settlement of Villa Hermosa.
136.3	218.1	These are the Quitovac Mountains.
138.1	221.0	Rancho San Antonio down side road (left). Then Rancho Las Torritos at right.
141.3	226.8	Top of pass. Now down.

REMEMBER: On downhill stretches, brake with your motor – not your brakes. A burning smell means you've used your brakes too much. If you can, pull over and let them cool for ten minutes or so.

142.8	228.5	Here's another Customs Check station name of San Emeterio. Outbound traffic should make like a stop and he'll probably wave you on. This is the limit of the Baja California "Free Zone." In other words, you can move around freely between this point and Tijuana without tourist cards, car permits, etc. (unless you're there more than 72 hours).
146.8	234.9	Roadside rest area and little shrine at right.
147.6	236.2	Past Ejido Patria Mexicana. Then Ejido Lázaro Cárdenas. Those really rocky mountains off to right are called the Cubabis.
159.1	254.6	Curve right and enter town of Sonoyta, sometimes spelled Sonoita. Tierra del Sol Restaurant at left. Then Motel Nora at left (23 A/C units; restaurant; pool; MC, VI). **GAS** station at left.
159.6	255.4	Pass Motel Desert Sun (30 A/C units) at left. Motel Gilmer at left (26 units; pool) and Excelsior Motel (10 A/C units) next door. Slow now! Then come to junction (left) with Hwy #8 down to Puerto Peñasco.

IF TO: Pto Peñasco, start Sonoyta- Pto. Peñasco Special (page 87).

IF TO: San Luis Colorado (Yuma), Mexicali, Tijuana, etc., take LEFT FORK just beyond **GAS** station at right and start Sonoyta - San Luis Rio Colorado Log (page 98).

IF TO: Puerto Peñasco, turn left and start Sonoyta - Pto. Peñasco Log (page 87).

Bear in mind that the U.S. border is only 2 miles (right fork) where there's U.S. gas and a restaurant and motel. If you're tired of traveling in Mexico you can head for home here, take in Pipe Organ National Park, and continue on up to Ajo and Gila Bend, Arizona and on to Phoenix or Yuma. Incidentally, the Sonoyta-Lukeville border is open from 6 AM till midnight.

End of Special II

SPECIAL JJ *START:* S Luis R. Colorado, Son *END:* Sonoyta

UD-019

126.0 MI or 201.6 KM
DRIVE TIME - 2 1/2 - 3 HOURS
SCENIC RATING — 1

NOTE:- If you're heading south into Mexico on Hwys #2 and #15, you must clear immigration at Sonoyta. And you'll need proof of citizenship to obtain your tourist card (and proof of ownership of your vehicle to obtain your vehicle permit at San Emeterio). Better check with a Sanborn's office if you're not sure of your documentation because it's a nuisance to be turned back when applying for Mexico entry papers.

MI	KM	
0.0	0.0	In San Luis at junction Hwy #2 and main street that leads (north) to USA border (and on to Yuma) proceed ahead down wide highway. Watch for stoplights. At second light, pass side road (right) to El Golfo (70 miles) on Sea of Cortés.

El Golfo, short for "El Golfo de Santa Clara," is a small fishing village with a white sand beach that extends for almost 35 miles, and where high northern October tides rise to 40 feet (second highest in world) creating a difference of almost a mile when receding between high and low tides. Consequently, fishermen must anchor more than a mile away from the shoreline.

MI	KM	
1.5	2.4	Motel Continental at right (restaurant, pool, bar). Then Motel El Rey and Sirroco Restaurant at left.
2.0	3.2	Careful as road narrows. Then **GAS** at right. Then Motel Silvia (fair) at left.
3.3	5.3	Baseball stadium and then cemetery, both at right, and industrial park and Coca-Cola at left. Take leave of San Luis and ahead on long, straight stretch into fringe of Altar Desert ("El Desierto del Altar"). Pass livestock quarantine station (left) and school.
14.5	23.2	Make like a stop at plant inspection station at right - you'll probably be waved on.
18.8	30.1	You're only a hop-skip-jump from U.S. boundary - yonder mountain range off to left is in state of Arizona.
27.0	43.2	Desert ejido of Aquiles Serdan at right. Then curve right past lava beds at left.
32.8	52.5	Ejido of Aquiles Serdan #1.
34.5	55.2	And ejido of Aquiles Serdan #2. (Aquiles Serdan, 1876-1910, was a Mexican revolutionary and forefather of Mexican Revolution.)
45.5	72.8	Rest stop and past little shrine at left.
47.0	75.2	Pass truck stop settlement of La Joyita at right. Then easy winding stretch. That mountain at right is Cerro Pinto (2,260 feet). Note microwave relay station on top.
49.5	79.2	Rugged mountain dead ahead (part of Sierra de los Viejos range).
60.5	96.8	Note lava beds at left.
67.0	107.2	Sonora mines and truck stop at left. Then thru El Puerto Pass.
79.3	126.9	Pass volcanic crater over to left and then microwave relay station, also at left.
82.3	131.7	Several craters over to right and another ahead at left.
84.5	135.2	Now thru lava beds for couple of miles.
89.1	142.6	Come now to oasis of Los Vidrios. **GAS** at left (next gas, 37 miles). Slow for vado.
90.3	144.5	Another long mile of lava beds.
93.5	149.6	Cerro Pinacate (3,957 feet), an extinct volcano, is 17 miles off to right.

Before their first lunar mission, American astronauts trained in this area because of the volcano's similarity to the surface of the moon, with mesas and craters and cones and black lava. The old lava flow covers an area near 45 miles long and 30 miles wide. The Papago Indians once called this volcanic region "Tjuktoak" meaning "Black Mountain." Its present name, "Pinacate," came from the name of a local beetle that leaves broad paths in the sand around the extinct volcano when moving in great droves.

MI	KM	
104.8	167.7	Slow a little for fairly sharp left curve.
107.8	172.5	Pass side trail (right) to Ejido Cerro Colorado.
114.0	182.4	Wide spot of El Papalote at right.
116.0	185.6	Past trail right to Santo Domingo.
125.0	200.0	At long last! There's Sonoyta (population 10,000) ahead at right. Or maybe we should say "Sonoita." However, it seems to be spelled both ways on various maps, etc., so we'll stick with the "y" version inasmuch as we started out spelling it that way.

MI   KM

126.0 201.6 Careful now! Come now to important junction. Pass **GAS** at right and TURN LEFT and then wind up over and ahead to border (2 miles) where immigration office is. Just ahead is La Granja Feliz ("The Happy Farm"). This is "Ciudad de los Niños" or Boys Town (or orphanage, not to be confused with Boystown of the red-light district).

IMPORTANT NOTE:- DO NOT TURN RIGHT at junction. You MUST go back to border here and get tourist cards because you won't be allowed to pass San Emeterio customs-Immigration check stop, 17 miles down Hwy #2, if you don't have them. (Although they issue them at San Emeterio, they sometimes run out and then of course you would be forced to return to the border to get them -better not take a chance.)

If you already have your tourist cards, TURN RIGHT and head for San Emeterio where you'll get them validated and also obtain your vehicle permit from BANJERCITO and get inspected by the ADUANA.

IF TO: Santa Ana, Start Sonoyta - Santa Ana Log (page 91) at mile 2.0.

Having driven the 2 miles from junction up to border, stay on Mexican side and drive in and park in median (in front of MIGRACION on west side). This is where you'll get your tourist cards.

There are several eating places in Sonoyta, but there are better ones in Caborca.

There're a couple of fairly good motels ahead in Sonoyta, the NORA and GILMER. Also, there's a third motel, the EXCELSIOR, that's fair and inexpensive with a fairly good restaurant open all night. In addition, the Motel Nora has a dozen spaces for RV's with hookups.

End of Special JJ

SPECIAL KK *START:* Sonoyta, *END:* S L Río Colorado, Son

UD-019

125.0 MI or 200.0 KM
DRIVE TIME 2 1/2 – 3 HOURS
SCENIC RATING – 1

NOTE: Between here and San Luis you'll cross a flock of dips ("vados") for flashflood runoff. As a rule, you can zip right thru them at normal speeds, but we'll try to warn you if and when you can't. Also their is no gas from Sonoyta to San Luis Río Colorado, so fill up before you start.

0.0   0.0   Having taken LEFT FORK at junction of road that goes up to border (right fork) proceed ahead on Hwy #2 and take leave of Sonoyta. Then on straight stretch thru desert.
2.0   3.2   Motel Colores at left (not for you) and airport of sorts.
5.3   8.5   Pass side road (left) to Ejido Morelia.
7.1   11.4   Pass side road (left) to Ejido Josefa O. de Domínguez.
8.5   13.6   Curve left and up and right and down and left again and straight.
9.3   14.9   Pass side road (left) to Santo Domingo.
11.1   17.8   Wide spot of El Papalote at left.
18.0   28.8   Note that we're now right next to U.S. border - you can see fence over at right.
19.3   30.9   Slow a little for fairly sharp left.
20.5   32.8   Curve sharp right alongside base of hill and then up, left, down, right, and straight.
32.5   52.0   Cerro Pinacate (3,957 feet), an extinct volcano, is 17 miles off to left.

Before their first lunar mission, American astronauts trained in this area because of the volcano's similarity to the surface of the moon, with mesas and craters and cones and black lava. The old lava flow covers an area near 45 miles long and 30 miles wide. The Papago Indians called this volcanic region "Tjuktoak" meaning "Black Mountain." Its present name, "Pinacate," came from the name of a local beetle that leaves broad paths in the sand around the extinct volcano when moving in great droves.

36.3   58.1   Down thru little cut and a bit slower for a dip (45-50 MPH) and pass little "oasis" of Los Vidrios.
37.5   60.0   The "R.C." after San Luis mileage sign means "Río Colorado" - the full name of the town is "San Luis Río Colorado."

MI	KM	
41.5	66.4	Lava rock quarry at right.
42.8	68.5	Note we're gradually getting into sandy desert country as you enter a 7-mile stretch of "El Desierto de Altar." Microwave station at right.
49.5	79.2	Now out of dunes and back into brush.
52.5	84.0	Curve left around base of mountains and slow for "vado." Truck stop and restaurant at right.
58.0	92.8	Thru El Puerto Pass and right and left. Then Sonora mine and truck stop at right.
64.1	102.6	Now right and continue on up.
66.1	105.8	Right again and on up and over and alongside fringe of mountain range for 6 miles.
72.5	116.0	Now down and straight stretch. Then pass rest stop at right (tree and table).
77.0	123.2	Sahuaro Restaurant at left (only fair).
78.3	125.3	Note road over at left up to microwave station of Cerro Pinto (2,260 feet).
79.3	126.9	La Joyita Restaurant at left (fair). Then little shrine at right and past rest stop.
88.5	141.6	Long desolate straight stretch thru here.
90.0	144.0	Ejido Aquiles Serdán #2.
91.8	146.9	Ejido Aquiles Serdán #1.
95.5	152.8	Now back again into sand country. Thru Ejido Sinolense (strange name).
100.5	160.8	Sand dunes. Then wide right curve.
103.0	164.8	Curve left and note U.S.A. border fence again over at right.
105.8	169.3	Another microwave station at left.
107.5	172.0	Good old U.S.A., just a couple hundred yards to right.
110.5	176.8	Careful now! Pull up and stop at right for fruit and plant inspection (you'll probably be waved on). Then long, straight stretch alongside border to San Luis "R.C."
118.3	189.3	San Luis Gun Club at left. Then Charro Club.
119.5	191.2	Quarantine center for livestock at right and school at left.
121.5	194.4	San Luis cemetery at left, ball park at right, and industrial park and Coca-Cola at left.
122.0	195.2	Now into Mexican border town of San Luis (population 135,000) which has boomed recently.
122.5	196.0	Motel Silvia (fair) at right. Then OK gas at left and Casa Blanca Motel at right.
123.0	196.8	El Rey Motel at right. Affiliated Sirroco Restaurant next door.
123.3	197.3	Good economical Motel Continental at left (restaurant; bar; pool). Bear in mind that Yuma's only 25 miles away and there are dozens of good motels there plus some excellent restaurants.
123.5	197.6	Another gas station at right and another at left. Continue on into San Luis and up their wide main stem. Watch for traffic lights. **GAS** at left (next gas across border in U.S.A., and in Mexicali, 40 miles ahead on Hwy #2).
124.8	199.7	Careful now! If you're planning to go back into U.S.A. and up to Yuma, TURN RIGHT at street just before tall CANADA sign at right. Then go a block and turn left at Hotel Internacional (OK) onto wide blacktop street alongside border fence. Proceed along this street next to fence at right for another block and then stop and TURN IN YOUR CAR PERMIT AND TOURIST CARD(S) - even if you have to get out of your car and take them to the Mexican Immigration officers at the little building ahead.

After you've turned in your entry papers, turn right and into U.S.A. and proceed up to U.S. Customs office. Yuma is 20-odd miles up the pike (US-95) and our affiliated Sanborn's agency in Yuma is located at 670 E. 32nd, suite 11.

Oops! You folks who do not plan to return to U.S.A. here at San Luis Río Colorado, do NOT turn right at tall CANADA sign at right (which is in front of the Canada shoe store), but continue another block till you come to junction with their main north- south street that leads up to border gateway to right.

125.0	200.0	Here's that north-south street that leads (right) to border gateway.

IF TO: Mexicali, Tijuana Continue ahead on Hwy #2 and start San Luis Río Colorado - Mexicali Log (See Mexico's Baja book, page 65). There's an excellent hotel in Mexicali, The Lucerna, plus a Holiday Inn and several good ones in El Centro, California, 10-odd miles beyond Mexicali. Or, you can continue on Hwy #2 and cross over into U.S.A. at Tecate or through Tijuana and on up to San Ysidro and San Diego.

End of Special KK

Puerto Peñasco

UD-019

Area Code — 638
See map on page 90

SLEEPING IN PUERTO PEÑASCO

ALMA MARINA – MOD – 5 A/C rooms across from Sunrise RV Park. Ph: 383-5202 or 383-2590.

CASA DEL MAR — MOD — Beach side apartments in exclusive Las Conchas. Restaurant with international cuisine. Reservations: Clifton Management, 6420 E. Broadway, B300, Tucson, AZ, Ph: (520) 886-5716.

COSTA BRAVA – MOD – Paseo Victor Estrella #41. Best in town. 4 stories, 41 room, 3 suites hotel. All have balconies. Great view of ocean from all rooms. Piano-bar overlooking the sea. Limited secured parking. Restaurant adjacent also excellent, seats 100. MC, VI. Ph: 383-4100, 383-3130 Fax: 383-3621.

EL CID – ECON – Rather spartan 12 unit A/C, 2 story motel a block off highway. No restaurant. Parking.

EL DORADO – ECON – Small, strictly emergency north-end motel. No restaurant.

ELSA – ECON – Good motel with 7 room, 2 apts at Madero # 251 and Calle 25. Weekly and monthly rates. Parking. No credit cards Ph: 383-2406

FIESTA DE CORTEZ – UPPER – Baja California and Ramos Arizpe. Worth the extra money. Beautiful building. 36 rooms are actually small apartments with kitchen facilities. Nice restaurant. (P.O. Box 441 & 448, Lukeville, AZ 85341) Ph: 383-3424, 383-2524 Fax: 383-3788. Phoenix: 674-1804 Tucson: 622-4825

GRANADA DEL MAR – MOD – Av. 18 and Sinaloa final Sur. 18 A/C room hotel next to disco. For the party-hearty crowd. Ph: 383-2742. P.O. Box 30806, Tucson AZ 85751, Ph: 622-4825.

MANNY'S BEACH CLUB – MOD – Calle Primera and Coahuila. Popular with party-hearty folks. 8 room A/C motel near beach. Pricey. Beachfront restaurant, outside tables, atmosphere. MC, VI. Ph: 383-3605 Fax: 383-4472. Sign: "No Shoes, No Shirt, No Problem" and "If our food & drinks aren't up to your standards, please lower your standards." You get the picture.

MAR Y SOL – MOD – Nice, comfy, 15 unit A/C (and heat) motel at north end on highway KM 94. Friendly management. Relatively quiet. We like the place. Ceiling fans. SATV. Restaurant. Bar. Patio BBQ. MC, VI. Parking. Ph: 383-3188, Fax: 383-3190.

PARAISO DEL DESIERTO – MOD – Av. Constitución and Simón Morua. 70 A/C (& heat) beautiful modern rooms. Not on the ocean, but nearby. SATV. Pool. Restaurant. Bar with pool table. Secure parking. MC, VI. Ph: 383-2175 Fax: 383-5272.

PLAYA BONITA – MOD-UPPER – Paseo Balboa #100. 41 A/C rooms on fine sand beach with every room facing the water. Next to Puesta del Sol restaurant. North of Playa Hermosa on beach. MC, VI. Ph: 383-2586, 383-2199. Fax: 383-5677.

PLAYA HERMOSA – ECON – Calle 13 and Armada Nacional behind plaza Las Glorias. 2 stories. 40 A/C rooms plus some kitchenettes. Originally beachfront but landfill spoiled it. MC, VI. Ph: 383-5616 Fax: 383-3714.

PLAYA INN SUITES (Best Western) – MOD-UPPER – Calle 18 and Sinaloa. 2 stories. 80 rooms. Not on beach, but nearby. Continental breakfast and happy hour. Pool. Jacuzzi. Suim up bar. Bar-B-Q court. AE, MC, VI. Ph & Fax: 383-5015. US PH: (Phoenix) 602-899-3722 or 1-800-952-8426.

PLAZA LAS GLORIAS – UPPER – Calle 13 final. 210 A/C rooms. Restaurant. Pool. Jacuzzi. Beach. AE, MC, VI. Ph: 383-6010 Fax: 383-6015.

POSADA DE LEON – MOD – Av. Abasolo and López Mateos on left near stadium as you enter town. 40 A/C rooms. Posada's acceptable restaurant adjacent. Parking. MC, VI. Ph: 383-3997 Fax: 383-3455.

SEÑORIAL – MOD – Calle 13 and Francisco Villa #81. 60 A/C rooms, 2 stories. Dining room specializing in Oriental food and seafood. Pool. Parking. MC, VI. Ph: 383-2065, 383-2120 Fax: 383-3055.

VILLA GRANADA – MOD – Francisco Madero #47 east of main stem. 2 stories, 32 A/C rooms. Restaurant. MC, VI. PH & Fax: 383-2775.

VIÑA DEL MAR – MOD-UPPER – Malecón Kino and Victor Estrella on the waterfront. Popular. 100 A/C rooms. Cafeteria. Bar. Disco. Pool. Small jacuzzi with tepid water. SATV. Sports bar. Boutique. Parking. MC, VI. Ph: 383-3600, 383-3601, 383-3602, or 383-3603 Fax: 383-5361.

EATING IN PUERTO PEÑASCO

COCODRILOS — On Armada Naciona in front of Plaza Las Glorias. Party atmosphere. Seafood. Ph: 383-6376.
COSTA BRAVA – UPPER – On Malecón, faces the sea. Very popular. Mexican or American food, consistently good. A/C. AE, MC, VI. Ph: 383-3130. Fax: 383-3621.
EL ESPACIO – MOD – A 24-hour Restaurant, uphill from El Delfín. Mexican and seafood.
HAPPY FROG – ECON – Restaurant and Taco stand near Hotel Señorial.
LA CASA DEL CAPITAN — MOD — Av. del Agua #1. On top of hill overlooking town and bay. Great views. Seafood appetizer and combination beaf and seafood entries and tacos Open 11 AM till 10PM. AE. Ph: 383-2698, 383-5558.
LA CURVA – MOD – More popular than Los Arcos but just as clean, and same type of cuisine. Serve generous portions. VALUE. Open Mon-Thurs 8 AM till 10:30; Fri-Sun 8 Am till 11 PM Ph: 383-3470
LILY'S – MOD – Next to fish market. Excelent food. Wonderful staff. Open 7 AM till 11 PM. MC, VI. Ph: 383-2510
LOS ARCOS — MOD — Mexican-American steak house and seafood. In attractive brick building on Blvd E. Kino. Signs near railroad crossing on main stem direct you there.
MARISCOS KENO'S – ECON – Across from Señorial. Seafood and tacos. Palapa dining. Across the street is an unnamed taco stand with both seafood and beef tacos. By the way, we eat at taco stands like these if they are busy, which pretty much insures that the food is fresh. Check the kitchen in these places and see if it's clean enough for you.
MR AMIGO'S – On Freemont Rd. turn left at municipal bldg. Mexican/American food. 4 pool tables. Open 11 AM till 10 PM, 7 days a week. Specialties: Shrimp, fish and steaks. Ph: 383-5079.
POSADA – MOD – Near stadium, on left as you enter town. Adjacent to Posada De Leon Motel. Mexican and American food.
PLAYAS DEL REY – MOD – In same area as La Curva and Los Arcos. Good Mexican and seafood. Ph: 383-3821.
PUESTA DEL SOL – MOD – More of a bar on the beach toward Cholla Bay. Mexican-American service, but spotty quality control. Next to Playa Bonita RV Park.
ROCKY GARDEN — Av. Matamoros #146, col El Mirador. Great steaks and fish a la Veracruzana. Live music. Ph: 383-5442. Fax: 383-3550.
THE FRIENDLY DOLPHIN – MOD – Small place on hill in the old part of town. Mexican and seafood. Reasonable. Nothing fancy, but good. Open daily 11 AM till 10 PM. Ph: 383-2608.
THE SMOKEHOUSE — Next to Playa Miramar. Open 7 AM till 11 PM. Ph: 383-2208
VILLA LAS PALMAS – UPPER – Armada Nacional and Pino Suárez. Pricey. Seafood & American food. Live music. CATV. Parking. No credit cards. Open 7 AM till 11 PM. Ph: 383-4311.

CAMPING & RV PARKING

EL SEÑORIAL – MOD – 65 spaces. Cable TV. Laundromat. Showers. Pool. Across the road from Playa Miramar, El Mirador and Playa de Oro. Ph: 383-3530.
EL MIRADOR VILLAGE – MOD – Beachfront park at Av. Matamoros #140-B. 26 spaces with EWS. Toilets. Showers. Bar. Ph: 383-6333.
LAS PALMAR —Next to Playa Bonita. Brand new under developement. 88 spaces.
PLAYA BONITA – MOD – 24 space park north of Playa Hermosa on beach, next to Puesta del Sol restaurant. EWS. Showers. Toilet. Laundry. Rec. room. Boat ramp. Refreshments. Ph: 383-2596, 383-5566.
PLAYA DE ORO – UPPER – Nice big 330 space beachfront park south of town at Matamoros and Sinaloa. All hookups (20-30 amp electricity). Showers. Library. Security. Toilets. Laundry. Storage. Boat ramp. RV supplies. Ice. Fishing supplies. Restaurant. **One of the best in Mexico.** Ph: 383-2668.
PLAYA ELEGANTE – MOD – On the beach near Playa de Oro and owned by Tom & Lucille Juanarena who

originally developed Playa de Oro. The newest and probably the best equipped RV Park in town. Apdo. Postal #101. 205 spaces with EWS. Showers. Spic & span toilets. SATV. Boat ramp. Storage. Library. Coin laundry. Rec. hall. Weekly & monthly rates. Senior discount. Ph: 383-3712. Fax: 383-6071.

PLAYA MIRAMAR – UPPER – 120 EWS space beachfront park past El Mirador. All hookups. Showers. Toilets. Laundry. Ice. SATV. MC, VI. Ph: 383-2587 Fax: 383-2351.

ROCKY POINT RV PARK — 3 miles north of town. 28 spaces. EWS. SATV. Showers Baths. Laundry. Rec. hall. 9-hole golf course. Ph: 1-800-762-5956.

SAN RAFAEL – MOD – Very nice and private RV Park located in Playa Mirador area. Laundromat. 55 spaces with complete hookups. Showers (hot & cold). 24 hour Security guard. Ph: 383-5044

SUNRISE PARK – MOD – Across the road from Miramar and Playa de Oro. 16 spaces. All facilities. Pool. Jacuzzi. BBQ pits. laundry. Library. Kitchen. New, neat and eager to please. Ph: 383-4450

OTHER SERVICES

EMERGENCY NUMBERS – Chamber of Commerce, 383-2848; City Hall, 383-2056; Fire Department, 383-2828; Hospital, 383-2110; Police, 383-2626; Red Cross, 383-2266; Tourism, 383-4129.

FESTIVALS – The Big annual event in Rocky Point is the Día del Marino Carnival, held Feb 20-25.

NOTE : It is illegal (and enforced) to drive an ATV or motorcycle after 6 PM if you are under 18. It is also prohibited to drive an ATV on the beach.

End of Puerto Peñasco Eat & Stray!

Hermosillo

UD-019

Area Code — 662
See map on page 11

HERMOSILLO is a nice town, its founding dating back to the beginning of the 18th century. Today it is the capital of the rich state of Sonora and has an official population of 500,000. It is a principal agricultural and industrial center as well as home of the University of Sonora.

The city offers many fine museums including the beautiful new *"Costumbrista"* (See map on page 11 for location.), converted from the old prison. *Cerro de la Campana* (Hill of the Bell) is also nearby. Of interest downtown is the cathedral and government palace (and mural in central patio) and their beautiful gardens, the plaza and its pretty kiosk, and many old picturesque mansions. Don't hesitate to stroll through downtown and along the town's boulevards shaded by huge Yucateco (Indian Laurels). These trees become the roosting place for literally thousands of birds at dusk. Quite a sight!

SLEEPING IN HERMOSILLO

ARAIZA INN — MOD — Blvd. Eusebio Kino #353 — 60 rooms with A/C. Restaurant. Snack bar. Pool. Tubs. Jacuzzi. Tennis. Golf. AE. Ph: 210-4541, 210-2717. Fax: 210-4541.

BUGAMBILIA HERMOSILLO — MOD — Blvd. E. Kino #712 — Good 60-unit A/C motel on north Hwy #15. Restaurant. Pool. No pets. Parking. AE, MC, VI. Ph: 214-5050. Fax: 214-5252. Mex: 91-800-62333.

CALINDA HERMOSILLO QUALITY INN — MOD — Av. Rosales #86 and Morelia — Highrise 12-story, 110-room A/C hotel in midtown just north of San Alberto. Rooftop gourmet restaurant. Coffee shop. Disco. Bar. Pool. Shops. Parking. AE, MC, VI. Ph: 217-2396. Fax: 217-2424.

EL ENCANTO — MOD — North Hwy #15 — 39-unit A/C motel. No restaurant. Pool. Parking. MC, VI. Ph: 214-4730.

FIESTA AMERICANA — UPPER — Blvd. E. Kino #369 — Highrise 221-room A/C motel at north end of town on Hwy #15 just south of Kino Circle. Restaurants. Bar. Disco. Pool. Shops. Parking. AE, MC, VI. Ph: 259-6000, 259-6011. Fax: 259-6060.

GÁNDARA — MOD — Blvd. Kino #1000 — 180-room A/C motor hotel at Blvd. Kino #1000, Col. Pitic. Restaurant. Coffee shop. Bar. Pool. Parking. AE, MC, VI. Ph: 214-4414, 214-4623. Fax: 214-4241. Mex: 91-800-62-344

HOLIDAY INN HERMOSILLO — UPPER — Blvd. Kino and Ramón Corral #369. 132 rooms. Restaurant and Cafeteria. Lobby bar. Pool. AE, MC, VI. Ph: 214-4570, 214-4206 Fax: 214-6473. US: 1-800-HOLIDAY Mex: 01-800-00999.

KINO — ECON — Pino Suárez #151 Sur — 140-room, 4-story downtown A/C hotel. Restaurant. Parking. AE, MC, VI. Ph: 213-3131 or 213-3151. Fax: 213-3852.

LA FINCA – MOD – Matamoros and Gastón Madrid s/n. 80 A/C rooms. Restaurant. Pool. Sauna. Parking. AE, MC, VI. Ph: 217-1717.

LA SIESTA — ECON — 26-unit A/C motel on north Hwy #15, Blvd. Kino and Primero de Mayo. Good restaurant. Parking. MC, VI. Ph: 214-3989 Fax: 214-3043.

PITIC VALLE GRANDE — MOD — Blvd. Kino and R. Corral — Good 144-unit, 2-story A/C motor inn out on north Hwy #15 across street from Norotel Bugambilia. Supper club. Coffee shop. Lobby bar, live entertainment. Pool. Parking. AE, MC, VI. Ph: 214-4570. Fax: 216-6473.

SAN ALBERTO — MOD — Serdán and Rosales — Big 160-room, 4-story A/C hotel in midtown (basic, some complaints). Restaurant. Coffee shop. Ladies bar. Pool. Gift shop. Beauty and barber shops. Bookstore. Parking. AE, MC, VI. Ph: 213-1840, 212-6314, 213-3736. Fax: 213-1897.

SAN ANGEL – UPPER – Blvd. García Morales #104, Col. El Llano. 184-room A/C motel. Restaurant. Bar. Pool. Parking. Ph: 260-3339.

EATING IN HERMOSILLO

BLOCKY'O CLUB — MOD — Off Blvd. Rodríguez — Nice restaurant and club. Good Sonora beef and Mexican dishes plus salad bar. Disco Friday and Saturday till dawn. Open noon till midnight daily for dining. AE, MC, VI.

EL PALOMINO — MOD — Blvd. Transversal at corner of Calle Bahía — Steakhouse in east part of town. Features wide variety of beef cuts.

FREEDOM — MOD — Blvd. E. Kino #1012, Col. Pitic, across from Fiesta Americana. International Cuisine. Ph: 215-0640 Fax: 215-1300.

HENRY'S — MOD — Blvd. E. Kino #904. Very good restaurant converted from old home on Hwy #15 at far north end across from and beyond Bugambilia Valle Grande. Extremely varied menu. Children's menu. *Tounge Española* — great. Charbroiled steaks a specialty. Seafood. Salads. Open 1 PM till midnight. Mon. - Fri. 1 PM till 5 PM Sat. Ph: 214-7393.

JO-WAH — MOD — Rosales Street — Chinese restaurant on south Hwy #15. Open noon till midnight.

LA SIESTA — MOD — Specializes in huge 2 pound steaks. Located in hotel of same name.

MANNIX — MOD — Blvd. Kino — Popular short-order restaurant just south of Chevrolet agency.

MERENDERO LA HUERTA — MOD — (Eating Place in the Orchard) — Calle 11 #136 Ote. — Seafood restaurant.

MIYAKO — MOD — Carr. Bahía Kino KM 4 — Japanese restaurant atBlvd Encinas #537, Col El Torreón, established by a wealthy local business man who imported chefs from Japan. Surrounded an acre of formal Japanese gardens. Service from counter or from private rooms where you sit Japanese style. Ph: 218-540.

RODEO — MOD — Blvd. Morelos and Av. Deanza — Cafe with open-air patio. Specialties include *carne asada* "Sonora" style and chicken. Open noon till midnight.

SANBORN'S DE HERMOSILLO – MOD – Blvd. Navarrete #182, Col. san Benito. International cuisine. Ph: 215-7515, Fax: 214-7201.

XOCHIMILCO — MOD — Calle Obregón #51 — Package special all parts of cows. Villa de Seris. Ph: 250-4089. Fax: 250-4052.

VILLA FIESTA — MOD — Blvd. Rodríguez and Yañez #33 — Typical gourmet. Ph: 212-1840.

End of Hermosillo Eat & Stray

Kino Bay

UD-019

Area Code — 662
See map on page 46

KINO BAY (Bahía Kino) is divided into two areas — Old (Viejo) Kino southwest of El Desierto gas station and New (Nuevo) Kino where most of the accommodations are located. The area has an easygoing and relaxed atmosphere with excellent sunny weather year 'round, especially during winter when the area fills with long-term tourists. It offers fishing, diving, crabbing, clamming and beachcombing — as well as a very interesting nearby Seri Indian settlement.

The Seri Indians, numbering approximately 500, live primarily in Desemboque (also known as Desemboque del Seri and not to be confused with El Desemboque situated farther north on the coast west of Caborca) and in Punta Chueca on the desert coast of Sonora. The Seris are known for their physical strength and power and have firmly resisted all attempts by the Mexican government to integrate them into today's society. They still preserve something of their pre-Hispanic religion, worshiping such gods as the god of the Center of the Earth (represented as a mole), the god of the Hills, and the god of the Seas. Their main festivals are held in May when the "caguama," or giant turtle, arrives on the shores to nest and in July for the gathering of the pitahaya fruits. (The "pitahaya" is a tall and very spiny cactus with purple flowers and bears an edible scarlet fruit.) On both occasions the tribe gathers to celebrate and feast on the giant turtle and pitahaya honey. The celebration continues with dancing and singing until dawn.

The Seri women weave heart-shaped baskets called *coritas* made from a fiber of the torote plant, which they strip off with their teeth. Then with the aid of a deer bone awl and natural dye, they make baskets valued by tourists and collectors alike. The men make a living from fishing and handicrafts, especially their carvings of animals made from *palo fierro* (ironwood). However, ironwood is be coming scarce, so the Indian craft may soon become a thing of the past. Some of these carvings are works of art and are often considered collectors' items. A smaller female industry bringing in quick cash is that of making shell jewelry. Shell necklaces of intricate design are inexpensive and attractive to tourists.

Punta Chueca, 16 miles from Motel Kino Bay, is the closest of the two Seri villages and can be reached via a dirt road. However, a trip to Desemboque, a rather depressing place 65 miles north of Kino, should be attempted only with a truck or four-wheel drive vehicle. This once self sufficient tribe, its life, history and culture may be seen and studied at the Seri Museum on Mar de Cortés.

Also of interest (especially to nature lovers) is Isla Tiburón. Tiburón is Mexico's largest island and is approximately 29 miles long and 15 miles wide, while its highest point is 4,000 feet. It is a wildlife refuge, rich in plant and animal life, and belongs to the Seri Indians. However, due to its ecological importance, the Mexican government has placed the island "off limits" to the Seris and to tourists. Incidentally, *tiburón* is Spanish for shark.

FISHING — All season fishing from Bahía Kino is one of the major lures to the area. Bottom fishing around nearby rocky points is an experience even a novice may enjoy, especially when reeling in a sea bass or a yellowtail. Launching permits and fishing licenses may be obtained from the Club Deportivo.

EMERGENCIES — Club Deportivo's Rescue One is a group of volunteers who can help in just about any kind of emergency, providing monitoring services and information on CB Channel 4 or VHF Channel 06. If someone is lost or needs assistance at sea or on land, they can mobilize aircraft and seacraft to handle it. Contact them at club, which is across from Kunkaak RV park. (About 1/4 mile off beach, by landing strip.)

There is a resident doctor at the clinic in Old Kino 24 hours a day for emergencies. Besides that there are three other doctors: Raul Figueroa Canizales, located behind the Farmacia Aquario; José Luis González located at Topolabampo and Padre Kino Blvd.; and Jorge Grijalva on Calle Altata; All in Old Kino. Drs. González and Grijalva speak English.

SAFETY — The narrow channel between Isla Tiburón and the mainland is subject to changing winds, strong currents and shifting sandbars. It's no wonder that area is known in Spanish as *El Infiernillo* (Little Hell). Ocean conditions may change rapidly, especially during the summer months. Diving and snorkeling around rocky areas north of Kino Bay can be worthwhile but not spectacular. Sediments cloud the water. Swimming at Kino Bay's beach is relatively safe. At times there are strong currents and beware of the small clear-blue stinging man-of-war Stingray fish (or Jellyfish). If you see them, especially at incoming tide, stay out of the water.

ECOLOGY — The ecological system of the Gulf of California has been deteriorating due to overfishing by large fishing trawlers. In June, 1993, President Salinas de Gortari declared two large areas at the northern Gulf as biosphere reserve. In the most northern area, from San Felipe north to Santa Clara, no fishing or oil drilling will be allowed. In the second area from San Felipe to Puerto Peñasco, shrimp nets will not be allowed and the size of gill nets will be restricted. These measures will be strictly enforced in order to protect the Totoaba, Vaquita and other species from extinction.

VISITOR'S GUIDEBOOK — An excellent handy guide for Kino Bay and vicinity is called *Your Place in the Sun* by Joan Stenberg and Gloria J. McDonagh, published by Kino Publications, Apdo. #135, Bahía de Kino, Sonora.

SLEEPING IN OLD KINO

RV PARK and CABINS — ISLANDIA MARINA — ECON-MOD — Nice folks! **ON** the fishing beach. Follow signs through town. Office at gate. 73 space RV park and 8 cabins on beach, (old, but well-maintained now, value). All hookups. Showers. Restrooms. 8 kitchenettes with 2 beds and 3 cots. Boat ramp and storage. Fish cleaning. 20 AMPS. Pets OK. Ph: 242-0081.

EATING IN OLD KINO

MARLIN PLACE — MOD — Clean, reasonably priced restaurant near Islandia Marina. Seafood specialties. Very good food and service. George, a singing waiter.
DORITA — In front of police station. Serve breakfast and lunch. Open 7:00 AM till 3:00 PM
EL PULPO NUEVO — In town. Seafood specialties.
TAQUERIA PRADO — ECON — Great tacos on the road into town across from park. Open late.

SLEEPING IN NEW KINO

ANCHOR HOUSE — MOD — Bed and Breakfast on beach at 3525 Mar de Cortés. 1 room with king size bed, 1 with 2 double beds and 1 with one double bed. Includes full breakfast and use of all home amenities. All rooms A/C and private bath. Owner, Gloria and Chuck McDonagh. Ph: 242-0141.
BELLA VISTA — ECON — 2 Two-room kitchenette units with double beds. Microwave. Refrigerator A/C. Ph: 242-0139.
KINO BAY — MOD — 8-unit, 2 story A/C motel at north end. Good deal. Small restaurant. 8 kitchenettes. Boat rentals. MC. VI. Ph: 244-0216 or (6) 214-1492 in Hermosillo.
EL SAGUARO — ECON — 4 kitchenette units. Ph: 242-0165
POSADA DEL MAR — MOD — Good value. 48-unit, 2 story A/C motel across from beach. Restaurant. Pool. AE. MC. VI. Ph: 242-0155 or (6) 218-1221 in Hermosillo.
POSADA SANTA GEMA — UPPER — Mar de Cortés and Río Plata. Pricey 14-unit A/C apartment motel. Two bedroom split-level units with bath, kitchen and fireplace. MC. VI. Ph: 242-0024, 242-0002 or 242-0026.
SARO — MOD — 16 rooms. Simple but very neat. On beach. Laundry. SATV. Betty and Saro, owners. Saro is an interesting character, speaks English, Italian and Spanish. Ph: 242-0007.

EATING IN NEW KINO

EL PARGO ROJO — UPPER — Nice seafood and steak place on Av. Del Mar 1426. Across from beach. Green Angels hang out here sometimes. Open 10-12, 7 days. AE, MC, VI. Ph: 248-3340
KINO BAY — MOD — Only place for breakfast. On Beach. Mexican food. Nice atmosphere. Ph: 242-0049

Open 8 AM till 10 PM
VILLAS DEL MAR NAUTILUS CLUB — UPPER — international cuisine and seafood. Closed Tuesday.

CAMPING & RV PARKING

CAVERNA DEL SERI — UPPER — Small 30 spaces on beach at far north end on paved road. All hookups. 14 spaces with patios and shade. Potable water. Restrooms. SATV. Store. Laundry service. Ice. Apartments. English. Boat ramp. 30 AMPS. Club house. Ph: 244-7134 or (6) 214-7134 in Hermosillo.

EL CACTUS — MOD — 33-space park a half-mile off main street on sand road. All hookups. Concrete pads. Showers. Restrooms. Fenced. Some small covered patios. Pool. Laundry service. Pets OK on leash. SATV. Free launching service. Ph: 248-3180 or 244-7032.

KINO BAY — UPPER — Very good 200-space facility in conjunction with motel. All hookups. Shady pull-thrus. Showers. Restrooms. Rec hall. Restaurant. Palapas. Laundry. Dump station. Store. Shaded concrete patios. Boat ramp, dock and rentals. Ice. Bungalows. Fishing supplies and cleaning. English. Ph: 242-0216 or (6) 215-3197 in Hermosillo. 30 AMPS. Apdo. 857-83000, Hermosillo, Son.

KUNKAAK — UPPER — 54 large space with patio and all hookups. Across from Club Deportivo. Potable water. Restrooms. Showers. Rec hall. Laundry — coin. Fish cleaning area. Fishing. Boat launch 0.5 miles away. 30 AMPS. Ph: 242-0209 or 242-0088. Hermosillo: (6) 217-4474, 217-0683 Ph and Fax: 217-4453.

PARADOR BELLA VISTA — UPPER — 18 spaces with all hookups. Concrete pads. Restrooms. Showers. Laundry — coin. 6.5 KM from entrance to Kino Bay, past Posada Santa Gemma. English spoken. Owner Sr. Lorenzo Penelli and his wife, María are very nice hosts. Children welcome. Pets OK. 20 AMPS. 2 furnished bungalows. P.O. Box NR 27. Ph: 242-0139.

POSADA SANTA GEMMA — MOD — Small 14-space park next to motel. All hookups. Restrooms. Showers. Palapa covered patios. Boat ramp. On beach. Store. Grills. 20 AMPS. Ana María, manager. English spoken. MC. VI. Ph: 242-0024, 242-0002 or 242-0001.

SARO — MOD-UPPER — 7 spaces with all hookups. First park on main road to town. Across from hotel by same name. Opposite beach. Owner speaks Italian, English, Spanish. Laundry. SATV. 30 AMPS. Boat access. Beach. Rec hall. Nice management. Ph: 242-0007.

End of Kino Bay Eat & Stray

San Carlos

UD-019

Area Code — 622
See map on page 61

SAN CARLOS (or Nuevo Guaymas, its official name) is a unique resort community nestled between the beaches of the Sea of Cortés and the Bacochibampo Mountains. It was developed as an alternative to the more crowded Mexican vacation spots such as Puerto Vallarta and Acapulco and offers a wide variety of outdoor activities and attracts those looking for a different kind of vacation.

Rafael Caballero, a developer from Nogales, Sonora, is the man behind the San Carlos boom. Having camped near Guaymas as a Boy Scout, he returned as a very young man to buy 17 miles of beachfront along Bacochibampo Bay (Bay of the Sea Serpents) and a 45,000-acre spread. But anticipating land problems, he formed his own *ejido* and ceded some 28,000 acres, including more than four miles of beachfront, to the government for future settlers. The rest was his, free from pressure felt by resort developers all the way to Acapulco.

Today San Carlos is a community with scenic shorelines and calm waters, hotels, motels, condominium apartments, RV facilities, a gas station, a police station (*comisaría de policía*) which is the only authority in San Carlos, fire department, potable tap water and several well-stocked mini-markets.

The San Carlos Country Club (Ph: 226-1102) facilities include a contemporary clubhouse with open terraces looking out onto the bay, a restaurant and lounge, a tennis and golf pro shop, a sauna and a pool. The tennis center is the pride of the country club. There are 13 tennis courts all lighted for night use, including an amphitheater exhibition court. There is an 18-hole, 6,617-yard golf course, designed by Roy Dye, overlooking the sea and small islands rising on the horizon.

San Carlos is famous for its deep-sea fishing. One will find not only an abundance but a bewildering variety of game fish in the Sea of Cortés. Summer offers the most spectacular fishing, but the weather following May is sometimes oppressively hot. The big runs of marlin and sailfish come in the spring, between April and June, but there is game fishing to satisfy the soul of the average angler during fall and winter months, such as roosterfish, trigger fish, sea bass, barracuda, grouper, red snapper, cabrilla, sea trout, yellowtail, dolphin, Pacific whitefish, sierra, giant ray, totuava, and corvina among others. The annual San Carlos International Deep-Sea Fishing Tournament is held in September.

Water sports are excellent here. The beach by most of the hotels is somewhat gravelly with coarse sand. As you go out toward Algodones, though, there are miles of uncrowded, sandy beaches for swimming, strolling, snorkeling, and startling blue water for diving. Skin diving gear is sold and rented at a very good shop adjoining the Creston Motel.

The Marina San Carlos (Ph: 226-1230, Fax: 226-0565) is one of the largest in Mexico with 400 slips for boats from 14-50 feet long. Water, power, concrete ramp and tractor service are available for larger slips. Fishing craft and power boats can be rented, fishing gear can be purchased or rented, and pleasure cruises around the bay area are available. For those wanting to leave their boat in dry storage here, contact the super nice people, Tere and Eddie Grossman at the Marina San Carlos Dry Storage. They will help you with the paperwork.

Located 1/4 mile before the San Carlos Marina entrance is Tetabampo Charter boats. The owner, Sr. Bustamante, has worked in San Carlos for over 30 years and knows all the aspects of the Sea of Cortés sporting arena: fishing trips, scenic cruises and margarita sunset cruises. Yacht charters are $25-40 per boat per day and sunset cruises are $15 per person. Ph: 226-0011.

Pearls of Guaymas - An ocean pearl farm! Gorgeous pearls and mabe pearl creations mounted in Taxco silver or gold made locally. Free tour (Apdo. Postal #484 Bahía de Bacochibampo, Guaymas, Sonora, Mexico, Ph: 221-0136, Fax: 221-0243, Web page on the internet: http://www.perlas.com.mx E-mail: perlas@campus.gym.itesm.mx Exit off Hwy 15 in north Guaymas at intersection to Miramar and Playa de Cortés Hotel. Go about 1 1/2 miles and turn left at the guard gate just left of the arched entrance to hotel. Tell the guard you are visiting the college or pearl farm and you will be admitted. The show room is in the first large building to the left with entrance from the parking lot.

Of interest to scuba divers is the following information: A plane, trains and ferry boats have been sunk in the San Carlos Bay area providing unique and spectacular underwater scenery for divers to explore. The train is located at Punta Doble about 5 miles southeast of Marina Real in about 50 feet of water with an average of 30 feet visibility. The DC-3 plane is located at Los Tres Presidentes about 4 miles southeast of Marina Real in about 45 feet of water and average visibility of 30 feet.

Activities in San Carlos are not confined to fishing, swimming, golf and tennis. One can also hunt from September through March or go horseback riding along the beaches or in the almost barren desert among giant stands of Saguaro cacti. Or one can climb the Cerro del Vigia, a 2000-foot mountain whose summit is reached by a winding and steep dirt road. A few miles north around the bend from San Carlos Bay is Playa de Los Algodones (Los Algodones Beach) where you can enjoy the white sand dunes and beach.

For indoor exercise try Club Verde Gymnasio "Just Do it." It has top-notch equipment, showers, sauna, jacuzzi and an Olympic size out door pool (cold in winter and spring) at a reasonable price (Ph: 226-1206). Turn north at corner of Santa Rosa Market and follow road out to the Ranchitos area toward Loma del Mar subdivision.

San Carlos, where the bare mountains in the background rise to 2,000 feet reflecting themselves in the warm, smooth waters of the harbor, is designed not just as a vacation retreat but also as one of Mexico's retirement communities. In the winter months one will see campers, trailers, and automobiles with license plates from almost every state in the Union. In fact, trailer spaces will be hard to find in winter but are easy to find and less expensive in nearby Guaymas.

Some will find San Carlos a comfortable introduction to Mexico because it is small, well organized and much English is spoken. Others will find it too Americanized for their taste. If that describes you, check out Guaymas, which has a more "Mexican" flavor.

If you are just passing through, consider the Guaymas RV parks. They cost about half as much and are not crowded at all. It will take you about 1/2 hour to drive to them.

Services available in San Carlos include: 4 Pharmacies, 5 doctors, 1 lab clinic, Rescate ("rescue") ambulance, San Carlos Wellness Center, Rotary Club, AA weekly meetings at the Catholic Church, 2 hardware stores, copy and fax center, art galleries, several real estate agencies, and many gift, arts and craft shops.

SLEEPING IN SAN CARLOS

CRESTON — MOD — Very good 24-unit A/C motel on beach. Pool. Shuffleboard. Parking. Pets OK. MC, VI. Ph: 226-0020. Excellent value. Good comments from readers.

FIESTA SAN CARLOS — MOD — Carr. San Carlos KM 8.5 — Nice 33-unit, 3-story A/C motor hotel on beach. It resembles a modern Mayan temple when viewed from the beach. Dining room. Circular pool. Parking. MC, VI. Ph: 226-093 Ph and Fax: 226-0229.

HACIENDA TETA KAWI — MOD — Best Western hotel at Blvd. Manlio Fabio Beltrones. Very nice. 26 Rooms as well as 4 suites with refrigerator. Restaurant. Pool. Parking. AE, MC, VI. Ph: 226-0220, Ph and Fax: 226-0248.

LOMA BONITA — UPPER — At entrance to Country club and shopping center at corner of Paseo de los Yaqui and Av. de los Seris. Great place for families. 69 - 2 bedroom apartments. Pool. Water slides. Jacuzzi. Tennis. Bowling. Parking. AE, MC, VI. Ph: 226-0713. Ph and Fax: 226-0413. US: 1-888-790-0366.

LOS JITOS HOTEL & SPA – MOD – Manillo Fabio Beltrones Km11. 28 rooms. Ph: 226-0092. US: 1-888-790-0366.Fax: 226-1413. E-mail: losjitoshotel@hotmail.com

PLAZA LAS GLORIAS —UPPER — Blvd. Gabriel Estrada s/n, Sector Creston. 33 Deluxe A/C suites (8 with jacuzzi). Tubs. Very nice. Restaurant. Bar. Gym. Tennis. Parking. AE, MC, VI. Ph: 226-1029, 226-1021 Fax: 226-1035. US: 1-800-515-4321 Mex: 01-800-800-2424.

POSADA DEL DESIERTO — MOD — Privada del Delfín #10, close to the marina. 97 A/C rooms. Parking Ph: 226-0072, 226-0122. Fax: 226-0451.

SAN CARLOS PLAZA — UPPER — Mar Bermejo Nte #4, Playas Los Algodones — 172 room hotel. 3 restaurants. Snack bar. Bars. Pool. Night club. Cold water jacuzzi (has to be turned on by staff). Tennis. Health center. Water sports. Horseback riding. Car rental. Boutiques. Ph: 227-0077, 227-0778 227-0779. Fax: 227-0098. US: 1-800-854-2320, Mex: 01-800-716-4368. e-mail: scplaza@tetakawi.net.mx

SUITES MAR ROSA — MOD — On left just before Country Club going into town. 6 A/C units. Kitchenettes. Some queen-size beds, some twin. Ph: 226-0250 Fax: 222-1117.

VILLA SUNSET — Furnished apartments with kitchenette behind El Paradise Restaurant. Ph: 226-0304

EATING IN SAN CARLOS

BLACKIE'S - UPPER - On north side near Banamex. Hogan-style atmosphere. Seafood specialties. Great salads.

CHARLY'S ROCK (Former La Roca) - MOD- Across from Hacienda Teta Kawi. Great waterfront scenery and live music till midnight. Fish and seafood fare only. Ph: 226-0667.

EL BRONCO — UPPER — Across from Gary's. Specialties are steaks, bone marrow soup, pork loin and seafood (not on menu, ask). Good grilled lobster. Open 5 PM till 11 PM. Closed Monday. Sat and Sun, open 1 PM till 10 PM. Ph: 226-1130.

JAX SNAX - MOD - On north side past Banamex. Family atmosphere with daily specials including pizza. No alcohol. Ph: 226-0270.

PELICANO PALAPA - MOD - At Hacienda Teta Kawi by the pool. Good food. Breakfasts are a great "filling"

deal. Open 6 AM til 12 PM. Live music 5-9 PM. Ph: 226-0248.

ROSA'S CANTINA — ECON — Calle Aurora #297 — CABRITO Steak, enchiladas. Casual place, popular with younger folks. Bulletin board for buying, selling, renting or local events. Parking. Open 6:30 PM till 1:30 AM daily. MC, VI. Good value. Ph: 226-1000, 226-0989.

SAN CARLOS GRILL — UPPER — Varied menu. Chicken, fish, steak, crepes. Live music. Trendy. Open 7 days, 1 PM till 11 PM. MC, VI. Ph: 226-0509, 226-0888.

TEQUILA'S BAR & GRILL — ECON — Calle Plutón #27. Great place for breakfast, lunch or early dinner. Fresh toasted whole wheat bread, eggs, sandwiches, smoked bacon, seafood, Mexican dishes. Outside tables with view of Yacht harbor. Across from Lanchas de Pesca de Ostión St. Open 7:00 AM till 11:00 PM Mon, Thurs, and Sun; till 2:00 AM with live music, Tue, Fri and Sat. Good value. MC, VI (with 5% service charge). Ph: 226-0545. E-mail: slice@chipmail.com

THRIFTY ICE CREAM SHOP - Next to Paradise Restaurant, on the right side just past Hacienda Teta Kawi. Treats when you are "hot!"

CAMPING & RV PARKING

EL MIRADOR - UPPER - On Mirador Escencio, Parcela #43, just before the Marina Real. 90 spaces with electricity,water and sewer. Restaurant. 30 amp electricity. CATV. Showers. Tennis. Pool. Clubhouse. Night security. Ph: 227-0213, 227-0107. Fax: 227-0108. e-mail: mirador@tetakawi.net.mx Web page: www.elmiradorrv.com

HACIENDA TETA-KAWI — Across street from the largest San Carlos Beach. Very nice 45 space facility. All hookups. Pull-thru slots. 20 AMPS. Showers. Jacuzzi. Toilets. Self-service laundry. Fish-cleaning room. Concrete patios (some covered). Rancho Grande restaurant at front of hotel is very good. 4 furnished apartments. Mailing address: Apdo. Postal # 71. Ph: 226-0220 Fax: 226-0248.

TOTONAKA — UPPER — 130 space park next to Teta-Kawi. All hookups. 30 AMPS. Showers. Restrooms. Rec-hall. 2 laundries — coin. Restaurant. Bar. Concrete patios. Beach across street. 25 furnished apartments, some with kitchens. SATV. Phone, mail service. Ph: 226-0323, 226-0481, 226-0531 Fax: 226-0523. E-mail: totonakarv@yahoo.com

OTHER SERVICES

AMBULANCE — CUERPO DE RESCATE across from Pemex station, between Venus and Del Gary streets.

FISHING BOATS are available at the Marina San Carlos in a variety of sizes as well as a diesel or gas-operated, fully equipped party boat.

GIFT SHOP — KIAMY'S — next to Creston. Good selection. Open 9 AM till 6 PM. AE, MC, VI. Ph: 226-0400

PHYSICIAN — Dr. Manuel Andueza Quiros. Plaza La Mar #4. Ph: 226-0129 Fax: 226-0097. Home: 221-1081.

REAL ESTATE — H. D. REALTY – Edificio Hacienda Plaza, Luna and Pasoe San Carlos #264. Ph: 226-0297. Fax: 226-0313. e-mail: hdtours@prodigy.net.mx Heriberto Duarte, director.

HACIENDA TOUR AGENCY — National and international flights, tours to famous cities of Mexico and Copper Canyon tours Ph: 226-0297 Fax: 226-0313 Attn.. Heriberto Durante. Apdo. 110, San Carlos, Son. 85506.

SCUBA DIVING gear is available at EL MAR Diving Center on Del Gary St. (next door to Creston Motel) PH: 226-0404. They also offer diving classes, bicycle and kayak excursions and fishing trips.

CANNON BARRITAS, just 12 miles north of San Carlos, is a village with 8 cabins and a clubhouse and offers scuba packages which include transportation, meals accommodations and other amenities, as well as hiking snorkeling, fishing, astronomy, kayaking, bird watching and concepts of ecology. Ph: 226-1414.

KAYAKING and HIKING — A 4-hour trip to Nacapuli Canyon or a visit to the Arches and natural aquarium are available at the Sonora Sports Center. Ph: 226-0929. Ask for Vince or Carl.

End of San Carlos Eat & Stray

Guaymas

Area Code — 622

See map on page 14

SLEEPING IN GUAYMAS

ARMIDA — ECON — Excellent value! On Blvd. García López. 125-unit A/C hotel on Hwy 15 in town practically at junction with main stem. One jacuzzi suite. Restaurant. Bar. Pool surrounded by two-century-old Yucateco trees. Boutique. Parking. AE, MC, VI. Ph: 224-3035, 224-1302 Fax: 222-0044. USA: 1-800-732-0780. Mex: 01-800-647-0500. E-mail: harmida@son1.telmex.net

FLAMINGOS — ECON — North Hwy #15 — 55-unit surprisingly nice motel. Some A/C. Good beds. Restaurant. Bar. Pool. Parking. MC. VI. Ph: 221-0961. Fax: 221-2061.

IMPALA — ECON — Calle 21 #40 — 46-room, 3-story A/C downtown hotel. Restaurant. On-street parking. Ph: 222-6056, 224-0922.

LEO'S INN — ECON — VALUE! Bacochibampo Bay — Small 15 A/C rooms. Beachfront inn in Colonia Miramar. Very pretty grounds No restaurant (but Venenos next door). Parking. Ph: 221-0104, 222-1337, 222-9490. (Turn west just before De Cortés. It's about a mile on left, just before beach. Popular with Europeans).

PLAYA DE CORTÉS — UPPER — Bacochibampo Bay — Colonial atmosphere with oil paintings and tropical gardens. Famous 132-unit, 3-story A/C hotel, originally built by Southern-Pacific Railroad. 3 elegant dining rooms. Pool. Tennis. Boat ramp. Boutique. Parking. 8 bungalows. AE, MC, VI. Ph: 221-1224, Fax: 221-0135. US: 1-800-732-0780. Mex: 01-800-647-0500 RV park.

SANTA RITA — ECON — Serdán and Calle 9 — Budget, 3 story A/C downtown, 1 block off main street, across from Rest. Del Río. Parking. VI. MC. Ph: 224-1919, 224-1617, Fax: 222-8100.

EATING IN GUAYMAS

BIBLIO CAFE — ECON — Av. Serdán — Typical restaurant between Calles 13 and 14. Mexican food, seafood.

CARAMBA'S GRILL — MOD — Av. Serdán #664 — Next to supermarket. Owner is Alejandro Maksabedian R. Good food and service. PH: 2-9606. Thanks to B and A Abraham, Sun Lakes, AZ.

DEL MAR — UPPER — Av. Serdán and Calle 17 — Very good downtown restaurant. Excellent seafood and prime cuts from Sonora. Terrific seafood cocktails and clam and fish soups. Open 12:30 PM till 11:30 PM daily. AE, MC, VI. Ph: 224-0225.

HELADOS BING — ECON — On Serdán just east of 5th — Ice-cream, sundaes and more!

MEXICO — ECON-MOD — Hwy #15 — "Typical" eatery, 1/8 mile East of Flamingos. *Al fresco* dining. Owned by same folks as in Hermosillo. The conventional can stick with ribs and steaks. Ph: 222-7810.

PLAYA DE CORTÉS — UPPER — At hotel of same name. Elegant dining room. Romantic.

CAMPING & RV PARKING

BAHIA — MOD — On Playitas Peninsula — 80 space park. All hookups. 20 AMPS. Apartments. Restrooms. Showers. Patios. Rec. hall. Boat ramp. Ph: 1-5030.

PLAYAS DE CORTÉS — UPPER — Bacochibampo Bay — By hotel with same name. 55 spaces, all hookups. Use of hotel facilities. Hunting fishing arranged. PO Box 66. 30 AMPS. Restrooms. Showers. Restaurant. Bar. SATV in bar. Pool. Tennis. Laundry service. Beach. Boat ramp and storage. AE, MC, VI. Ph: 221-0142, 221-1224, 221-1121, 221-1047, 221-0148. Fax: 221-0135. US: 1-800-782-7608.

HELPFUL INFORMATION

MECHANIC — TETO'S — Family-run business with prompt competent service, some English and a fair price at Calle 9 #278 Sur. Ph: 222-1605.

TOURISM OFFICE AND INFORMATION — Now on Av. Serdán #441. Ph: (6) 224-4114; 1-800-4-SONORA (in U.S.)
BOATS — In town on waterfront across from city hall, Playa de Cortés Hotel, or Las Playitas RV Park.
LA CASONA SHELL SHOP — Across from cathedral plaza on 24th Street. Nice collection of sea shells and nice jewelry. Rents videos. English spoken. Ph: (6) 222-0199.

End of Guaymas Eat & Stray

Ciudad Obregón

UD-019

Area Code — 644
See map on page 17

CIUDAD OBREGÓN was named for General Alvaro Obregón who along with Pancho Villa helped Carranza defeat Huerta in the 1913 revolution — and then had to whip Villa (for his boss, Carranza) at Celaya, where Obregón lost an arm. Later, he fell out with Carranza and defeated him, and became president (1920). Eight years later, when he was reelected (after he changed the rules to permit a second term) he was assassinated. Obregón came from these parts, so they renamed this nice town in his honor. A big dam was built up on the Yaqui River about 30 miles northeast of town and with irrigation they've made this fertile Yaqui valley into a fabulous producer of cotton and vegetables, which accounts for all the gins, fertilizer factories, insecticide plants and vegetable sheds hereabouts — it's just about the fastest growing town on the West Coast, with a population of about 300,000.

SLEEPING IN CD. OBREGÓN

COSTA DE ORO — MOD — M. Alemán and Allende #201 — 2-story, 103 room A/C motel on highway (Miguel Alemán) thru town. Restaurant. Disco. Bar. Pool. Parking. AE, MC, VI. Ph: 414-1775. Fax: 413-3475.
DAYS INN — MOD — At gas station on Miguel Alemán.
HOLIDAY INN — UPPER — Miguel Alemán and Tetabiate — 2 story, 132 room A/C motor inn on north end on highway thru town. Dining room. Coffee shop. Pool. Parking. AE, MC, VI. Ph: 414-0940. Fax: 413-4194.
OBREGON PLAZA MOTOR INN – MOD – Located at 200 Norte and Allende. AE. MC. VI. Ph: 414-3830.
SAN JORGE — Mod — Miguel Alemán #929 — Older 60 room A/C motel on north end. Small restaurant. Bar. Pool. Parking. Ph: 414-4353. Fax: 414-0110.
TRAVELODGE — MOD — Jalisco #350. Restaurant. Pool.
VALLE DEL YAQUI — MOD — M. Alemán and Cájeme — Nice 84 room, 2 story A/C motel inn on north end on Hwy #15. Coffee shop. Bar. Club (best in town). Pool. Parking. AE, MC, VI. Ph: 414-1300 or 414-8389.

EATING IN CD. OBREGÓN

EL CORTIJO — MOD — Calle 5 de Febrero — Nice restaurant just 2 blocks west of Hwy #15 thru town. Cabrito and paella are specialties.
MR. STEAK — MOD — Miguel Alemán and Mayo — Pleasant Western-style rustic restaurant just south of Norotel Nainiri Valle Grande. Specializes in *carne al carbón*. Open for lunch and dinner. Ph: 413-3570.

CAMPING & RV PARKING

If you have a generous and compassionate heart and would like to visit an orphanage, you will find Hogar de Refugio Infantil Villa Juárez by turning right onto side road to Villa Juárez, go 26 miles on paved road, turn right for another mile, then turn left following signs to the orphanage. They are able to accommodate motor homes, trailers etc. and have a crude dumping station as well as electrical hookups.

End of Cd. Obregón Eat & Stray

Navojoa

UD-019

Area Code — 642

NAVOJOA, the center of a major cotton and wheat-producing area, lies on the left bank of the Río Mayo. Originally a settlement known as "Navojoa" inhabited by the Mayo Indians, it was discovered in 1620 by the Jesuit missionary P. Diego de La Cruz.

With the building of the railroad station at the turn of this century, white families moved in and the town began to flourish; but in 1915 a terrible flood virtually wiped out the city, and a new town was then rebuilt on higher ground. Today Navojoa boasts a population of 100,000 and is a rapidly growing city surrounded by agricultural wealth.

Navojoa is also the largest center of the Mayo Indians, a tribe related to the once potent Yaqui tribe. The Mayos fought long and hard for their liberty and tribal land, but today are almost entirely integrated, having turned to farming. They are slowly losing their identity although they still retain some old beliefs and rituals. A reenactment of these rituals highlights religious festivities during Easter Week and on June 23-24 when the Indians honor St. John the Baptist. Most memorable are the *danza del venado* (deer dance) and the *matachines* (coyote dance).

Navojoa is the departure point to colonial Alamos and to Presa (dam) Mocuzari, famous for its bass fishing and duck hunting. On the south side of Navojoa, a paved road southwest connects to Huatabampo 23 miles away on the Mayo delta where ex-President Alvaro Obregón is buried. Another 12 miles away is the little village of Huatabampito with nearly 13 miles of beautiful, unspoiled, sandy beach. The waters are mild, and the beach is so wide and firm that small airplanes often use it for a landing strip.

SLEEPING IN NAVOJOA

COLONIAL — MOD — 34 room A/C motel at south end of town. Restaurant-bar. Club (*mariachis* on Thurs. and Fri.). Parking. Ph: 422-1919. Fax: 4223413.

DEL RÍO — UPPER — Pesquería #228 — Very nice 62 room A/C Best Western motel just beyond Alameda. Restaurant. Bar. Pool. SATV. Tennis. 5 Kitchenettes. Parking. RV park on north end. AE, MC, VI. Ph: 422-0331. Fax: 422-5601.

EL MAYO — MOD — Motel most recommended by customers. A good deal. One block off main highway at Otero and Jiménez. 47 rooms. Bungalows with carports, nice, clean, comfortable and quiet. Ph: 422-6054, 422-6828 Fax: 422-6515.

EL RANCHO — MOD — Carr. Internacional KM 1788 — 62 room A/C ranch-style motel at far north end. Restaurant. Bar. Pool. Disco (F-Sat till wee hours of morning, making sleep impossible). Parking. MC, VI. Ph and Fax: 422-0004 or 422-0310. Fax: 422-3584.

FENIX — ECON — Hidalgo and Angel Flores #365 — Economy hotel. MC, VI. Ph: 422-2623.

MONTE CARLO — ECON — Corner of Independencia and Angel Flores — Good enough hotel. Ceiling fans. TV. Bar. Parking. MC, VI.

POSADA REAL — MOD — 154 room hotel. Continental breakfast free. A/C, nice but cold. Pool. TV. Parking. AE, MC, VI. Ph: 422-2179.

EATING IN NAVOJOA

EL GRANERO — MOD — Corner of Serdán and Zaragosa — Specializes in beef dishes. MC, VI. Open daily.

LAS BRASAS — Fine steak house on main street next to Danesa ice cream parlor. Bar. AE, MC, VI.

MARLIN'S — Good restaurant on main street thru town. Specializes in seafood dishes.

QUINTA EL ASADERO — Very good restaurant (town's best) 1 KM south of Del Río on left. Specializes in charbroiled meats. Open noon till midnight daily. AE, MC, VI. Ph: 422-0941, Fax: 42-4437.

End of Navojoa Eat & Stray

Alamos

Area Code — 647
See map on page 62

ALAMOS (cottonwood trees) is an interesting old town, sort of a national park like Taxco and the construction of buildings with modern architecture is not allowed. The town is one of the oldest in North America — Coronado's army camped here in 1530. Alamos once had a gold-silver-lead mine population of 40,000 but the mines played out some 70 years ago and the town was soon on its downswing. However, *Norteamericanos* have discovered this quaint place and quite a few have moved here and rebuilt the magnificent ruins, some of which are open to the public.

GUIDED TOURS — Solipaso Excursions and Tourist Services, at La Ciudadela on Calle Cárdenas #15, is run by the MacKay family and they arrange and conduct customized small group tours to abandoned mines, ghost towns and through beautiful forests. Tours include guided hiking trips, mountain biking, birdwatching, a float down the Río Mayo or an excursion to the Sea of Cortés. Ph: 8-0466. Website: www.Solipaso.com

There's also a lifelong resident, Emiliano, that speaks English and offers tours of distinction, ghost town tours, bird watching, Indian and mining village tours. He can be reached at Las Palmeras Hotel (428-0065) or Casa Los Tesoros (428-0110). Local guide, Joseph Yucopicio is at the Tourist Information office across from the main plaza. He is a Mayo descendant and knows all plus where the movie stars live.

HOUSE TOURS — Check at your hotel. 10 AM Saturday, October 1 till May 1. They meet at the museum. Money goes to Alamos Scholarship Fund. For special tours for group of 10 or more during the week contact Dolores Parker at 428-0348 or write her at Calle Juárez #25, Alamo, Sonora, Mexico 85760. Some guides offer tours, but they can't get into houses, so be careful.

CRAFTS AND GIFTS — "Curiosidades y Regalos" gift shop located on Calle Morelos #1D has an excellent selection of crafts from all over Mexico and also offer professional transalation services.

Incidentally, Alamos is where the Mexican jumping beans originate. They aren't beans at all, but little three-section nuts with a tiny worm in each section, and it's the movement of the worms that makes the "bean" jump. A man from Alamos, Señor Joaquín Hernández, was once considered the jumping bean "king," because he used to buy up all the beans from natives who gathered them and then shipped them in drums to the States and all over the world. The beans start jumping in midsummer and keep hopping till late September when the worms apparently become just too pooped to hop anymore (can't blame them) so they burrow their way out, curl up and die.

You'll enjoy old Alamos — don't hesitate to run over and stay the night. Incidentally, if no accommodations are available, it's only 33 miles to Navojoa.

SLEEPING IN ALAMOS

CASA DE LOS TESOROS ("House of Treasures") — UPPER — It is not cheap and has less quality than other hotels in town However, it includes breakfast and is the only one that takes credit cards. Obregón #10, 1 1/2 blocks from Plaza. 14 A/C rooms, and ceiling fans, converted from an 18th-century convent. Restaurant. Pool. One room with tub. Good water pressure in showers. Fireplaces. Parking. AE, MC, VI. Apdo. 12, Alamos, Son., Mexico. Ph: 428-0010. Fax: 428-0400.

CASA ENCANTADA — UPPER — The most expensive hotel in town. If you want atmosphere, you've got to pay for it. It's a really charming but expensive bed and breakfast located at Juárez #20, a nice Antilysin style mansion built over 250 years ago. The owners are very friendly and accommodating. 10 rooms. Pool. No credit cards. Ph: 428-0482, 428-0221.

CASA OBREGÓN #18 — MOD — Value! 3 suites (more like apartments, 2 with tubs, 1 with full kitchen. You won't believe the place. Great courtyard. Enclosed parking. Monthly discounts. Often full. Less expensive than others in neighborhood. Owner speaks English. No credit cards but accepts personal checks. No phone.

DOLISA — ECON — VALUE! Reasonable prices. Comfy 8-unit motel at Madero #72 on highway just before town (within walking distance to downtown). For those on a budget, you can't do better. No restaurant. Most rooms A/C; others with ceiling fans. Fireplaces. Coin laundry. Water purifying plant. Parking. Ph: 428-0131.

HACIENDA DE LOS SANTOS — UPPER — Sixteenth century, elegant, luxurious, spa hotel located in town. E-mail: hacienda@hipernet.com.mx Website: haciendadelossantos.com Ph: 428-0222 Fax: 428-0367.

LA CIUDADELA — UPPER — Calle Cárdenas #15. Built in the 1680's,* it was originally constructed as a garrison for Spanish troops. It was turned in to a private residence by a prominent silver baron. It has 4 well-appointed guest rooms furnished with antiques and local crafts, each with its own fireplace. There is also a kitchen, living room and dining room. It is also headquarters of Solipaso Excursions and Tourist Services run by Jennifer and David Mackay who arrange and conduct customized small group tours to abandoned mines, ghost towns andthrough beautiful forests. Tours include guided hiking trips, mountain biking,birdwatching, a float down the Río Mayo or an excursion to the Sea of Cortés. Ph: 428-0466 US message: 1-714-908-9865.

LOS PORTALES ("Covered Walks") — MOD — Older hotel. 14 rooms on Juárez #6 at Alamos' main plaza. No A/C; ceiling fans only. No restaurant. Fireplaces. Parking. Bar. Pleasant courtyard. Formerly private house of mine owner. Apdo. 31, Alamos, Son., Mexico. Ph: 428-0211.

MANSIÓN — UPPER — Some rooms are good enough and others are plain. Obregón #2, down from Tesoros. 14 rooms. Ceiling fans and fireplaces. No credit cards. Ph: 428-0221.

POSADA — MOD — Less expensive than many and nice enough. A remodeled old mansion on Prol. 2 de Abril. Good ambience and food. 20 rooms, one with tub. A/C and ceiling fans. Rooms are designed for families. Some have a loft bedroom and three beds. 3 kitchenettes. Pool on the roof. Secure parking. No credit cards or personal checks. Ph: 428-0045. Fax: 428-5763. In Tucson, (520) 327-4683.

POLO ACOSTA — MOD — 6 rooms in conjunction with RV park on east side of town beyond cemetery. Restaurant which prepares food by reservation only. Pool. Parking. Ph: 428-0246 or 428-0077.

SOMAR — ECON — 16 room hotel on Madero #110 at entrance to town. No restaurant. Parking. Pleasant courtyard. Ph: 428-0195. The unusual feature of this hotel is the beds whose bases are made of *tucuruguari*, a mixture of slaked lime, calcium, oxide, and sand.

EATING IN ALAMOS

CASA DE LOS TESOROS — UPPER — Courtyard dining area. Sonora specialties,and international cuisine.

EL CARACOL — MOD — Restaurant on a hilltop in conjunction with RV park of same name, 9 miles west of town. International and Mexican food. Live music on Sunday afternoons. Open noon till 9 PM; closed Mondays. Ph: 428-0117, Fax: 428-5760.

LA BARRANCA — ECON — Tacos and tortas. Across the barranca up on hill (inquire locally to get there).

LAS PALMERAS — MOD — On plaza. Good breakfasts.

POLO'S — MOD — Downtown seafood restaurant located at Zaragoza #4 behind church. American and Mexican food. Specialty is Mexican plate. Ph: 428-0001.

SIETE MARES — MOD — Between Casa de Los Tesoros and Mansión. An unbelievable place — an old mansion with huge marble columns, lush gardens and fountain. They serve seafood (from 7 seas). You might think you're in Italy, Greece or Spain. Open 10 AM till 10 PM. Owner, Antonio Del Pardo.

CAMPING & RV PARKING

DOLISA — UPPER — West side — 50 space facility on highway, Madero #72, within walking distance to town. (Just before the road forks). Owner really cares about the place and it shows. 25 spaces with all hookups; 25 with water and electricity. Pull-thrus. Patios. Bungalows/Apartments. Restrooms. Showers. Security. Dump station. Laundry. Water purifying plant. Pets on leash OK. Tenting permitted. Friendly. Ph: 428-0131.

EL CARACOL — MOD — West of town, KM 37 — Big 65-space park on highway 9 miles west of town. All hookups. 30 amps Showers. Restrooms. Laundromat. Pool. Drive-thru spaces. Pets on leash OK. Friendly. SATV. Ph: 428-0117

ACOSTA — UPPER — East side — Older 18-space trailer "rancho" on far east side of town beyond cemetery. Get to it by the river, not thru town, very pretty. All hookups. 30 amps. Patios. Restrooms. Rec hall palapa. Pool.

Horses. Hunting and fishing. SAT TV. Lodge/Bungalows. Pets on leash OK. Friendly. Ph: 428-0246.
REAL DE LOS ALAMOS — UPPER — 51-space park on right 1 1/2 miles before town. Full hookups. Potable water. 30 AMP. Restrooms. Pool. Laundry. Hot showers. BBQ areas. Caravan rates. Ph: 428-0002.

End of Alamos Eat & Stray

Los Mochis

UD-019

Area Code — 668
See map on page 21

LOS MOCHIS is rather interesting and offers good accommodations and excellent seafood (only 14 miles from the Sea of Cortés). One of Mexico's most up-and-coming agricultural towns, Los Mochis houses one of the largest sugar refineries on the West Coast in addition to its cotton and vegetable production. Strangely enough Los Mochis was founded in 1893 by an American family, the Johnstons, who came from Virginia to build a sugar refinery — and they laid out the town, building the first church, the lighthouse atop Cerro de la Memoria (Memory Hill), and later an airport. Mr. Johnston died in Hong Kong in 1938, and the family later moved back to the States. The sugar refinery is now owned by Mexican interests.

Mr. Johnston hired very capable Americans to help him run the sugar mill. Among these was Dr. Chapman, the medical doctor for the sugar company and American colony. Following Mr. Johnston's death, Dr. Chapman stayed on and built the Motel Chapman.

Even before the Johnstons founded Los Mochis, there was a Utopian colony established by Albert Kinsey Owen in 1872, the man who conceived the railroad over the Sierras. There are still descendants of these Utopian colonists in and around Los Mochis.

FISHING — Freshwater largemouth black bass fishing is available only 55 miles from Los Mochis at either Presa (dam) Miguel Hidalgo or Domínguez near the picturesque colonial town of El Fuerte (see EL FUERTE SPECIAL). Deep-sea fishing (grouper, yellowtail, roosterfish, and cabrilla, all year; dolphin, sailfish, and marlin, June-September) is available at Topolobampo, only 14 miles from Los Mochis.

HUNTING — Los Mochis boasts a very good hunting season from November 1st to February 15th. Duck, speckled geese, quail, and white-tailed dove are plentiful. Hunting arrangements can be made through your hotel or RV park.

FERRY — "Topo" is a typical Mexican fishing village with its fleet of shrimpers and freezing plant, and it's also where the Baja car-passenger ferry operates. 6 weekly departures to La Paz, Baja California Sur: Mon thru Sat at 10 AM. The "Baja Express," a passenger only hydrofoil/catamaran deal will zip people across the bay. (When it works.) Check for schedules — it changes a lot.

MECHANIC — A good one who specializes in VW's is Taller García, Blvd. Jiquilpan #640 (between B. Domínguez and 20 de Noviembre) near the university.

CYBERCAFE – If you need to check your e-mail a good place is located on the corner of Cárdenas and Leyva across the street from Plaza Inn.

SLEEPING IN LOS MOCHIS

CORINTIOS — MOD — Obregón #580 Pte. Very nice, quiet 3-story 52-room hotel. Restaurant. Bar. CATV. Jacuzzi. Gym. Secure parking. AE, MC, VI. Ph: 818-2224, 818-2300 Fax: 818-2277. Mex: 91-800-69030.
PLAZA INN — UPPER — An attractive and quiet Balderama hotel on corner of Leyva and Cárdenas — 125 units. 2 restaurants. Lobby bar. Pool. Disco. Parking. Ph: 818-1042, 818-1044 Fax: 818-1043 US: 1-800-862-9026.

SANTA ANITA — UPPER — Corner of Leyva and Hidalgo — 5-story, 133-room downtown hotel. Town's largest. Dining room. Bar. Club. SATV. Travel agency. Parking. AE, DIN, MC, VI. Ph: 818-7046, 818-7184 Fax: 812-0046. Mexico City: 5-510-3398.

EATING IN LOS MOCHIS

EL BUCANERO — ECON — Allende and Alfonso Cano, Inexpensive eatery. Surprisingly good sea food.
EL FARALLÓN (The Rocky Island) — UPPER — Corner of Obregón and Flores — Nautical decor (fish nets, seashells, and murals depicting Sea of Cortés). Excellent seafood (the best in town) cocktails and dishes. Open 7 days, 8 AM till 10 PM. AE, MC, VI. Ph: 812-1273, 812-1428.
EL QUEMADO — MOD — Blvd. Macario Gaxiola #372 Sur, Topolobampo Hwy 3 block northeast of Obregón. Sometimes Cabrito, Carne asada, steaks. Down-home place with thatched roof. Very popular with locals. Quesadillas on wheat tortillas are huge. MC, VI. Open 7 AM till 11 PM. PH: 815-1833.
ESPAÑA — MOD — On Obregón #525 Pte. Spanish cuisine. Very nice atmosphere. It has a waterfall and aquarium. Open 10 AM till 11 PM. AE, MC, VI. Ph: 812-2221, 812-2335.
LA PARRILLA DORADA — MOD — Leyva #222 Sur — Attractive restaurant converted from old home. Serving Swiss cuisine as well as *menudo* and other Mexican dishes and Charbroiled steaks. Open 7 AM till midnight. Ph: 812-2603.
PALACIO CHINO — On Blvd. Rosales #350. Ph: 818-1914.
PLAZA INN — On corner of Leyva and Cárdenas. Good food and a swinging place, great for young people who like to party.
SANTA ANITA — MOD — Located in Hotel Santa Anita. It's the only late-night place to eat downtown. Quiet Good. Langostino Pango (fish), steaks, chicken. Serves Peña Fiel agua mineral. Open 6 AM till 11:30 PM. Ph: 818-7046.
TACOS LOS FEOS — Callejón Sinaloa and Gabriel Leyva — A taco lover's delight. Tacos al pastor, carne asada, and tripita.

CAMPING & RV PARKING

COLONIAS — MOD — South end near bullring — 67 spaces (EWS). ENGLISH. Shower, toilets laundry. 30 AMP. PH: 811-8111 or 818-8222 Fax: 811-8181.
COPPER CANYON RV PARK — MOD — 1/2 mile off freeway. 120 spaces with all hookups. Mail address: Apdo. Postal #1201 Los Mochis 81200, Sin. Personal checks accepted. Ph: 812-6817 Fax: 812-0046.
LOS MOCHIS — MOD — 120-pull-thru-space park at north entrance to town. All hookups. Showers. Toilets. Rec. hall. Laundry. Brick patios. Security. Restaurant (seasonal). Pets OK. Ph: 812-1388 or 812-6817.

End of Los Mochis Eat & Stray

El Fuerte

UD-019

Area Code — 698
See map on page 64

EL FUERTE, accessible by a nice paved road, is a quaint colonial town still undiscovered by tourists. Originally named "El Fuerte de Montes Claros," the town was founded in 1564 by the Spanish conquistador Francisco de Ibarra and soon became the most important military post of the Spaniards in their conquest of Northwestern Mexico and California. El Fuerte, meaning "fort," was a stronghold of fortification built to protect the soldiers and settlers from the continuous fierce raids by the Yaqui, Mayo and other Indian tribes. The Yaqui tribe lives on the north side of river and the Mayo tribe on the south side. The settlement eventually flourished and for three centuries it was the principal commercial and farming center and the major trading post for silver miners as well as gold seekers. At one time there were more than 400 mines in the area. In 1855 it even became the state capital for a short period.

Today, El Fuerte has retained its old Mexican character and atmosphere — cobblestone streets, old houses with "*portales*" (arches), patios filled with beautiful tropical foliage, wrought-iron windows and doors, an ancient plaza with its ornate kiosk, a century-old church (with a cactus growing on its steeple), and much more. Of particular interest when in the area is a visit to the Ocolome Jesuit Mission and to the old Mayo Indian village where ancestral customs still prevail.

El Fuerte is a paradise for fishermen and hunters. Fishing at Domínguez and Hidalgo Lakes is great. Black bass and catfish are plentiful and both "*presas*" (dams) are only a 30-minute drive from downtown El Fuerte. For the hunter there are duck, mourning and whitewing dove and blue pigeon. It's not uncommon to shoot the daily limit of ducks and to catch the daily limit of bass the same day along the banks of Domínguez Lake.

Remember, you can take the train through to the copper canyon from here. We recommend you do that instead of going all the way to Los Mochis. You save three hours.

SLEEPING IN EL FUERTE

EL FUERTE — UPPER — Very friendly place with 25 rooms and nice courtyard in old mansion. Excellent restaurant with fantastic meals. No credit cards. They can arrange tours and train tickets Owner, Robert Brand used to own La Paloma in Nuevo León state. Ph: 3-0226
HIDALGO LODGE — Lupi Nieblas and Tom Jenkins, Nice lodge for hunting/fishing. 24 units. A/C. Ph: (706) 813-0657 in El Fuerte, Box 11. In U.S. P.O. Box 3036, Burbank, CA 91504, Ph: (213) 388-4157.
POSADA DE HIDALGO — UPPER — Hidalgo #101, Centro Histórico de la Ciudad — Nice 37-room hotel a half-block from main square, once the largest and most beautiful colonial mansion in El Fuerte. Restaurant. Bar. Filtered pool. Street parking (with security). AE, MC, VI. (This hotel has been declared a historical landmark as it's where President Venustiano Carranza slept in room 7 in September, 1913.) Ph and Fax: 893-0242 in El Fuerte, or 812-0046 in Los Mochis, or 1-416-5950 in Chihuahua. A Balderama hotel.
SAN FRANCISCO — MOD — Av. Obregón #201 — OK 18-room hotel centered around a flowered patio on the cobblestone street into town. Restaurant. Bar. MC, VI. Ph: 893-0055.
VILLA DEL PESCADO — MOD — On Obregón. Restaurant.

EATING IN EL FUERTE

CAPRI — ECON — Next to San Francisco hotel. Open 7 AM till 11 PM. On Mondays, 8 AM till 4 PM. MC, VI.
EL MESON DEL GENERAL — MOD — Benito Juárez #202, one block towards highway from square. Seafood, steaks. Locally popular. MC, VI.
LA PALOMA — Restaurant in Posada de Hidalgo. Romantic, overlooking flower garden. Has crayfish soup, black bass (Lobina), panela asada — grilled goat cheese.
PASEO DE LAS AVES — Go 2 blocks past main plaza, then look for sign saying to turn left. Follow the signs. It's on the river and has swings for kids. Specializes in Lobina. Open 9 AM till 11 PM. MC, VI. Ph: 893-0986.

End of El Fuerte Eat & Stray

Culiacán

UD-019

Area Code — 667
See map on page 24

SLEEPING IN CULIACÁN

COLONIAL — ECON — Madero #730 Pte. — 47-room, 3-story A/C hotel. Restaurant. Parking. Pets OK. Ph: 712-8500.
DEL VALLE — MOD — Blvd. Solano #180 Ote. — 3-story, 42-room A/C motel on boulevard thru town.

Restaurant. Beauty shop. Pharmacy. Ice machines. Parking. Small pets OK. AE, MC, VI. Ph: 713-9020, 713-9120, 713-9180, or 713-9170. This hotel is being renovated.

EJECUTIVO — UPPER — Corner of Obregón and Madero — Very good 6-story, 229-room A/C downtown hotel. Cafeteria. Restaurant. Bars. Pool. Servibars. Tennis. Gift shop. Solarium. Parking. AE, MC, VI. Ph: 713-9300, 713-9301 or 713-9310. Fax: 713-9487.

LOS CAMINOS — MOD-UPPER — South end of Solano Boulevard — Remodeled 51-room, 2-story A/C motel thru town. Restaurant. Bar. Pool. Night security. Parking. AE, MC, VI. Ph: 715-3300.

SALVADOR — ECON — Solano Blvd #297 — 40-room, 7-story A/C hotel thru town practically across from bus station. No restaurant. On-street parking. MC, VI. Ph: 713-7462.

SAN LUIS LINDAVISTA — MOD — Av. De Las Palmas #1 — 45-unit A/C motel atop hill ("Lomas de Culiacán") on the south end of Obregón next to Basilica of Guadalupe Church. Rooftop dining room. Pool. Parking. AE, MC, VI. Ph: 713-1600, 713-1400, 713-1500 or 716-7010. Fax: 715-0815.

TRES RÍOS — MOD — KM 1423 Carr. Internacional — Good, recommended by readers, as not fancy but good, 68-unit A/C motor inn at north end. Pleasant restaurant. Bar. Pool. Parking. AE, MC, VI. Ph: 750-5279, 715-4140, 715-4540, 715-4340 or 715-4440. Fax: 716-4435.

VALLE BONITO — MOD — Corner of Solano and Carranza — 40-room, 3-story A/C motel. Restaurant. Servibars. Parking. Small pets OK. AE, MC, VI. Ph: 713-9320 or 713-9220

EATING IN CULIACÁN

EL CHAPARRAL LOMITA — UPPER — Obregón #1244 Sur — Nice restaurant on far west end of Obregón just below San Luis. Specializes in steaks.

LA TAVOLA — MOD — Popular restaurant across from Plaza Ley, almost behind bus station. Pizza and Spaghetti a la Bolognesa plus draft beer.

TRES RÍOS — MOD-UPPER — Recommended restaurant in hotel of same name. Thanks to R. Heller of Green Valley AZ.

CAMPING & RV PARKING

TRES RÍOS — UPPER — North of town on Hwy #15 — Good 18-space park in conjunction with motel at north end. All hookups. 20 amps. Restrooms. Showers. Pool. Laundry service. Several patios. Restaurant. Boat ramp. Ice. Disco. TV lounge. Tennis. AE, MC, VI. Ph: 712-3030.

LOS CASCABELES — MOD — 13 miles south of town on Hwy #15, KM 1401 and 3.5 miles on Hwy #19 toward Costa Rica City. 20 acres with surrounding fence. Cabins. Boats. Restaurant. Pool. Store. Sport field. Phones. Hunting and fishing nearby. Ph: 713-6418 or 713-6822.

END OF CULIACÁN EAT & STRAY

Mazatlán

UD-017

Area Code — 669

See maps on pages 27 and 28

Altitude: 16 feet. Population: 500,000. Least crowded — Aug-Sept. Rainiest — July-Aug. Coolest — Jan-Feb.

MAZATLÁN, meaning "Land of Deer" in Nahuatl, is on the same latitude as Honolulu and has an average temperature of 80° F. It's Mexico's largest Pacific coast seaport, a major vacation resort city and the closest one to the USA.

Spaniards officially founded the city in 1513 at the foot of Cerro de la Nevería. Here they loaded the Spanish galleons with gold and silver from nearby gold and silver mines for transport back to Spain — that is, if they managed to survive the storms and outwit the English privateers. It later became known as the Athens of the West and was finally incorporated in 1806.

Today, Mazatlán, nicknamed the "Pearl of the Pacific," is a thriving seaport on the international trade routes and the center of one of the largest fishing industries in Mexico. More than 37 million pounds of shrimp are processed yearly and tons are frozen daily and shipped to the USA. Tourism has developed quickly into the second largest industry behind fishing. Mazatlán currently has more than 140 hotels and 8,500 hotel rooms and more are to come as new hotels are built and others expand.

Some people prefer to get away from the "Golden Zone" and walk along the "Olas Altas" promenade. Here's where the first "beachfront" hotels were. If you want an area where peddlers and condo salesmen don't besiege you, this is the place. The 17 KM boulevard is the 2nd longest beachside promenade in Latin America.

Other areas are infested with timeshare sales people. Many have "tourist information" kiosks. They are there to make an appointment for a "free" breakfast. Use your own judgement. Also, people who ask "Are you enjoying your vacation?" are also sales people.

WHAT TO SEE AND DO

AQUARIUM — One of the largest in Latin America, it's off Av. Reforma, near Av. De los Deportes.

FISHING — Mazatlán enjoys a reputation as an outstanding deep-sea fishing port and is known as the billfish capital of the world. Several world records have been set here. Striped marlin abound from December thru April and sailfish from May thru November. There are several reliable fishing outfits in Mazatlán. BILL HEIMPEL'S STAR FLEET is one of the best. He has 5 boats — 2 / 34 feet (2 fishing chairs; maximum 4 persons); 38 feet and 40 feet (3 fishing chairs; maximum 5 persons); and 43 feet (4 or 5 fishing chairs). His boats meet U.S. Coast Guard standards, are equipped with life preservers and are quite comfortable. The crews know their stuff. Cost is $70.00 per person to secure a back booth. 4 or 5 people and $240 to $300 to rent the whole boat. They'll fix you a box lunch (tuna or ham and cheese sandwiches) for a small fee. The fishing license is $7.00. For reservations call 982-3878 or 982-2665 Fax: 982-5155.

The Avis fleet is also very good with modern boats and safety equipment. They have 10 boats 2 - 28 feet, 3 - 31 feet, 2 - 33 feet, 2 - 36 feet, 1 - 45 feet. Cost: 28 feet - $290; 31-33 feet - $325; 36 feet - $375; 45 feet - $430. Fishing license $7.00. Will pick up at hotel at 6:30 AM. Ph: 916-3468. 1-800-525-1925, 1-800-634-3085.

For those willing to chance it, the El Dorado fleet certainly doesn't meet any safety standards, nor are their boats in good shape, but they are less expensive. They are single engine boats. Ph: 981-6204, 913-5820.

Another outfit is FLOTA FARO with a fleet of boats — 35 feet (2 fishing chairs); 35 feet (3 fishing chairs); and 42 feet (4 or 5 fishing chairs). Ph: 981-2824 or 982-4977 for reservations. Fishing trips are from 6:30 AM till 3 PM and include bait, tackle and crew (fishing licenses extra). Beer and soft drinks are available on board. Remember that "catch and release" is the smart way to fish.

SHOPPING — For dresses, shirts, rugs, etc., an easygoing place is *"EL GENERAL."* Market Bugambillas, Sabalo and Costa Azul #14 (in the Gold Zone). Owner Arturo Castro G. is a nice guy, speaks English and not pushy.

ARTS AND CRAFTS CENTER — A block north of Playa Mazatlán on Las Gaviotas, is worth a visit to see artisans from several parts of Mexico work at their crafts. Large selection of gifts. Open from 9 AM till 6 PM, 7 days. THE DESIGNER'S BAZAAR, TEQUILA TREE and CASA PACÍFICA (in the "Golden Zone") feature interesting clothes, leather goods, crafts and jewelry.

SIGHTSEEING — The MAZATLÁN FIESTA CRUISE (3 hours) departs daily at 10:30 am from north end of main docks and features Mexico's largest fishing fleet, Seal Islands, La Paz Ferry, beaches from offshore, French Cannon, second-highest natural lighthouse in the world and more. As with most of these deals, lots of booze and music. The **CITY TOUR** (2 1/2 hours) departs daily at 9:30 AM and at 2:30 PM and features the basilica, municipal palace, Fisherman's Monument, Spanish fort, residential areas, market, etc. The **COUNTRY TOUR** features a visit to some rural villages back in the foothills including Concordia (leather goods and furniture) and Copala and Rosario (old silver-mining towns). **LOS CHIVOS ISLAND TOUR** departures are daily at 11 AM, 1 PM and 3 PM from Restaurant La Palapa (short distance up beach from Mazatlán) and next to Suites Las Flores by amphibious truck *La Barca de Oro*. To book any of the tours mentioned above, contact Agencia de Viajes ABZ (see INSURANCE).

The Stone Island Bay and Beach Tour - a six hour package including lunch is great fun. Also the Mazatlán Ecological Jungle tour is a bird lover's paradise just 4 miles south of Mazatlán. See David Pérez of King David Travel Agency at Camarón Sabalo #333 Ph: 914-1444 Fax: 914-0451 e-mail: kingdavid@acnet.net

BULLFIGHTS — Nov.-Apr. on Sun. Bullring on Blvd. Rafael Buelna. Buy tickets there, at El Camerón Motel or a travel agency. Ph: 984-1666.

SEA LIONS — Oct-May. Hire a boat to take you to the island where they winter.

PULMONIAS (Pneumonias?) — Open-air three-wheeled carts with only a canopy found all over town. They carry 3 persons and their fares are less expensive than taxi — and they're *mucho* fun!

ICE BOX HILL *Cerro de la Nevería* — So named because many years ago the ice brought from San Francisco by ship was stored in the two tunnels. In the very early days (during the 16th and 17th centuries) this "hill" was used as a lookout for pirate ships. Perhaps the most interesting part in history played by this "hill" was during the revolution in 1914 when Mazatlán became the second city in the world to be bombed by an airplane (first was Tripoli, Libya). General Carranza's forces sent an old biplane to bomb the lookout fort atop Ice Box Hill. The story has been told that the pilot overflew the target and the bombardier, overcome by airsickness, lost his grasp on the bomb. It fell into the streets below killing two civilians and injuring several others. We've heard that this crude bomb was dynamite and pieces of old iron packed in pigskin. How true? *¿Quién sabe?*

CARNIVAL — This is Mazatlán's main event, held during Mardi Gras (but really starts the preceding Friday and peaks the Sunday before). It's a mixture of New Orleans and Río de Janero with parades, coronation parties, street dances, floats, fireworks and costumed merrymaking. There is no sleep during those days and reservations must be made for hotels at least 6 months in advance. SPECIAL EVENTS (Besides Carnival) — May 1-10 — Rosario holds "Spring Festival," during which typical dishes and folklore shows are enjoyed. Sept. 4-10 — Escuinapa celebrates the "Feria del Mango and Mazatlán celebrates the "Week of Commerce." Every store in Mazatlán develops a different event or promotion.

EATING OUT – **If you want to save money,** look for places that have a *"Comida Corrida,"* which is the traditional Mexican lunch. The menu will be set and you'll get maybe 2 choices of main courses, beans or rice, soup, a salad and maybe coffee or tea. Another way is to drink (eat?) a *"licuado"* for breakfast. They're fresh fruits (papaya, melón, mango, banana etc.) blended before your eyes with milk, sugar (or honey — *"miel de abeja"*). You can add wheat germ — *"trigo,"* oatmeal — *"avena,"* nuts or whatever they've got. It's quick and inexpensive — a dollar or two for enough to fill you up. You'll find a good *licuado* stand (the only one that's open late at night) downtown, near the market, on Juárez, across from a bank. Make sure you specify *"con leche"* (with milk) instead of water. You'll find them everywhere in Mexico.

STATE TOURISM OFFICE — Av. Camarón Sabalo #59 and Tiburón on the fourth floor of the Banrural bank building in the North Beach area across from el Quijote Inn. They speak English and are very helpful. Ph: 915-5160, 915-5165.

MONEY EXCHANGE — La Farga at Sabalo # 508 in the Gold Zone, also sells stamps and has long distance phone and fax service Ph: 914-2199, 913-1560. Open 8 AM till 8 PM week days Sat and Sun 10 AM — 3 PM. Near El Cid, Holiday Inn and other hotels there are several. Aquilles Serdán, A. Serdán #1225, Centro. Ph: 982-2688. The Shrimp Bucket, Olas Altas.

CRESTON LIGHTHOUSE — On hilltop near fishing fleet harbor, reportedly the second highest lighthouse in the world (515 feet above sea level) — and quite a hike to the top!

CLIFF DIVERS — Local divers leap from rock cliffs near tourist office. Times vary, so check with tourist office for details.

LAUNDRY — EL SABALO — In Gold Zone at Sabalo #1666 across from Sr. Frog. Ph: 914-2634.

NEARBY ATTRACTIONS — TEACAPAN is only 56 miles south on Hwy #15, then 26 miles west, a little off the beaten track. Go there if you have a spirit of adventure and you are tired of the party atmosphere of Mazatlán. Naturalists will enjoy the place and the (so far) unspoiled beaches. You can fish, go bird watching and loaf. Wildlife includes white and pink heron and pichihuila and deer. This is a small town with friendly folks and beautiful scenery. There are two good hotels: In town is Hotel Denisse, which is small (5 rooms) and inexpensive; farther out is the Rancho Los Angeles with the best restaurant in town, perhaps in Mexico. It is for a more affluent crowd with private bungalows and a swimming pool. The only RV park is The Oregon, on the beach, near Sr. Wayne's restaurant.

COPALA is only 15 1/2 miles south on Hwy #15, then 27 miles east on Hwy 40. It's an old mining town and Daniel's restaurant is worth the trip. Daniel Garrison is the owner and serves the best California-Tex-Mex-Arkansas style food in the world. His dad was born in Gravit, AR, but Daniel is Mexican. He lived in CA and came home, after working 15 years in the oil fields and realizing life in Mexico was better. Be sure to try his banana creme coconut pie.

CYBERCAFE – If you need to check your e-mail there's a good place at Cameron Sabalo 2 blocks north of Burger King.

SLEEPING IN MAZATLÁN

The oceanfront boulevard, which has most of the hotels, changes names several times, so don't become confused. Since Mazatlán is a popular resort with Mexicans, as well as Americans and Canadians, advance reservations are mandatory during the two weeks before and after Christmas and Easter. They're pretty smart from mid-December onward, too. If you don't make them, you'll still find a place to sleep, but you'll have to be flexible. Facilities are air-conditioned unless otherwise noted. Budget places (as anywhere) are located near the bus station, between the beach and downtown and near the ferry terminal.

AMIGO PLAZA (Formerly, Las Brisas) — MOD — 53-room, 7-story hotel at Av. Del Mar #900 across from beach. Restaurant. Pool. Tennis. Parking. MC, VI. Ph: 983-03339, 83-6699 Fax: 983-7282.

AMMACZATLAN — MOD — Nice 3-story, 40-condo complex on beach at Sabalo Cerritos #576 at north end. One and two bedroom units. Pool. Parking. AE, DI, MC, VI. Ph: 914-1219.

AQUA MARINA — MOD — Rambling 100-unit, 2-story motel at Av. Del Mar #110. Restaurant. Bar. Pool. Parking. MC, VI. Ph: 981-7080 to 85 or 981-6909. Fax: 982-4624. Best Western.

AZTECA INN — MOD — Good Value! Av. Rodolfo T. Loaiza #307 — 74-room, 3-story motel across from Playa Mazatlán. Noé at front desk speaks English and is helpful. Restaurant-bar. Pool. Jacuzzi. Parking. MC, VI. Ph: 913-4655, 913-4477. MEX: 91-800-69770 Fax: 913-7476. www.aztecainn.com.mx E-mail: aztecainn@acnet.net

BALBOA CLUB – MOD – Camaron Sabalo. 18 A/C rooms and 22 A/C suites. Restaurant. Heated pool. Ph: 913-2222. Fax: 914-1287. Mex: 01-800-716-9707. E-mail: hinsunspree@red2000.com.mx

BALBOA TOWERS — UPPER — Delightful 52-unit hotel on Camarón Sabalo next to Balboa Club on beach. 30 rooms, 15 suites and 11 master suites, all with kitchenettes. No restaurant. 2 pools with bar. Gym. Sauna. Travel agency. Curio shop. Parking. AE, MC, VI. Ph: 913-7784, 913-7290, 913-7144, or 913-5558.

BELMAR — ECON — 200-room, 6 story old-time hotel near downtown on Olas Altas #166. Secure parking. Pool. Some rooms have good views. It's a little down at the heels but inexpensive. A sort of "faded grandeur" place. AE, MC, VI, Ph: 985-1111 AL 13, Fax: 981-3428.

BUNGALOWS MAR-SOL — MOD — Av. Camarón Sabalo #1001. Very clean, double and single beds with kitchenettes. Just beyond Posada la Misión. Real nice management. Parking for cars, MC, VI. (A. Verhulst, Grandview MO). Ph: 984-01-08.

CASA CONTENTA – MOD – Av. Rodolfo Loaiza #224 on Playa Gaviotas just north of Playa Mazatlán. 8 1-bedroom kitchenettes. 5 A/C units. Pool. Parking. MC, VI. Reserve well in advance. Ph:913-4976 Fax: 913-9986.

CAMINO REAL — UPPER — Nice 170-room, 4-story beach hotel on north end up on knoll *Punta del Sabalo.* 2 restaurants. 2 lounges. Club. Disco. Inviting pool. Tennis. Travel agency. Shopping arcade. Putting green. Masseuse. AE, MC, VI. Ph: 913-1111. US: 800-722-6466. Fax: 914-0311. E-mail: mtz@caminoreal.com

COSTA BRAVA — UPPER — Lovely 164-condo complex on Camarón Sabalo Cerritos next to Paraíso Mar. One- and two-bedroom units. Restaurant. Bar. Club. Nice pool. Tennis. Parking. AE, MC, VI. Ph: 983-6444.

COSTA DE ORO – UPPER – Av. Camaron Sabalo, Zona Dorada. 290 A/C rooms. Private beach. Pool. Tennis. Secure parking. USA: 1-800-342-2431. Fax: 914-4209. E-mail: info@costaoro.com

DAMY'S BUNGALOWS — ECON — 28-unit, 3-story motel on Av. Del Mar #1200 at Camarón Glorieta. 19 kitchenettes. Some A/C. Pool. Parking. Pets OK. Ph: 983-4700, 983-4766.

DAYS INN (POSADA DE DON PELAYO) — MOD — 160 unit, 10 story hotel at Av. Del Mar #1111 across from beach. Restaurant. Bar. Club. Pool. Tennis. Car rental agency. Travel agency. Parking. AE, MC, VI. Ph: 983-1888 or 983-2233. Fax: 984-0799. E-mail: daysinnmzt@mazatlan.com.mx

DE CIMA — ECON-MOD — Big 4-story, 140-room hotel on Av. Del Mar #48. Some quieter rooms. Restaurant. Cafeteria. Club. Pool. Tennis. Book Shop. Curio shop. Tunnel from hotel to beach. Parking. AE, MC, VI. Ph: 982-7400. Fax: 982-7311.

DEL SOL — ECON-MOD — 20 rooms, 12 kitchenettes at Av. Del Mar #800. Bar. Pool. Parking. AE, MC, VI.

Ph: 985-1103 or 985-2603.

DOUBLE TREE (formerly CARAVELLE) — 128-room, 7-story beachfront hotel on Camarón Sabalo. Restaurant. Bar. Tennis. Parking. AE, MC, VI. Ph: 913-0200, 9130377, 913-0288. Fax: 916-6261. US: 1-800-222-TREE MEX: 1-800-69559.

EL CID MEGA RESORT — UPPER — Av. Camaron Sabalo s/n. EL CID GRANADA has 120 rooms, a 27-hole golf course, 9 tennis courts. 2 restaurants. Pool. — EL CID CASTILLA has 600 rooms with panoramic views. restaurants. Bars. Disco. Giant pool. Water sports. — EL CID MORO has 390 family-size suites. Pool. Jacuzzi. — EL CID MARINA has 210 suites. Restaurant. Pool. Jacuzzi. Yacht club. AE, MC, VI. Ph: 913-3333. Fax: 914-1311. Mex: 01-800-716-9800. www.elcid.com E-mail: sales@elcid.com

EL QUIJOTE INN — UPPER — On beach at corner of Av. Camarón Sabalo and Tiburón. 67 rooms, kitchenettes. Pool. SATV. Restaurant. Bar. SATV. Jacuzzi. AE, MC, VI. Ph: 914-3621, 914-3609 or 914-1134. Fax: 914-3344.

FIESTA INN — UPPER — Lovely new hotel with beach on Av. Camarón Sabalo #1927. 117 rooms. 2 pools. Ph: 989-0100 Fax: 989-0130.

HACIENDA MAZATLAN — MOD — 95-room, 9-story air-con hotel on corner Av. Del Mar and Flamingos. Pool. Restaurant. Bar. Parking. AE, MC, VI. Ph: 982-7000 Fax: 985-1579.

HOLIDAY INN SUNSPREE RESORT — UPPER — 204-room, 6-floor beach front hotel on Camarón Sabalo #696. 3 restaurants. Bar. Disco. 2 pools. Tennis. Tobacco shop. Boutiques. Barber and beauty shops. Drug store. Parking. AE, MC, VI. Ph: 913-2222 Fax: 914-1287. US: 800-465-4329 Mex: 91-800-00-999.

INN AT MAZATLÁN — UPPER — Located at Camarón Sabalo #6291. 142 rooms. Ph: 913-5166, 913-5354, Fax: 983-4782.

ISLAS DEL SOL — MOD-UPPER — Good 75-unit, 19-story condo-hotel tower on Camarón Sabalo #696 on beach next to Holiday Inn. 2-bedroom units. Restaurant. Bar. Pool. Parking. Use of Holiday Inn's facilities. AE, MC, VI. Ph: 913-0088, 913-0199, 913-0044, 913-0066, 913-0022, Fax: 913-5666.

JACARANDAS — ECON — Av del Mar across from noisy disco. 160 rooms, kitchenettes. Restaurant. Bar. 2 pools. Tennis courts. Ocean view. Parking. AE, MC, VI. Ph: 984-1177, 984-1277, Fax: 984-1077.

LA SIESTA — ECON-MOD — 57-room, 2-story hotel at Olas Altas 11 Sur. A/C and ceiling fans in some rooms. Quiet with views. Shrimp Bucket Restaurant. Bar. No pool. Shops. Parking. AE, MC, VI. Ph: 981-2640, 981-2334. Fax: 982-2633. Mex: 01-800-711-5229. www.lasiesta.com.mx E-mail: lasiesta@mazatlan.com.mx

LAS PALMAS – UPPER – Camarón Sábalo #304. 200 A/C rooms and suites. SATV. Restaurant. Pool. Tennis. AE, MC, VI. Ph: 913-4255. Fax: 914-3477.

LOS ARCOS — MOD — 20-apartment, 2-story beachfront motel on Playa Las Gaviotas beyond Playa Mazatlán. 1 and 2 bedroom kitchenette units. Pool. Parking. Ph: 983-5066.

LOS SABALOS — UPPER — Luxurious 185-room, 8-story beachfront hotel on Playa Las Gaviotas between Playa del Rey and Playa Mazatlán, on Rodolfo T. Loaiza #100. Some rooms are noisy from a nearby disco. Check first. Dignified. Restaurant. SATV. Bar. Club. Pool. Tennis. (Access to jacuzzi, sauna, steambath at health club in front of hotel — for a fee). Parking. AE, MC, VI. Ph: 913-5333, 983-5409. Fax: 983-8156. US: 800-528-8760. www.lossabalos.com E-mail: sabalos@red2000.com.mx

LUNA PALACE – UPPER – KM 12 on camarón Sabalo. 72 A/C rooms. 8 stories. Restaurant. SATV. Pool AE, MC, VI. Ph: 914-6366. Fax: 914-9666.

MARINA EL CID – UPPER – Av. Sabalos Cerritos. 103 rooms, kitchenettes. 2 tennis courts. SATV. AE, MC, VI. Ph: 983-0000.

MARLEY — MOD — 16-kitchenette, 2-story beachfront motel on Playa Las Gaviotas. One and two-bedroom units. Pool. Parking. Ph: 913-5533.

MILÁN — ECON — J.M. Canizales Pte. #717 — A popular backpacker's place. 24 rooms, some with A/C. Ph: 981-3588.

OCÉANO PALACE — UPPER — 200-room, 6-story hotel on beach just beyond Holiday Inn on Camarón Sabalo. Restaurant-bar. Roxy Disco. 2 pools. Tennis. Shopping arcade. Travel agency. Parking. AE, MC, VI. Ph: 913-0666, 913-0777, 913-6605, 913-0688 or 913-0755. US: 800-352-7690. Fax: 913-9666. Mex: 91-800-69678

PARAÍSO DEL MAR — UPPER — 153-unit, 10-story condo-hotel on Av. Sabalo Cerritos next to Costa Brava on beach. Restaurant. Bar. Club. Pool. Billiards. Tennis. Bowling. Shops. Parking. AE, MC, VI. Ph: 983-6444.

PLAYA MAR — ECON — 60 unit, 4 story hotel at Av. Del Mar #139 across from beach. 25 kitchenettes. Disco. Pool. On street parking. MC, VI. Ph: 914-0617.

PLAYA MAZATLÁN — UPPER — Av. Rodolfo T. Loaiza #202 — Good 435-room, 5 story beachfront hotel on Playa Las Gaviotas. Many restaurants and bars. Pool. Water skiing. Scuba diving. Shopping arcade. Parking. AE, MC, VI. Ph: (6) 913-4444 Fax: 914-0366 US: 800-762-5816. Mex: 91-800-69567.

PLAYA REAL BEACH & GARDEN – UPPER – Punta de Sabalo s/n. 165 room and 4 suites. SATV. Restaurants. Pool. Tennis. Water sports. AE, MC, VI. Ph: 913-111. Fax: 914-0311.

PLAZA GAVIOTAS — UPPER — 66-room, 3 story motel across from Playa Mazatlán on Playa Las Gaviotas, Bugambillas #100. Restaurant. Bar. Pool. Boutiques. Parking. AE, MC, VI. Ph: 913-4322, 913-54233, 913-4754,134496, Fax: 913-6685.

POSADA COLONIAL — ECON — Older 18 unit motel at Alemán #11, about a half-mile from ferry terminal. Some A/C. Parking. AE, MC, VI. Ph: 913-1888. Budget.

POSADA LA MISIÓN — ECON — 96 unit, 2 story hotel on Camarón Sabalo across from beach. 54 kitchenettes. Restaurant. Bar. Pool. Parking. MC, VI. Ph: 913-2444 or 913-2533.

POSADA SANTA FE — MOD — 3 story, 28 unit beachfront apartment-motel on north beach. Pool. Parking. Ph: 83-5444.

PUEBLO BONITO — UPPER — On beach at Av. Camarón Sabalo #2121 — 245 rooms, kitchenettes, SATV. 3 restaurants. Bar. Pool. A/C. AE, MC, VI. Ph: 914-3700. Fax: 914-1723. US: 800-262-4500. www.pueblobonito.com.mx E-mail: reserva@pueblobonito.com.mx

RIVIERA MAZATLÁN — UPPER — 258-room, 4-story hotel at Camarón Sabalo #51 on beach. Restaurant. Bar. Club. Pool. Jacuzzi. Tobacco shop. Car rental. Travel agency. Shopping arcade. Parking. AE, MC, VI. Ph: 983-4822. Fax: 984-4532. US: 1-800-782-4298. Mex: 91-800-69555. E-mail: riviera@mail.red2000.com.mx

ROYAL VILLAS RESORT – UPPER – Av. Camarón Sabalo #500. 12 stories shaped like a pyramid. 130 kitchenettes. 2 restaurants. Bar Jacuzzi. Gym. Pool. AE, MC, VI. Ph: 916-6161. Fax: 983-8156. Mex: 01-800-696-7000. www.royalvillas.com.mx E-mail: royal@red2000.com.mx

SANDS/LAS ARENAS — ECON — 67-room, Fairly quiet 3 story hotel on Av. Del Mar #1910 across from beach next door to disco. Restaurant. Bar. Pool. Parking. AE, MC, VI. Ph: 982-0600, 982-0800, 982-1015, 982-0000. Fax: 982-1025. www.sandsarena.com E-mail: hotelsandsarena@red2000.com.mx

SOLAMAR INN — MOD — 40-room, 4 story condo-hotel across from beach at Camarón Sabalo #1942 next to Las Brisas. Restaurant. Bar. 2 pools. Parking. AE, MC, VI. Ph: 983-6666.

SUITES CARIBE — MOD — 122-suite, 12 story condo-hotel on Loaiza next to Las Brisas. Pool. On-grounds parking. AE, MC, VI. Ph: 981-7288.

SUITES LAS FLORES — MOD — On beach, 119-kitchenette, 12 story hotel near arts-and-crafts center on Loaiza #212. Restaurant. Bar. Pool. Tennis. Parking. AE, MC, VI. Ph: 913-5100, 913-5122, 9135011. US: 800-452-0627. CA: 800-252-0327. Fax: 914-3422.

SUITES LINDA MAR — MOD — 12-suite, 3 story hotel at Playa Las Gaviotas #222 on beach. Kitchenettes. Pool. Parking. AE, MC, VI. Ph: 983-5533.

SUITES LOS ARROYOS — MOD — 38-room, 4 story hotel at Camarón Sabalo #308. Restaurant. Pool. Tobacco shop. Travel agency. Parking. MC, VI. Ph: 913-4277.

SUITES MARCOS — ECON — 12-kitchenette, 2-story layout on Av. Del Mar #1234. Pool. Parking. Ph: 983-5998.

SUITES TECALI — ECON — 14-kitchenette, 3-story complex at Gabriel Ruiz #3 in El Dorado Subdivision. Pool. Parking. MC, VI. Budget. Ph: 914-7754 Fax: 914-7755.

TORRE TROPICANA — MOD — 169-room, 10-story hotel at Loaiza #27 overlooking Playa Gaviotas. Restaurant. Bar. Pool. Tubs. Parking. AE, MC, VI. Ph: 983-8000. Fax: 983-5361. MEX: 91-800-69600. www.torretropicana.com.mx E-mail: torretropicana@red2000.com.mx

VIDALMAR — MOD — 14-suite, 3-story hotel at Av. Las Palmas #15 between downtown and north beach. Pool. No parking. Ph: 981-2190, 981-2197, 981-2820.

VILLA DEL MAR — ECON — A. Serdán #1506 Nte., near 21 de Marzo. 26 ceiling-fanned rooms. Parking. Rocking chairs in lobby. Simple, clean. Budget. Ph: 981-3426 Fax: 981-1952.

EATING IN MAZATLÁN

ANGELO'S — UPPER — Camerón Sabalo #2121 in Hotel Pueblo Bonito. Superb Italian gourmet food in an elegant setting. Live entertainment. Open 7 AM till noon and 6 PM til midnight. AE, MC, VI. Ph: 914-3700.

CAMARON — MOD — Camerón Sabalo #406 open-air and enclosed restaurant just down from Panamá Restaurant. Mexican food, seafood. Party atmosphere. Open 11 AM till Midnight. Ph: 913-2040.

CASA DEL COUNTRY — MOD — On Camerón Sabalo in front of Hotel El Quijote Inn. A lively place with loud music and dancing. Serves seafood, cabrito al horno and lots of drinks. Like Carlos 'n Charlie but with more class. Ph: 916-5300.

CASA LOMA — MOD — Nice restaurant at Las Gaviotas #104. Secluded dining room plus informal outside patio. Variety of international dishes. Poached fish with 3 wine sauces is the specialty. Reservations suggested. Open Oct. — Apr. Hours: 1:30 PM till 10:30 PM. AE, MC, VI. Ph: 913-5398. www.restaurantcasaloma.com

CLUB NATURAL – ECON – Camerón Sabalo #204-1. Delicious fresh fruit cocktails with yoghurt or cream if desired, granoa and oney. Good breakfasts and sandwiches. Good for early morning or late night snacks. No credit cards. Ph: 916-5109.

COPA DE LECHE — ECON — Next to Belmar Hotel in Olas Altas. An open-air restaurant on Malecón. Popular with backpackers. Seafood and Mexican food. Open 7 AM till 11 PM. MC, VI. Ph: 983-5753

DONEY — MOD — ATMOSPHERE — Av. Mariano Escobedo 610. Downtown. Very good restaurant east of cathedral. All types of Mexican food including seafood and steaks — also **cabrito!** But only at lunch and only sometimes. Comida Corrida! French bean soup, alubias. (It's an Italian name and it's like a little bit of Rome with strolling violin, accordion and base trios.) Open noon till midnight. Popular with locals and tourists alike, having served Mazatlán since 1959. AE, MC, VI. Ph: 916-5888, 981-5441.

ERNIE'S TOMATOES — MOD — At Adolfo T. Loiasa #403. 1/2 block from Azteca Inn. A lively place with a little bit of everything including loud music and a big screen TV. Pizza, ribs, seafood and Mexican food. Open Noon till Midnight. AE, MC, VI. Ph: 914-2474, 916-5426.

EL PARAJE — ECON — Great inexpensive food and friendly atmosphere. Wednesday Bingo and a Jazz band some nights. American Legion rents it the first and third Wednesday of month. Quite a social gathering place. All you can eat for a low price. Blvd. Camarón Sabalo between Luna Palace and Océano. Pool table and CATV. Open 7 AM till 11 PM. MC, VI, AE. Ph: 916-1301. Meme and Mary Lou, owners, speak English.

EL PATIO — UPPER — Av. Camaron Sabalo #2 601. Good, tropical-style restaurant across from Océano Palace. Lobster, steak and Mexican specialties. Strolling musicians. Good margaritas and excellent wine selection. Open 11 AM till midnight daily. AE, MC, VI. Ph: 916-5196 or 982-1709.

EL SHRIMP BUCKET — UPPER — Well-known seafood restaurant at Olas Altas #11 in La Siesta, the original restaurant of the Anderson chain. Marimba band. Open 7 AM till 11 PM. AE, MC, VI. Ph: 981-6350 or 982-8019.

GRILL LARIOS — ECON-MOD — Rodolfo T. -Loaiza #413. Mexican food. Casual. MC, VI. Ph: 984-1767.

HARLEY'S — ECON — Av. Las Garzas #8. Everything charbroiled, botanas, hamburgers, salads. Owner owns a Harley. Open 12 Noon till 1 AM Ph: 916-5414.

JADE — MOD — #412 Morelos — Chinese, Cantonese food. Closed Monday. Noon till 10 PM.

KARNES EN SU JUGO — ECON — Av. Del Mar #550 Small family-run restaurant. Specializes in Mexican Stew with chopped beef, onions, beans and bacon. Home-made tortillas. No credit cards. Ph: 982-1322.

LA CONCHA — UPPER — Av. Camarón Sabalo in El Cid Resort. Very attractive enclosed palapa with three level seating. Open for breakfast. Also outdoor tables on the beach. AE, DC, MC, VI. Ph: 913-3333.

LA COSTA MARINERA — MOD — Next to Oceano Palace hotel and close to Holiday Inn in North Beach. Superb fish filet in garlic and butter. A Mexican favorite.

LA FONTANA — MOD — Av. Laguna #306 (or can enter from gift shop on Camarón Sabalo. Excellent seafood and service in a outdoor palapa.

LA MANZANA — MOD — Vegetarian restaurant at Belisario Domínguez #1809 and corner of Calle 21 de Marzo, Ph: 982-6143. Another is also located at Av. Del Mar between Gral. Pesqueíra and Flamingos. Open for lunch only, 11 AM till 2 PM.

LA MURALLA CHINA — MOD — For a diffe5-rent taste, this restaurant has great food at a resonable price. At Juan Carrasco Y Aguascalientes 518, Ph: 982-6143.

LOS ARCOS — MOD — Tropical open-air restaurant on Del Mar. Seafood fresh from ocean. Open noon till 10 PM. AE, MC, VI. Ph: 913-9577 or 914-0999.

MAMUCA'S - MOD-UPPER — Simón Bolívar #404 — Popular downtown seafood restaurant a block off waterfront. A real down home seafood place, no frills, great food. It's like a New Orleans seafood restaurant and since 1961 is known as "Rey de Mariscos." Features Parillada de Mariscos plus "seafood explosion," a variety tray and seafood dishes such as Paela, Langostinos (craw fish). Open 10 AM till 10 PM. MC, VI. Ph: 981-3490.

MR. "A's" —UPPER — Across from Costa de Oro. One half block off Camarón Sabalo. White table cloths, elegant with soft music. Excellent.

MIKIKO — UPPER — In the golden zone by Banamex. Japanese food and drinks. Sushi, teppan yaki, sake and beer. AE, MC, VI. Ph: 981-6590.

PANAMÁ — MOD — On Camarón Sabalo next to Guadalajara Grill and across from Lobster Trap. Popular breakfast and lunch place and pastelería. Omlettes and nopales, tacos, submarine sandwiches, sopes, BBQ, licuados and a nice variety of fruit drinks, cakes and breads. No smoking. Open 7 AM till 11 PM. MC, VI. Ph: 913-6977.

PARAÍSO 3 ISLAS — MOD — Rodolfo T. Loaiza, on the beach across from Seashell City and next to Las Cabañas shopping center. Seafood. Great lobster. Casual. 8 AM till 11 PM, MC, VI. Ph: 914-2812.

PEDRO'S FISH and CHIPS — ECON — Open air restaurant on Camarón Sabalo next to Cavanderia. Breakfast specials on Mexican food. "El Sabalo" seafood. Open 9 AM till midnight.

PEPE Y JOE'S — ECON — Punta Camarón. Lots of (home-made) beer. Also good hamburgers, hot dogs and sandwiches. AE, MC, VI. Ph: 984-1666.

RANCHO LAS MORAS — UPPER — this 150-year -odl hacienda consistas of six bedroms, 5 cottages, a tequila processing area, storage facilities and an open air church over looking teh mountain coutryside. For reservations & information call Ph: (69) 16-50-44 or Fax: (69) 16-50-45. Av. Camaron Sabalo 204, Suite 6, Zona Dorada 82110.

ROCAMAR — ECON — Av. Del Mar next to Pizza Hut across from beach. Seafood with daily lunch speials. Open daily. Ph: 81-6008. Also at Av. Del Mar and Isla de Lobos. Ph: 981-0023.

SHEIK — MOD — Av. Camarón Sabalo. International food Beautiful view. Ph: 984-1722.

SHRIMP FACTORY — MOD — On Adolfo T. Loaiza, near North Beach on east side of Playa Las Gaviotas just north of Azteca Inn about 100 yards. Seafood, shrimp and lobster. Open 11 AM till 11 PM. MC, VI. Ph: 916-5318.

SR. FROG — UPPER — Popular disco/restaurant on Del Mar Between Hotel Del Sol and Suites Caribe. Popular with "party-hearty" crowd. Decent food, especially ribs and Oysters Madrazo. Excellent drinks. Open noon till midnight daily. AE, MC, VI. Ph: 985-1110 or 982-1925.

SR. PEPPERS — MOD — Av. Camarón Sabalo across from Hotel Camino Real. Elegant yet unpretentious. Specialty lobster grilled on mesquite. Dancing and live music. No lunch. No credit cards. Ph: 914-0101.

SUPER TACOS LA CARRETA — ECON — #325 Av. Gutiérrez Nájera — next to electrical store. Look for **neon pig** sign.

TONY'S PLAZA — UPPER — Nice restaurant in Plaza Las Gaviotas. Another is located on the beach at Plaza Bonita next to Océano Palace. Good international cuisine and excellent service. Open noon till 4 PM and 6 PM till midnight. MC, VI. Ph: 983-4233.

CAMPING & RV PARKING

HOLIDAY RV PARK (formerly PLAYA ESCONDIDA) — MOD-UPPER — Tropical 232 space park out on far north end beyond Camino Real. Showers. Toilets. Saltwater pool. Rec hall. Store in office. 15 amps. Concrete patios. Pets OK on leash. Ph and Fax: 988-0077.

LA POSTA — MOD-UPPER — Nice place. It's a 210 space park at Calz. Buelna #7, just east of Camarón Glorieta (on bypass road to Hwy #15). All hookups. Showers. Toilets. Pool. 3 rec halls. Shuffleboard. Concrete patios. Car and boat rentals. Convenience store. Beach nearby. Pets OK on leash. Ph: 983-5310.

LAS PALMAS — UPPER — 66 space park at Camarón Sabalo #333. All hookups. Noisy from nearby clubs. Unconcerned management. Some rodent problems. Apartments. Showers. Toilets. Rec hall. Pool. Beach 11 KM. Pets OK on leash. Ph: 913-6424.

MAR ROSA — MOD-UPPER — 65 small spaces at north end next to Holiday Inn on beach. All hookups. New showers and toilets. Night security. Patios. Rec. area. Some pull-thrus. Small store. Pets OK on leash. Permanents have ocean fans (16 lots). Ph and Fax: 13-6187.

MARAVILLAS — MOD — 34 space park on secluded beach at far north end of town Between DIF and Quinta del Mar on Cerritos beach. Some spaces a little difficult for big rigs. All hookups. Showers. Toilets. Rec hall. Concrete patios. Pets OK. Ph: 984-0400.

POINT SOUTH MAZATLÁN TRAILER PARK — MOD — Value! In Zona Dorada on Camarón Sabalo #109 across the street from Hotel Riviera and Hotel Sabalos and next door to Los Venados Restaurant and Casa de Cambio. 50 spaces with full hookups. 30 Amp electricity. Cement patios. Baths. Hot showers. Beach nearby. Often full with caravans. English spoken. Emergency medical service. Full security parking. Ph: 983-2157 Fax: 984-1833 US: 1-800-421-1394 US Fax: (909) 924-3838.

SAN BARTOLO — MOD — 46 space north end park off Camarón Sabalo across from beach. All hookups. Showers. Toilets. 15 amps. Rec. area. Friendly place. (Closed June to October) Ph and Fax: 913-5755.

OTHER

ABZ TRAVEL AGENCY — Located at Hotel del Sol on Av. Del Mar #800. Ph: 981-7442. Open 8 AM till 12 Noon, Mon-Fri.

CLÍNICA LOMAS — Fracc. Lomas de Mazatlán, Buena Nevada #130. Dr Juan José Porras MD. speaks English. Ph: 916-5555. 983-3523, Fax: 986-3162.

MAIL BOXES ETC. — full service operation (very professional)- phone, fax, copies, mail handling, office supplies, etc. Ave. Camaron Sabalo 310, Mazatlan, Sin. Ph: 16-40-09 & 16-40-10. Fax: 16-40-11.

SHARP HOSPITAL — Located at corner of Av. Buelna and Doctor Kumate. Excellent facility for major or minor operations or plastic surgery.

End of Mazatlán Eat & Stray

Creel & the Copper Canyon

UD-017

Area Code —635

CREEL'S a great place to relax and return to a QUIET, unhurried life. Set against the backdrop of imposing mountains, you know you're in a special place. Like Alamos, Son; Bisbee, AZ; Real de Catorce, SLP; or Palenque, CHI, it attracts a special type of searcher. More for visionaries (or those whose life-vision has become limited) than excitement seekers. This is a place where you can find yourself by losing yourself. Let the Canyon work its magic on you. You'll be glad you came. You can walk around town in less than an hour. Remember, though, that you're at 7,000 feet. Take it easy. Some spots listed below you can drive to but others you'll have to take a tour. As in the US, please lock your car and don't leave any valuables in it before heading off. Your hotel can arrange a tour for you. Here's a list of some of the spectacular things to see.

BASASEACHIC FALLS — 900 feet of cascading waterfall! A day trip.

BATOPILAS — Old mysterious mining town below La Bufa. Semitropical vegetation.

CUSARARE WATERFALL — Out by the Copper Canyon Lodge, you can walk from there in a hour each way. It's a couple of miles by dirt path.

EL TEJABÁN — Perhaps the best view of the canyon — pretty remote. Allow a day to get there and back.

LA BUFA — Mysterious site of Spanish mine. One story has silver the size of basketballs coming out of here. Some stories have hordes of silver hidden by the Tarahumara Indians in special places. Steep descent from 7,000 to about 2,500 feet.

RECOHUATA HOT SPRINGS — 2 to 3 hours steep strenuous hike (see Pensión Creel).

VALLEY OF THE GODS — Wind, rain, sun and climate have carved some magnificent expressions in the rocks.

CHRIS HALL — A good tour guide. He speaks English, French, Italian and Spanish. A great guy. He can be found at Burger Creel or at Margarita's (use her fax #) or call Presidio Information Center 1-800-597-4168 in Presidio, TX

PAPELERIA DE TODO — A good office and photo supply store. #30 Lopez Mateos, Creel.Ph.: 60-122 & 60-222

SLEEPING IN CREEL

CASA VALENZUELA — ECON — Least expensive in town. Rooms with bath in private house across from Abarrotes LaCombe

CASCADA INN — MOD — Next to Parador. 32 Rooms. Good beds. Heaters. Steak house restaurant. Parking. Indoor pool. Ph: 456-0151 Fax: 456-0253.

COPPER CANYON LODGE — MOD — 12 miles south of town beyond lake. 29 rooms. Old-world atmosphere. Rustic. Wood-burning stoves and kerosine lanterns. Fireplace in lobby. Fine restaurant. First lodge in Creel, restored by Skip McWilliams, open since 1965. Popular with hikers and Europeans. Reservations advised through travel agent in Chihuahua, Ph: 412-8893. US Reservations: 1-800-776-3942 He also owns inn at Batopilas. A great experience.

KORACHI — ECON — Francisco Villa #116 next to bus station — 20 rooms (12 with bath). There are also 14 cabañas in back with wood stoves and large private baths. Ph: 456-0207.

LA POSADA DE CREEL — MOD — Av. López Mateos #25, on left as you go into town. 21 units, some with private bath. Ph and Fax: 456-0142.

MARGARITA'S — ECON — Very nice 17 Cabañas, 3 bedroom and various layouts, 1 suite and 1 cabañita. With breakfast and dinner. Ph and Fax: 456-0245. Good guide — Chris Hall.

MARGARITA'S PLAZA MEXICANA — ECON — Hostel-like (Casa de Huéspedes) Calle Chapultepec s/n All with breakfast and dinner. BBQ and great atmosphere. For backpackers and those on a budget Ph and Fax: 456-0045

NUEVO BARRANCAS DEL COBRE — MOD — Very nice hotel in town, behind train depot — 22 heated and carpeted rooms. Very good management. Lots of hot water. MC, VI. Ph: 456-0022.

PARADOR DE LA MONTAÑA — MOD — Av. López Mateos #44 — In town, just across tracks and 1 block right (South) past station on left side of street — 36 rooms, 3 Jr. suites, 1 Presidential suite, which sleeps 8 with kitchen. Can house 125 people. Restaurant. Bar. Tours. Gift shop. House doctor. Very nice. Phones in room. Second oldest lodge in Creel, open since 1971. Ph: 456-0075 or 456-0085. Chihuahua: 410-4580. Fax: 415-3468. Eugenio Cuesta, owner.

SIERRA BONITA CABAÑAS CLUB – UPPER – Situated on hill overlooking town. 21 cabins with kitchens and fireplaces. SATV. 1 Jacuzzi suite. Restaurant. Disco-bar. Jeep rental. E-mail: esbonita@chih/.telmex.net.mx Ph: & Fax in Chihuahua: 410-4015, 410-4557 or USA: 1-899-713-4460.

THE LODGE AT CREEL (Best Western) – UPPER – Lopez Mateos #61 (the main street of Creel) Stylish log cabins with fireplaces, porches on secluded grounds bordered by dramatic rocky point. Atmosphere dining. meditation meeting lodge. E-mail: bwcreel@prodigy.net.mx Ph: 456-0071 Fax: 456-0082 USA: 1-800-879-4071.

EATING IN CREEL

Both the Copper Canyon Lodge and the Parador have good restaurants with varied menus.

EL CABALLO BAYO — MOD — Nice restaurant and bar next door to La Posada de Creel. Varied menu Open 2 PM till 10 PM. Ph: 456-0136.

ESTELA — ECON — Very nice little place. Home cooking, guisado and good soups. Cook — Manela. Open 7 AM till 9 PM.

LUPITA — ECON — Across from Parador 1/2 block toward town, same side as train station. Great Mexican food. Neat. Clean. Comfy with old fashioned jukebox.

CAMPING & RV PARKING

KOA CREEL RV PARK — UPPER — Located just off the main highway on Calle López Mateos in Creel. Business Office in Chihuahua at Av. Tecnológico #4904, Col. Grandes Ind. Chihuahua, Chih CP 31160. Owner: Fernando Cuesta. 73 RV spaces all with E/W and 35 with sewer. Most have 30 amps. 20 camping cabins, 30 tent sites. Camping kitchen. Restaurant. Bar. Ph: 421-7088 Fax: 421-7089. Toll-free US : 1-888-610-2095 Mex: 01-800-710-6422. E-mail: fcuesta@infosel.net.mx

PARADOR DE LA MONTAÑA — MOD — In connection with hotel. Accepts RV's in secured parking area.

NO HOOKUPS, but owner will let you use facilities if not full. Can arrange for tours and rail trips. English. Friendly. Ph: 456-0075 or 456-0085.

BEYOND CREEL

EL TEJABÁN

TEJABÁN — MOD — Isolated with stupendous view on the rim of canyon. Difficult to get to, you must have a vehicle with high clearance. 12 rooms with fireplaces and small tubs that have jacuzzi jets. Excellent restaurant, where you'll undoubtedly eat as it's too much trouble to go back to town. Pool. 2 casas with tub jacuzzi. Own generating plant. Also has dormitory rooms with bunk bed space for 40 people. Altitude 7,200 feet.

DIVISADERO:

HOTEL DIVISADERO BARRANCAS — UPPER — The first hotel you come to. You pay for the fact that they are on the canyon rim. 52 rooms. Meals included in price. In Chihuahua: Apdo. Postal #661 C.P. 31238 MC, VI. Chihuahua Ph: 415-1199 Fax: 415-6575. E-mail: hoteldivisdero@infosel.net.mx

LA MANSIÓN TARAHUMARA — UPPER — Go about 3 1/2 miles past the Hotel Divisadero Barrancas. It's the second hotel you'll see (the first is the Misión). It's on a hill to the left.15 cabins. Restaurant. Bar. Ph: 415-4721 Fax: 416-5444 in Chihuahua. E-mail: mansion@buzon.online.com.mx Owner María Barriga is very friendly and knowledgeable and a good friend of Sanborn's. **RV's can park here!** There is even a honeymoon suite! Be careful for railroad crossing at entrance to her place. Sometimes they are uneven.

MISIÒN — UPPER — 30 rooms. Very nice place with good restaurant. Reservations thru Santa Anita hotel in Los Mochis. Ph: (6) 815-7046. In Chihuahua: 416-5950.

PARAÍSO DEL OSO — UPPER — 15 rooms with bath. Rustic hotel at the foot of a toothy mountain with a natural rock profile of a bear. Offers a Urique Canyon trip by four-wheel drive vehicle.

POSADA BARRANCAS MIRADOR — MOD-UPPER — An extension of Rancho Posada Barrancas. 30 rooms and 2 suites. Fantastic fireplace view of Canyon. Restaurant. Bar. Gift shop. Soft beds. Dining room. Group rates. Reservations thru Santa Anita in Los Mochis. Ph: (6) 818-7046 Fax: (6) 812-0046. In Chihuahua: (1) 416-5950 or 416-6589.

RANCHO DEL OSO CAMPGROUND — 5 km north of Cerocahui. Buried cave and archeological sites. Owned by Doug.

RANCHO POSADA BARRANCAS — MOD-UPPER — A Balderama hotel. 35 rooms. Wood-burning fireplaces. Garden, vineyard and orchard. Reservations thru Santa Anita in Los Mochis. Ph: (6) 818-7046 Fax: (6) 812-0046. In Chihuahua: 416-5950 or 416-6589.

BATOPILAS: Area code 645

SLEEPING IN BATOPILAS

BATOPILAS — ECON — On road into town. Good water pressure. Ceiling fans. Public bathrooms. Primitive.

CASA BUSTILLOS — ECON — On the plaza, look for "Indian Curios" sign. 4 rooms, rather Spartan, but with hot water and gardens. River behind sounds nice. No screens on doors. Popular with the backpackers. Owner has a washing machine.

CHULA VISTA — ECON — On road into town. 8 room. Common bathroom. Spartan, but will do in a pinch.

MARY — ECON — On Calle Juárez, across from the church. Many long term guests. Well run. 12 rooms, two stories. Nice garden courtyard. Hot water.

PALMERA — ECON — The first hotel as you enter town. 6 rooms. My favorite. The best of the economy hotels. It's clean, the owner is nice and the place is clean. Nice restaurant.

RIVERSIDE LODGE (formerly Hacienda Batopilas) — UPPER — Staying at this luxury resort is like stepping back into another century. The old-world furnishings, oriental rugs, feather beds. Ceiling fans and lush gardens make you feel like you are in a turn-of-the century hacienda, which is the desired effect. You'll be served gourmet meals to boot. The sitting room might remind those who know of a bordello with its oil paintings and furnishings. The ceiling is painted with cherubs and churches like in a cathedral. Tubs. Tours. It's pricey and you must stay for three days. Make reservations in the U.S. at 1-800-776-3942. If you didn't plan ahead, try making a reservation at the Copper Canyon Lodge back in Creel since all guests originate from there. Price includes transportation from Creel to Batopilas and you might as well take advantage of it and save the wear and tear on your vehicle. The owner, Skip McWilliams promised a small discount to members. Reservations in Chihuahua. Ph: 414-1582. Ph: and Fax: 414-1505.

EATING IN BATOPILAS

Hotels Palmera, Mary and Casa Bustillos have restaurants. Food is mainly tacos, enchiladas, guisados and chicken. Guests at the Riverside Lodge, have excellent meals, but if you aren't a guest, you can't eat there. You can make deals with individuals to cook for you in their homes. You can also make deals to rent rooms.

DOÑA MICA'S — This isn't really a restaurant. You eat on the lady's front porch. Mica's been serving guests for 25 years. To get there, walk past the basketball court to the dead end, turn right, then walk a long block. Her house is on the right, just before the walkway goes uphill and narrows. Look for a house with a big porch. There are two tables with plastic covers over colorful tablecloths and little wooden chairs. You can't just drop in. You have to go by in the morning and tell her you want to eat. She has to buy the food for you for the next day for breakfast, lunch or dinner. Although she has electricity, like gourmet cooks the world over, she doesn't trust it for cooking and uses her gas stove. She says she doesn't have much money, but is rich in friendship. Eating there is like making a new friend or grandmother.

GENERAL INFO

Things to do here include visiting the Shepherd mansion, now in ruins, hiking the many trails and visiting the old cathedral at Satevó. Some guidebooks refer to this as a lost cathedral, but it was never lost. It's on the royal road to Alamos, so its location was never a mystery. It has been neglected, though. To get there, go to the end of town (to the left of the plaza), turn left to the river. This is a steep embankment, so be careful. Follow the only road around until you see the cathedral on your left. It will take about 45 minutes. Ask for the key at the first house on the left. There are very old drawings and an air of decay inside. It's worth a visit.

End of Creel & Copper Canyon Eat & Stray

Tepic

UD-019

Area Code — 311
See map on page 33

SLEEPING IN TEPIC

BUGAMVILLAS – UPPER – Very nice 50-room hotel at Av. Insurgentes and Libramiento Pte. Family restaurant. Pool. CATV. Suites with jacuzzi. Ph and Fax: 218-0225.

CORITA – MOD – 34-room, 3-story hotel on Hwy #15 one block south of sports center. Restaurant-bar. Pool. Disco. Enclosed parking. MC, VI. Ph: 212-0477.

DEL SOL – MOD – 25-unit motel a few blocks south of Hwy #15-200 junction. No A/C. Small restaurant. Enclosed parking. Pets OK. MC, VI. Ph: 212-2828.

FRAY JUNÍPERO SERRA – MOD – Lerdo #23 Pte. – Good 5-story, 85-room downtown hotel across from main plaza (on south corner). Some A/C. Restaurant. Bar. Parking. AE, MC, VI. Best hotel in town. Ph: 212-2525. Fax: 212-2051.

LOS PINOS – MOD – Comfy little 17-kitchenette motel and RV park a couple miles south on Hwy #200 next to Linda Vista. Pool. Parking. Pets OK. Ph: 213-1232.

SAN JORGE – MOD – Lerdo #124 – 3-story, 39-room downtown hotel, a couple of blocks back of main plaza.

Restaurant. Parking. MC, VI. Ph: 212-1755 or 212-1709.

SANTA FE – MOD – Calzada de la Cruz #385 – 2-story, 36-room hotel a block off Hwy #200, across from normal school. No A/C. Restaurant. Parking. Ph: 213-1966.

SIERRA DE ALICIA – MOD – Av. Mexico #180 Pte. – Fair 3-story, 60-room hotel a block before main plaza. No A/C. No restaurant. Parking. Pets OK. AE, MC, VI. Ph: 212-1040. Fax: 212-1309.

VILLA LAS ROSAS – MOD – Insurgentes #100 Pte. – 30-room motel, old Hwy #15 thru town. Restaurant. Bar. Enclosed parking. MC, VI. Ph: 213-1800 or 213-1857.

EATING IN TEPIC

BEACHCOMBER – MOD – Insurgentes and Durango – Thatched-roof restaurant on Hwy #15 across from Loma Park. Delicious carne asada and seafood. MC, VI.

CENADURÍA LUPITA — MOD — Av. Allende #276 Pte. More than fifty years serving authentic "Antojitos Mexicanos." Free home delivery. Open 1:00 PM till 10:30 PM daily except Monday. Ph: 212-2579.

FONDA HUICOT – MOD – Colonial restaurant on Hwy #200 (toward Puerto Vallarta). Serves basic Mexican food, but menu includes some American dishes. MC, VI.

FU SENG – Cantonese food and take out, in historic building 1 1/2 blocks from plaza. Ph: 212-0010

INTERNACIONAL (ROBERTO'S) – MOD – Militar and Insurgentes – Good restaurant a half-block from La Loma across from north side of Loma Park. International cuisine. Excellent food and service. Open 1 PM till 1 AM. MC, VI. Ph: 212-2717.

LA TERRAZA – MOD – Insurgentes Pte. #98 – Restaurant-soda fountain (Hwy #15 thru town) across from park. Specialties include Pollo Asado (grilled chicken). Newsstand with U.S. publications. Open 7 AM till 11 PM. MC, VI.

LOS MOLCAJETES – MOD – Calle Mexico – Popular place serving Mexican and American food (main street into downtown) a block from state capitol.

TIN JAO – MOD – In front of Loma park at Paseo de la Loma #199-A. Unpretentious Chinese food. Shank fin soup very good. Open 1 PM till 11 PM. Owner speaks English, Spanish and Taiwanese. No credit cards. Ph: 214-0944

CAMPING & RV PARKING

KAMPAMENTO KOA – UPPER – 87-space park about 3.5 miles east of town and about a half-mile off Hwy #15 down cobblestone road just beyond Lázaro Cárdenas tobacco plant ("Planta Despitadora Lázaro Cárdenas"). 34 spaces with all hookups; 31 with electrical and water only; 12 tent spaces. Laundry. Showers. Restrooms. Pool. Dump stations. Rec hall. Store. Ice. Ph: 213-2699. Fax: 213-3113.

KOALA BUNGALOWS and T.P. – MOD – 52 KM Southeast of Tepic and 20 KM from Tepic/Guadalajara Highway on Laguna de Santa Maria. Near crater lake. 730 M above sea level and 2 KM in diameter. 65 spaces with electricity and water. Camping. Boat ramp. Swimming. Boating. Fishing.

LOS PINOS – UPPER – From south bypass, follow road to city for 2 KM. Located on left. 24-space RV park with all hookups. Showers. Toilets. Concrete pads. Ph: 212-2427.

End of Tepic Eat & Stray

San Blas

UD-019

Area Code — 323

See map on page 70

SAN BLAS used to be an important port for Spanish fleet and had galleons unloading from the Far East regularly. Now it's popular with surfers, bird watchers and laid-back Gringos. Matanchén beach is delightful, though Playa Borrego at the end of town is more easily accessed.

TOURIST OFFICE – next to McDonald's. Fishing licenses – Pesca office beyond Las Garzas Canela.

NEARBY ATTRACTIONS

LOS COCOS BEACH – between Aticama and Santa Cruz. Very nice. "Police" permanently stationed in small building in front of restaurant La Manzanilla and w ill help with car problems!

Two places nearby are of particular interest. Closest is Santiago Ixcuintla, home of the Huichol Center for Cultural Survival. From the junction with Hwy #15 and San Blas turnoff, it's 14 miles north, then west 8 KM. If you have an interest in these native peoples' way of life or would like to learn some of their unique bead work or weaving techniques, you should check it out. Their eye-socket popping bead work is prized by collectors everywhere. You may see some of it in Pto. Vallarta. If you're truly interested, call Susana Eger Valadez (3) 235-1171. If she can, she'll arrange a class for you. Since this is also a medical center for the Huichol people, she discourages drop-ins, but if you have an honest interest in learning, helping with the hospital, or buying a lot of Huichol artwork, you couldn't ask for a better opportunity. In the U.S. or Canada, you can order a color catalog of the Huichol works for sale from: Huichol Center, P.O. Box 1430, Cottonwood, AZ 86326. PH: (602) 634-3946.

The other is Mexcaltitán, the "Venice of Mexico" and traditional home of the Aztecs. It was here that Aztec priests saw a snake in a cactus, which directed them to build the great city of Mexico. Turnoff is 23.7 miles north of the San Blas junction with Hwy #15. Annual "Feria de Mexicanidad" celebrates the event in Tepic, Nay., Nov. 16 – Dec 2.

LOCAL EXCURSIONS

JUNGLE BOAT TRIP #1 – departs from next to the bridge over Río San Cristóbal as you enter town. It takes about 3 hours and goes down the river for a short way and then up La Tobara Tributary to beautiful La Tobara Springs with amazingly clear water. Take your swim suit as the boat stops for an hour there. Refreshments are available.

JUNGLE BOAT TRIP #2 – is shorter than #1 (1.5 hours) because the boat is boarded farther up Río Tobara where the gravel road to Matanchén beach crosses the river.

JUNGLE BOAT TRIP #3 – leaves from the same place as #2, but goes to jungle zoo – crocodile farm – same price as #2.

BIRD TRIPS – San Blas is renowned among bird watchers! More than 300 species of birds can be seen here. They come in groups just for the bird watching. Manuel works with Audubon groups and will take you out. Ask at the Las Garzas Canela hotel. While you're there, a great book on the feathered friends who visit the area is for sale – *Finding Birds in San Blas*. It's reasonably priced and excellent.

FISHING – Great! Get a guide and go river or deep-sea fishing. Just make sure you both agree on a price before you set out (always a good idea anywhere). Also, check the boat to make sure they have enough safety features for your liking. Call Pipla 285-0362 or ask for Tony Aguayo or Tony P. at the docks or Las Garzas Canela.

AA – English. M–W–F 6 PM 9:30 Sun. Comes and goes. Check at restaurant McDonald's to see if any are going on.

JEJENES – Well, folks, we'd be remiss in our responsibility to you if we failed to tell you about the reason why San Blas has been saved from becoming a Cancún or Ixtapa. It's the home of a pesty little gnat called a "jejene," pronounced "he-he-nee." These nasty little gnats are most prevalent during the summer months, but they can show up at any time – early morning, late evening, night. They don't even take a siesta at midday. They're a sort of sand fly and are quite tiny, but they bite BIG. Don't worry, they won't really hurt you, and they're quite democratic, biting locals and tourists alike. A citronella candle might help. (It does wonders with mosquitoes.)

LONG DISTANCE PHONE AND FAX – If you need to send a message home, inquire at Farmacia Económica, 1 block from the plaza on Calle Batallón, toward beach. PH: (3) 215-0111.

We hope you have a most enjoyable time here in old San Blas.

SAN BLAS isn't Puerto Vallarta or Mazatlán. There's no "Gold Zone." That's why some folks love it. If a rustic, off-the-beaten-track place is your cup of tea, then you'll drink your fill in old San Blas. If discos are for you, San Blas isn't.

SLEEPING IN SAN BLAS

BUCANERO – ECON – Juárez #75 – 2-story, 33 room emergency-economy hotel converted from old warehouse mansion on main street a long block beyond plaza. Restaurant. Very loud, in-and-out bar. Parking. Pets OK. MC, VI. Ph: 285-0101.

CASA ROXANNA - MOD - Callejón del Rey #1 and Comonfort just behind Posada del Rey. 3 very nice bungalows with A/C and kitchenettes. Screened-in porch. Pool. Run by Roxanne Summers. Ph: 285-0573.

LAS GARZAS CANELA – UPPER – Paredes S/N – The nicest place in town! 42-rooms. All A/C; some ceiling fans. Breakfast included. Very nice restaurant-bar. SATV. Pool. One and two-bedroom kitchenette. Enclosed parking. Pets OK. Fishing and tours arranged. Bird watchers' headquarters. English, French, German spoken. Nice book and souvenir shop with unique items. AE, MC, VI. Ph: 285-0112. Fax: 285-0308.

LOS FLAMINGOS – ECON – Calle Juárez #163 – 2-story, 24-room emergency-economy hotel converted from German consulate on main street a block beyond Bucanero (and like the Bucanero, has seen better days). Some A/C; mostly ceiling fans. No restaurant. Parking. Pets OK. Ph: 285-0448.

MARINO INN – ECON – Av. Heróica Batallón de San Blas – 54-room air-con hotel across from Centro de Salud on road thru town. Restaurant. Disco. Pool. Parking. MC, VI. Ph: 289-1321 or 285-0340.

POSADA DEL REY – MOD – Simple, clean 12-room A/C motel. Restaurant/bar serves snacks. English spoken. Pool. Night watchman. Parking. MC, VI. Ph: 285-0123.

SUITES SAN BLAS – MOD – Fracc. Palmar De Los Cocos, 3 miles – 3-story, 23-unit hotel (17 one-bedroom and 6 two-bedroom kitchenette suites at south end of town. No air-con; ceiling fans only. No restaurant. Pool. Playground. Disco. On-street parking. Monthly rates. AE, MC, VI. Ph: 285-0047 or 285-0505.

EATING IN SAN BLAS

EL DELFIN – UPPER – At Las Garzas Canela Hotel. Elegant white tablecloth place. A/C. Fish fillet with oyster and pecan sauce or oysters, mushrooms and shrimp. English spoken.

LA HACIENDA – MOD – Calle Juárez #33 – Across street and down a few doors from bank. Charming decor. Wonderful carnitas (deep fried pork)! Can buy by kilo or 1/2.

LA FAMILIA – MOD – Batallón #18 – Very attractive authentic Mexican-style restaurant housed in an old restored colonial home in town. Domingo Gutiérrez is your gracious host, an educated man who once studied to be a veterinarian. Hand painted menus by Rafael Gutiérrez, (his father) whose paintings adorn the wall. They are for sale. Try pescado or shrimp quetenque. Soothing dinner music. Open 5 PM till 10 PM daily; closed Sunday. Ph: 285-2058.

McDONALD'S – MOD – Calle Juárez #36 – (Not the golden arches type) Good restaurant a block west of main plaza. Good Mexican-style beef filets, fish filets, broiled lobster, shrimp, tacos, and enchiladas. Reasonable prices. Local gathering spot for local Gringos, including Friends of Bill W. Open 7 AM till 10 PM daily. Ph: 285-0432.

PEPI'S PLACE — ECON — On Juárez north of old customs house ruins and across street from El Bucanero Motel. Lumber-jack style breakfasts and great fresh cooked lunches and dinners. Produce is fresh daily. English spoken.

ROSY'S – MOD – Typical and clean family restaurant. Mexican food, including sopes, enchiladas, tacos, tostadas. On plaza, near church.

TONY'S INN LA ISLA – MOD – Paredes Sur – Small, decorated with nets and shells, restaurant with excellent shrimp, fish, lobster, and steak. Open from 2 till 10 PM daily. Ph: 5-0407.

TORINO'S – MOD – Town's largest restaurant located downtown a block beyond plaza across from Bucanero, on main stem. Open 8 AM till 10 PM daily. MC, VI. Seasonal.

SLEEPING IN LOS COCOS

CASA MAÑANA – MOD – 9.7 miles south of junction of "Santa Cruz – Aticama" highway and San Blas road (same as Playa Amor T.P.). 7 rooms, 2 bungalows. Nice views. Owned by nice German fellow.

EATING IN LOS COCOS BEACH

SOUTH COCOS – MOD – Good seafood, hamburgers – "*estillo* USA." Open 9-1, 5-9.

CAMPING & RV PARKING

LOS COCOS – ECON-MOD – 100-space park off main stem near beach. All hookups. Pull thru spaces. Showers. Restrooms. SATV in bar. Laundry service. Rec hall. Bar. Boat ramp, nearby. 20 amps. Pets OK. Nice place. Ph: 285-0055.

PLAYA AMOR – MOD – Between San Blas and Santa Cruz – Highly recommended! 40-space facility on beach. 25 with all hookups. 15 with electricity and water. 30 amps. Showers – hot water. Toilets. Security wall and guard. English spoken. Fishing. Hiking. Boat ramp. Laundry service. Rooftop patio rec hall. Just before San Blas, take left to Alicama/Santa Cruz, go 6 miles south on paved road. On right. Look for "papelia" tree at entrance.

End of San Blas Eat & Stray

Rincón de Guayabitos

UD-019

Area Code — 327

SLEEPING IN RINCÓN DE GUAYABITOS

CASA DE ORO — Bungalows with kitchenette and pool.

COSTA ALEGRE — 72 room, 2 story beachfront motel on Tabachines. 19 kitchenettes. Some A/C. Pool. Parking.

DIANA BUNGALOWS — 19 bungalow, 2 story motel a half-block away from beach on Av. Del Sol Nuevo. Restaurant. Pool. Parking. Pets OK.

EL DELFIN BUNGALOWS — 14 bungalow, 2 story motel on Ceibas near beach. Pool. Parking. Pets OK.

EL RINCONCITO — 10 bungalow, 2 story beachfront motel on Ceibas. Restaurant. Bar. Club. Pool. Parking. Reservations suggested. Pets OK.

FIESTA MAR — Nice 24 room, 2 story A/C hotel two blocks from beach. Restaurant. Bar. Enclosed parking. MC, VI. Ph: 621-3535 in Guadalajara.

LAS HACIENDAS — 19 room kitchenette motel on Laureles on beach. Pool. Parking. Pets OK.

MARIA TERESA — 15 kitchenette complex a block from beach. No restaurant. Parking. Small pets OK.

PEÑA MAR — 86 room A/C hotel on north entrance to town near beach. Restaurant. Piano bar. Disco. Pools. Tennis. Parking. Ph: 614-9871 in Guadalajara.

PLAYA DE ORO — NEW HOTEL UNDER CONSTRUCTION ON BEACH.

POSADA DEL SOL — 10 bungalow, 3 room complex on Del Sol Nuevo near beach. Restaurant. Pool. Parking. 4 RV spaces.

QUINTA TERE — 7 kitchenette, 2 story complex in residential area on beach. No restaurant. Pool. Parking. Pets OK.

SAN CARLOS — 32 bungalow, 27 room, 2 story complex on Laureles on beach. Restaurant. Bar. Pool. Parking. Pets OK. Ph: 277-0025 in Compostela, NAY.

TITO'S — Some suites. Restaurant. Bar. Pool.

EATING IN RINCÓN DE GUAYABITOS & VICINITY

BEACHCOMBER — Rustic beachfront restaurant near Trópico Cabañas. Seafood specialties.

ROBERTO'S — Another rustic beachfront restaurant specializing in seafood, of course.

VILLANUEVA'S — Seafood restaurant in conjunction with RV park of same name.

CAMPING & RV PARKING

DELIA — 16 space facility across from Paraíso del Pescador. All hookups. Showers. Toilets. Laundromat.

Coffee shop. Grocery. Curio store. LP gas. Ice. Pets OK.

EL CARACOL — 22 space facility in Lo de Marcos on beach. All hookups. Dump station. Showers. Toilets. Concrete patios. Pets OK. 5 bungalows with kitchenette.

EL DORADO — Nice 21 space facility set in an acre of tropical flowers and coconut palms on beach. All hookups. Showers. Toilets. Boat ramp. Pets OK.

EL FLAMINGO — 20 space facility north of El Dorado on beach. Showers. Toilets. Pets OK.

EL NUMBER UNO — 20 space facility on beach next to Roberto's. Showers. Toilets. "Plazita" with benches and tables. Ice. Refreshments and beer. Pets OK. Ph: 625-7627 in Guadalajara.

LA PEÑITA — 200 space facility just north of La Peñita 2.3 miles north of Rincón de Guayabitos on Hwy #200, west side of road between km 91 and 92. Some with all hookups; others with electricity (115 V.) and water only. Showers. Toilets. Pool. Laundromat. Brick patios. Cooking area. Ice. Refreshments. Palapas. Pets OK. Ph and fax: 274-0996.

MARY'S — 13 space facility next to Motel Russell. All hookups. Toilets. Pets OK.

PARAÍSO DEL PESCADOR — 90 space facility among fruit trees on beach. All hookups. Showers. Toilets. Fish cleaning station. Pets OK.

POSADA DEL SOL — SEE ABOVE.

RUSSELL — 11 space facility 2.3 miles north of Rincón de Guayabitos in La Peñita. Shower. Toilet. Concrete patios. Laundry service. Ice. Refreshments. Pets OK.

SAYULA — 10 space facility 1.5 miles off highway on serene, secluded beach. 10 spaces with hookups. Space for 40 more. Showers. Toilets. Concrete patios. Dump station. Pets OK. Not recommended for large RV's as access road is very bad.

TROPICO CABAÑA — 30 space facility next to Villanueva's on beach. All hookups. Showers. Toilets. BBQ pit. Rec room. Pets OK.

VILLANUEVA'S — 30 space facility on beach. Showers. Toilets. Restaurant. Pets OK. Ph: 11 in La Peñita, NAY.

End of Rincón de Guayabitos Eat & Stray.

Puerto Vallarta

UD-019

Area Code — 322

See map on page 36

PUERTO VALLARTA is a medium-sized town that blends into the countryside and climbs the mountainside overlooking the Pacific. It's a very popular winter resort (December 1 – May 5), especially during holidays (both U.S. and Mexican. If you plan to be in "Vallarta" then, advance reservations are pretty smart. In summer, there are lots of discounted deals.

Known as the "Poor Man's Riviera" in the early 1960's, "Vallarta" offered a certain charm. It was serene, and only a handful of fisherman and vacationers visited regularly. Later it became a popular spot to "get away from it all." In those days only DC-6 props flew into and out of the area utilizing a small ramshackle old terminal held together by bailing wire and hope. In the 1970's, however, Vallarta "was discovered" by Hollywood and has since become an increasingly popular resort with Europeans and Canadians as well as with Americans. Today, Vallarta is perhaps a bit too tourist-oriented for some, but there's still a lot of the old charm if you stay out of the "Golden Zone." The surrounding countryside and beaches are breathtakingly beautiful.

The Tourist Office is located in a Banamex building in the northeast corner of Puerto Vallarta's main plaza and city hall.

GALLERIES

GALERÍA UNO – Moreles 561. Established in 1971 and consistently features the finest Mexican artists. Open 10 AM till 8 PM. Ph: 222-0908 or 222-4559.

GALERÍA OLINALA – Lázaro Cárdenas # 274 in south end of town between Vallarta and Constitución. Owner

Nancy Erickson possesses a wealth of information about origins and symbolisms of Indian Tribal art and has the widest range of ceremonial and combat masks representative of most Indian groups. Open daily 10 AM – 2 PM and 5 PM – 9 PM. Ph: 222-4995.

GALERÍA MUVIERI – At 177 Libertad 2 blocks south of main plaza. Specializes in Mexican tribal art of the Huichol and Cora tribes. Open daily 10 AM – 2 PM and 4 PM till 8 PM. Ph: 223-2695

GALERÍA PACÍFICO – Insurgentes #109 (second floor). Open Mon – Sat. 10 AM till 9 PM. Ph: 222-1982

GALERÍA RAC – Lázaro Cárdenas 286. Gallery featuring paintings, collage, ceramics and masks. Rita Zanoni Burns, famed master ceramicist/sculptor from Oklahoma and Bowie, Texas, is an exhibitor at the gallery. Ms. Zanoni can be reached by calling 222-5984 in Puerto Vallarta.

GALERÍA VALLARTA – Juárez 263. Ph: 222-0290. Gene and Barbara Peters, owners, are very hospitable and knowledgeable and will help you make an intelligent purchase. They like to encourage young artists. They're from Texas. Stop in and visit them. Open Mon – Sat 9:30 AM till 8 PM. Sun. 10 AM till 3 PM.

GALERÍA TALENTO MEXICANO - Westin Regina Hotel, Local D Ph: 1-1100

GALERÍA LEPE - Lázaro Cárdenas #237.

GALERÍA EM - Paseo de la Marina, Local 17 Ph: 222-1172.

SERGIO BUSTAMANTE - Juárez #27/Paseo Díaz Ordaz #542 Ph: 222-1129

SIGHT-SEEING

LUIS GUTIÉRREZ – Ph: 222-4939 or 222-5535. Tours with bilingual guides. A very good fellow. Recommended.

JACK'S WATER TAXI – Round trips from Los Muertos pier to Mismaloya, Boca de Tomatlán, Las Animas, Quimixto, Las Caletas and Yelapa (great waterfall!) every day.

BIKE MEX ADVENTURES – Mountain biking adventures for the active traveler. Equipment provided. Bilingual guides. Call 223-1680.

HORSEBACK RIDING – Rancho Ojo de Agua, 224-8240 o22r 4-0607; Rancho El Charro, 224-0114.

MAYAN PALACE WATER PARK – Cruises, Tours, Mexican Fiestas, Horseback riding, 4 high speed slides. 2 tube slides, 6 kiddie slides, lazy river and the second largest pool in North America. Restaurant. Open 11 AM till 7 PM. Ph: 221-1500 ext. 608 or 221-1155. Two locations – Pto. Vallarta and Nuevo Pto. Vallarta.

MILLER TRAVEL SERVICE – In Sheraton – Bus sight-seeing tours. Professionals. Recommended. YATES YELAPA, S.A. – Four different cruises. Contact Servicios Mexicanos Turísticos S.A., Av. Juárez No. 174 Despacho No. 104 and 105. Ph: 222-0026 or 222-1003. Departures daily from the marina pier 9:30 AM. Music, dancing and lots of drinking. Sun deck.

SCUBA DIVING AND SNORKELING - Bass Fishing Viva Tours Ph: 224-0410. Chico's Dive Shop on Díaz Ordaz #770-5 Ph: 222-1895.

GENERAL INFO

CONSULAR AGENCIES: USA - Zaragoza 160, 2nd floor Ph: 222-0069; Canada – Zaragoza 160, First floor, Ph: 222-5398; British – Guadalajara, 013-761-6021; Holland – Guadalajara, 013-673-2211; Germany – Guadalajara, 013-613-9623.

AIRLINES: Aeromexico 224-2777, American 221-1799, Canadian 221-0736, Continental 221-1025 and Delta 221-1032.

LAVANDERÍA DE CINE BAHIA – 357 Francisco Madero. Open 8 AM till 2 PM, 4 M till 8 PM M–F, 8 AM till 4 PM Sat. Other location next to Junto Rest Place Van Dome. English spoken.

RICARDO LEÓN, DVM – Venustiano Carranza No. 254. Ph: 222-3564 and 222-3584. Full service hospital for cats and dogs, cages, vaccinations, etc.

POST OFFICE LOCATIONS – Main office 2nd block north of main plaza; on Malecón – Paseo Díaz Ordaz; At airport, north of town; and on Columbia, 2 blocks south of Hidalgo Park.

SHOPPING CENTERS – Plaza Marina, just south of airport at north end of town. Plaza Caracol across from Fiesta Americana. Villa Vallarta, on Hwy to airport at 2nd stoplight north of bypass around town.

SPANISH LANGUAGE CLASSES – The University of Guadalajara has set up an extension of its very successful program at the main campus in Guadalajara. The Puerto Vallarta center is conveniently located downtown at

Jesús Langarica #200 (about 2 blocks from the Malecón McDonald's) in the penthouse suite. For more info call Lic. Carlos de la Torre at 223-0043, Fax: 222-4419.
FIRST BAPTIST CHURCH – Argentina 181, next to Hidalgo Park. Sunday "All English Service," 10 AM. All faiths welcome.

SLEEPING IN PUERTO VALLARTA

NOTE — Most of the hotels here have SATV, so we didn't specify. Also, rates vary a lot from winter (high season) to summer (low season).

BUENAVENTURA – MOD – 210-room, 4-story A/C hotel at Av. México #1301 near waterfront boulevard on beach. Restaurant. Lobby Bar. Club. Pool. Tennis at nearby club. Shops. Travel agency. Car rental. Laundromat. Sauna. Parking. AE, MC, VI. Good buy. Ph: 222-3737 or 222-3742 Fax: 222-3546. e-mail: benaven@pvnet.com.mx

BUGANVILIAS SHERATON – UPPER – KM 1 Paseo de las Palmas, CP 48300, Puerto Vallarta, Jalisco, Mexico. Luxurious 500 rooms. 169 suites with kitchenettes. 14 story (actually 6 towers) A/C Beachfront hotel. 4 restaurants. 5 bars. Club. Disco. Lovely pool. Shops. Boutiques. Travel agency. Car rental. Laundromat. Water sports. Tennis. Parking. AE, MC, VI. Ph: 223-0404. Fax: 222-0500. US: 1-800-433-5451. e-mail: sheraton@pvne.com.mx

CALINDA PLAZA LAS GLORIAS QUALITY INN – UPPER – 243-room, 4-story A/C hotel on beach on Av. De las Garzas. 2 restaurants. 3 bars. Pool. Travel agency. Car rental. Sauna. Tennis. Golf nearby. Children's activities. Water sports. Parking. AE, MC, VI. Ph: 222-2224.

CASA MAGNA MARRIOT – UPPER – Paseo de la Marina #5. 433 rooms. 29 suites. Restaurant. Pool. Tennis.AE, MC, VI. Ph: 221-0004. US: 1-800-228-9290.

CAMINO REAL – UPPER – Terrific 10-story A/C hotel a mile south of town, KM 2.5 on Hwy 200 in beautiful tropical seaside setting on beach. Playa de las Estacas, P.O. Box 95, 48300. Their Royal Beach Club tower is luxurious. 87 rooms for those who can afford to be pampered. The 337 rooms in the rest of the hotel are pretty nice, too. 3 restaurants. Health club, aerobics, tennis, golf, sauna, steam room and two pools. Convention facilities. AE, MC, VI. Ph: 221-5000. Fax: 221-5200. USA: 1-800-7CAMINO. e-mail: reserva@pvnet.com.mx

CONTINENTAL PLAZA RESORT – UPPER – 438 room, 4 story beach front hotel on Airport Boulevard. 4 restaurants. 2 bars. SATV. Club. Nice pool. Shopping arcade. Travel agency. Beauty shop. John Newcombe tennis club. Health club. Parking. AE, MC, VI. Ph: 224-0123. Fax: 224-5236. e-mail: hcont@pvnet.com.mx

COSTA ALEGRE – ECON – 30-room, 3-story budget hotel downtown at Fca. Rodríguez #168. No restaurant. Small pool. 1 block to beach. Parking. MC, VI. Ph: 222-4888 Fax: 222-0583.

COSTA DEL SOL – MOD – 48-room, 3-story A/C hotel on Paseo de las Palmas across from Plaza Vallarta. No restaurant. Parking. MC, VI. Ph: 222-2055. Fax: 222-4985.

COSTA FLAMINGOS – ECON-MOD – 113-room, 2 story A/C layout on Hwy #200 about 15 miles north of town on nice secluded beach. Restaurant. Bar. Pool. Tennis. Parking. MC, VI. Ph: (3) 298-0226 Fax: 228-0333.

COSTA VALLARTA BEACH CLUB – UPPER – Paseo de los Cocoteros, corner Paseo Cancún in Nueva Vallarta. Everything you'd expect at a resort like this. 1201 bedroom suites that sleep 8. Fancy, high-rise surroundings with tennis, club, bars, pools, TV's, golf, a marina for your yacht, horses for riding, sauna, child-care. Ph: 227-0515.

COSTA VIDA – UPPER – Located on the beach. Timeshare project & hotel 2.5km on Hwy. to Barra de Navidad. 208 A/C rooms. 2 restaurants. Pool. PH: 221-5059 Fax: (714) 643-7614

EL CONQUISTADOR VALLARTA CLUB – UPPER – 104-kitchenette, 2 story A/C hotel on north beach on Airport Boulevard. Restaurant. Bar. Pool. Travel agency. Parking. MC, VI. Ph: 222-2088 or 222-2764.

ELOISA – MOD – 75 room, 6 story (some) A/C hotel on Lázaro Cárdenas on south side near waterfront. Restaurant-bar. Pool. Parking. MC, VI. Ph: 222-6465.

ENCINO – ECON – One block south of Insurgentes Bridge. 4 story, 75 room inexpensive but nice place. Elevator. Phones. Rooftop restaurant. If you like blue and coral decor, you'll like this place. Rooftop pool. No parking, but on street parking appears OK. MC, VI. Ph: 222-0051. Fax: 222-2573. E-mail: info@hotelencino.com

FIESTA AMERICANA – UPPER – Beautiful 291 deluxe rooms, with 33 junior suites on 12th floor, A/C hotel on beach at Los Tules, KM 2.5 Paseo de las Palmas. 4 restaurants. 4 bars. Olympic pool. 5 night lit tennis courts.

3 KM jogging track. Shopping arcade. Car rental. Travel agency. Beauty shop. Parking. AE, MC, VI. Ph: 224-2010 Fax: 224-2108 US: 1-800-FIESTA-1

GARZA BLANCA (White Heron) – UPPER – LUXURY layout 4.5 miles south of town on beautiful secluded beach near Mismaloya. Nice, tropical 57 unit and villa A/C. Open-air restaurant. Natural pool at nearby waterfall. Private pools with villas. Tennis. Putting green. 9-hole, par-3 golf course. Parking. AE, MC, VI. Ph: 222-1023.

HOLIDAY INN – UPPER – On beach at Blvd. Medina Ascencio. 231 rooms. Restaurant. Pool. AE, MC, VI. Ph: 226-1700, Fax: 224-5683. USA: 1-899-322-2343.

KRYSTAL VALLARTA – UPPER – Terrific 438 room, 3 story A/C hotel north of town on airport boulevard on beautiful section of beach. 6 restaurants (including 24-hour coffee shop). 6 bars (some with live entertainment). 2 pools. All villas with private pools. Tennis. Horses. Shopping arcade. Travel agency. Art gallery. Beauty shop. Water sports. Parking. AE, MC, VI. Ph: 224-0202 Fax: 224-0222. A village in itself!

LAGUNITA (YELAPA) – Tropical 23-unit cottage-style layout 17 miles south of town at Yelapa reached only by boat. Open-air restaurant. Contact Miller Travel Service at 222-1197.

LA SIESTA – 24-unit, 2-story hotel at corner of Domínguez and Matamoros in town. Restaurant. Bar. Club. Small pool. Nice view of town. Parking. MC, VI.

LAS PALMAS – MOD-UPPER – Tropical 230-room, 5-story A/C layout on north beach off Airport Boulevard. Restaurant. Bars. Pool. Travel agency. Boutiques. Car rental. Parking. MC, VI. Ph: 224-0650. Fax: 224-0543. e-mail: palmaspv@pvnet.com.mx

LOS ARCOS VALLARTA (formerly Fontana del Mar) – MOD – 45-room, 5-story A/C hotel on dead end at Manuel Diéguez #171. Pool. Parking. AE, MC, VI. Ph: 222-0712 Fax: 222-0583

LOS CUATRO VIENTOS ("Four Winds") – MOD – Plenty of character, but lots of stairs at this 13-unit inn high at Matamoros 529 (3 blocks east of lighthouse). Open-air patio dining at Chez Elena Restaurant. Small pool. Parking. Ph: 222-0161.

LOS TULES – UPPER – Very good 450 unit, 4 story A/C layout at north end on airport boulevard. Some suites with full kitchen. Pool-side restaurant. Pools. Travel agency. Car rental. Laundromat. Sauna. Mini-super. Beauty shop. Tennis. Water sports. Parking. AE, MC, VI. Ph: 222-2990.

MELIA – Marina Vallarta – UPPER – Located at Paseo de la Marina Sur. One of the Spanish chain of grand hotels. 403 rooms, all ocean view. Tennis, squash, volleyball. Rooms have safes. Health club. 2 Pools. 2 restaurants. Convention center. Was dedicated by the King of Spain, Dec. 1989. At the same time all the city streets were improved. AE, MC, VI. Ph: 221-0200, 221-0126, 221-0715. Fax: 221-0118. Western US/CANADA: 800-888-5515, Eastern US 800-336-3542, Fax:: 305-854-0660.

MOLINO DE AGUA – MOD – After you go over bridge over Río Cuale, it's IMMEDIATELY on your right. To park, take 1st street to right after bridge. P.O. Box 54. Parking is secured behind gate. Beachside restaurant. It has a good Jacuzzi. Enclosed by a stone wall, it's absolutely QUIET! 29 bungalows, 8 seafront apartments, 4 suites and 12 junior suites. Bar. Pool. Laundromat. Lovely gardens. Parking. MC, VI. Ph: 222-1957. Fax: 222-6056. Reservations in U.S. Ph: US: 1-800-826-9408, CA: 2-800-423-5512.

ORO VERDE – MOD – 162 room, 8 story A/C hotel on Calle Rodolfo Gómez #111, Playa del Sol in heart of old "Vallarta." Restaurant. Bar. Pool. Boutique. Travel agency. Car rental. Parking. AE, MC, VI. Ph: 222-3050.

PELÍCANOS – MOD – 186-room A/C hotel next to Playa Las Palmas north of town. 15 bungalows. Restaurant. Bar. Beachside restaurant-bar. Disco. Pool. On-street parking. AE, MC, VI. Ph: 224-1010 Fax: 222-1414.

PESCADOR – ECON – 42 unit, 4 story A/C layout downtown at corner of Paraguay #1117 and Uruguay. No restaurant. On-street parking. Use of Rosita's facilities. AE, MC, VI. Ph: 222-2169 or 222-1884. e-mail: hpescador@pvnet.com.mx

PLAYA CONCHAS CHINAS – MOD – 19 room, 5 story A/C hotel on Hwy 200 south of town. 2 restaurants. Bar. Pool. Boutique. Laundromat. Parking. AE, MC, VI. Ph: 222-0156.

PLAYA DE ORO – MOD-UPPER – 410-room, 5-story A/C hotel on beach at far north end near airport at de las Garzas #1. Restaurants. Tahitian-style beachside bar. Pool. Tennis. Horses. Book and drug store. Shops. Travel agency. Car rental. Laundromat. Water sports. AE, MC, VI. Ph: 224-6868, Fax: 226-6810. e-mail: playadeoro@pvnet.com.mx

PLAYA LOS ARCOS – MOD – 135 room, 4 story air-con hotel at Olas Altas #380 in town on beach. 10 master suites. Restaurants. Bar. Pool. Car rental. Gift shop. Water sports. Parking. AE, MC, VI. Ph: 222-1583. Fax: 222-

2418. e-mail: losarcos@pvnet.com.mx

PLAZA IGUANA MARINA RESORT – MOD – KM 7.5, Carr. Aeropuerto. In Marina Vallarta, on north side of town. 3-4 story, 100-room, peach-colored place that tries to blend into the natural scenery. Pool. Tennis. Golf. Yacht club access. Ph: 221-0880. Fax: 221-0889. e-mail: iguana@pvnet.com.mx

PLAZA LAS GLORIAS – MOD – Located at Villa Vallarta Center KM 2.0 Carr. to Aeropuerto 48300. Marina and hotel – 320 rooms. 91 villas with kitchenettes. SATV and service bars. Restaurant. Bar. Golf course. Tennis club. Beach club. 2 Swimming pools surrounded by beautiful gardens and with view of the marina. Travel agency and car rental. Ph: 224-4444. Fax: 224-6559. US: 1-800-342 AMIGO USA. Mexico DF Ph: 514-3420 and 514-5240. GUAD: 652-1126 and 652-3818. e-mail: hcont@pvnet.com.mx

POSADA DEL ANGEL – ECON – 36-room, 2-story A/C hotel on airport boulevard 3 blocks from beach. Restaurant. Bar. Pool. Parking. AE, MC, VI. Ph: 222-1229 in Guadalajara.

POSADA RÍO CUALE – ECON-MOD – 25 room, 2 story A/C hotel in south part of town at Aquiles Serdán #242. Restaurant. Bar. Pool. Lots of character and nice rooms, with winding iron stars to rooms. Walking distance to beach. Parking. AE, MC, VI. Ph: 222-0914. Fax: 222-1148

POSADA ROGER – ECON – Basilio Badillo #237. Upper budget price, favorite of many economy travellers. 50 rooms in two and a half stories. Some have ceiling fans, some A/C. Nice garden courtyard. Most rooms very pleasant, but some are a bit dark, so look first. "El Tucán" bar/restaurant downstairs. Pool on second story. MC, VI. Ph: 222-0836. Fax: 223-0482. E-mail: pdroger@pvnet.com.mx

PRESIDENTE INTER-CONTINENTAL – UPPER – Carr. a Barra de Navida KM 8.5. 120 deluxe A/C rooms including 19 junior suites and 3 master suites. 2 restaurants. Pool. Gym. Jacuzzi. Golf. Tennis. AE, MC, VI. Ph: 228-0507. Fax: 228-0116. E-mail: puertovallarta@interconti.com

QUALTON – UPPER – KM 2.5 Paseo de las Palmas. 300 deluxe rooms. 8 master suites and 2 presidential suites with jacuzzi. Health club with first class facilities, including hydromassage, eucalyptus inhalation, herbal wraps, salt and mud treatment. Gymnasium decorated in pastels with mini-mirrors, and has every exercise machine imaginable. Ph: 224-4446. Fax: 224-4445. e-mail: qualton@pvnet.com.mx

RAMADA PLAZA – UPPER – 466-room, 17-story A/C hotel on beach at KM 3 Paseo de las Palmas. 2 restaurants. Piano bar. Club. Nice pool. Travel agency. Car rental. Laundromat. Golf nearby. Shopping arcade. Tennis. Water sports. Parking. AE, MC, VI. Ph: 224-1700.

ROSITA – ECON – Older 112 room hotel downtown. Restaurant. Pool. On-street parking. MC, VI. Ph: 222-0033 or 222-1033. E-mail: reserva@hotelrosita.com

SIERRA PLAZA PUERTO VALLARTA (Formerly Bel-Air) – LUXURY – UPPER – Marina Vallarta, north of town near airport. Pelícanos #311 Marina Vallarta, Puerto Vallarta 48300, Mexico. One of the nicest hotels in Mexico. **67 rooms – all suites. The Grand Class suites have jacuzzis in room. 25 villas, with private small pools. Restaurant. Golf and tennis privileges with other hotels. No swimming pool, or public jacuzzi, but use of another hotel's facilities. AE, MC, VI. Ph: 221-0800. Fax: 221-0801. RESERVATIONS: GUAD: (3) 652-0000. USA: 1-800-362-9170.

SIERRA RADISSON – UPPER – A 350-room all inclusive hotel at Paseo de los Cocoteros #19 in Nuevo Vallarta, Nayarit. 5 restaurants. Water sports. Fitness center. Ph: (3) 297-1300 Fax: (3) 297-0082.

VALLARTA SHORES — UPPER — Condominium/hotel at Calle Malecón #400 on the beach at the south end of downtown. Large A/C rooms. Pool. Parking. Ph: 222-3838.

VILLA DEL MAR/PALMAR – MOD – 315 room, 10-story A/C hotel at KM 3 Paseo de las Palmas a mile from airport at north end of town. Restaurants. Bar. 2 pools. Boutique. Travel agency. Beauty shop. Gym. Tennis. Sauna. Parking. MC, VI. Ph: 224-0635.

VILLA DEL ORO – UPPER – 135-room, 4 story A/C condo-hotel on beach on Airport Boulevard. Restaurant. Bar. Pool. Parking. AE, MC, VI. Ph: 222-3306.

VILLA TIZO – ECON-MOD – 23 unit, 2 story hotel situated high above road south of town. Very steep entry although you can park at road level on opposite side of curve and ride cable car up. No restaurant. Pool. Parking. Ph: 222-1570.

WESTIN REGINA RESORT – UPPER – Paseo de la Marina Sur #205. 280 deluxe rooms. 14 suites. Pool. Water sports. AE, MC, VI. Ph: 221-1100. Fax: 221-1141. E-mail: info@westinpv.com

EATING IN PUERTO VALLARTA

ARCHIE'S WOK – Francisco Rodríguez #130. Across from the Hotel Marsol. Regional Asian cuisine. Owner Cynthia Alpeuia really nice, mellow. Archie's Wok became legendary when he was chef for John Huston. His legacy lives on. "They did their own thing in their own time," to borrow a line from "Easy Rider." Excellent food, white tablecloth. New Age music and vibrations. Highly recommended. Ph: 222-0411.

BASKIN & ROBINS – 31 flavors – downtown on Paseo Díaz Ordaz just one block north of main plaza.

Best tamales in town – On the town side of the one-way North bridge, the lady on the left (as you're driving towards the Gold zone) has three flavors. About a buck a tamale. Good. One thousand stars.

BOGART'S – On Hwy 200 and in Hotel Krystal. Very pricey. International food. Unique Arabic atmosphere. More waiters than you can shake a stick at. Romantic dining. Open 5 PM till Midnight. Ph: 224-0202.

BRAZZ – Good, casual restaurant at corner of Morelos and Galeana, another of the renowned Guadalajara chain. Excellent charcoal-grilled meats and fish. Good bar and *mariachi* music daily. Open noon till midnight. AE, MC, VI. Ph: 222-0324.

CAFE EUROPA – MOD – New European style cafe at Basilo Badillo # 252 Complete french pastry line. Open 9 AM till 10 PM. Ph: 223-1925.

CAFE DES ARTISTES – Guadalupe Sánchez #740. Serves gourmet cuisine in an artistic setting. Superb dishes prepared by award-winning Chef Thiery Blouet. Ph: 222-3228.

CARISMA CAFE – MOD – Basilio Badillo 283, across from Roberto's. Italian cuisine. Open 5 PM till 12 AM. Ph: 222-4959, 222-6533.

CARLOS O'BRIAN'S – Bar-grill at Díaz Ordaz #786 on waterfront downtown. International cuisine. Open for lunch and dinner. AE, MC, VI. Plenty of atmosphere where there's never a dull moment! For the "party-hearty" crowd. Ph: 222-1444

CASABLANCA – UPPER – Díaz Ordaz #570. EXPENSIVE. Among PV's fanciest restaurants. Specialties include lower star, Coquilles St. Jacques, Chateaubriand, and Mahi-Mahi. Excellent service. Popular bar. Upstairs dining overlooking ocean. Open 8 AM-4 PM; 5 PM-1 AM. AE, MC, VI. Ph: 222-1723.

CASA DEL ALMENDRO – International restaurant at Galeana #180 a half block off Díaz Ordaz. Specialties include shrimp scampi, almond lobster and chicken dishes. Open 5 PM till midnight. AE, MC, VI. Ph: 222-4670.

CHEF ROGER'S – Agustín Rodríguez #267. "Fine food for simple prices," is what they advertise and deliver. Swiss and French cuisine. Chef Roger is Swiss and a Vallarta personality. English spoken. Open 6:30 PM till 1 AM. Closed Sundays. VI, MC. Ph: 222-5900.

CHEZ ELENA – Below the Hotel Cuatro Vientos at Matamoros #520. Courtyard dining by pool or inside, international and Mexican. Really elegant food but not a stuffy atmosphere. Live musician, ballad singer, paid by the house, wanders around. "El Nido" (The Nest) rooftop bar a hefty climb, but worth it. Wonderful sunsets. Ph: 222-0161.

CHICO'S PARADISE – Remotely located restaurant about 12 miles south of town on Hwy #200 above Mismaloya Beach – Jungle atmosphere. Delicious spareribs and crawfish; coconut pie is a special treat. Open 11:00 AM till 11:30 PM. AE, MC, VI. Ph: 222-0747.

CUETO'S – Marisquería, Brasilia 475. Dinners only, 7 days a week. Family owned and run by José and Irene Cueto. Serves only fish, but menu is enormous, every conceivable fish and seafood served every way. Large servings beautifully presented and reasonably priced. They serve FREE DRINKS and usually have at least one group of musicians to entertain the people while they wait. Linen tablecloths and napkins. Ph: 3-0363.

DAIQUIRI DICK'S – Olas Altas #314 and Basillo Badillo on Los Muertos beach. Open daily 9 AM till 10:30 PM. MC, VI. Ph: 222-0566.

DENNY'S – In Marina Vallarta – just south of airport at north end of town.

DOMINO'S PIZZA – 2 locations: Next to main plaza, downtown on Zaragoza by Los Arcos. – On Hwy to airport at Lucerne #101. Open daily 12 Noon till 2 AM. Home delivery. Ph: 224-1222 or 224-2222.

EL DORADO – Tropical open-air beachside restaurant at Amapas and Pulpito. Good for a snack as well as Mexican and seafood – "Old Vallarta" atmosphere. Open 8 AM till 7 PM. MC, VI.

EL SET – Mountainside restaurant overlooking bay near Camino Real. Seafood and broiled steaks. Pool. Open 4 PM-midnight. AE, MC, VI. Ph: 221-5342.

HOT ROD CAFE – On Hwy 200 North end of town, just South of Sheraton. Supreme Court of Rock'n'Roll.

Cafe and bar has something for everyone. Town's tallest beers. For the "Party Hearty" crowd. For those who like to dance, be there about 10 PM. A party every night! Open 24 hours a day.

IL MANGIARE – Mexican-European-style restaurant (no foolin') at corner of Abasolo and Díaz Ordaz on waterfront. Romantic and elegant. International food with accent on Italian specialties. Open 5 PM till midnight. MC, VI.

KENTUCKY FRIED CHICKEN – At Juárez and Zaragoza on main plaza. No parking. No credit cards. Open daily 9:30 AM till 11 PM. Ph: 222-3813

LA CASA DE MARISCOS – B. Badillo, Pino Suárez PTO. Vallarta, Jalisco. Features good seafood at reasonable prices. Open 4 PM till 11 PM daily. Ph: 222-33-17.

LA CEBOLLA ROJA ("The Red Onion") – Popular restaurant-bar on waterfront at Díaz Ordaz #822 adjacent to Carlos O'Brian's. Seafood specialties plus soups, chicken and pork dishes, etc. Open 1 PM till 1 AM – MC, VI. Ph: 222-1087.

LA CHATA – Located on Paseo Díaz Ordaz #700. Traditional Mexican cooking. Live Marimba music. Open 8 AM till late evening.

LA FUENTE DEL PUENTE – Corner of Insurgentes #107 and Agustín Rodríguez at foot of northbound bridge. Mexican and international food. Live music. Mariachis. Ph: 222-2987 or 222-1141.

LA HACIENDA – Elegant restaurant decorated in greenery at Aguacate #274. Specialties include snails, papillote of fish, Crepes St. Jacques, Lobster a la Hacienda, plus good salads. Open 6 PM till midnight. AE, MC, VI. Ph: 222-0590.

LA IGUANA MEXICAN FIESTA – Famous indoor-outdoor restaurant a couple of blocks South of Río Cuale at Lázaro Cárdenas #311. Used for semi-private *noche buenas*. Open 7 PM till 11 PM. Ph: 222-0105

LA JOYA DE MISMALOYA – Palapa-style restaurant off Hwy. #200 near Mismaloya. Seafood specialties including crab crepes au gratin, lobster, octopus, etc. Open 9 AM till 7 PM. AE, MC, VI. Nice view of Mismaloya Bay. Ph: 228-0660.

LA PALAPA — UPPER — At Pulpito #103 on Los Muertos Beach. Enjoy seafood with waves lapping at your feet. Specialty is grilled lobster and shrimp. Ph: 222-5225. www.lapalapapv.com

LA PERLA – International cuisine in the Camino Real – "Not cheap, but oh so nice," according to one patron. One of the best views. Ph: 221-5000.

LAS CAZUELAS – Very good restaurant at Basilio Badillo #479. Reservations suggested. Mexican and international cuisine including shrimp, roast pork and other delicious entrees. Excellent service. Open 6:30 till 11 PM. Ph: 222-2498 or 222-1658.

LAS PALOMAS – Waterfront restaurant on corner of Díaz Ordaz #610 and Aldama, downtown. Good breakfasts as well as seafood and Mexican specialties. One of the most popular sunset watching spots in town. Find movers and shakers at early breakfast in back room. Live music nightly. Open 8 AM till 1 AM. AE, MC, VI. Ph: 222-3675. Fax: 223-054. www.laspalomaspvr.com

LE BISTRO – Easygoing restaurant at Isla Cuale #16-A. Dine indoors or on outside patio. Sea food, meats, good salads and soups. Open daily 9 AM till 12 AM; closed Sundays. AE, MC, VI. Ph: 222-0283.

LE GOURMET – French restaurant at Aquiles Serdán #242. French cuisine including lobster, shrimp, Steak Diane — many dishes prepared at your table. Live piano music. Open daily 6 PM till midnight. AE, MC, VI. Ph: 222-1148.

LOS ARBOLITOS – Camino de la Rivera #184 and the Río Cuale. Good seafood and Mexican food. Handmade tortillas and good mole. Reasonable prices. Ph: 223-1050.

KAMAKURA – UPPER – Elegant restaurant at the Kristal Hotel, serving excellent Japanese cuisine in high style. Open 6 PM till midnight. Ph: 224-0202.

McDONALD'S – At North end of Malecón, Paseo Díaz Ordaz at 31 Octubre. – In Marina Vallarta, just south of airport. Open 9 AM till 11 PM. Ph: 222-5966.

MR. FISH – Seafood restaurant on airport boulevard across from several major hotels. Open 12 noon till midnight. AE, MC, VI. Ph: 222-1962.

MOBY DICK – Seafood restaurant at Octubre #31 downtown a half block off main boulevard. Seafood (natch) served family style. Open noon till 1 AM. MC, VI. Ph: 222-0655.

MOCAMBO – Corner of Díaz Ordaz and Abasolo. Restaurant/grill/bar club at International cuisine including terrific prime rib and Italian sandwiches. Piano music. Open 7 AM till 12:30 AM. MC, VI.

PALACIO – 302 Lázaro Cárdenas, corner Constitución, across from "La Iguana." Chinese. Very good, especially the butterfly shrimp. Seafood. Open daily, 1:30 PM till midnight. VI, MC. Ph: 222-0580.

PIETRO'S PIZZA – Italian restaurant at corner of Hidalgo and Zaragoza downtown. Try "Piatto del Giorno" (dish of the day). Open noon till midnight. MC, VI.

PIZZA HUT – Avenida de las Palmas at plaza Caracol, across from Fiesta Americana.

PIZZA JOE'S VILLA – Basilio Badillo #269. Moved up in the world. Couldn't have happened to two nicer folks. Joe and Claire will treat you right at this authentic Italian place. Spaghetti, lasagna, pizza, etc. Courtyard or indoor dining. Classical music. Open 5 PM till 11 PM. Closed Mondays. Ph: 222-2477.

RICO MAC TACO — ECON — On the corner of Uraguay and Mexico (the main south route in town) just down from the Pemex. Caters to Americans. Serves the best fresh squeezed orange juice and cinnamon laced coffee. Also barbacoa.

RIVER CAFE – MOD – Isla Río Cuale Local #4. Fine cuisine. Open daily 9 AM till 11:30 PM. AE, MC, VI. Ph: 223-0788. E-mail: rivercafe@rivercafe.com.mx

RITO'S BACI – At Domínguez #181. Features handmade pizza dough and breads stuffed with Italian sausage. Also pasta favorites. Top service, reasonable prices. Ph: 222-6448.

ROBERTO'S PUERTO NUEVO – MOD – Basilio Badillo #284. Fresh seafood home cooking. Open12 AM till 11:30 PM. Ph: 222-6210, 222-6533. www.robertosptonuevo.com

RODOLFO'S – F. Madero, #406. VALUE. Pozole Estillo Guerrero with onions (chili piquine on the side), avocado con chicharrón. Interesting photos of food on wall to tell you what you're ordering. Blue tablecloth restaurant.

SANTOS – Francisco Rodríguez #136. Across from the Mar Sol and next to Archie's Wok. White tablecloth on place-mat budget. Mexican food. Good value. Open 4 PM til 11 PM. Ph: 222-5670

SEÑOR CHICO'S – Open-air restaurant at Pulpito #37 south of town. Chateaubriand, prime rib, sirloin, frog legs, red snapper, etc. Open 5 PM till midnight. MC, VI. Ph: 222-3570.

THE PANCAKE HOUSE – Basilio Badillo #289. This place is very simple, clean and fairly attractive. English is spoken. "The" breakfast place where local North Americans and tourist in the know catch up on "what's new" over a great cup of coffee and over 70 breakfast possibilities. What a choice! Very, very imaginative. Served with fruit, lots of good butter, jams, syrups, and portions are quite large. Open daily, 8 AM till 2 PM only. Ph: 222-6272.

ZAPATA BAR & GRILL – Mexican-style restaurant at Díaz Ordaz #522. Live music nightly in Latin American atmosphere. Open 11 AM till 4 PM and 6 PM till 1 AM. AE, MC, VI. Ph: 222-4748.

CAMPING & RV PARKING

PUERTO VALLARTA – Very good 70 space park out on north edge of town across road and down from Pelícanos. All hookups. Showers. Toilets. Laundromat. Pool a block away. Long-distance phone service. Ph: 222-2828.

TACHO'S – Very good 155 space facility out on north end across from marina. All hookups. Showers. Toilets. Laundromat. Brick pads. Bus service to town.

OTHER SERVICES

V.D. CAMACHO, M.D. – General Practitioner – 1 block from City Hall, 437-2 Juárez – Ph: 222-1854.

AGUSTÍN FERNÁNDEZ – Orthopaedic Surgery and Traumatology – Ph: 222-6894 or 22-6923 (Emergency calls through radio 2-4448, operator of Hotel Plaza Vallarta) – Postgraduate training in Switzerland.

MÓNICA GÓMEZ – Ophthalmologist – Allende 190 – Ph: 222-2316 – Treatment for diseases of the eyes and contact lenses and fitting. English spoken.

ÓPTICA ITALIA – Ph: 222-1431 – Glasses and contact lenses. Eye tests by a licensed optometrist. DR. JORGE TREJO – Specialist in Cardiology and Internal Medicine – Ph: 2-6894 or 2-6923 (Emergency calls through radio 222-4448, operator of Hotel Plaza Vallarta) – Postgraduate training in Baltimore, Johns Hopkins University Hospital.

EMERGENCY PHONE NUMBERS: Red Cross 222-1533, IMSS hospital 224-0824, Regional hospital 224-4000, Paramedics 225-0386, police 222-0123. Federal highway police 221-1065, immigration office 221-1380,

Federal Tourism bureau 222-0242.

BAY MEDICAL SERVICES – 24-hour bilingual service including patient evacuations, ambulance, X-rays, pharmacy, dentist, gynecologist and various specialists. Located at Km.1, Paseo de las Palmas #500. Ph: 222-2627, 222-5152, or 223-1600.

HOSPITAL MEDASIST VALLARTA – 24-hour, bilingual, private hospital with emergency room, laboratory, X-rays, and full staff of specialists. Located at Manuel Diéguez #360, near south side gas station. Ph: 223-0656, 223-0444, 223-0497, Fax: 222-3301.

CHIROPRACTORS – Dr. Paul J. Constante. California licensed. English spoken. Calle Jesús Langarica #200-22 Ph: 3-0081 Emergencies after 10 PM call 224-5420 or 224-5025 ext. 1216.

DENTIST – Dr. Martha Peña. General dentistry. Francisco Madero #372 Ph: 222-0174.

HOLISTIC MEDICINE – Dr. Abel Jiménez M.D. Manuel Diéguez #322. Ph: 223-1505, or 222-3772.

MASSAGE – Stress reduction, pain relief, reflexology. Calle Amapas #114, just around the corner from Hotel Oro verde. Ph: 223-0132.

PSYCHOLOGICAL SERVICES – Psychotherapy. Abuse recovery. Colleen McDonald, M.S., MFCC or Lic. Miguel Angel Sosa Cravlota. Affiliated with CMQ Medical offices Ph: 222-5660 or 90-329-4-0078

End of Puerto Vallarta Eat & Stray

Guadalajara

UD-019

Area Code — 33

See map on page 43

DEGOLLADO THEATRE —East side of Plaza de la Liberación. Its facade is lined with Corinthian columns, and below the frieze, which depicts the Nine Muses of Greek Mythology, are engraved these words: "The Rumors of Discord Shall Never Arrive." Named after the governor who ordered its construction in 1865, the Degollado Theatre is home of the Guadalajara Symphony Orchestra and the University of Guadalajara Folkloric Ballet. Concerts, plays, operas, and special performances are also presented in the theatre. Open 10-1 and 4-7. Ph: 3613-1115.

LIBERTY MARKET ("Mercado Libertad") — Just east of downtown section at corner of Calz. Independencia and Av. Javier Mina. Guadalajara's largest market, also known as "Mercado San Juan de Dios" because San Juan de Dios River runs underneath, covers an area of 430,400 square feet and is open daily. Bargaining is the name of the game here (and be sure to hang on to your purse/wallet).

FLOWER MARKET (*Mercado de Flores*) — West side of Parque Agua Azul on Calz. Independencia around corner from Casa de Artesanías near Sheraton Hotel. This market is open from mid-morning to early evening and always offers an impressive display of colorful flowers. Bargaining is also customary here.

ZAPOPAN — Suburb of Guadalajara a couple of miles northwest of downtown on Calzada Avila Camacho (5 mi or 7.5 km). This is the location of the 17th-century Franciscan shrine where the Blessed Virgin of Zapopan is venerated. Famous throughout Mexico, the statue of the Guadalajara patroness is made of corn husks with a wooden carved face and hands. On October 12, a spectacular procession takes place ending at night with music, dancing and fireworks. At the right of the shrine entrance is an interesting Huichol and Cora Indian Museum. Open daily 10 AM till 1:30 PM and 4 till 7 PM.

CABAÑAS ORPHANAGE ("Hospicio Cabañas") — One block behind Liberty Market at corner of Calle Hospicio and Av. Cabañas across from Plaza de Toros Progreso ("Progreso Bullring"). Founded in 1803 by Bishop Ruiz de Cabañas, the dwelling was an orphanage for 178 years but has now been converted to a cultural center called "Centro Cultural de las Americas" where artistic and cultural events are held. Resembling the more famous "Monastery de El Escorial" near Madrid, the center features 23 flower-filled patios and outstanding murals by Orozco, among them the "Conquest of Mexico," the "Four Horsemen of Apocalypse," and his masterpiece, the "Man of Fire." Small fee. Open Tues-Sat 10:15 AM till 6 PM, Sun 10:15 AM till 3 PM.

CATHEDRAL — Av. 16 de Septiembre downtown in center of four plazas which form a cross around the structure. Started on July 31, 1571, the cathedral's original twin towers were destroyed by an earthquake in 1848.

It is a product of many architectural styles including Gothic, Corinthian, Ionic, Doric, Byzantine, and Mudejar, and displays fine paintings of Paez, Uriarte, Castro, and Cabrera, and in the sacristy is Murillo's finest work, the "Assumption of the Virgin." Closed Thurs and Sun at noon for confirmations.

GOVERNMENT PALACE — East side of Plaza de Armas. The building dates from 1643 and features some of Orozco's earlier murals including "Man and His Philosophies," "Progress in a Spiritual and Material World," and "The Ghost of Religion in Alliance With Militarism." In this building in 1810, Hidalgo decreed the abolition of slavery in Mexico. Free admission. Open 8 AM till 8 PM.

REGIONAL MUSEUM OF GUADALAJARA — North side of Plaza de la Liberación (behind cathedral) at Calles Corona and Hidalgo. Once a seminary, the museum now houses a display of regional arts and crafts, archaeological artifacts, and an excellent collection of European, colonial, and modern paintings. Small fee. Open 9 AM till 3:45 PM daily; closed Mondays.

ENGLISH AA — Go to any lengths way out in Sector Providencia. Filadelfia #2015. Near Av. de las Americas and López Mateos. Up from highrise office building, Torre Americas. Down side street from Brazz restaurant, across from the Roosevelt School. M, W 7:30 PM. Call Bill: (33) 3663-1417 or Vick 3625-2613. Spanish-AA M, TH 7 PM; Ph: 3641-2935 or 3623-1317.

CHAPALA, JAL – AJIJIC AREA – Sun, Jocotepec, call Bill (376) 765-2575. Mon – Little Chapel, 4 PM. Tues – Río Zula #1, Wed – ACOA, Hidalgo #63, Ajijic, ALANON, Río Zula #1, 4 PM. Thurs – Río Zula #1, 4 PM. Sat – ALANON, Río Zula #1, 9:30 AM.

MECHANIC — European Car Service. Excellent, hard working and conscientious. Alberto Rivas C. Depto. Volkswagen, Prol. Alcalde 2144 Ph: 3624-5612. English spoken. Jeep, Nissan (Datsun), VW, Chrysler, Chevrolet, and Ford.

SLEEPING IN GUADALAJARA

ARANZAZU – MOD – (part of Hoteles Vista chain) 540-room, 10-story twin-tower A/C hotel just off Av. 16 de Septiembre at Revolución #110. Restaurant. Cafeteria. Bars. Fancy clubs. 2 pools. Barber shop. Beauty shop. Travel agency. Tobacco shop. Parking. AE, MC, VI. Ph: 3613-3232 Fax: 3614-5445; US 800-882-8215.

CAMINO REAL – UPPER – Deluxe 205-room A/C hotel in west end of town at Av. Vallarta #5005. 4 restaurants. Coffee shop. Bar. Club. 5 heated pools. Tennis. Putting green. Travel agency. Car rental. Boutiques. Horses. Lovely grounds. Parking. AE, MC, VI. Ph: 3134-8000, 3134-2424, Fax: 3134-2404; U.S. 800-228-3000. E-Mail: gdl@caminoreal.com

CASA GRANDE – UPPER – Located in front of the International Airport of Guadalajara, connected by a joining bridge between the hotel and the airport. 160 luxury rooms, 27 suites. SATV. Restaurant. Spa gym. Business center. Ph: 3678-9000, Fax: 3678-9002. E-mail: cgrande@mail.udg.mx

CHAPALITA – MOD – 79-room, 2-story A/C hotel at López Mateos #1617 across from Posada Guadalajara. Restaurant. Shakey's Pizza and Chicken Restaurant adjoining. Bar. Pool. Beauty shop. Parking. AE, MC, VI. Ph: 3622-4484.

COLÓN – MOD – 6 story older hotel near downtown on Av. Revolución #12. A/C, servi-bars, TV, phones. Sometimes has specials. Ph: 3613-3753.

CROWNE PLAZA GUADALAJARA – UPPER – Av. López Mateos Sur 2500, near Plaza del Sol. 293 A/C rooms with full baths. 3 restaurants. Bars. Pool. Health club. Children's playground. Parking. AE, MC, VI. Ph: 3634-1034, Fax: 3631-9393. E-Mail: crownegd@crownegdl.com.mx

DEL PARQUE – MOD – VALUE. 845 Av. Juárez. 77-room, 4-story A/C downtown hotel just west of Parque de la Revolución. Dining room. Parking. AE, MC, VI. Ph: 3625-2800.

DE MENDOZA – MOD – Attractive 104-room, 5-story A/C hotel right in heart of town adjacent to Degollado Theater at Carranza 16. Restaurant. Bar. Pool. Travel agency. Parking. AE, MC, VI. Ph: 3631-9393, Fax: 3613-7310.

DON QUIJOTE PLAZA – MOD – Nice, reasonably-priced hideaway. Niños Héroes #91. 32 rooms (15 with tubs!) and 1 suite. TV. A/C. Carpets. Lobby bar that closes 9-10 PM. Parking 5 blocks away. Ph: 3658-1299.

EL TAPATIO – UPPER – Overpriced 120-room A/C hilltop hotel out on Blvd. Aeropuerto #4275 (Hwy #44), on road to Chapala. Restaurants. Bar. Disco. Club. Pool. Boutiques. Tennis. Putting Green. Playground. Horses. Bullring. Parking. Advertises a spa, but no facilities. AE, MC, VI. Ph: 3635-6050 Fax: 3635-6664; U.S. 800-

431-2822. e-mail: info@htapatio.com

EXELARIS HYATT REGENCY GUADALAJARA – UPPER – Beautiful 350-room, 14-story A/C hotel resembling a pyramid at Av. López Mateos #2500 across from Plaza del Sol shopping center. Several restaurants and bars. Club. Pool. Ice skating ring (only one in town). Physical fitness center. Spectacular atrium with panoramic elevators. Parking. AE, MC, VI. Ph: 3678-1234 Fax: 3622-9877; U.S. 800-233-1234 or 800-228-9000.

FENIX – MOD – 259-room, 12-story A/C downtown hotel at Corona #160 a block south of Juárez. Continental restaurant. Lobby bar. Disco. Pool. Boutiques. Travel agency. Car rental. Jewelry store. Boutiques. Parking. AE, MC, VI. Ph: 3614-5714. Best Western Hotel.

FIESTA AMERICANA – UPPER – Terrific 391-room, 22-story A/C deluxe hotel at Aurelio Aceves #225, overlooking Minerva Fountain. 4 Restaurants. Bars. Disco. Clubs. Pool. Tennis. Shopping arcade. In-room movies. Travel agency. Car rental. Parking. AE, MC, VI. Ph: 3625-4848 or 3825-3434 Fax: 3630-3725; U.S. 800-FIESTA-1; Mex. 91-800-36302.

FIESTA INN – MOD – Av. Mariano Otero #1550, Rinconada del Sol. 158 rooms and suites. Restaurant. Lobby bar. Pool. Ph: 3669-3200, Fax: 3669-3247.

FRANCES – MOD – The city's oldest hotel (original structure dates from 1610) and a declared national monument at Maestranza #35, off of Plaza de la Libertad. 60 rooms. Restaurant. Bar. Ph: 3613-1190. Fax: 3658-2831.

FUTURA DEL SOL – MOD – 18-apartment complex complete with housekeeping facilities a block from Plaza del Sol. No restaurant. Parking. Weekly and monthly rates. Ph: 3621-8566.

GUADALAJARA PLAZA (Expo) – MOD – Av. Mariano Otero #3261 at the corner of Topacio near Plaza del Sol. Restaurant. Bar. Club. Pool. Tennis. Sauna. Green area. Security. Parking. AE, MC, VI. Ph: 3669-0215, Fax: 3122-2850. e-mail: reservaexpo@hotelesgdlplaza.com.mx

GUADALAJARA PLAZA (Lópes Mateos) – MOD – Av. López Mateos Sur #2128.142-room A/C hotel ner Plaza del Sol. Restaurant. Pool. Ph: 3647-5300 Fax: 3122-1842. Mex: 01-800-363-4500. E-mail: reservalm@hotelesgdlplaza.com.mx

HILTON GUADALAJARA – UPPER – Ave. de la Rosas #2933. 422 Rooms. 2 restaurants. Lobby bar. Pool. Fitness center. US: 1-800-774-1500. www.hilton.com

HOLIDAY INN – UPPER – 305-room, 2-story (plus 9-story tower) motor inn on López Mateos just beyond Plaza del Sol shopping complex. Restaurants. Clubs. Disco. Pool. Curio shop. Tennis. Putting green. Beauty shop. Kennel. AE, MC, VI. Ph: 3634-1034; U.S. 1-800-HOLIDAY.

ISABEL – MOD – 60-room motel at Montenegro #1572 a block off Enrique de León some 7 blocks south of Av. Vallarta from university corner. 10 kitchenettes. Restaurant. Pool. Parking. AE, MC, VI. Ph: 3626-2630.

LA ESTANCIA DEL SOL – MOD – 2-story, 64-room motel on Mariano Otero #2407 just beyond Plaza del Sol. Some kitchenettes. Restaurant. Pool. Parking. MC, VI. Ph: 3631-8025.

LAFAYETTE – UPPER – 181-room, quiet 17-story A/C hotel at Av. de la Paz #2055 known as "first hotel" because of its original works of art decorating rooms (no two alike) and public areas. Restaurant. Cafeteria. Bar. Pool. Shops. Parking. AE, MC, VI. Ph: 3615-6750 Fax: 3630-1112.

LAS CALANDRIAS – MOD – 18-kitchenette suite hotel 3 miles south on Hwy #15 and a half-block east on Calle Nebulosa. No restaurant. Parking. MC, VI. Ph: 3621-0216.

LAS PERGOLAS – MOD – 200-room, 4-story A/C hotel at Av. Morelos #2244, 3 blocks east of Minerva Circle in nice residential area. Restaurant. Coffee shop. Bar. Pool. Boutique. Beauty shop. Barber shop. Parking. AE, MC, VI. Ph: 3630-0629.

MALIBU – MOD – 180-room, 9-story A/C hotel at Av. Vallarta #3993. Restaurant. Bar. Pool. Boutique. Tennis. Car rental. Beauty shop. Parking. AE, MC, VI. Ph: 3621-7676.

MISION CARLTON – UPPER – Very nice 200-room, 20-story A/C hotel near downtown on corner of 16 de Septiembre and Av. Niños Héroes #125. Restaurants plus elegant rooftop restaurant with live entertainment. Club. Bar. Pool. Boutiques. Parking. AE, MC, VI. Ph: 3614-7272. Fax: 3613-5539; U.S. 800-871-5278. E-mail: fm981008@ja11.telmex.net.mx

NUEVA GALICIA – MOD – 95-room at Av. Corona #610 Ph: 3614-8780 Fax: 3613-9089.

PLAZA GÉNOVA – UPPER – A Best Western 185-room hotel at Av. Juárez #123, between Degollado and Molina. Three restaurants. Gym. CATV. Travel agency. Parking. MC, VI. Ph: 3613-7500. Fax: 3614-8253. Mex: 01-800362-2400.

PLAZA LOS ARCOS – UPPER – Av. Vallarta #2452 at corner of Francisco de Quevedo. Ph: 3615-1845, Fax: 3616-3817. Mex: 01-800-368-3200. E-mail: lumirojas@infosel.net.mx They also run **MORALVA SUITES**

across the street.

POSADA DEL SOL – MOD – 54-room, 2-story motel at López Mateos #4205 across from Holiday Inn. Some kitchenettes. Restaurant. Bar. Pool. Parking. MC, VI. Ph: 3631-5205, 3631-5620, 3631-5514 or 3631-5133.

POSADA GUADALAJARA – MOD – 180-room, 8-story A/C hotel on López Mateos near railroad underpass not far from Minerva Circle. Restaurant. Bar. Club. Pool. Parking. Ph: 3621-2022 or 3621-2424.

POSADA SAN ISIDRO – MOD – 45-unit, 3-story motel out on Hwy #54 at San Isidro Golf Course subdivision development. Restaurant-bar. Pool. Golf. Tennis. Country club privileges. Parking. Weekly and monthly rates. AE, VI. Ph: 3624-0622.

PRESIDENTE INTERCONTINENTAL – UPPER – A 12-story deluxe hotel at Av. Lopez Mateos Sur and Moctezuma. 411 A/C rooms. 2 restaurants. Pool. Health club. Skating rink. AE, MC, VI. Ph: 3678-1234, Fax: 3678-1222. E-mail: guadalajara@interconti.com

PUERTO VALLARTA – ECON – 32-room, 2-story motel at Vallarta #4003. Some A/C. No restaurant. Parking. Small pets OK. MC. Ph: 3621-7361. Budget motel.

QUALITY INN CALINDA ROMA – MOD – Old-time 174-room, 4-story A/C downtown hotel on east end of Av. Juárez #170. Restaurants. Bar. Secretary service. NO SMOKING ROOMS! Telex service. Pool. Travel agency. Parking. AE, MC, VI. Ph: 3614-8650. Fax: 3614-2629.

QUINTA REAL – UPPER – On corner of López Mateos and Av. México #2727. Magnificent and romantic. 76 suites. Has jacuzzi suite. Restaurant. Pool. Parking (go 1 block toward Minerva and take first right). Ph: 3615-0000 Fax: 3813-1797; US: 1-800-445-4565. E-mail: reservaciones@quintareal.com

RANCHO RÍO CALIENTE – MOD – 36-unit vegetarian hot springs health layout about 3 miles off Hwy #15 thru village of Primavera (follow winding road to its location alongside Río Caliente). Homegrown food. Pools (cool and hot). Steam and massage room. Yoga and meditation. Horseback riding. Hiking. Volleyball. No children under 15. American plan only. Charge for visiting and using facilities. Advance reservations suggested. USA: 1-800-200-2927. In Guadalajara call Elizabeth Hill 3634-3890.

SAN FRANCISCO PLAZA – ECON – VALUE! Charming little place. 76 spacious rooms – 6 with tubs. Degollado #267 across from little plaza. Go 2 blocks toward Tapatia Plaza from Fenix or towards downtown from Aranzazu – which is where you'll park if you stay there. It's just up from (and less expensive than) Don Quixote. It has a courtyard with fountain. Restaurant – reasonable. Dark wood, polished tile, hanging plants. This could be a romantic place. AE, MC, VI. Ph: 3613-8954, Fax: 3613-3257.

VISTA PLAZA DEL SOL – UPPER – Pricey. 352-room, 9-story A/C hotel on premises of Plaza del Sol shopping complex on Av. López Mateos. Restaurants. Bars (live music – noisy). Pool. Shops. Solarium. Car rental. Parking. AE, MC, VI. Ph: 3616-7274.

BUDGET

If you really want to save pesos, look around the old bus or train stations. The usual caveats apply – look at your room, expect it to be fairly noisy (thFough you can say the same about any first class hotel with a disco) and count on your mattress being as old as you and sagging even more. You'll often get large rooms and get to meet some nice folks, or you'll hate it. Water is not always very hot and towels have seen better days. Some of the below are better than the run-of-the-mill ones, though. You may find a good inexpensive hotel to be a real bargain as well as a chance to meet younger European and Mexican tourists.

CONTINENTAL – ECON – OK. 450 Corona – corner with Libertad. 128-rooms, 7 floors, elevator, lobby. TV, no bar. Restaurant. Parking. Street noise, but no discos nearby. Ph: 3614-1117.

NUEVO VALLARTA – ECON – 14-room, 2-story motel at Vallarta #3999 at corner with Degollado. No restaurant. Parking. MC. Budget motel.

POSADA REGIS – ECON – Charming little place (10 rooms) across the street from the Fenix. Corona 171. Old mansion carved into rooms. Bird-cages and tropical plants make the lobby a wonder. Big projection TV with movies each night. Little restaurant. Friendly staff. Owner speaks English. Does laundry for a reasonable price. No parking but a reasonable lot next door. Hotel begins on 2nd floor. You must walk up a flight of steps. Ph: 3613-3026.

GENOVA – ECON – 63-room, 6-story A/C hotel on Juárez between Molina and Degollado. Restaurant. Parking. AE, MC, VI. Ph: 3613-7500 or 3613-0403. Being remodeled.

POSADA ESPAÑA – ECON – BASIC. Small place, 12 rooms. Courtyard. Cheap. López Cotilla #594. Ph:

3613-5377.

POSADA DE LA PLATA – ECON – BASIC. Small, 9 rooms. Inexpensive. López Cotilla #619. Ph: 3614-9146.

UNIVERSO – MOD – VALUE. QUIET. 137-rooms, 7 stories at López Cotilla, corner with Degollado. TV. PH. Laundry. Elevators. OK restaurant. AE, VI, MC. Ph: 3613-2815.

EATING IN GUADALAJARA

ACUARIUS – ECON – Priciliano Sánchez # 416. Vegetarian fare. Good price and good food. Soyburgers Milanesa de Trigo. Fruit drinks. The most famous veggie place in town. Open 9:30 AM till 8 PM. Ph: 3613-6277.

ALBATROS – MOD – Good open-air restaurant set in beautiful home on Av. de la Paz #1840, three blocks from Av. Chapultepec. Seafood specialty and international cuisine. Open noon till midnight. MC, VI. Ph: 3625-9996 or 3625-7723.

ARTHUR'S – MOD – Excellent English pub and steak house at Av. Chapultepec sur #507. Good steaks and ribs prepared to order, lobster, and lavish salad bar. Open for breakfast serving menudo on Saturday mornings. Beautiful bar in Victorian decor where you can enjoy a drink and a tortuga adobada. Terrific wine list. Open Monday-Saturday, 8 AM till 1 AM. AE, MC, VI. Ph: 3626-0167 or 3626-1505.

ASAHI – ECON – Av. de la Paz #2056 near Lafayette Hotel. Japanese food. Reasonable prices. Subdued atmosphere. Open daily 1:30 till 11 PM. MC, VI. Ph: 3616-3203.

BRAZZ – MOD – Chain of 3 restaurants (Av. López Mateos #1195; López Mateos Sur #6022 (next to English AA, corner Filadelfia); and Av. 16 de Septiembre #720), each with different atmosphere but all specializing in grilled meats including New York steaks, rib eyes, and sirloin. Ph: 3647-5050 or 3647-9231; 3641-4827.

CAPORALES – MOD – Mexican-style restaurant with regional Jalisco atmosphere at López Mateos Sur #5290 south of hotel zone. Mexican cuisine with floor shows and mariachi music. Parking. Open 2 PM till 1 AM daily; Sun, 2-7 PM. AE, MC, VI. Ph: 3631-4543, 3631-4596 or 3631-4139.

CARNITAS URUAPAN – ECON – Colón #338 corner with Libertad. Tacos, carnitas, and gorditas – a good taco place. Open 10 AM to 7 PM.

CASA de PAELLA – MOD – Since 1952. Spanish, Mexican, International. Nice place. Americas #930, across from Torre Américas. Jazz 9 PM – 1:30 AM. Ph: 3641-5669, 3641-6853.

CHALET SUIZO – MOD – Swiss-style restaurant at Hidalgo #1983 near Minerva Circle. Swiss and International dishes. Piano bar upstairs. Open 1 PM till 11 PM; closed Monday. AE, MC, VI. Ph: 3615-7122.

CHE MARY – UPPER – Spanish restaurant at Av. Guadalupe #596 at corner of San Rafael, Colonia Chapalita. Open 1 PM till 12 Midnight daily. Ph: 3621-2951 or 3622-2505.

COLOMBO – MOD – Av. López Mateos #131 near Minerva. Good lunch buffet. Since 1957, good Italian food (chicken cacciatori, cannelloni) and pizza (also with anchovy). Can make strictly vegetarian dishes. Piano music at night. Open 1:30 till midnight; till ten, Sunday; closed Wednesday. Very friendly owner. Ph: 3615-7900.

COPA DE LECHE – ECON – Downtown restaurant at Av. Juárez #414, a Guadalajara institution since 1932. International cuisine served in traditional and typical Tapatian (Guadalajara) atmosphere. Sidewalk cafe and balcony dining. Open daily 7 AM till midnight for breakfast, lunch, and dinner. AE, MC, VI. Ph: 3614-5347 or 3614-7976.

COPENHAGEN – MOD – Intimate, relaxing and romantic restaurant on López Cotilla #750 corner of Mario Castellano in front of Parque Revolución. Soft jazz music (9 AM till 1 AM, 3:30 - 4:30 PM and 8 PM - 1 AM). International food with specialties such as paella, zarzuela and pepper steaks. Open daily 1 PM till 1 AM. AE, MC, VI. Ph: 3625-2803. Jazz Club off Federalismo.

D'ELYS – MOD – 456 Corona. Sandwich shop and bargain eatery. Across from Hotel Continental. Mexican food, hamburgers, cheap breakfasts.

DON QUIJOTE – MOD – Hotel San Francisco Plaza, Degollado 267. Restaurant. Bar. Ph: 3658-1299.

DURÁN DURÁN I – MOD – Av. Vallarta #1543-A, Ph: 616-4095. Music and video bar. Incredible assortment of "stuff" hanging from ceiling. Tacos, steaks, hamburgers, drinks. Decent prices. Open 1 PM to 11:30 PM.

EL ABAJEÑO – MOD-UPPER – Typical Mexican restaurant at Av. López Mateos #4796, La Calma; serving Jaliscan specialties including delicious tacos, carnitas, chalupas, enchiladas. Open 8 AM till 11 PM daily. MC, VI. Ph: 3631-30097. Also another at Av Vallarta #2802. Ph: 3630-2113 or 3630-0307

EL CHE – ECON – Argentine-style charcoal-beef restaurant at López Hidalgo #1798 specializing in El Churrasco. South American guitars and vocalists. Open 1 PM till midnight. AE, MC, VI. Ph: 3652-0325.

EL DELFIN SONRIENTE (The laughing dolphin) – ECON – Good seafood. Reasonable prices. Frog legs. Ceiling fans. Try *"Pachanga de Mariscos"* (Seafood party – octopus, squid, shrimp in soup). Family place. Av. Niños Héroes #2239. VI, MC. Ph: 3616-0216, 3616-7441.

EL GRULLO – MOD – NW corner Plaza del Sol. Vegetarian fare. A little pricier than others but good. The fanciest in town.

EL MESON DE SANCHO PANZA – MOD – Marcos Castellanos #114. Spanish, Mexican, and international food. Open 1 PM till 9 PM TUES. - Sun, closed Mon. Ph: 3625-2898 or 3626-5886.

EL OSTIÓN FELIZ (The Happy Oyster) – MOD – Seafood restaurant at Av. Las Américas #1301 serving a fresh, dazzling array of seafood, from cold platters to Alaskan catfish specialties. Also features good Mexican food. Indoor and outdoor dining rooms. Bar with large TV screen. Open noon till midnight daily. AE, MC, VI.

EL PARGO DEL PACÍFICO – MOD – Av. de la Paz #2140. Seafood. Popular. Ph: 3626-7150 or 3615-7465. Another on Federalismo #876. Ph: 3610-5285.

GUADALAJARA GRILL – MOD – For young, boisterous, "party-hearty" types. Sponsors drinking contests. One of the Anderson chain, at López Mateos Sur #3771, near Plaza del Sol and Holiday Inn. Several dining rooms plus outdoor terrace. Spare ribs, chicken, meats, shrimp and oysters. Homemade bread and biscuits (from outside oven). Open Monday-Saturday 1 PM till midnight; Sundays 1 PM till 5 PM.

KOPPEL HAUS – MOD – Av. America # 764 German food. Seafood. Mon- Fri 7 AM - 11 PM. Sat. 8 AM - 11 PM, Sun. 8 AM - 3 PM. Simple, could be intimate if TV not on. AE, MC, VI. Ph: 3641-4563.

LA CHATA – ECON – Mexican food. López Mateos and Otero. Another by Zoo and train station. Ph: 3632-1379 or 3632-4532.

LA MISIÓN – MOD – Mexican restaurant housed in elegant mansion at Pedro Moreno #1125 in residential area. Good Mexican cuisine. Open noon till 1 AM daily. MC, VI. Ph: 3626-1133.

LA PIANOLA – MOD – Mexican restaurant at Av. Mexico #3220 serving Mexican and International cuisine. Piano music. Open 8 AM till 1 AM daily. AE, VI. Ph: 3647-7881. Another at Miguel de Cervantes Saavedra #86 Ph: 3630-2774.

LA TRATTORIA – MOD – Good Italian restaurant at Niños Héroes #3051 just off López Mateos (Hwy #15) featuring homemade pasta, spaghetti, lasagna, Veal Scallopini and Parmesan, salad bar and more. AE, MC, VI. Ph: 3622-4425.

LAS CALAS – MOD – Av. Tepeyac #1156, Chapalita. Ph: 3647-0383 or 3647-0270

LAS MARGARITAS – MOD – Moroccan-style restaurant and store featuring vegetarian cuisine at López Cotilla #1477 (corner Av. Chapultepec). Open 8 AM till 9:30 PM (8 PM Sunday). Ph: 3616-8906.

LOS ITACATES – ECON – VALUE! Av. Chapultepec Nte. #110 Family restaurant. Nice refined decor, especially if you like blue. Cuisine Mexicana. Open 8 AM - 11 PM M-F, 8 AM - 10 PM Sun. Ph: 3625-1106.

LUSCHERLY – MOD – Duque de Rivas #5 corner of Morelos. Good Swiss food. Romantic atmosphere. Open Tues.–Sat 1:30 PM till Midnight, Sun 1:30 till 6 PM. Ph: 3616-2988 or 3615-0509.

NUEVO LEÓN – ECON – Inexpensive Mexican fast food. Specialty: Cabrito al Pastor. Independencia Sur #223 Ph: 617-2081, Av. Libertad #1586, Ph: 3625-4700 or 625-7827. Another on Calz. Independencia sur #223 Ph: 3617-2740 or 3617-2081.

PILECA – MOD – Colonias #279 (near Lafayette Hotel) Vegetarian food, daily buffet 1 - 5:30 PM. Ph: 3625-3544

PIPIOLO – ECON – Bargain food. Carne asada, Mexican fast food. Open 1 PM – 1 AM. All over town.

RECCO – MOD – Nice restaurants at Av. Libertad #1981 a half-block off Av. Chapultepec and at Circunvalación Providencia #1090. Italian cuisine as well as international including Chicken Cacciatore, lasagna, and shrimp Casamona. Open daily 1 PM till midnight. AE, MC, VI. Ph: 3625-0724 and 3641-4932.

SAINT MICHEL – MOD – Vallarta #1700 Crepes, sandwiches, capuchino. Intimate, romantic. Open 8 AM till Midnight.

SIROCCO – MOD – Fine restaurant at Libertad #1906 featuring seafood and steaks, including Lobster Thermidor and Filet New Orleans Style. Also offers sea grill. Open 1 PM till midnight daily. AE, MC, VI.

SUEHIRO – MOD – Excellent, authentic Japanese restaurant with bar and many dishes prepared at your table by Japanese chefs, at Av. de la Paz #1701. It's quite a kick ordering Japanese food in Spanish to a Japanese-Mexican waitress in a kimono! Specialties include tepperiyaki, teriyaki, and shabu-shabu. Open 1:30 PM till 11 PM daily. AE, MC, VI. Ph: 3626-0094 or 3625-1880.

SUSHI NORI – Next to Quinta Real. Shushi bar with satsumi and a few other Japanese dishes like the Mexico Maki. Open 1:30 PM till midnight Mon – Sat and 1:30 till 11 PM, Sun. AE, MC, VI. For home delivery call 3616-3135.

CAMPING & RV PARKING

HACIENDA – MOD – 100-space facility out in west end of town. All hookups. Pool. Laundromat. Showers. Toilets. Rec hall. Daily activities seasonally.

SAN JOSE DEL TAJO – UPPER – 225-space restful wooded layout some 7 miles southwest of town on Hwy #15-54 to Colima and then a half-mile off highway to right by cobblestone road. All hookups. Dump. Pool. Toilets. Showers. Coffee shop. Rec hall. Store. Daily activities. Several motel rooms and one-bedroom kitchenettes available on monthly basis. Ph: 3622-2193 or 3621-2902.

End of Guadalajara Eat & Stray

Chapala & Ajijic

Area Code — 376
See map on page 82

LAGO DE CHAPALA – Sung by composers, immortalized by poets – and because of its mild climate, the lovely countryside, and the nearby interesting Indian fishing village, Chapala has become one of Mexico's favorite vacation and retirement spots.

Chapala is distinct – it possesses a unique "ambiente" (atmosphere) all its own. It's "ambiente" is in the air, impregnated with the music of mariachi bands, the fragrance of flowers, the smell of delicious whitefish frying, and the aroma of "michi" soup (a local dish prepared with "charal," another fish of the lake). Chapala's "ambiente" is also present in its streets, park, and lakefront boulevard and is more evident on Sunday afternoons when the town is invaded by hordes of weekend tourists. Even President Porfirio Díaz enjoyed Chapala; matter of fact, Villa Montecarlo was his vacation place. Across from Chapala sits the island of the Alacranes ("scorpions") where there's a restaurant –but no scorpions.

Two miles west of Chapala is Chula Vista, and although administratively linked to Chapala, the town is a self-contained American settlement. And there is Ajijic ("ah-hee-heek"), an old Tarascan Indian fishing village with cobblestone streets, its church dating back to the 16th century, and lovely flower-filled gardens. Ajijic, quiet and peaceful, is home to many writers, painters, poets, and just plain retirees. At the west end of the lake, having passed "Balneario" (spa) San Juan Cosalá with its hotel and modern condominium lies another sleepy fishing village, Jocotepec. Founded in 1528, this slow-paced town comes to life every Sunday, its colorful market day. Along with fishing, hand- loomed "serapes" are its main industry.

And for those who enjoy golf, there are three courses in the area. In conjunction with Hotel Brisas de Chapala is a 9-hole layout overlooking the lake; in Chula Vista Subdivision is another 9-hole, par-31 course lining a mountainside with the lake below; and in Vista del Lago Subdivision (5 miles east of Chapala just beyond San Nicolás) the Country Club de Chapala offers still another 9-hole course (although regulation length) with two par-5, two par-3, and five par-4 holes and with two entirely different sets of tees (also on a mountain slope overlooking Lake Chapala).

Families will enjoy the Tabolandia Water Park at Carretera Chapala - Ajijic KM 7 Ph: 6-2120

SLEEPING IN CHAPALA & CHULA VISTA

CHAPALA HACIENDAS – MOD – 18-unit hotel on north end toward Guadalajara. Some kitchenettes. Dining room. Pool. Parking. MC. Ph: 765-2116.

LAKE CHAPALA INN — MOD — Paseo Ramón Corona #23. Six spacious rooms cheerfully decorated. Full breakfasts. Garden terraces on each floor. TV room. Library. Pool. Garden. Jacuzzi. Parking. Phone and fax: (day) 765-4786 or (night) 765-2624.

MONTECARLO — MOD — Av. Hidalgo #296. Formerly a private club. 3 stories. 46 rooms. 1 suite. Spacious lawns with strolling peacocks. 2 pools with thermal water. Parking. AE, MC VI. Ph: 765-2216, 765-2120 Fax: 765-2124

NIDO – MOD – Av. Madero #202 – Old-time 30-room downtown hotel (a landmark) on main stem near pier. Restaurant. Bar. Pool. Parking. MC, VI. Ph: 765-2116.

QUINTA QUETZLCOATL — UPPER — At Zaragoza #307. In case you can't pronounce it, it is also known as "QQ." 8 suites with colorful antiques. Rates include breakfast (except Sundays). For high season - 7 day packages (2 dinners and 1 barbecue included). A minimum 3-night stay. Deposit required by check. 2 bars. Pool. Jacuzzi. No credit cards. Ph: 765-3653 Fax: 765-3444. In the US Fax: 415-8898-1184. Checks can be mailed to Box 27 Point Richmond, CA 94807.

EATING IN CHAPALA & CHULA VISTA

CAFE PARIS – MOD – Restaurant on Chapala's main street. Specializes in whitefish, steaks, hamburgers, and short orders. Open 8 AM till 11 PM for breakfast, lunch, and dinner.

CAZADORES CHAPALA – MOD – Paseo Ramón Corona at Madero – Very good restaurant converted from old mansion in downtown Chapala next to church on main street. Enjoy eating on a balcony facing the lake. Specializes in meats cooked over hot coals, chicken in banana leaves, and cheese fondue. Open 1 PM till midnight. Part of the Cazadores chain with restaurants scattered throughout Guadalajara area. AE, MC, VI. Ph: 765-2162.

COZUMEL — MOD — Paseo Corona #22, lakeside of road near Yacht Club. Excellent selection of seafood plus chicken and steak. Bar. Pleasant atmosphere with live music. Closed Monday. MC,VI. Ph: 765-4606.

GRAN LAGO CHAPALA — ECON — Madero #236 main street in downtown Chapala facing the plaza. International food. Excellent barbecue ribs. Good breakfasts. Open 9 AM till 9 PM Ph: 763-9627.

HOSTERIA CHAPATLI — ECON — Hidalgo #303. Restaurant and art gallery. Daily full meal specials. Sunday, paella. Open 1:30 PM till 11 PM.

LOS CAMPANARIOS — ECON — On Paseo Ramón Corona just west of Lake Chapala Inn. It can also be entered from Hidalgo #236. Open air restaurant facing lake. Good Mexican food. Bar. Open 9 AM till 9 PM. Closed Monday. No credit cards. Bilingual menu.

SUPERIOR — MOD — Madero #415. Good downtown restaurant serving international food. Outside cafe. Breakfasts. Open 8 AM till 10 PM.

CAMPING & RV PARKING

PAL – MOD – Very nice 140-space facility between Chapala and Ajijic. All hookups. Very clean showers. Toilets. Fresh flowers. Recreation room. Pool. Laundromat. Purified water system. Picnic area. Security. Pets OK on leash. Satellite TV hookups. 37% discount from March 15 to Oct 30 on a minimum 2 month stay. Ph: 766-0040, 766-0220 or 621-8878 in Guadalajara.

SLEEPING IN AJIJIC & RANCHO DEL ORO

DANZA DEL SOL – UPPER – Zaragoza #165 – Unique 95-unit hotel in Rancho del Oro scattered over lovely spacious grounds. Units include living room with fireplace, breakfast nook, fully equipped kitchenettes, patio, and one, two, or three bedrooms. Restaurant. Bar. Pool. Tennis. Sauna. Parking. AE, MC, VI. Ph: 766-0220, 766-0640 in Ajijic or 621-8982 or 621-8878 in Guadalajara.

LA NUEVA POSADA — UPPER — Donate Guerra #9 facing the lake. 17 suites. Pool. Large tropical garden with exotic flowers. Parking. MC, VI. Ph: 766-1444 Fax: 766-1344.

LAS CASITAS — MOD – 11-unit, fully furnished one-bedroom apartment complex on west side of Ajijic, Poniente #10. No restaurant. Small pool. Parking. One day free for those who stay a week. Ph: 766-11-45

MARIANA – ECON – 22-room, 3-story downtown hotel at Guadalupe Victoria 10 behind church. Restaurant specializing in Italian, Mexican, and American food. Bar. MC, VI. Ph: 766-1060.

NUEVA POSADA AJIJIC – MOD – 17-unit tropical lakeside patio-style inn, once a tequila still. Restaurant. Lounge. Pool. Shops. On-street parking. MC, VI. Ph: 765-3395.

POSADA LAS CALANDRIAS – MOD – 29-unit complex at Poniente #8 consisting of 14 efficiencies and 15 two-bedroom furnished kitchenettes. No restaurant. Small pool. Has laundromat in front. Parking. MC, VI. Ph: 766-1052.

REAL DE CHAPALA – UPPER – Paseo del Pardo 20 – Good 2-story, 85-room secluded, garden-like lakefront hotel. Restaurant. Sunday buffet, noon. Cafeteria. Piano bar. 5 suites with small private pool. Boutique. Pool. Tennis. Game room. Playground. Horses. Enclosed parking with security. AE, MC, VI. Ph: 766-0007, 766-0014, 766-0021 Fax: 766-0025.

VILLA DEL GALLO CANTADOR — UPPER — Av. Colón #117. 4 rooms with magnificent views. 2 with private kitchens. Pool. Parking. No credit cards. Ph and Fax: 766-0308.

VILLA FLORES – MOD – Very nice restored 200-year old villa with 4 suites at Colon #43 just above central plaza. Breakfast included. Parking. Ph: 765-3665.

EATING IN AJIJIC & RANCHO DEL ORO

AJIJIC GRILL — MOD — Morelos #5 (down from the plaza). Specializes in Japanese lunch specials 12 - 3 PM. Mesquite grilled meats prepared at your table. Open moon till 8:30 PM, Mom - Sat. Sunday 1 to 8 PM. MC, VI. Ph: 766-2458.

BORSALINO RESORANTE ITALIANO — UPPER — 16 de Septiembre #5A (behind old Posada). Italian cuisine served in a garden atmosphere. Open noon till 10 PM. Closed Wednesday. Ph: 766-2368.

BRUNO'S — UPPER — Carretera Oriente #20. Cozy and charming. International food. Opens at 1 PM, Tues - Sat. Closed Sunday and Monday. Ph: 766-1674.

DANNY'S – ECON – VALUE. Good restaurant with pleasant home atmosphere. Breakfast, lunch. Serves hamburgers and garlic bread. Open 8 AM till 6 PM Mon thru Sat. 8 AM till noon Sun. Closed on Tuesdays.

LOS TELARES — UPPER — International cuisine in a lovely garden setting. Full bar. Open Sun - Thurs noon till 9 PM; Fri - Sat noon till 11 PM. Ph: 766-0428.

TRATTORIA DE GIOVANNI — MOD — Carretera Oriente #28. Specialties - Breast of chicken made many different ways. 18 varieties of beef. 22 varieties of fish filets plus pastas, salad bar and pizza. Open daily noon till 10 PM.

POSADA AJIJIC – MOD – Located at the old Posada. Serves Mexican food. Breakfast.

SLEEPING IN SAN JUAN COSALA & JOCOTEPEC

Area Code — 387

BALNEARIO SAN JUAN COSALA – UPPER – 34-unit, 2-story lakeside "spa" near village of San Juan Cosalá. Restaurant. 4 pools for adults; 3 for children. Parking. MC, VI. Ph: 763-0302.

POSADA DEL PESCADOR – MOD – 22-kitchenette motel just east of entrance to Jocotepec. Cafeteria. Pool. Carports.

VILLAS BUENAVENTURA SPA – UPPER – 16-rooms. 6 with private jacuzzis. 4 public wading pools. 2 pools. Balneario temp. 89° C. Crystal clear water. Lots of families. MC, VI.

End of Chapala & Ajijic Eat & Stray

LOG 13   START: Guadalajara, Jal   END: Tepic, Nay

143.3 MI OR 229.3 KM
DRIVE TIME 4 HOURS
SCENIC RATING – 3

MI	KM	
0.0	0.0	Starting with cathedral at your right, proceed ahead down Av. Corona. Cross Morelos, one-way your left. Parking lot, right. Turn RIGHT onto Hidalgo, one-way, right. Cross Pino Suárez right, Belén, left, Degollado Theatre to your right. Narrows to 1 lane. Stay right. Cross Carranza.
0.3	0.5	1 lane. Pizza Express, left. MEXICO, SALTILLO, LEFT.
0.4	0.6	RIGHT ONTO INDEPENDENCIA. Go under park. 4 lanes each way. Cross Juárez right. Light.
0.6	1.0	Pass Hotel Los Reyes, right. Cine Avenida, left. Streets crossing or dead-ending into Independencia will alternate one-way left, right.
0.8	1.3	Come to circle with Angel on top. Street right 2 way. Go around and straight ahead.
1.0	1.6	Cross divided 2-way Calzada Revolución. Next 1-way right. Gas right. Av. La Paz, right. Around little circle. Gas left. Airport, Bomberos signs. STAY OUT OF LEFT LANE. Hotel 13,000 – not for you.
1.6	2.6	Gas left. Cross wide González Gallo. (If you were going north, you could turn here with a protected left arrow.) Left 2 lanes can turn left. Pass Biblioteca Nacional. Follow signs for train. Beautiful park left. Right 3 lanes MUST go around *glorieta*. LEFT lane MUST turn left onto González Gallo – don't do that. You'll dead end into Curiel. Railroad station dead ahead.
1.8	2.9	Federal Express on left. Straight. Market, left. Plaza, right. CALZ. GOV. CURIEL STRAIGHT.
2.0	3.2	TRAIN STATION, RIGHT.
2.4	3.8	Up, then over railroad crossing (LOOK & LISTEN). DANGEROUS INTERSECTION. PPG industries de Mexico right. Banco Nacional, left. 4 lane divided street. No dividing strip.
2.8	4.5	Get into right lane for right turn ahead.
3.1	5.0	Should be in right lane for right turn onto Lázaro Cárdenas. Turn RIGHT onto L. Cárdenas. Signs: Clínica IMSS, ZONA INDUSTRIAL SIGNS AHEAD. Pass LP gas tank and satellite dish vendor.
3.5	5.6	Cárdenas is 3 lanes each way divided parkway. Right turn arrows DO NOT mean your lane dies – YET. It will in about 2 miles.
4.5	7.2	Pass Av. Cruz del Sur exit (left).
5.3	8.5	Pass Farmer's market, *Centro de Abastos*, right.
5.6	9.0	Road narrows. RIGHT LANE DISAPPEARS! Under overpass.
5.8	9.3	Come to small glorieta at Av. Mariano Otero. Stop sign. Go 3/4 around and veer right. Straight. Valencia restaurant and La Mansión a *cabrito* restaurant, right. Ahead on wide divided Av. Cárdenas.
5.9	9.4	GAS, right.
6.4	10.2	Cross wide divided López Mateos. Renault dealer on left. *Todo Fácil* – a neat place like a Handy Dan superstore, right.
6.5	10.4	Teléfonos de México, left. Banco del Atlántico.
6.8	10.9	Soccer field in middle of street!
7.0	11.2	Movie theater at right. GAS, left.
7.2	11.5	Hotel Malibu, way over to right.
7.4	11.8	Tutankhamen bar and rest, right. General Tires on left.
7.6	12.2	Cross Av. Del Niño Obrero.
7.8	12.5	Chrysler dealer on right. Veer a little to left. Right lane for local traffic. Nogales sign overhead. Down and under overpass. Street changes name to Av. Vallarta. Pretty brick. Pass electrical generating station, right.
8.0	12.8	Block sculpture in middle of street. Mayoral restaurant on right. Volks Vallarta, left. Road narrows. Interesting townhouses, right. Banco Atlántico, right. Right goes to Universidad Autónoma de Guadalajara, on Av. De la Patria. Goodyear right.
8.5	13.6	Coca Cola dealer right. Hotel Nuevo Real Vallarta, right. GAS, right. Car dealership, left. Road narrows – 2 lanes each way. No longer divided. El Gallo Pope right. Chevy right.
9.5	15.2	Left is to Trailer park, Hacienda. Protected left turn, but better turn ahead. Corona Vallarta right.
9.7	15.5	Protected left turn. Nissan dealer, left. Traffic light.
10.7	17.1	Pass nice cemetery, left.
11.0	17.6	Conasupo warehouses. Road divides again. Hospital Dr. Angel Leano, right. Straight. Could take right here for Saltillo and Hwy #54. Straight for Nogales. Stoplight. Intersection with Periférico.

IF TO: Chapala, Turn left and join Guadalajara Bypass Counterclockwise Log (page 78) at mile 8.3.

IF TO: Zacatecas, turn left and join Guadalajara Bypass Clockwise Log (page 76) at mile 16.5.

MI	KM	
12.0	19.2	Pass side road (right) to Ocotán Air Force Base – also called "Zapopan" Air Force Base – one of Mexico's largest. **GAS,** right. Often cops here, so obey traffic laws. Still divided.
12.6	20.2	Gamesa plant, right. Good cookies and crackers. Divided 4 lanes.
14.0	22.4	"Rancho Contento" at left – nice retirement condominium deal for Americans – has its own golf course.
15.8	25.3	Slow a little for a sharp right-left "S" curve and alongside the railroad. Turnoff for botanical institute.
17.0	27.2	Hunting club of Jalisco, right.
17.4	27.8	Thru village of La Venta del Astillero. Careful for farm machinery. **GAS,** right.

IF TO: Río Caliente Spa, a vegetarian health spa, turn off to the left just ahead at town of Primavera and follow stub log below. These folks frown on drop-in guests. Although they probably won't shoot you, it is best to call ahead and make a reservation, USA: 1-800-200-2927, Fax: (415) 615-0601.

RÍO CALIENTE SPA

0.0	0.0	After left turn, go thru village of Primavera. When road dead ends, turn right. At "T", turn left and cross bridge. At "Y" take middle fork with gate and sign that says Las Tinajitas 2.2 km.
2.8	4.5	Come to a fork. Do not take right fork. It goes to Al Río del Valle. Take left fork, Go over cattle guard.
3.0	4.8	Pass road (right) to Balneario La Primavera and road (left) to Hogar Betania. This is where nuns give mud baths and iridology readings.
3.1	5.0	Come to gate. If gate is locked, don't despair. There is a little opening to left. Park and walk up hill to office. If you look respectable, they will let you in. Ask for Dr. Ricardo Heredia or Javier Contreras.
3.2	5.1	Cross bridge over steamy river into Río Caliente Spa.

END STUB LOG

19.3	30.9	Wind past village of Primavera "Spring" (the season) in Spanish.
20.7	33.1	Cattle inspection station then roadside restaurant at right.
21.5	34.4	Grain silos at right.
21.8	34.9	Note deep arroyo (gulch) over to the left. Don't you agree that "arroyo" is a much prettier word than our English "gulch"?
22.0	35.2	Road narrows. There may be a guy selling highway signs here! Now you see why folks (even us) get lost sometimes! Then bumpy railroad crossing (LOOK-&-LISTEN). **KM 25.**
22.5	36.0	Curve right (take right fork) past side road (left) to town of Ameca. Come to junction with toll road to Tepic. For toll road veer left and up over overpass and follow stub log below. For free road stay in right lane. If you want to visit the town of Tequila take the free road.

Toll Road to Tepic

22.6	36.2	Having veered left onto overpass for toll road, proceed ahead on 4-lane.
24.0	38.4	Come to toll house and pay toll (Car, $44, extra axle, $22). There's a snack shop and restrooms.
27.0	43.2	To the left are fields of Blue Agave cactus, the plant from which the finest tequilas are distilled. The Guadalajara area produces most of Mexico's tequila.
32.0	51.2	Over puente Tequila. Sorry folks, that doesn't mean that tequila flows in the stream below.

MI	KM	
35.0	56.0	Up over puente Gorgorrones.
40.0	64.0	Pass exit (right) to Magdalena.
42.0	67.2	Note town of Magdalena over to right with pretty church dome.
54.0	86.4	Come to another toll house and pay toll (cars, $51). You'll find a 24-hour emergency medical service, cafeteria and clean restrooms here.
60.0	96.0	Slow and curve over puente Platamar.
64.0	102.4	Cross state line. Leave state of Jalisco and enter state of Nayarit. Also come to a new time zone. Leave Central Standard time and start Mountain Standard time. Turn you watch and dash clock back one hour. Then pass monument dedicating this toll road.
65.0	104.0	Over puente Ocote. Ocote is a strip of pine wood, dripping with sap, used by the farmers as a catalyst to start a fire.
66.0	105.6	**GAS** right. Then under overpass of Hwy #15 free road.
71.0	113.6	Pass exit (right) to Ixtlá del Río.
78.0	124.8	Pass exit (right) to Jala and Ahuacatlán.
85.0	136.0	Cross bridge over gully of black lava rock down below and over mountain side.
91.0	145.6	Come to last toll house and pay toll (cars, $24, extra axle, $12).
96.0	153.6	Come to junction with free road.
97.0	155.2	Now come to junction with turnoff to Pto. Vallarta.

IF TO: Pto. Vallarta, turn left and start Chapalilla - Las Varas Special (page 73).

IF TO: Tepic, straight ahead on free road. Join free road log at mile 116.2.

End Toll Road

		Continuation of free road.
23.0	36.8	Slow a little for bumpy railroad crossing (LOOK-&-LISTEN) – Ameca branch line.
24.5	39.2	Thru village of Santa Cruz del Astillero.
27.3	43.7	Bumpy stretch begins.
27.7	44.3	Note the maguey ("muh-gay") growing on the hillsides. The heart or core of the maguey cactus is used to make tequila.
29.0	46.4	Little tequila distillery town of Arenal (11,594 folks), left – note the cone-shaped grain silos. Sharp left curve.
30.5	48.8	CAREFUL. EVEN TRUCKS STOP FOR THIS railroad crossing! LOOK-&-LISTEN. Then over fancy bridge.
34.7	55.5	Tequila Orendain plant, right. Pass cemetery, right, and skirt town of Amatitán, left. **GAS**, right and at far end. Pass bullring on right. Clean restrooms at store beside gas.
37.3	59.7	Cross the railroad again.
41.5	66.5	Burlap and carton factory on left. If your windows are open, you'll know that you're coming into the famous Tequila-distilling town by the same name – TEQUILA (mostly off to left). Curve right at the fountain (left fork to downtown). Gas at left. Can you catch a whiff of the tequila smell in the air? On right just ahead is Mario's Restaurant and Tequila Shoppe. Mario sells all kinds from grade A on down at competitive prices. If you'd like a tour of this interesting town, Mario will take you on one – he's on a first-name basis with just about everybody at the SAUZA and CUERVO tequila distilleries and speaks enough English to get by (see SPECIAL REPORT ON TEQUILA and map, pages 37-38). After Mario's leave Tequila. Note small distillery over at right. Then nice panorama with deep Barranca de Santiago off to right.
42.0	67.2	**GAS**, left. Village of Teresa down at right.
44.9	71.8	**CAREFUL! DANGEROUS, ALMOST HORSESHOE CURVE.** Then up hill. **KM 66.**
47.0	75.2	**CAREFUL! DANGEROUS, ALMOST HORSESHOE CURVE.** Then up hill. Climbing lane!
50.8	81.3	You've climbed about 800 feet in the last 7 miles. Along here you'll spot some jet-black rocky stuff called OBSIDIAN.
54.3	86.9	Quinta Minas hotel, Ph: (386) 864-0560. Plan on taking it easy through Magdalena, an opal town with a population of 11,021. Congestion is amazing. The reason is there's only one stop sign at the end of the square, so be patient. Across on right is the regional hospital. Altitude 4,200 ft. Opals de Magdalena store at right. TURN RIGHT at end of plaza at traffic light and proceed on up thru town.

By the way, *La Unica*, the largest opal mine in the area, is located 7 miles from town atop Ocatera Mountain.

MI	KM	
54.3	86.9	Curve right. Bank of Promex. Restaurant Evangelina.
54.8	87.7	**GAS**, at far end of town. Airport, left.
60.0	96.0	Come to cross roads, Hostotipaquillo to right.
62.8	100.5	Pretty little village of El Zapote down at right. Police check point. You've climbed another 600 feet!
65.4	104.6	Exit left for Tepic toll road. Veer right for free road. Veer left if you want to take the toll road.
72.0	115.2	Lavender and mauve colored mountains. Free S.O.S. phones positioned throughout.
73.7	117.9	Pull off point. Altitude 4,500 ft.
76.9	123.0	Top. And come to state line – leave state of Jalisco and enter state of Nayarit. Also come to a new TIME ZONE – leave Central Standard Time and start Mountain Standard Time, so set your watches and dash clock BACK one hour.
77.0	123.2	Pass monument on right. Longitude 22 degrees. Go under pedestrian bridge.
77.4	123.8	Pull-off on right.
78.1	125.0	Sharp decline. Veer left to Tepic. Topes. Dangerous intersection.
80.0	128.0	Cross bridge over the railroad.
82.0	131.2	Railroad village of Ranchos de Arriba off to right. Toll road crosses to right. **KM 129**.
85.0	136.0	Hotel Hacienda, right. Balneario Casida, for home folks.
85.7	137.1	La Sidia restaurant to left. **KM 134**.
86.0	137.6	Up high on yonder mountain ahead you'll see the famed huge statue of CRISTO REY or "Christ the King." There's a side road up to it but don't tackle it – it's in very poor shape and we can't recommend it.
87.0	139.2	Slow now. To right and just over railroad tracks are IXTLÁN Archeological Ruins, on which very little is known (except that they are post-Classic, 900 A.D. and later). If you wish to drive over tracks and into the compound, hop to it. It's quite nice. (Admission is charged and zone is open from 9 AM – 4 PM daily.)
87.1	139.4	Truck stop to right. Hotel Vacancy Ixtlán to right.
88.0	140.8	Hotel restaurant Colón, right. It's OK by me. Clean restrooms, good food. If it's late, consider staying here, because you're 110 hard miles from PV, and 47 easy ones from Tepic. Then stoplight. Slow thru town of Ixtlán del Río (population 24,064). **GAS**, at end of town on right. Altitude 3,400 feet.
90.0	144.0	Ixtlán del Río's railroad station at right. International airport to right.

When it rains, this road has invisible puddles that will give you an unpleasant surprise. Please slow down.

91.0	145.6	Thru village of Mexpán. Then note railroad tunnel ahead at right. Baskets and woven chairs for sale.
92.2	147.5	Over narrow bridge over railroad. Note at the right where the train comes out of the tunnel.
94.0	150.4	Pass side road (left) to Amequita and La Ciénega (The Swamp).
95.0	152.0	Pass side road (right) to Jala.
96.2	153.9	Pass town of Ahuacatlán over to left on railroad. There's a road to the volcano around here. You can drive within 2 km of top, then walk. It's an active volcano. **GAS**, left. Then alongside railroad at left. **KM 152**.
99.5	159.2	Settlement of Copales. In 3 miles, you're in for a treat!

Now here's Something Special – Have you ever wondered what it's like on another planet? Well, here's your chance to be a space man (and space lady) and land on Mars or Jupiter or somewhere. Now you go thru a short mile of the famous LAVA-BEDS-OF-CEBORUCO caused by the eruption of Ceboruco volcano in 1885. Sort of eerie, no? Like something out of this world – but bear in mind that it's against the law to pick up the little green one-eyed men or to stop and swipe lava samples.

101.0	161.6	Parador turístico at right. **KM 161**.
105.0	168.0	Uzeta off to left. **KM 167**.
105.5	168.8	Pass side road (left) to Estación Tetitlán and Balneario Acatique Springs.

IF TO: Springs – Turn left at Balneario sign just beyond school. Over bumpy railroad tracks, 3/4 mile on right. Fresh water not hot. Large pools. Balneario Acatique. Proprietor J. Trinidad Dueñas A., a former taxi driver in Tijuana and former owner of a KFC in Phoenix. Space for self-contained RV's and trailers. Nice flat parking. They'll run a water hose for you. Very nice folks and a nice restful place.

109.0	174.4	Past a sugar mill on right. Then into little town of Santa Isabel. Pottery.
114.0	182.4	Past village of El Torreón on left. Emergency Motel La Cumbre and Restaurant at right. Then thru Chapalilla. **GAS**, right. **KM 175**.
116.2	185.9	Careful now! Here's the turnoff for Puerto Vallarta on Hwy #200. You will climb 200 feet in the next few miles. Altitude 3,300 ft. **KM 113**.

IF TO: Puerto Vallarta take "PUERTO VALLARTA CUOTA and COMPOSTELA CUOTA" slot.

Exit right, curve around and start Chapalilla - Las Varas Special (page 73). THIS IS A FINE ROAD. There's **GAS** at end of toll road as well as a neat hole-in-the-wall restaurant. Take right after **GAS**, go 1/4 mile toward town. Just before pavement ends is white iron-fenced hacienda on left. "El Rincón del Montero" is there. Sign says *Mariscos*. It's plain and for the adventurous. Inexpensive too.

MI	KM	
116.5	185.6	Past village of El Ocotillo. Altitude 4,250 ft.
118.2	189.1	Rest stop. Altitude 3,800 ft.
121.6	194.6	Pass side road (right) to Santa María del Oro and La Laguna, with neat motel and trailer park Koala. Tepic straight ahead.

IF TO: Koala Bungalows and trailer park is 52 KM SE from Tepic and 20 KM from Tepic/Guadalajara Hwy on Laguna de Santa María near Crater Lake (730 M above sea level and 2 KM in diameter). High entrance. 15 spaces with all hookups. Showers. Swimming. Boat ramp. Boating. Fishing. Ph: (327) 272-3772 or (311) 214-0509 (in Tepic).

128.0	204.8	Pass little town of La Labor over to left. Mechanic. **KM 200**.
133.0	212.8	Pass El Refugio at left.
134.0	214.4	That's Tepic in distance ahead.
139.2	222.7	Pass side road (left) to Pantanal and thru village of San Cayetano. Slow for "topes."
140.2	224.3	Come now to nice divided bypass around Tepic. Take LEFT FORK. Under railroad overpass. Straight ahead is old congested Hwy #15 thru town.
141.0	225.6	Over Río Mololoa (also known as Río de Tepic).
141.3	226.1	**GAS,** right. A right here goes to KOA RV Park. Paradise Motel, nice. Ph: (311) 214-0334.
142.7	228.3	Just before overpass, turn right for Puerto Vallarta or downtown Tepic. **KM 5**.
143.3	229.3	Come now to junction with Hwy #200.

IF TO: Downtown Tepic turn right (follow TEPIC CENTRO signs). For accommodations see Tepic Eat & Stray (page 129).

IF TO: Puerto Vallarta, turn right here and start Tepic – Puerto Vallarta Log (page 34).

IF TO: San Blas, Mazatlán, etc. continue straight ahead under double railroad overpass and start Tepic – Mazatlán Log (page 157).

You'll like Tepic, capital of the state of Nayarit, an interesting, colorful, and friendly town of 238,101. If you look closely, you might get a glimpse of the Cora and Huichol Indians in their native costumes, especially on Sunday, Tepic's market day. Of interest are the cathedral, finished in 1750, with its two perfect Gothic bell towers, and the Regional Museum of Anthropology with its excellent collection of Indian crafts and archeological items.

End of log 13

LOG 14	*START:* Pto Vallarta, Jal	*END:* Tepic, Nay

UD-019

102.3 MI OR 163.7 KM
DRIVE TIME 3 1/2 — 4 HOURS
SCENIC RATING — 3

0.0	0.0	Starting here at the fabulous Hotel Camino Real at left, proceed on up Hwy #200, winding thru residential area alongside the Pacific. Then pass El Set Restaurant — great food in Mexican atmosphere.
1.5	2.4	**GAS,** at left. Periférico (loop) at left around PV.
1.8	2.9	Now pass Hotel El Mesón de los Arcos at left. Then *Supermercado* Gil at left on corner with Av. Lázaro Cárdenas. Then Cine Bahía at right.
2.0	3.2	Up over bridge over Río Cuale. Note houses up at right built up alongside river. That's famous "Gringo Gulch", a colony of expatriate Americans and plush homes. On left, there's a park in the river with good restaurant, Hacienda del Sol, and an anthropological museum.

MI	KM	
2.3	3.7	Bend right and pass *Mercado Municipal* (city market) at left. Go 2 blocks beyond market and turn right onto Juárez at Banco Industrial de Jalisco.
2.5	4.0	Aviación Mexicana offices at right. Then AeroMexico ticket office at left. Helados Bing (town's best ice cream parlor) at right, and Banamex at left on corner with Calle Zaragoza.
2.8	4.5	PV's main plaza and city hall at left. Then supermarket El Gallo Marinero at right. In next block you'll see Las Margaritas, one of PV's best restaurants, and Vallarta Pharmacy on next corner.
3.3	5.3	Careful Now! Here at this wide cross-street (Calle 31 de Octubre), turn left. You can see Hotel Rosita down at right. Go one block and turn right onto Morelos, then straight.
3.5	5.6	Big **GAS**, station at left. Then after a couple of blocks, turn right and merge with Hwy #200. Then cross bridge over Arroyo Camarones and out.
4.0	6.4	Pass Sheraton Hotel at left. Sports field at right.
4.2	6.7	Careful at stoplight. *Libramiento* at right, a bypass around Vallarta. Then pass side road (right) to Puerto Vallarta RV Park.
4.5	7.2	Disco at left and side road (left) to Economical Hotel Los Pelícanos and Hotel Las Palmas.
4.8	7.7	Los Tules Resort and Fiesta Americana (outstanding), at left.
5.3	8.5	Highrise Ramada Inn at left. Then over Arroyo Pitallil and pass side street (left) to big Hotel Krystal and Hotel Playa de Oro, and Miller Travel Service, located across the street from Hotel Krystal.
5.5	8.8	Car-passenger ferry and cruise ship terminal at left. Paved side road (right) to Tacho's RV Park.
6.3	10.1	Naval base ("Armada de Mexico") over at left. Cross bridge over part of Río Ameca delta.
6.5	10.4	Marina to left.
7.0	11.2	Las Iguanas Marina and Resort hotel at right. Then LP gas at right.
7.3	11.7	**GAS**, at right.
7.5	12.0	Puerto Vallarta International Airport at left.
9.8	15.7	Pass side road (right) to Las Juntas, 2 km.
10.8	17.3	Pass Policía Federal de Caminos. Then up and over big, long toll bridge over Río Ameca. This is also state line — leave Jalisco and enter Nayarit. Likewise, this also marks a time zone — leave Mountain Time and enter Central Time. You lose an hour — set your watches and dashboard clock AHEAD an hour (you become an hour older).
11.8	18.9	Pass side road (left) to Jarretaderas.
12.5	20.0	Pass side road (left) to Nuevo Vallarta, an exclusive private and residential resort.
14.5	23.2	Pass side road (left) to San José del Valle, Valle Banderas, and San Juan de Abajo. Then thru settlement of Mezcales.
16.0	25.6	Nice Country Club de Golf Los Flamingos at left, open to public. Restaurant-bar. Pool. Pro shop. Sauna. Massage. Green fee. Electric cart fee. Caddie fee. **GAS**, on left.
17.5	28.0	Pass side road (left) to A/C Hotel Flamingos (restaurant, pool) and to Bucerias RV Park. 25 spaces with hookups, 30 more with electricity and water, showers, toilets, laundromat, rec room.
18.0	28.8	Costa Dorada at left, a very nice a/c 5-story, 15-apartment condominium (ocean-view rooms; piped-in music; pool; restaurant-bar; laundromat).
18.5	29.6	Over Río de Bucerias and thru seaside village of Bucerias.
19.5	31.2	Bungalows Vista del Bahía at left on beach. 8 nice kitchenettes. Pool. Pets OK. Portable fans only. 5 RV spaces, all hookups, shower, toilet. Bungalows Los Picos, also at left on beach. Complex of 6 buildings, each with two 3-bedroom, 2-bath apartments. Portable fans only. Pets OK.
20.5	32.8	Pass side road (left) to La Cruz de Huanacaxtle and to its nautical institute. There is also a Japanese resort Pinta Mitaketmar.
28.5	45.6	Tropical settlement of San Ignacio at left. Then curve right.
29.5	47.2	Pass side road (left) to Sayulita and Sayula RV Park on beach, 1.5 miles.
32.5	52.0	Settlement of San Francisco at left with its own hospital and vocational fishing school. Also Hotel Costa Azul Sport Resort. Adriana's Bed and Breakfast is one block from plaza. Then thru banana plantations.
39.3	62.9	Pass side road (right) to Lo de Marcos and to nice El Caracol RV Park (22 spaces; all hookups; showers; toilets; concrete patios; beach).
41.8	66.9	Thru settlement of Chula Vista.
44.0	70.4	Pass edge of village of El Monteón at left.
47.3	75.7	Pass side road (left) to Rincón de Guayabitos (see Eat & Stray, page 133), a popular resort development.
48.0	76.8	Over Río de Jaquey. Icehouse a few blocks off to left. Then over Río La Peñita.
48.5	77.6	Slow for topes and into seaside brick-making village of La Peñita de Jaltemba (simply known as "La Peñita"). Pass divided boulevard to left to downtown La Peñita.

IF TO: Russell RV Park, go to end of boulevard and then a block north (or right).

MI	KM	
49.3	78.9	Pass side trail (left) to La Peñita RV Park (274-0996), a nice cliffside layout overlooking the Pacific. Then **GAS**, at left.
54.8	87.7	Over Río de la Lima. Then pass side road (left) to Lima de Abajo and Puesta de la Lima. Note tobacco-drying racks.
56.3	90.1	Pass side road (right) to El Capomo, 5 kilometers away.
60.3	96.5	Over Río Las Varas. Then pass side road (left) to Chacala — an old pirate hangout. This used to be magnificent jungle — but look at the price of progress.
60.5	96.8	**GAS**, at left. Now thru booming little tobacco town of Las Varas. Note red brick tobacco factory and Tabaco Mexicano office ahead on right. Side road (left) to Zacualpan.

IF TO: San Blas via Zacualpan and Santa Cruz, turn left and start Las Varas - San Blas Special (page 71).

63.5	101.6	Over Río Viejo and careful for topes as you go thru little settlement of La Cuata (The Female Twin). Then over Río Las Piedras and thru village of Las Piedras (The Stones).
71.0	113.6	Thru village of Mesillas.
81.5	130.4	Come to junction right with toll road that cuts across east to Chapalilla on Hwy #15, a nice shortcut for motorists traveling between Puerto Vallarta and Guadalajara (or vice-versa). Then pass Autonomous University of Nayarit branch over at left.

IF TO: Guadalajara, turn right and start Las Varas — Chapalilla Special (page 73).

82.8	132.5	Cross Río Compostela. Then gas at right.
83.3	133.3	Take LEFT FORK here and curve left thru cut for bypass around town of Compostela (10,000 population), biggest place between Tepic and "PV" with a couple of emergency hotels on plaza. Of interest here is the old church built with red *tezontle* (volcanic rock) in 1539.
87.5	140.0	Over bridge over Río Refilión. Then pass side road (right) to coffee-growing El Refilión.
93.5	149.6	Pass settlement of Emiliano Zapata over to right.
97.0	155.2	Thru settlement of El Testerazo, mostly at right.
100.0	160.0	Thru little town of Xalisco. Pretty plaza at left. Then **GAS** at left. Careful now as you come to junction with Periférico (Loop) and Hwy #15 around Tepic. For accommodations see Tepic Eat & Stray (page 129)

IF TO: Mazatlán, San Blas, etc. turn left (take Mazatlán exit) and start Tepic — Mazatlán Log.

IF TO: Guadalajara, turn right and start Tepic — Guadalajara Log (page 35).

IF TO: Tepic and to Linda Vista and Los Pinos RV Parks, La Loma Motel, Fray Junípero Serra Hotel, or excellent Roberto's International Restaurant, continue straight ahead.

End of Log 14

LOG 15	*START:* **Tepic, Nay**	*END:* **Mazatlán, Sin**

UD-019

173.5 MI OR 277.6 KM
DRIVE TIME 4 1/2 – 5 HOURS
SCENIC RATING – 2

Some divided, mostly two lane. Heavy truck traffic. Stretches of poor surface.

0.0	0.0	Here just north of the double railroad overpass, the highway from Pto. Vallarta joins the bypass, proceed ahead. Radiator distributor "Sanher" at left. **KM 5**.
0.4	0.6	Thru rock cut. **KM 6**.
1.1	1.8	Cuauhtémoc suburb to left.
1.4	2.2	Cement block factory to right.
1.5	2.4	Colonia del Bosque to right. Curve left. **KM 8**.
2.5	4.0	Pass side road (right) to downtown Tepic.
3.7	5.9	School and suburb to right. Housing project to left. Mazatlán straight. Hotel BugamVillas on right. **GAS** station (under construction) at left. **KM 12**.

MI	KM	
4.2	6.7	Curve left under overpass. Right goes to Tepic.
4.4	7.0	Begin divided.
4.8	7.7	Free road exit at right. Toll road straight ahead.
7.4	11.8	Mazatlán *Libre*, straight. Mazatlán *cuota*, Hwy #15D, go straight. Libre exit right. 280 KM from Mazatlán. Altitude 3,000 ft.
9.0	14.4	Sharp downhill slope. Use your motor to break. KM 3. 3 miles. Toll booth now at 2,500 ft. Pay toll (car – $12; 2 (rear) axles – $24; extra axle – $6).
11.2	17.9	Summit at 2,600 ft. Community of Trapachillo.
16.3	26.1	Mazatlán, veer left. Tepic veer right. This is where the free highway intersects toll. 4 lanes.
16.9	27.0	Divided highway begins.
18.9	30.2	Pass Restaurant Amalia at right at TOME FANTA sign – cold cokes, package snacks, plus a zoo of sorts including jaguars, parrots, etc. Careful now! GAS, left and come to junction (left) with side road down to famed old-time seaside town of San Blas. If you have a couple of hours to spare, run down for a quick look-see at this tropical historic place. Friends of Bill W. sometimes in town. **KM 32**.

IF TO: San Blas, see Jct. Hwy #15 - San Blas Special (page 68).

IF TO: Mazatlán, straight. 260 KM. Santiago 30 KM.

22.2	35.5	El Paraíso at left. Note big stand selling freshly squeezed fruit juices.
27.5	44.0	Pass side road (left) to tobacco town of Villa Hidalgo. Mazatlán straight, 240 KM.
28.0	44.8	Wind past another tobacco town of Valle de Lerma at right. Note tobacco fields thru here. Many Huichols make their living as field workers harvesting tobacco.
29.0	46.4	Estación Nanchi to right.
29.5	47.2	Cross Río Grande de Santiago on big steel bridge. This is a bad-acting river. Flooded in 1927 and 1992.
29.9	47.8	La Luz Del Mundo (The light of the world). A fancy new school to right just before you enter Del Capomal.
30.0	48.0	Pass side road (right) to Estación Yago on railroad.
30.5	48.8	Thru village of Capomal.
32.4	51.8	Pass side road (left) to Santiago Ixcuintla and on to Los Corchos (The Corks) on beach. GAS, in town. Mexcaltitán to right. Mazatlán straight.

If you're interested in the Huichol Indians' weaving and bead work, this is the place where the Huichol Center for Cultural Survival and Traditional Arts is located. Susana Valadez, who helps organize things will be glad to arrange classes for interested groups. She runs a hospital and cultural center there, so please be considerate. She's not ready for troops of tourists to drop by and visit, but if you have a sincere interest or if you're a fledgling importer who wants to buy some really unique art, please call and make an appointment to see her. She's usually gone in late June-July. She'll put on demonstrations for tour groups also. The hotel Bugamvillas is the best, just on the outskirts of town. There is an OK hotel, Casino, in town, basic, but clean. You can call her at (323) 5-1171 Fax: 5-1006, or write: 20 de Noviembre #452, Santiago Ixcuintla, Nay.

When you get back, if you want to buy some of their art work, they have a US outlet: 801 2nd Ave., Suite 1400, Seattle, WA 98104 Ph: (206) 622-4067 Fax: (206) 622-0646. The Huichols are shy, artistic people who are becoming extinct due to TB and other diseases. They have a 50% infant mortality rate. IF you want to help with medical supplies or donations, they are tax-exempt: IRS # 95-3012063.

35.6	57.0	Community of Heróico Batallón de San Blas up road, right.
40.6	65.0	Cross Río San Pedro and thru roadside market community of Peñitas. Careful for side road, left, to Tuxpan. GAS, right.
41.6	66.6	Come now to side road (left) to little island town of Mexcaltitán, Mexico's mini-Venice.

If you insist on visiting Mexcaltitán, go approximately 29 miles over a rough gravel road to a place called "El Embarcadero" where you'll park, then hire a dugout canoe for the 15-minute trip to the island town of about 3,500 inhabitants, many of whom have never left the island. This side-sortie is suggested only for the adventuresome as Mexcaltitan isn't ready yet for the normal course of tourist traffic, but the shrimp is fresh, jumbo-size and delicious.

44.1	70.6	Banana Plantation on right.
44.8	71.7	Cross bridge over Río El Bejuco. Road bad for while after rains. Pass side road (left) to Chilapa. **KM 77**.
52.3	89.6	Railroad town of Rosamorada (Purple Rose), right. Cross Río Rosamorada. Railroad bridge, right.

MI	KM	
53.2	85.1	**GAS**, left.
53.6	85.8	Couple of bridges and railroad at right. Truck stop of El Mil (1000) at left. Gas, left.
65.8	105.3	TOPES. Be careful of people selling stuff on topes! Thru village of Tierra Generosa (Generous Land).
70.1	112.2	Village of San Miguel, mostly to right.
77.1	123.4	Thru San Francisco and over Río Acaponeta.
78.5	125.6	Now slow for sharp curve and over narrow and very bumpy steel bridge. Pass side road (left) to Sayulita. Then right curve.
80.4	128.6	Then pass side road, right, to Acaponeta, founded in 1584 by the Franciscans (about 1.3 miles away where there's OK motel Cadenales at entrance to town). Then paved side road, left, to Tecuala and on to Novillero (22 miles), a rather solitary village on the Pacific coast with miles and miles of open beaches known as "Playas de Novillero." You'll find the accommodations somewhat inadequate and primitive – Margarita 2-story, 33-room hotel within walking distance of beach; ceiling fans, restaurant, covered parking and Bungalows Paraíso 12 kitchenette units on beach, space for few RV's with no hookups, tenting permitted. Hotel and Restaurant Miramar across street, a little more humble but nice
80.7	129.1	**GAS**, left.
81.2	129.9	Up and over bridge over railroad.
82.2	131.5	Inspección de Sanidad Fitopecuaria Y Forestal. No pigs allowed!
86.1	137.8	Over Río Cañas and cross state line – leave Nayarit and enter Sinaloa. Then curve left and stop at truck inspection, right. Thru village of La Concha.
90.1	144.2	Pass railroad village of Copales.
94.4	151.0	Careful for couple of sharp curves ahead. Community of Las Mulas (The Mules).
95.4	152.6	Now slow for sharp left curve. Up alongside mountain with salt marshes on left.
98.6	157.8	Thru village of Palmillas.
103.6	165.8	Big Ejido La Campaña, right. Pick up railroad on left.
110.5	176.8	Village of Tecualilla, off to left, behind trees.
112.5	180.0	Santa Anita fumigation station at left.
115.6	185.0	LP gas, right. Now thru a mile-long mango grove. Chapel at left. **KM 195**.
116.9	187.0	Thru Escuinapa. Mall to right. Clean restrooms ($1 peso). Try lunch at El Rodeo Restaurant (shrimp and Quesadillas).
117.1	187.4	Follow one-way street thru town. **GAS**, to right on one-way the other way. Come to junction with road (left) to Teacapan.

IF TO: Teacapan, turn left,

TEACAPAN, Sinaloa is a little off the beaten track, 26 miles away, a sleepy tropical village with nice white beaches. This is a birder's paradise area. Efforts are underway to have the government declare it a sanctuary and park. A great place to go if you have a spirit of adventure. Naturalists will enjoy the place and the (so far) unspoiled beaches. You can fish, go birding and loaf. Wildlife includes white and pink heron, pichihuila and deer. This is a small town with friendly folks and beautiful scenery. There are two good hotels. In town on plaza is Hotel Denisse, which is small (5 rooms) and inexpensive. Farther out is the Rancho Los Angeles (after 15.8 miles, turn right at mini-Super Los Angeles sign; use gate entrance to right of arch; enter and veer right, follow dirt road 1.5 miles to hotel) with the best restaurant (excellent Bar-B-Q fish) in town, perhaps in Mexico. It is for a more affluent crowd with private bungalows and a swimming pool. The only RV park is The Oregon, on the beach, near Señor Wayne's restaurant. Hotel Palmeras (under construction) will be a nice place once it's finished. Jejenes (no-see-ems, or sand fleas) do exist here but are not as bad as in San Blas. They only come out for about an hour in the morning and an hour at dusk. When the city sprays, there are few mosquitos.

		Back on one-way Hwy #15.
117.9	188.6	CAREFUL. Merge right onto Hwy #15. Over bridge and leave town of Escuinapa (population 60,000).
119.0	190.4	Good enough Motel Virginia on right.
122.9	196.6	Cross south fork of Río Baluarte.
125.2	200.3	TOPES. Pass side road (left) to Chametla.
130.0	208.0	Over bumpy, long steel bridge over another fork of Río Baluarte.
131.0	209.6	Up past village of Chilillos. Past LP gas, right. Up, down and cross Río Baluarte on 1/2-mile-long bridge. **GAS**, right. Skirt town Rosario (population 47,497). Nice snack stands and icehouse, left. Hotel Los Morales at left.
134.0	214.4	That's Mount Yauco dead ahead.
137.0	219.2	Thru settlement of Los Otates (The Bamboos), right. Over bridge.

160

MI	KM	
141.0	225.6	Cross río and pass village of Las Higueras off to right. Side road (right) to Presa (dam) Las Higueras.
142.5	228.0	Then experimental fruit station. Village of Potrerillos down at left.
143.5	229.6	Thru Tablón #1.
144.4	231.0	Ejido El Tablón, mostly at left.
146.1	233.8	Village of El Huajote, at left, with its baseball field.
149.0	238.4	Sometimes there's an immigration stop here.
157.0	251.2	Motel El Pino, right, OK. **GAS**, left.

IF TO: Hwy #40 to Durango, Torreón, Saltillo, Monterrey, etc., turn right here. Start Mazatlán - Durango Log. (See Mexico's Central Route book, page 103).

IF TO: Mazatlán, ahead on Hwy #15 for you.

157.5	252.0	Curve right and into town. Slow thru town of Villa Unión. Speed 30 KMPH. Topes.
158.5	253.6	Divided highway begins. **KM 271**.
158.8	254.1	Hotel El Kino and OK restaurant, right. Topes. Leave town. Cross Río Presidio.
161.3	258.1	Pass side road (right) to Mazatlán's airport. **KM 272**.
164.1	262.6	Large penitentiary, right. Speed limit 80 KMPH. Pass "el Zipi-Zape" veggie packers. **KM 275**.
164.4	263.0	**GAS**, left. **KM 279**.
165.9	265.4	Large thermoelectric power plant, left.
166.6	266.6	Colonia La Sirena, left. Salt flats, left.
168.1	269.0	Under overpass with sign "Bienvenidos A Mazatlán" (Welcome to Mazatlán). Up hill.
168.3	269.3	Golf course, right. Tractores de Occidente, right. Look alive! City traffic begins.
168.7	269.9	LP gas, right. Coke distributor at left. John Deere at right. Goodyear at left.
169.1	270.6	Curve right. Stoplight. **GAS**, left. Sign says "Culiacán straight. Mazatlán Centro, Playas and Ferry to left."

IF TO: Ferry, turn left here. Go this way only if planning to take the ferry. Otherwise, continue straight.

169.7	271.5	Curve left and past school at right. Thru suburb of Rincón de Urias. Pass Café Marino plant right. Farmer's market (Central de Abastos), right.
169.9	271.8	Bimbo to the right.
170.2	272.3	Euzkadi tire distributor. **KM 209**.
170.7	273.1	Over bridge. Then pass multicolored Colonia (subdivision) Lic. Mario A. Arroyo and cemetery at left.
171.1	273.8	Pass up motel Real, a motel *del paso* (rents by the hour), to left.
171.9	275.0	For Culiacán toll road curve right here. Playas left.
172.1	275.4	**GAS**, left. Road narrows here.
173.5	277.6	Culiacán toll road, right. Libre road, straight.

IF TO: Mazatlán, turn left. Follow "Playas" signs.

IF TO: Culiacán, straight. Follow Mazatlán - Culiacán Log. Having turned left off Hwy #15, (following Tepic, Aeropuerto signs) ahead on nice divided bypass around Mazatlán.

IF TO: North end RV parks, Hotel Camino Real, go 6.7 miles to sign "Mazatlán Playas", turn left, go to beach and turn right.

End of Log 15

LOG 16 *START:* Mazatlán, Sin *END:* Culiacán, Sin

UD-019

135.4 MI or 216.6 KM
DRIVE TIME 3 — 3 1/2 HOURS
SCENIC RATING — 2

Note: This log also covers the toll road. The toll road is rather expensive. There are 2 toll booths, one at entrance just north of Mazatlán and the other at KM 122. Some say it's worth it (if you're in a hurry) saving at least an hour of driving time, and is safer. The free ("*Libre*") road is OK and is more scenic.

Stub Log From Downtown to Hwy 15

MI	KM	
0.0	0.0	Starting at ocean blvd. with McDonald's on left and Hotel San Diego at right, proceed ahead.
0.1	0.2	La Posta Trailer Park at right. Then **GAS** at right. They accept credit cards.
0.3	0.5	Sharp Hospital, right.
0.5	0.8	Gigante at left. Then bullring at left.
1.0	1.6	Come to intersection with stoplight. Turn left here for Hwy 15.
1.2	1.9	Stoplight and then up and over railroad tracks.
1.5	2.4	Pacific beer distributor at right and Motel Relax at left. Come to junction with Hwy #15.

End stub from Downtown

0.0	0.0	At junction of bypass around Mazatlán and Hwy #15, proceed ahead (north). **GAS**, left. Restaurant La Palmita, right.
0.7	1.1	**GAS**, left. *Centro de Bodegas* at right. Then at right, *Ciudad de los Niños* ("boys' town" or "orphanage," not to be confused with the "red-light district"). Gamesa Plant right.
1.0	1.6	Luenaillo, left. **KM 2**.
1.3	2.1	Carta Blanca Agency at left. Federal Police Highway. Ph: (669) 911-6355.
1.9	3.0	Come to junction with toll road. For accommodations, see Mazatlán Eat & Stray (page 118).

IF TO: Toll road, take first left after bridge and start stub log below.

IF TO: North end hotels, do not take the toll road.

IF TO: Free road, straight. Road narrows to 2 lanes.

MAZATLÁN - CULIACÁN TOLL ROAD

0.0	0.0	Cross over free road on nice divided toll road.
1.0	1.6	Pass police station at right.
4.5	7.2	Careful for traffic merging from right from the north end entrance to Mazatlán.
14.5	23.2	Over Río Quilete. You are now passing thru rolling hills and farm country.
17.2	27.5	Come to tollhouse and pay toll. Cars - $61, extra axle - $30, they accept AE, MC, VI. **KM 26**.
60.0	96.0	Pass exit (right) to La Cruz and Cueta. This is also the exit to take if you want to go to Cosalá.

Cosalá, founded in 1516, is a small Spanish colonial town with cobblestone roads and churches over 250 years old. There are two OK hotels and some restaurants. The Sabinal river feeds the *Vado Hondo* spa (not reviewed) with clear water. 20 KM north is Lake Comedero chock-full of largemouth bass. There is also a Museum of the History of Mining. The balneario and waterfall are 8 km off the highway on a dirt road. Do not attempt this road when it's been raining. It is 6.5 miles before town, on the left.

PRESA LÓPEZ PORTILLO (LAKE COMEDERO) — One of Mexico's two hottest lakes, Comedero was opened to fisherman only since in 1987. Comedero has fast become a legend in the number of fish caught per man per day. With catches from 100 to 200 bass per day common, it is easy to see why this remote lake has become a prime destination for the traveling angler. Turn east on the Cosalá turnoff to the town of Cosalá. (50 miles). The lake is 30 miles from town on a dirt road that winds up in the steep mountains to the village of Higueras de Urrea. The San Lorenzo river is the source of Lake Comedero and the lake is one of the prettiest in the northern hemisphere. Towering mountains surround the lake with lush subtropical jungle right up to the waters edge. Comedero's banks are lined with some brush and cover; however, the lake is large and very open and it's also very deep. With depths approaching 300 feet in places, Comedero's fish tend to school up and suspend sometimes in water as deep as 60 feet. At present there's only one full time camp on the lake. Full packages are available as well as room and board. Contact: Ron Speeds S and W Tours, 1013 Country Lane, Malakoff, TX, 75148 (903) 489-1656.

MI	KM	
96.0	153.6	Pass exit (right) to Quila and El Dorado.
109.8	175.7	Come to second tollhouse and pay toll (Car - $63, extra axle - $31). **GAS** on left.
111.3	178.1	Exit to Culiacán and Costa Rica and Los Cascabeles. After exit, get in left lane for Culiacán. Curve up and around and rejoin Hwy #15 on still divided 4-lane.

There is a nice pastoral spot 4.1 miles west of here on Hwy #19. It's Los Cascabeles on the lake of the same name. 20 fenced acres with 10 cabins, boats, pool, hunting and fishing. RV section (MOD) with 44 spaces, electricity and water. Dump station. Medical services. Palapa. BBQ pits. Security. Store. Self-service laundry. Restaurant. FAX: (67) 13-6418 or in Culiacán (671) 3-6418, 3-6822.

114.0	182.4	Agricultural experimental school at right.
116.5	186.4	Villa Juárez, left and **GAS**, left.
117.9	188.6	LP gas on right just before village of El Quemadito.
121.1	193.8	To Guasave and Los Mochis, left. Veer left and follow Guasave sign. Right goes into Culiacán. Start Culiacán - Los Mochis Log (page 163).

END OF TOLL ROAD

2.9	4.6	Highway police station at left. Big mango grove at right.
4.1	6.6	Hilltop restaurant at right. **KM 7**.
6.0	9.6	Come to crossroads, left to El Habal and right to La Noria.

IF TO: Beach. Take side road (left) to Playa Cerritos and shortcut beach road to Mazatlán. (If heading to north beach hotels, RV parks, etc., go ahead and turn here. When you come to ocean, turn left and head toward town.)

IF TO: Culiacán, points north, straight.

9.9	15.8	Pass side road (right) to La Palma.
10.0	16.0	Pass side road (left) to El Potrero. Note bust of General Juan Carrazco at left.
10.4	16.6	Roadside food at left. **KM 16**.
14.7	23.5	Come now to TROPIC OF CANCER — note marker at left.
15.5	24.8	Los Zapotes off to right and El Recreo off to left.
20.5	32.8	Over Río Quelite, then curve left past side road (left) to Mármol (marble). Is there's any marble?
21.9	35.0	Pass side road (right) to El Quelite.
25.5	40.8	Straight stretch ends. Begin curves. El Moral off to right. Climbed 400 ft. at this point.
37.6	60.2	Pull off for view watches to right.
37.9	60.6	Pass side road (right) to El Limón and more winding with sharp curves.
41.7	66.7	**GAS** right. Watch the kids here. Pass side road (right) to San Ignacio, 32 KM.

San Ignacio is a very picturesque town. Founded in 1582 and named after San Ignacio de Loyola. Palm trees line the road into town with a grand mauve entrance that, when you pass through it, opens to a bridge that crosses a rather large river.

46.0	73.6	Pass side road (right) to Hacienda Piaxtla. Then settlement of Crucero de Piaxtla.
49.9	79.8	Village of Piaxtla off to right.
53.0	84.8	La Minita (The Little Mine) up at right. The mill here grinds ore brought in from Mexico's interior, separating zinc, copper and lead.
56.0	89.6	Left and wind down. Pass so-so-restaurant-bus stop. Then slow for sharp left curve.
57.0	91.2	Cross Río Elota. Then pass side road, right, to nearby town of Elota.
65.5	104.8	Pass side road (left) to La Cruz. Red Cross. **KM 105**.
MI	KM	
66.5	106.4	Pass side road (right) to picturesque ex-mining town of Cosalá, 33 miles, on Hwy #D-1. See description in the toll road stub log (page 161).

68.0	108.8	Thru Agua Nueva.
68.7	109.9	Cemetery at right.
69.5	111.2	Pass Glass House Resort Hotel — MOD — 36 rooms, restaurant, pool, English spoken, looks brand new and very nice. **KM 112.** Curve left, then thru El Aguaje.
73.0	116.8	Thru El Espinal. Topes. **KM 118.**
81.0	129.6	Thru settlement of El Avión. **KM 130.**
87.5	140.0	Pass side road (left) to Estación Abuya.
89.5	143.2	Pass village of Higueras de Abuya, then cross south fork of Río Obispo and curve left.
93.0	148.8	Pass side road (left) to Obispo (bishop).
95.7	153.1	Over north fork of Río Obispo and curve left. Thru village of Las Flores.
97.5	156.0	Pass side road (left) to Oso (bear).
102.7	164.3	Thru Tabala. Note ruins of ancient church at left with burial tombs. Then curve left and up over Río San Lorenzo. **KM 165.**
108.7	173.9	**GAS**, right. Cross a couple of bridges Río Salado, then up thru town of El Salado. Topes! Topes!
108.8	174.1	El Dorado to the left. Culiacán straight.
114.8	183.7	Thru San Fernando.
117.5	188.0	El Carrizal, and Sebu cattle ranch at left.
119.3	190.9	**GAS**, both sides of the road. Danesa 33 Ice cream Store. Restaurant Centro Recreativo Los Cascabeles. Turn at Costa Rica to the left to get to Los Cascabeles.

There is a nice pastoral spot 4.1 miles west of here on Hwy #19. It's Los Cascabeles on the lake of the same name. 20 fenced acres with 10 cabins, boats, pool, hunting and fishing. RV section (MOD) with 44 spaces, electricity and water. Dump station. Medical services. Palapa. BBQ pits. Security. Store. Self-service laundry. Restaurant. FAX: (67) 13-6418 or in Culiacán (671) 3-6418, 3-6822.

120.0	192.0	Pass side road (left) to Costa Rica. Careful for slow-moving farm traffic. Seafood restaurant. This is where t oll road rejoins free road.

IF TO: Culiacán, Nogales, look alive! Junction with bypass coming up. The signs say "Los Mochis" or "Guasave Cuota." You'll turn left. Just don't get off onto the "Libre" route.

129.1	206.6	Come to junction with bypass around Culiacán. TURN LEFT to Guasave and Los Mochis. Culiacán (population: 602,100) is straight. For accommodations see Culiacán Eat & Stray (page 117).
130.1	208.2	Having turned left, pass little town of El Ranchito.
133.4	213.4	Motel Cabañas del Rey.
135.4	216.6	Guasave cuota (toll road) to left. **GAS**, right, LP gas at right, 1 mile ahead.

IF TO: Los Mochis, Nogales, turn left and start Culiacán — Los Mochis Log.

End of Log 16

LOG 17   START: Culiacán, Sin   END: Los Mochis, Sin

UD-019

129.5 MI or 207.2 KM
DRIVE TIME 2 — 2 1/2 HOURS
SCENIC RATING — 1

0.0	0.0	Having turned left at junction with Culiacán bypass and Hwy #15 (the "Libre", or free road from downtown), proceed ahead on 4 lane divided This is a very fertile farming regions in Mexico, thanks to irrigation projects.
0.7	1.1	**GAS**, right. Restaurant on left and right. Toll road is called: "Autopista Benito Juárez." Come to tollhouse and pay toll (Car - $15, Extra axle - $8). Restrooms at right just past tollbooth. Nursery at left.
7.0	11.2	Pass exits for San Pedro and La Curva on Hwy #280 to right. **KM 13.**
14.0	22.4	Under overpass.
16.3	26.1	Exit, right, to La Palma and Vitaruto a couple of miles over to right on Hwy #259. **KM 31.**
26.0	41.6	Over bridge, curve left — nice cattle farm over to right.
MI	KM	
29.5	47.2	Pass Restaurant Mar de Cortés, left.
39.4	63.0	Restaurant El Bacatete, right.

40.0	64.0	Pass side road (left) to La Reforma and Zapatillo, Hwy #70. **GAS** to left. **KM 63**.
68.5	109.6	Pass side road (left) to Angostura and right to Guamúchil. There is a hot/cold spring 18 km away in Mocorito (turn left at cemetery before town). Come to tollhouse and pay toll (Car - $15, extra axle - $8). **KM 109**.
73.4	117.4	Thru underpass. Straight ahead. Careful for traffic merging from old two-lane "libre" highway. **KM 123**.
75.0	120.0	Veer left to Guasave. Las Brisas exit right. **KM 125**.
82.5	132.0	Palos Blancos, left. Then another toll booth (Car - $10, extra axle - $5).
92.8	148.5	Over Río Petatlán. Now thru edge of boom town of Guasave, founded in 1595 (population: 257,821). Shopping center to right.

GUASAVE has three hotels and a great mechanic, Taller Bojórquez (see map inset). The best hotel is El Sembrador at Guerrero and Zapata. It has 85 nice quiet rooms, 10 suites, restaurant, bar, parking and is very reasonably priced. SATV (English and weather channel, HBO, CNN, etc). Ph: (687) 872-4062, 872-3141, Fax: 872-3131.

If you have a notion to go fishing at Lake Baccarito (Presa Díaz Ordaz), we recommend that you change your mind. There is no reason to go to that out-of-the-way lake. It has been gill-netted out, and there have been assaults on the road.

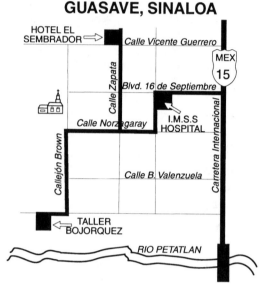

GUASAVE, SINALOA

94.5	151.2	Pass ball park at left (Guasave belongs to the powerful Mexican Pacific League).
96.0	153.6	Pass Trébol Park Motel, right.
99.0	158.4	Right to Estación Naranjo. **GAS** on road to Estación Naranjo.
105.0	168.0	Pass side road (left) to Huitusi over on Bahía de San Ignacio.
105.1	168.2	Batamote to right. Pass LP gas to right.
110.6	177.0	Little town of Ruiz Cortines, at left, named for a past president of Mexico (1952-58).
111.5	178.4	**GAS**, on right. Unfriendly (WATCH 'EM!)
113.2	181.1	Cerro Cabezón, to left.
118.3	189.3	Government agricultural experiment school (Ciapan), right. **GAS**, left. Big town of Juan José Ríos (the largest ejido in Mexico) at left. **KM 186**.
120.0	192.0	Curve left past Ejido *Las Vacas* (The Cows) at left. Cross Río Estero. Heading due west.
124.0	198.4	Pass entrance to industrial park at left. Then rice factory at left. Northrup-King seed plant, left. (*Arroz* is rice in Spanish, *Algodón* means cotton and *algodonera* means cotton gin.)
127.5	204.0	Up and over Chihuahua-Pacífico Railroad overpass, which is the same line that goes up into the Sierra Madres thru scenic Copper Canyon. Curve left around hill.
128.5	205.6	Note tomato packing sheds thru here. Mountain at left is called *Cerro de la Memoria*. Turnoff, right, is to nice Hotel Colinas and RV Park, right, on hilltop (67 spaces EWS, 30 AMP, Ph: (681) 812-0101, 812-0134)). It was formerly a Holiday Inn. *Lienzo del Charro* arena at left where the Mexican *charro* (cowboy) performs in the rodeo, usually on Sunday. **GAS**, left.
129.5	207.2	Careful now! Go under two overpasses. Come to junction with El Fuerte Hwy and Los Mochis. **GAS**, right (Watch them).

IF TO: Los Mochis or Topolobampo, take right lane (follow LOS MOCHIS signs) and then left and up and over highway. For accommodations, see Los Mochis Eat & Stray (page 115).

IF TO: Navojoa or Cd. Obregón, straight ahead, under overpass. Start Los Mochis — Navojoa Log.

IF TO: El Fuerte and Domínguez and Hidalgo Lakes, exit right and start Los Mochis — El Fuerte Special (page 63).

The twin lakes of Hidalgo and Domínguez are about 40 miles NE of the Pacific coast town of Los Mochis via a paved road, a few miles from the town of El Fuerte. The two lakes are about 5 miles apart. They have some of the best fishing south of the border. See El Fuerte Eat & Stray (page 116).

Incidentally, the Chihuahua-Pacific (Copper Canyon) Railroad passes near El Fuerte — you might wish to combine a little fishing with this very scenic train ride through the Sierra Madre Occidental.

End of Log 17

LOG 18 START: Los Mochis, Sin END: Navojoa, Son

UD-019

98.0 MI OR 156.8 KM
DRIVE TIME — 2 HOURS
SCENIC RATING — 2
Divided toll highway thru fertile farming country.

MI	KM	
0.0	0.0	Here at Los Mochis interchange, proceed ahead. **GAS**, right but watch them.
7.0	11.2	Cavalry's 18th regiment barracks at left. If you go through on leave day, don't be alarmed. There may be hundreds of soldiers hitchhiking.
9.9	15.8	Now thru edge of little town of San Miguel Zapotitlán. **KM 16. GAS**, right — sometimes they try to charge more for it, so watch them.

RV'ers take note: the exit to El Fuerte RV Park is 0.3 miles ahead. Get in left lane. Turn left at next left.

MI	KM	
10.2	16.3	Over Río Fuerte. Then just past overpass, Higuera Zaragoza turn off to left and El Fuerte RV park to left.
12.6	20.2	Prepare to pay Toll at "caseta puente San Miguel." Cars — $14, extra axle — $7. **KM 20.** Going north. Start uphill. Begin rolling hills.
16.3	26.0	Begin series of S curves.
18.2	29.1	Now pass very large Ejido A.G. Calderón, right.

By the way, an *ejido* is a government-sponsored community agriculture project — you'll pass many of these on your Mexico motor trip. They usually have fancy names, like famous revolutionary heroes, ex-presidents or historical dates. There are about 30,000 *ejidos* throughout Mexico. The concept of some land for every Mexican was one of the tenets of the Revolutionary struggle in Mexico. The *ejido* system has been eliminated in modern times, but the names and signs live on.

MI	KM	
23.0	36.8	Big Ejido Los Natochis at right.
26.7	42.7	Vast Ejido Chihuahuita at right.
32.2	51.5	Restaurant La Posta, right. **KM 52.**
33.4	53.4	El Fuerte to right and Choix turnoff.
38.0	60.8	Ejido El Carrizo at left, headquarters town for irrigation district of huge El Fuerte irrigation project. Red Cross. **GAS**, left. **KM 55.**
39.0	62.4	Big Ejido Talamantes at left. Pass side road (right) to San Francisco microwave tower.
39.5	63.2	Ejido Dolores Hidalgo at right. Cemetery at left.
40.2	64.3	Truck agricultural inspection station on left for south bound vehicles only.
42.0	67.2	Thru Desengaño ("Disillusion"). Slow for *vibradores* (ribbed topes).
43.1	69.0	Come now to state line, leave the state of Sinaloa, which is pretty lengthy — 397 miles. Enter the state of Sonora, the longest state in Mexico. It's 433 miles from here to Nogales; and if you go by way of San Luis Río Colorado, you'll be in Sonora for the next 665 miles. There is a very thorough drug inspection checkpoint here. Allow for a 20 minute delay. Pass thru Agricultural, Immigration inspection. **GAS**, right, diesel. Watch for monster topes.
46.0	73.6	Thru village of Estación Don. ("Don" is pronounced "Doan," sort of like Doan's back pills, except it's pronounced crisper.)
51.5	82.4	Ejido Manuel Caudillo at left. Roll up your windows thru here; it's very earthy country. **KM 72.**
58.0	92.8	Big Ejido Francisco Sarabia at left. Bumpy railroad crossing! Then huge Conasupo farmers' co-op at right. **GAS**, left — nice, clean restrooms, diesel. **KM 93.**
59.0	94.4	Railroad station community of Estación Luis at right. Then pass side road, right, to Ejido Tierra y Libertad (Land and Liberty).

"Tierra y Libertad" was Emiliano Zapata's cry as he seized and burned the haciendas in his home state of Morelos and divided the land among his white-clad Indian followers, paving the way for Article 27 of the Mexican Constitution, upon which all subsequent land reform laws have been based.

MI	KM	
63.0	100.8	Mexico's always attracted dreamers and visionaries, for instance Albert Kinsey Owens, who founded an American colony in Los Mochis. He wanted to grow sugar cane, build a railroad to the U.S. in 1872 and build a utopian community. **KM 100.**
67.7	108.3	Truck stop restaurant Carmelita, right.
71.7	114.7	Pass side road (right) to Masiaca, 6 miles and (left) to Las Bocas, 7.5 miles, a beach resort.
77.0	123.2	Toll road straight. **KM 128**. Turn left here for free road to Navojoa via Huatabampo.
78.0	124.8	At right is Ejido Luis Echeverría, named after one of Mexico's ex-presidents (1970-1976). Then pass side road left (free road) to Huatabampo which means "Willow Tree in the Water." It's a nice little city located in a large, prosperous irrigated district 28 km away. Four miles south of that town is Huatabampito, a little resort on the Gulf of California with miles of inviting sandy beach.
79.0	126.4	Slow for toll booth. Stop and pay toll (car - $32, extra axle no charge — trailers are the same price as cars in this state only). No restrooms here.
85.5	136.8	Curve left thru Ejido Bacabachi and school at left. Then cemetery off to right.
88.0	140.8	Rest area El Abajeno at left, popular with truck drivers. Then small shrine at left. **KM 140.**
89.3	142.9	Pass Restaurant Santa Ana, left.
90.0	144.0	Pass granja El Milagro, left. Railroad tracts follow road at right.
92.8	148.5	Pass airfield at right.
95.5	152.8	Pass **GAS**, left (watch them). Speed limit slows to 40 KPH. Electrical generating station to left. Tres Estrellas at right. Cotton gin.
96.0	153.6	Free road from Los Mochis joins highway here at left. **KM 153**.
96.7	154.7	Pass thru an industrial zone with Tecate Brewery to right. Then Pemex industrial to right.
97.7	156.3	Enter city of Navojoa. **KM 155**. Motel Colonial on left. Over railroad tracks. Social security hospital (ISSTE) on left. Curve left. Big flour mill (Conasupo) also on left.
98.0	156.8	Pass **GAS**, right. Motel El Mayo (Ph: 642-422-6828) on right. Tips' restaurant, right. On left, Goodrich, VW dealer and Chrysler/Dodge. Come to junction (right) with side road to Alamos and stoplight. For accommodations, see Navojoa Eat & Stray (page 112).

IF TO: Guaymas via toll road, proceed ahead and start Navojoa — Guaymas Log.

IF TO: Guaymas via free road, turn left and start Navojoa - Guaymas Free Road Stub Log.

IF TO: Alamos, turn right and start Navojoa — Alamos Special (page 59).

End of Log 18

LOG 19   *START:* Navojoa, Son   *END:* Guaymas, Son

UD-019

121.5 MI OR 194.4 KM
DRIVE TIME 2 — 2 1/2 HOURS
SCENIC RATING — 3
Easy flat drive on divided toll highway. Fertile farming country and glimpses of Pacific Ocean.

0.0	0.0	Here at junction with highway from Alamos, proceed ahead. At left is Goodrich. At right is MZ supermarket (good fast-food carry-out counter). General Tire on right. Stoplight. Pass Nissan dealer left.
0.3	0.5	Stoplight. Big auto parts and Telemex office on right. Another stoplight. Pass side road (left) to San Ignacio and Tetanchopo.
0.6	1.0	Firestone on left and Uniroyal on right.
0.9	1.4	Town of Tesia to the right. ISSTE clinic on right. Restaurant Pekin to left. Ph: (642) 422-8556. General tire on left. Chevy right. Nissan left. Goodyear right. 2 Smiling elephants at left. Restaurant/bar Los Coporales on right. **GAS**, right.
1.5	2.4	Then Asadero Restaurant (tasty *carne asada*), right. Straight on thru on nice wide main street. Very good **GAS**, right. If bypass completed around town, follow signs. If you want to go through town, feel free. Leave Navojoa.

Navojoa means "place among the tunas" in Mayo Indian, tuna being a prickly pear.

IF TO: Alameda RV Park, exit left immediately before bridge.

MI	KM	
1.6	2.6	Restaurant Los Arcos on left. Motel Del Río on left. Then turn left into RV Alameda just before bridge.
2.4	3.8	Then thru little community of Guaymitas. Motel Rancho down at left. Begin divided highway again. Left lane is for Navojoa free road, also Villa Juárez. Straight for toll road. If you choose to take the free road, begin the following stub log. Otherwise jump down to continuation of log (mile 7.3). Free road is OK. It takes 15 minutes longer. **KM 1.**

Stub Log: Navojoa - Guaymas Free Road

0.0	0.0	Having veered turned onto free road, continue ahead.
4.6	7.4	Pass village of Became Nuevo to right.
7.0	11.2	Pass sign that says "Ejido 7 Leguas."
10.4	16.6	Pass side road (left) to Buaysiacobe. **KM 20.**
13.5	21.6	Topes and pass farm equipment yard, right. Then thru Agua Blanca and more topes. **KM 24.**
14.0	22.4	Over canal at **KM 26.** Then pass village of Bacobampo and Calle 26 at left.
15.6	25.0	Come to junction. TURN RIGHT for Cd. Obregón; straight is to Villa Juárez. **KM 28.**
21.5	34.4	Texaco sign, right. Topes. Then thru village of Jecopaco, store with phone.
28.8	46.1	**GAS**, right.
29.6	47.4	Goodyear, right.
31.5	50.4	Come to junction with Hwy #15 toll and resume continuation of log at mile 25.0.

End of Stub Log

7.3	11.7	Straight for toll.
9.0	14.4	Pass side road (left) to Villa Juárez, 30 km. (18 miles).

If you have a generous and compassionate heart and would like to visit an orphanage, you will find Hogar de Refugio Infantil Villa Juárez by turning left onto side road to Villa Juárez, go 26 miles on paved road, turn right for another mile, then turn left following signs to the orphanage. Bob Mason, the director, welcomes visitors. They are able to accommodate motor homes, trailers etc. and have a crude dumping station as well as electrical hookups.

10.7	17.1	Cotton community of Sibolibampo.
23.6	37.8	Tollbooth. Stop and pay toll ($32). **KM 196.**
25.0	40.0	Pass another exit (left) for Villa Juárez.
29.1	46.5	Pass enormous statue to the Virgin of Guadalupe at left. **Turnoff to it is just past KM 203.**
31.5	50.4	Ejido Francisco Villa way over to left.
32.7	52.3	Pass side road (left) to airport.
37.5	60.0	**GAS**, left but watch them. **KM 210.**
38.0	60.8	Pass another side road (left) to Villa Juárez. Conasupo to left. Bumpy railroad crossing. At stoplight, straight ahead. General tire mobile on right. DHC left. Veer right at waterfall. Stoplight. Onto Ave. Alemán.
38.9	62.2	Petroleum tanks on right. **KM 219.**
39.5	63.2	Cayenne Fertilizer plant, right. Come to junction (left) with free road to Guaymas here at Cd Obregón. If you decide to take free road, turn left and ahead on narrow 2 lane road, but you're on your own.
40.0	64.0	Welcome to the prosperous town of Cd. (abbreviation for *ciudad* "city") Obregón, Industrial park, left. SLOW-LOOK-&-LISTEN at railroad. Plenty of cotton and grain-related industries here. Then big Gamesa (Galletas Mexicana, S.A.), right, one of Mexico's largest cookie producers — sort of like Nabisco in the States. Coca-Cola bottling plant, left. **KM 222.**

Cd. Obregón is the agricultural heart of the Yaqui Valley (known as the Bread Basket of Mexico) with a population of 450,000. This was formerly called Cájeme after the famous chief of the Yaqui Indians, but the name was later changed in honor of President Obregón. His family was originally of Irish lineage.

40.2	64.3	Ley shopping center, left.
40.8	65.3	To avoid town, take next right for bypass. At Guaymas - Cuota sign, make an immediate right. Ahead of you is a **GAS** station.
41.0	65.6	Having made an immediate right (before **GAS** station) at Guaymas - Cuota sign, proceed ahead on one-way stretch that takes you thru an industrial section of town.
41.2	65.9	Pass grain silos on right and tall MUNSA 3-tower grain Silo on left.

MI	KM	
41.7	66.7	Over railroad crossing (Look-&-Listen).
42.2	67.5	Stoplight. Railroad station on right.
43.0	68.8	Over another railroad crossing (Look-&-Listen).
43.5	69.6	Careful for dip in road. Tecate brewery at right.
43.8	70.1	Here is where the traffic from town rejoins log. There is a **GAS** station 1/2 mile towards town that takes credit cards (when manager is in), several new hotels, a Holiday Inn Ph: (644) 414-0936 Fax: (644) 413-4194, 91-800-62333 and a good restaurant, Mr. Steak, where they roll a cart of beef out and cut your steak to your request. See Cd. Obregón Eat & Stray (page 111) for more info on accommodations. Leave prosperous town of Cd. Obregón.
44.7	71.5	Prison to left. **KM 2**.
45.7	73.1	Pemex tank farm, right.
47.1	75.4	Military base, right.
48.0	76.8	Golf club on right.
48.2	77.1	**GAS**, on left. Topes!
48.7	77.9	**GAS**, left. Pass side road (left) to Cocorít, while side road right goes to Tezopaco de Rosario and to Presa (dam) Alvaro Obregón which has a reputation for the best bass fishing in North America. Skirt edge of Esperanza (Hope). Then onto Av. Miguel Alemán (Hwy 15), Cd. Obregón's main stem. Careful for stoplights. **GAS**, left. Stop at tollhouse and pay toll ($32).
50.7	81.1	Cross over famous Río Yaqui whose course from the state of Chihuahua to the Sea of Cortés is 419 miles long. This is also where the Yaqui Indian Reservation begins.
51.7	82.7	Bend left and slow for *Salida de Camiones* (yield to trucks merging with highway traffic). Pass side road (right) to Est. Corral, 3 km. CAREFUL! Settlement of Tajimaroa to left.
53.1	85.0	Under pedestrian crossing. **KM 23**.

Green Angel — Adalberto Rocnín Mendivil, Calle Mango #1707, Col. Fouisste 2. Cd. Obregón, Son. Ph: (644) 414-5894.

53.5	85.6	Thru scattered settlement of Loma de Guamúchil. Guamúchil is a very common tree in this part of Mexico, with thorny leafstalks, hairy white globe-shaped flower clusters and black shiny seeds in spirally twisted pods from 5-6 inches long.
58.6	93.8	Pass side road, right, to Bacum. Heading NE 60. Then come to junction where the FREE ROAD JOINS HWY #15.
59.7	95.5	Pass another road, left, into town of Bacum. Canal waterfall, left.
62.5	100.0	Yaqui masks are made of dissected deer heads, wood and dried goat skin.
67.4	107.8	Pass side road (left) to Torim.
69.0	110.4	Community of Cárdenas and come now to famous YAQUI INDIAN VOCATIONAL AND AGRICULTURAL SCHOOL, left where "knowhow" is taught to Yaqui Indian kids. "Ehwi" in Yaqui means yes.
73.5	117.6	Slow thru little town of Vicam. **GAS**, left and across street **GAS**, right.
77.4	123.8	Potam exit to left. Guaymas, straight.
79.0	126.4	Pass side road (left) to Potam. Note irrigated countryside thru here — very fertile soil. Main crops — cotton, wheat soya, sunflower oil sorghum.
84.8	135.7	Pass side road (right) to Pitahaya.
94.2	150.7	Slow for sharp left curve. Now heading NE.
98.7	157.9	Livestock-shipping community of Las Guásimas.
100.5	160.8	Thru rock cut of Boca Abierta (Open Mouth).
106.0	169.6	Pass Cruz de Piedra (Cross of Stone) over to right on railroad. Note disabled and outdated railroad cars used now as homes. Here is where a big Yaqui Indian reservation ends; it ran for about 50 miles from the Yaqui River just north of Ciudad Obregón. The Yaquis had a big uprising back in the late 20's and Mexico gave them this territory for a reservation.
106.5	170.4	Pass side road (left) to Playa del Sol, a beachfront development.
107.0	171.2	Veer left following Hermosillo signs. **GAS** on left.
108.5	173.6	Pass side road (right) to Ortiz. Down side road a short mile is where famous NASA space capsule tracking station was located (the place that a couple of the early astronauts referred to when they remarked as they passed over, "Hello, Guaymas! Send us up some enchiladas!"). This is no longer used by NASA.
111.0	177.6	Fertimex plant, right. Pass side road (left) to beachfront community of El Cochori, 2 miles (no accommodations). Then come to toll bypass around Guaymas to right. Continue ahead on the free bypass, which is OK, unless you're in a hurry.

IF TO: Toll Bypass of town. Take an immediate right at Guaymas-Cuota sign and follow stub log below. Otherwise continue straight.

Stub Log: Toll Bypass Around Guaymas

MI	KM	
0.0	0.0	Having turned right onto bypass, "topes" and over railroad, pass big Fertimex plant at right.
3.0	4.8	Up and over bridge over railroad.
9.0	14.4	Truck stop restaurant Los Faroles, left.
11.6	18.6	Over bridge.
12.0	19.2	Stop at tollhouse and pay toll (Cars $32, extra axle, $16). Then under overpass and come to junction with Hwy #15. **GAS**, diesel (SIN) and ice, left.

IF TO: San Carlos, and downtown Guaymas, Use retorno and go back on free highway for 4 miles to San Carlos turnoff, then follow San Carlos Special (page 59), for Guaymas continue ahead from there for 8 miles.

IF TO: Hermosillo, pick up Guaymas — Hermosillo Log (page 170) at mile 8.0.

End of Stub Log

113.4	181.4	**GAS** (watch them) on left. Highway patrol, right. **KM 113**.
113.5	181.6	Ferrocarril del Pacífico station (Pacific Railroad station), right. Railroad crossing.
114.2	182.7	TOPES. Then white palm trees lining highway. Then big Anderson-Clayton complex, left.
114.8	183.7	Restaurant to right. Mount Dolly Parton to left?
115.0	184.0	Big railroad shops, right. Then slow for another railroad crossing (LOOK-&-LISTEN). Begin causeway and over double railroad crossing. And one more railroad switch line. AHEAD on Hwy 15. Right fork is to railroad town of Empalme. And there, right, stands old engine 70 of the Ferrocarril de Sonora (Sonora Railroad), a monument to Empalme and its railroad industry.
116.2	185.9	Onto causeway alongside railroad track, left.
117.7	188.3	LP gas, right. Power plant, left. Guaymas Bay and Gulf of California on left.

Mexico calls the Gulf of California *Mar de Cortés* (Sea of Cortés).

118.0	188.8	Pass junction with side road (left) to ferries. Veer right.
119.0	190.4	SLOW FOR SCHOOL ZONE. Two big topes.
119.5	191.2	**GAS** right. You're skirting edge of town. Another SCHOOL ZONE.
119.8	191.7	Curve to the right. Exiting left here will take you to town. **GAS**, on left. **KM 139.**
120.0	192.0	Fruit and vegetable inspection.
120.2	192.3	SLOW thru SCHOOL ZONE. Thru light. Monument to Benito Juárez on hilltop to left.
120.4	192.6	Chevy dealer. Monument at left to Heroes of Guaymas.

IF TO: San Carlos, VEER RIGHT here. Start Guaymas — San Carlos Special (page 59).

IF TO: Guaymas, RV parks on bay, TURN LEFT and start Guaymas RV Stub Log (page 13).

120.5	192.8	Stay right and veer right at obelisk. Traffic light. Motel Armida, right.
121.0	193.6	**GAS**, left. Ice. Chrysler/Dodge and VW dealer. Then Nissan and Ford dealers, left. Zerimar supermarket, left. Stoplight. Las Villas Subdivision on left.
121.1	193.8	Shopping center, right. Plaza de Viola.
121.5	194.4	Continue ahead under overpass. Pass exit left for Bocachibampo Bay (Bay of the Sea Serpents). For neat hotel Cortés with large RV park, under overpass, exit right onto Col. Miramar and continue straight to beach. For info on accommodations, see Guaymas Eat & Stray (page 110).

IF TO: San Carlos, Hermosillo, start Guaymas — Hermosillo Log.

End of Log 19

LOG 20 *START:* Guaymas, Son *END:* Hermosillo, Son

UD-019

82.5 MI or 132.5 KM
DRIVE TIME 1 1/4 — 2 HOURS
SCENIC RATING — 3
Nice flat divided highway, tolls. Ocean on your left, mountains right.

MI	KM	
0.0	0.0	Pass Miramar exit (right) to Bacochibampo Bay, Playa de Cortés Hotel and RV Park, a wonderful old place with plenty of charm. Also down this road is Leo's Inn.
0.5	0.8	Leave city of Guaymas. Motel Flamingos at right. **GAS**, left.
2.5	4.0	There's Guaymas airport over to right.
4.2	6.7	Motel Casa Blanca, left — NO. That's one White House you don't want to say you've slept in.

IF TO: SAN CARLOS, exit here, then over overpass — it's quite a nice place, sort of a Gringo oasis. It's about 5 miles straight ahead on a fine divided road — you won't get lost. Watch your speed. They really have traffic cops now. Begin Guaymas — San Carlos Special (page 59).

8.0	12.8	Careful as you come to junction with toll bypass around Guaymas. Over overpass, then **GAS** and diesel, left.
9.0	14.4	Truck inspection station, right. Wide spot of El Caballo "The Horse", right.
10.9	17.4	Series of well-marked curves for a mile or two.
21.4	34.2	Watch out for posts on right side of road. DANGER!
28.2	45.1	Rancho Los Arrieros, left. Pass side road (left) to Kino Bay. **KM 168**.

IF TO: Kino Bay, turn left here and start Hwy #15 — Kino Bay Shortcut Special (page 48). It will save 1/2 hour.

30.8	49.3	White church on right. **GAS**, left.
38.2	61.1	Slow for brown-and-white cow in middle of road. This is the Dan's famous brown cow.
41.5	66.4	SHARP S-CURVE. There's about a mile more of them. Might as well tell you "heavy metal" fellows (and gals) that smokey (*el oso?*) is around and has radar! What's Mexico coming to?
44.2	70.7	Rest stop of Los Pocitos. Highway Patrol hangs out here sometimes. **KM 198**.
47.0	75.2	Whistle stop of La Pintada at left where there are supposed to be caves whose walls are carved with prehistoric hieroglyphics (though nobody seems to know about them, so look for them only if you are adventurous and speak Spanish). CAREFUL - there will be some fairly sharp curves ahead.
54.0	86.4	Those rugged mountains ahead to left are called El Pilar "The Pillar."
60.1	96.2	Sierra Madre mountains to right.
67.5	108.0	Over bridge over little dry Río La Poza, then SHARP right curve.
69.3	110.9	Notice camel hump hill over to right! Now say it 3 times, real fast.
75.3	120.5	**GAS**, left.
77.6	124.2	Police Institute right. Mexico is professionalizing its police force and some states have hired law enforcement consultants from the U.S. Welcome to Hermosillo sign.
78.0	124.8	Right to Hermosillo Ecological Park — a very worthwhile place.
78.3	125.3	Motel Del Fuego at right.
78.6	125.8	Corona distributor and ice on right. Motel Cid on left.
79.1	126.6	Shopping plaza to left.
79.2	126.7	Junction with Periférico west, right. "Periférico" means "bypass" or "loop." Right to Santa Ana and El Novillo Dam (lake), 95 miles (good bass fishing). **GAS**, right (watch them).

IF TO: Bypass town and on to Santa Ana, turn RIGHT and (skip Kino Bay stublog) start bypass stub log below. Otherwise skip down to mile 79.5.

IF TO: Kino Bay, turn left and start Kino Bay via Bypass stub log below.

Stub Log: To Kino Bay Via Bypass

0.0	0.0	Having turned onto Periférico heading west, pass Plaza Sur shopping center.

MI	KM	
0.4	0.6	Pass Palo Verde business park, left.
0.9	1.4	Pass automatic transmission repair shop, right.
1.1	1.8	Pass **GAS** station, left. Stoplight. Cemento Campana, left just before light.
1.2	1.9	Pass Calle Lázaro Cárdenas, left.
1.9	3.0	Amazing rock formation on left behind Las Palmas shopping center
2.1	3.4	Road goes over usually dry river and freeway to nowhere.
2.5	4.0	Another stoplight (You are now heading west). Long distance fax office on left just before light.
3.3	5.3	Another shopping center, left.
3.6	5.8	Stoplight. Plaza Satélite, left just past light.
3.8	6.1	Pass thatched mariscos palapa, right.
4.2	6.7	Pass big dry cleaner (*tintorería*) on left.

IF TO: Kino Bay, Turn left and begin Hermosillo — Kino Bay Special (page 43) at mile 2.0.

End of Stub Log

Stub Log: From Guaymas Highway to Nogales

0.0	0.0	Having turned right onto bypass go under overpass. Follow "Nogales" signs. **GAS**, left.
0.1	0.2	Goodyear on left. Uniroyal on right.
0.8	1.3	**GAS** on right.
1.0	1.6	VEER LEFT at Santa Ana sign (Straight ahead is to Yécora and Hwy 16 to Copper Canyon.). Right is to Sahuaripa. Industrial park on right. Then pass street left to downtown Hermosillo.

IF TO: Chihuahua or Copper Canyon, start Hermosillo — La Junta Special (page 48).

1.3	2.1	**GAS** on right. Cattle feed lot on right. Roll up your windows.
2.8	4.5	Railroad crossing. Curve right.
3.0	4.8	Cement plant to left.
3.6	5.8	Dangerous curve and over bridge. Railroad bridge overhead to right, then dangerous curve to left.
4.0	6.4	Get in right lane. Left lane turns to the bus station.
4.3	6.9	Baseball field on right. Soccer field on left. Careful for school zone.
4.5	7.2	**GAS** on right.
4.6	7.4	Veer right onto one-way street, *Las Vírgenes*. Farmacia, left. AA (Spanish) Buenos Amigos at right (Alanon meetings — 4:30 til 6:00 PM, Mon and Wed).
4.9	7.8	Curve left. Then under pedestrian crossing. Again on divided 4 lane.
5.0	8.0	Over railroad crossing. Curve right.
5.5	8.8	Pemex storage facilities on left and right. Ahead, to left, is Fiesta Americana Hotel.
5.6	9.0	Firestone on right. Goodrich, left
5.7	9.1	Mobile and Chevy dealer on left. **GAS** ahead on left.

IF TO: Nogales, turn RIGHT onto Hwy #15. Start Hermosillo — Santa Ana Log (page 172) at mile 2.2.

IF TO: Downtown, turn LEFT.

End of Stub Log

		Continuation of main log.
79.5	127.2	Welcome to Hermosillo, (population: 449,472), capital of the state of Sonora. It's named for Colonel D. José María González Hermosillo in 1828, a leader in the war for independence.
79.9	127.5	Restaurant a Hacienda, right. Then white double domed church.
80.7	129.1	Electrical generating station, left.
81.0	129.6	Gas, regular only, right. Note monument at left to *Los Tres Pueblos* in memory of three villages on Río Sonora that were washed away years ago by a big flood. Hotel Granada, left.
81.2	129.9	Over freeway. Pass cultural center at left. Nogales straight. Centro bus station to right.
81.4	130.2	Up and over usually dry bed of Río de Sonora. Big Rodríguez Dam and Lake upstream to right.
81.8	130.9	Hotel Kino, right.
82.1	131.4	Civic center, left. Down wide two-way Avenida Rosales.
82.2	131.5	Restaurant Jo Wah. Hotel San Alberto left. Then highrise hotel Calinda.

172

MI   KM
82.5   132.0   University Plaza ahead on left. Rodríguez Library and Museum, right. Bend left past mounted statue of Don Bautista de Anza, a Sonoran military hero and explorer. He founded a little village of San Francisco, CA. in his spare time. For info on accommodations, see Hermosillo Eat & Stray (page 102)

IF TO: Nogales, Santa Ana — STRAIGHT. Start Hermosillo — Santa Ana Log.

IF TO: Kino Bay — LEFT — following "AEROPUERTO" "KINO" signs. Start Hermosillo — Kino Bay Special (page 44). Left 2 lanes are left turn only. Right 3 lanes are straight, for now, stick to middle.

IF TO: Agua Prieta and Douglas (the scenic way by Ures, Moctezuma and Nacozari) — STRAIGHT — for 8 miles on Hermosillo — Santa Ana Log, to junction with turnoff. Then start Hermosillo — Douglas Log (page 64).

End of Log 20

LOG 21   *START:* Hermosillo, Son   *END:* Santa Ana, Son

UD-019

107.1 MI or 171.4 KM
DRIVE TIME 1 1/2 - 2 HOURS
SCENIC RATING — 2

0.0   0.0   Here at University Plaza, proceed ahead past Rodríguez Museum and Library, right, and plaza of University of Sonora, left. Monument of mounted Capitán de Anza (a native of Sonora and founder of San Francisco, California) is behind you.

Rodríguez Museum and Library, Rodríguez Dam and Lake, and Rodríguez Boulevard coming up, are all named for Abelardo Rodríguez, a Sonora boy who served as president from 1932-34.

0.1   0.2   Stoplight. Restaurant Mirikon (Japanese), right. Then, Av. Madrid
0.3   0.5   KFC at right.
0.6   1.0   Come to a monument (on right) to one-armed man — General Alvaro Obregón. He was president of Mexico from 1920-24, a native of Sonora. His arm was shot off during a revolutionary battle against Pancho Villa at Celaya. Hertz Rent-A-Car, left.
0.8   1.3   Sports Palace on right. Ford clock tower and Chevy dealer to left. Straight to Santa Ana. Right to downtown Hermosillo at light. Stay in left 2 lanes — right goes to lateral only. Pass shopping center, left.
1.0   1.6   **GAS**, right.
1.1   1.8   Veer left here. Right lane is a lateral. To the left is a grocery store, "Valle Petic."
1.2   1.9   Chrysler dealer on right. La Fiesta restaurant on left.
1.4   2.2   **GAS**, left. Laundromat on right. Mannix Cafeteria on left (fast service). Ford dealer on left. La Siesta Motel, right. Señorial Hotel on right.
1.5   2.4   Motel Bugambilla, left. Hotel Petic Valle Grande, right.
1.7   2.7   Motel Encanto just beyond at right. Excellent restaurant Henry's at left.
1.8   2.9   Pretty Bancomer at left. Then well-known motel Gandara at right, 1000 Blvd. Kino.
2.1   3.4   Big Ariaza hotel at right. Highrise Fiesta Americana on right.
2.2   3.5   Come to traffic light and junction with bypass around town. Huge **GAS**, left. Periférico north, right. "Periférico" means "bypass" or "loop." This goes to Guaymas. Welcome to those folks joining us from the bypass, here at what used to be Kino Circle, back before this traffic light. Chevrolet dealer, right.
2.4   3.8   Railroad station to right. Under pedestrian crossing.
2.5   4.0   Hotel Autoparador at right, nice. Under sign "Hermosillo wishes you a good trip."
2.6   4.2   Mercedes Benz dealer on left.
4.2   6.7   Pass Motel Costa Del Sol, right.
4.7   7.5   **GAS**, right.
5.2   8.3   Town of La Victoria over to right. This is a rich farming area with a lot of allied industry. Icehouse, right.
6.5   10.4   Sign to Nogales Hwy 15 Cuota (Toll).
7.2   11.5   Sign to Nogales Libre. Toll road to Nogales, VEER LEFT. Free road, VEER RIGHT, following URES sign. If you want to take the Libre (free) road, be aware that it is very congested, and we recommend the toll road.

IF TO: Douglas, AZ via Ures, Nacozari, turn right and start Hermosillo — Douglas Log (page 64).

MI	KM	
7.3	11.7	Having taken toll road (no tollbooth here), note statue of bull at right. **KM 9**.
7.4	11.8	ITESM (technical school) to right. Statue of Capitán de Anza to left.
7.6	12.2	**GAS** at left. Altitude 1,000 ft. **KM 10.**
23.0	36.8	Pass side road (right) to Pesqueíra, named after Ignacio Pesqueíra, a former governor of Sonora. Red Cross. Cafes on both sides.
33.5	53.6	Mount Cuervos over to left.
45.2	72.3	The Yaqui Indians are native to this area. Their "deer dance" is pretty neat. Of course, young folks of all tribes do "dear" dances. Like most Indians, they have a dance to celebrate the important transitions in life and in the seasons. It's also an excuse to socialize and relax. **KM 68**.
45.7	73.1	Up into El Oasis. **GAS**, left and ice. Emergency motel Oasis, also at left with bus station restaurant. Pass side road, right, to town of Carbo on railroad.
50.5	80.8	Mt. Amore dead ahead with radio tower.
51.5	82.4	Parador turístico to right.
52.7	84.3	Microwave tower at left, then Chapel and truck stop of "Los Chinos" (the Chinamen).
55.0	88.0	Water for radiator sign with place to right, but don't count on finding any water. **KM 84**.
55.7	89.1	Over bridge over dry Río Apache. A Texas Aggie had to make an emergency landing with his plane around here. He banged it up pretty badly. When he was pulled from the wreckage, he asked, "Why would somebody make a runway that's 100 miles wide and only 100 feet long?"
65.1	104.2	The Pápago Indians are desert dwellers. Their pottery and wood carvings are sold in "trading posts" in Phoenix and Tucson, AZ. **KM 100**.
72.5	116.0	Pass side road right to Querobabi on railroad. Hwy #82. **KM 113**.
78.2	125.1	Now up and over railroad overpass. **KM 123**.
79.9	127.8	The hand carved art works by the Seri Indians are done with *palo fierro* or iron wood. A non-Indian taught them the skill within the last 20 years. **KM 125**.
80.7	129.1	**GAS**, left and ice. Then past side road left that leads to railroad junction of Benjamín Hill. The town has an unusual name for a Mexican place especially since there's no "hill." It's named after a general in the Mexican Constitutionalist forces during the Mexican Revolution of 1910-1917. General Hill was the defender of the Mexican border town of Naco (south of Bisbee, Arizona) in 1914 and was of British descent.
91.7	146.7	**GAS** on right. Clean restrooms. Expensive refreshments.
92.0	147.2	Cross Río El Alamo (cottonwood). **GAS** and restaurant on right.
94.0	150.4	Cemetery with pearly gates on right. "Swing low, sweet chariot .... " Pass little railroad town of Estación Llano at left.
100.0	160.0	**GAS** at left. **KM 159**.
104.5	167.2	Pass side road (right) to Rancho Betania, an economical church-sponsored campground, that offers 26 RV spaces with full hookups (E/W/S) plus showers and restrooms. English spoken. It's about a mile down the road. (For more info inquire at 543 W. Curtis Street, Nogales, AZ 86521.)
105.0	168.0	Plaza Kennedy truck stop (RV parking sometimes allowed) and highway patrol station on left.
105.9	169.4	Sharp curve.
106.3	170.1	Restaurant El Zarape. Punta Vista RV Park, left. Run by nice folks, Ana and Edgar Osuña. Nice view at top of hill.
106.4	170.2	Turn right. Centro bus station. Over little bridge. At right is San Francisco Hotel, Ph: (632) 324-0322, and at left is Hotel Elba, —MOD— restaurant (open 6 AM till 11 PM) with good food (serve 1/2 orders for those who have a small appetite), MC, VI, Ph: (632) 324-0361, 324-0178. School to left then curve to left. Downhill.
106.9	171.0	Retorno Nogales/Magdalena. Then Motel San Carlos (50 rooms and less expensive than El Camino across the highway, PH: (632) 322-1300 or 322-3697)
107.0	171.2	Enter Santa Ana at junction Hwys #15 and #2, then pass **GAS** at left.

IF TO: Nogales, veer right and Start Santa Ana — Imuris Log.

IF TO: Caborca, Sonoyta, Puerto Peñasco, San Luis Colorado (Yuma), Mexicali, Tijuana and the Pacific Ocean, TURN LEFT and start Santa Ana — Sonoyta Log (page 95).

End of Log 21

LOG 22   *START:* Santa Ana, Son   *END:* Imuris, Son

UD-019

26.5 MI or 42.4 KM
DRIVE TIME 30 — 45 MINUTES
SCENIC RATING — 2

MI	KM	
0.0	0.0	Here at junction of Hwy #2 west (left) to Caborca, Sonoyta, San Luis Río Colorado, Mexicali, Tijuana, etc. and Hwy #15, proceed ahead. **GAS**, left. Uniroyal at right.
0.1	0.2	Under pedestrian crossing. Curve right. Uphill and out of town.
2.8	4.5	Sign says: Tucson, 200 KM (120 MI).
5.6	9.0	Granja Santa Regina granary. **KM 175.**
7.5	12.0	Get into right lane for toll (Cuota) road or left lane for free (Libre) road.
8.0	12.8	Butane gas at left.
8.5	13.6	Toll road or free road 1 KM ahead.
9.3	14.9	Left to Magdalena. Right to Toll Bypass, right 2 lanes. Left lane exit only. Free road begins with killer topes. The Saguaro Motel at right. Statue of "Christ" on hill on left. View of Magdalena to left. Thru Saguaro forest.
10.1	16.2	Pass turnoff (left) to Kino Hotel and Trailer Park. Then pass Ayabay Motel, right.
10.3	16.5	Enter Magdalena (population 41,000) famous as the place where the skeletal remains of the great PADRE KINO were discovered in 1966 — if you have an extra 20 minutes, don't miss this! Pottery sold here.
10.5	16.8	Slow over topes and pass Colegio de Sonora at right.
10.8	17.3	Monument to Padre Kino on right.
10.9	17.4	Pemex **GAS** on left.
11.0	17.6	Pass series of stoplights every couple of blocks.
11.2	17.9	**GAS** on right. Large pharmacy next on left. Moclamora Motel and restaurant, left, then Plaza del Sol with long distance phone booth. Then on right, AA Group.
12.1	19.4	Pass Tourism office, then cross bridge and past soccer field on right, then more topes.
13.1	21.0	If on toll road, stop and pay toll ($ 32), then ahead.
13.4	21.4	For Nogales veer right and bypass Magdalena (pop. 41,000), **KM 187.**
14.0	22.4	San Ignacio to left.
16.1	25.8	Under power line. Over bridge over Río Tasicuri.
20.0	32.0	Careful for sharp left and right curves. Careful for next 7 winding miles.
22.1	35.4	Careful for curves.
23.8	38.1	Stone cutters on right. Very interesting. Then flashing light. Enter the fringe of Imuris (population: 8,000).
24.2	38.7	Puente Babasac. **KM 205.** Curve right. Jct. with Hwy #2 to the right.
26.5	42.4	**GAS**, left. Red cross. Then down and over bridge over Río de los Alisos. Come to junction of Hwy #2 from Douglas, AZ at statue of Padre Kino.

IF TO: Nogales, AZ, start Imuris — Nogales Log.

IF TO: Douglas, AZ, turn right and start Imuris — Douglas Log (page 67).

End of Log 22

LOG 23   *START:* Imuris, Son   *END:* Nogales, AZ

UP-126

48.0 MI or 76.8 KM
DRIVE TIME 50 MINUTES — 1 1/4 HOURS

SCENIC RATING — 2

Easy, winding stretch of divided highway.

NOTE: The newer border crossing via the "loop" is open from 6 AM till 10 PM only; otherwise, you have to cross at the "old" gateway via Hwy 89 downtown. Since you're not driving at night, it doesn't matter — right?

MI	KM	
0.0	0.0	Here at junction RIGHT with Hwy #2 to Agua Prieta, Mexico and Douglas, Arizona. There is a VERY neat statue at right. Take a few minutes to stop and walk all the way around it.
1.2	1.9	Thru fringe of hilltop town of Imuris (e-moo-rees). Pass Imuris' railroad depot at left.
3.0	4.8	Down past Las Viguitas on left. By the way, Mexican smokeys have ears. That's radar, son, radar, so watch your speed. Speed limit is 90 KMPH.
8.5	13.6	Railroad settlement of Cumeral, left.
11.1	17.8	Thru falling rock zone.
13.1	21.0	We have climbed to 3,400 ft.
13.8	22.1	Topped 3,500 ft. Now down. Curve right. **KM 229**.
16.5	26.4	Thru settlement of La Casita. **KM 233**.
21.0	33.6	Bear LEFT thru Cibuta and slow thru school zone. Pedestrians.
29.0	46.4	Pass *MIGRACIÓN and ADUANA* inspections station, left.

If you will not return to Mexico before your vehicle permit expires, TURN IT IN HERE. Ask for "Banjército" office. Failure to do so may result in high fines.

MI	KM	
29.1	46.6	**GAS**, right.
31.0	49.6	Thru railroad workers' settlement of Agua Zarca.
34.0	54.4	Nogales' airport over at left. **KM 260**.
36.0	57.6	Over railroad and follow alongside railroad at left.
37.0	59.2	Frequent *retornos* (turnarounds). Highway patrol station at left.
37.5	60.0	Goodyear plant left. **KM 265**.
38.0	60.8	Thru traffic light. Pass Foster Grant Americana on left. This is a big industrial zone — some big-name American plants are located here. **KM 266**.

They manufacture the first part of their products in Mexico and then ship them to their stateside counterparts for finishing touches — less expensive this way. They are called *maquiladoras*.

MI	KM	
38.1	61.0	CAREFUL for TOPES, Pedestrian crossing and school on left. Plaza Kino to right.
38.2	61.1	Hotel Posada Real on right. Come to stop at intersection. General Tire ahead on left. TURN LEFT.
38.7	61.9	**GAS** and diesel station. Federal prison, left.
39.0	62.4	Electrical generating station to left.
39.7	63.5	Nogales Technical Institute, left.
40.6	65.0	3 story building on right. Victor Muir Aduanal Agency at top of hill.
40.7	65.1	New Municipal auditorium to left. **GAS**, left.
40.9	65.4	Pass warehouse complex on left. Chamberlin manufacturing plant to right. Radio station on right.
41.6	66.6	Downhill after passing Customs. Curve right.
41.8	66.9	Cross Mariposa Canyon.
41.9	67.0	Pass town of Nogales, Sonora, mostly to right.
42.0	67.2	Texaco and Fiesta market to left.
42.3	67.7	Thru housing development. Pass La Voz Del Norte newspaper, left. Pass turnoff (right) to downtown Nogales. Straight ahead thru cut. Under pedestrian walkway. School on right.
42.5	68.0	Veer right at bridge. Straight to "new" border gateway — you're entering USA. This is Nogales, AZ. The officer will ask you where you were born and where you have been in Mexico. I've found most of these officers to be reasonable with a tough job to do. They may ask you to pull over and inspect your car. After customs, USA to the right.
42.8	68.5	Flashing light. School on left. Stoplight. Straight ahead for you.

MI	KM	
42.9	68.6	Carl Jr's Burgers on left. Over bridge.
43.1	69.0	A right will take you downtown. This is Jct. #19. Left is to Tucson. Straight to Nogales Sanborn's office.
43.2	69.1	Vet supermarket to left. Loma Linda shopping center on right with Wal-Mart. Stoplight. Chevron at left then Mickie D's and Valley National Bank also at left.
43.5	69.6	KFC and Arby's on right.
44.0	70.4	Cross Mariposa Canyon. Motel 6 at right. Chevron at right. Stoplight. K-Mart left. Turn left. Exxon and K-Mart on left.
44.1	70.6	Railroad at right. Stoplight. Cross "Baffert Drive."
44.9	71.8	San Luis Truck terminal at right. Bell **GAS** on left. Stoplight. Circle K at left.
45.5	72.8	Come to junction.

IF TO: Tucson, points north, east, or west, get onto IH-19. Bye-bye.

IF TO: Nogales, Sanborn's office, veer east along truck route. Turn left to Sanborn's Mexican Insurance and RV park. Having elected not to go to Tucson, ahead on US #180 (Mariposa Road). Pass Best Western Inn Suites at right.

46.5	74.4	Pass K-Mart, Safeway, and Revco drug stores. Stoplight. Turn left onto US #89. Ahead 3 stoplights.
48.0	76.8	Pass Nogales Service Center Truck Stop at left. Arrive Sanborn's Mi Casa RV Travel Park.

We hope you had a dandy time. The next time someone tells you how unsafe it is to drive in Mexico, you tell them you know better! See us next time you go south!

End of Log 17